THE KNOWLEDGE BUSINESS

To Aoife

15th October 2004 – 15th July 2010

There is a light that never goes out

Love from Uncle Chris x x x x x

The Knowledge Business
The Commodification of Urban and Housing Research

Edited by

CHRIS ALLEN
Manchester Metropolitan University, UK

ROB IMRIE
King's College London, UK

ASHGATE

Educ.

Educ.
HT
110
.K65
2010

Published by
Ashgate Publishing Limited
Wey Court East
Union Road
Farnham
Surrey, GU9 7PT
England

Ashgate Publishing Company
Suite 420
101 Cherry Street
Burlington
VT 05401-4405
USA

www.ashgate.com

British Library Cataloguing in Publication Data
The knowledge business : the commodification of urban and
   housing research.
   1. Research and development contracts.
   2. Academic-industrial collaboration. 3. Universities and
   colleges--Graduate work. 4. Housing--Research. 5. Urban
   renewal--Research.
   I. Allen, Chris, 1969- II. Imrie, Robert, 1958-
   363.5'072-dc22

Library of Congress Cataloging-in-Publication Data
The knowledge business : the commodification of urban and housing research / [edited and contributed] by Chris Allen and Rob Imrie.
      p. cm.
   Includes index.
   ISBN 978-0-7546-7690-4 (hbk.) -- ISBN 978-0-7546-9387-1
(ebook) 1. Sociology, Urban--Research. 2. Housing--Research. 3. Business and education. 4. Research--Economic aspects. 5. Research and development partnership. I. Allen, Chris, 1969- II. Imrie, Robert, 1958-
   HT110.K65 2010
   306.43'2--dc22
                                                                    2010016245

ISBN 9780754676904 (hbk)
ISBN 9780754693871 (ebk)

Mixed Sources
Product group from well-managed
forests and other controlled sources
www.fsc.org Cert no. SA-COC-1565
© 1996 Forest Stewardship Council
FSC

Printed and bound in Great Britain by
MPG Books Group, UK

Contents

PART III CONCLUSIONS

List of Tables

Notes on Contributors

Chris Allen is Professor of Sociology at Manchester Metropolitan University where he works on issues of housing, urban regeneration, social class and knowledge production and distribution. Recent relevant publications include 'The Fallacy of Housing Studies: Problems of Knowledge and Understanding in Housing Research' which appeared in *Housing, Theory and Society* in 2009; 'Gentrification "Research" and the Academic Nobility: A Different Class', which appeared in the *International Journal of Urban and Regional Research* in 2008; and the book *Housing Market Renewal and Social Class*, published in 2008 by Routledge.

Gary Bridge is Professor of Urban Studies at the University of Bristol. His publications include *The Blackwell City Reader* (2nd edn, 2010) and *The New Blackwell Companion to the City* (2010, both edited with Sophie Watson); *Reason in the City of Difference: Pragmatism, Communicative Action and Contemporary Urbanism* (Routledge 2005); and *Gentrification in Global Context* (edited with Rowland Atkinson, Routledge 2005).

Noel Castree is a Professor in the School of Environment and Development and managing editor of *Progress in Human Geography*. Until recently he was also managing editor of *Antipode: A Journal of Radical Geography*. His main research interests are in society–environment relationships (from a Marxian perspective). However, he has also authored a string of commentaries and essays on modern universities and their social role. He's the author, co-author or co-editor of several books, most recently *The Point is to Change it: Geographies of Hope and Survival in an Age of Crisis* (Wiley-Blackwell 2010), *A Companion to Environmental Geography* (Wiley-Blackwell 2009), *Nature: The Adventures of an Idea* (Routledge 2005), *Questioning Geography: Key Debates* (Blackwell 2005) and *David Harvey: A Critical Reader* (Blackwell 2006).

Jon Coaffee is a Professor in Spatial Planning in the Centre for Urban and Regional Studies, University of Birmingham. He has published widely on the social and economic future of cities, and especially the impact of terrorism on the functioning of urban areas. He is the author of *Terrorism Risk and the City* (Ashgate 2003), and (with David Murakami Wood and Peter Rogers) *The Everyday Resilience of the City* (Palgrave, 2008). He currently holds a number of UK research council grants related to national security policy.

Vickie Cooper is a lecturer in criminology at Liverpool John Moores University. She has just completed her PhD in homelessness and is currently working her PhD findings into publications. Her main interest is in the management and administration of marginal populations of society. She is particularly interested in the use of assessment methods of control and how they produce disciplinary knowledge and subjugate ambiguous knowledge.

David Demeritt is Professor of Geography at King's College London. His research focuses on the articulation of environmental knowledges and the policy process. Relevant publications include: 'Harnessing Science and Securing Societal Impacts from Publicly Funded Research: Reflections on UK Science Policy' which is forthcoming in *Environment and Planning A*; 'Un-ethical Review? Why it is Wrong to Apply the Medical Model of Research Governance to Human Geography', published in *Progress in Human Geography* (2008); 'The Promises of Collaborative Research', in *Environment and Planning A* (2005); 'Research Training and the End(s) of the PhD', in *Geoforum* (2004); and 'The New Social Contract for Science: Accountability, Relevance, and Value in US and UK Science and Research Policy', in *Antipode* (2000).

Marian Hawkesworth was a Research Associate in the Centre for Urban Policy Studies, at the University of Manchester. Her research interests are in human geography, disability, urban design and governance. Relevant co-authored publications include: 'Organisational Change in Systems of Building Regulation and Control: Illustrations from the English Context', *Environment and Planning B: Planning and Design* (2009); 'The Visibility of (In)security', published in the international journal, *Security Dialogue* (2009) and 'Should We Regulate for Anti-Terror Design?', which appeared in the practitioner journal of *Local Authority Building Control*, SiteLines (Spring 2009).

Rob Imrie is Professor of Geography at King's College London. He is co-author of *Inclusive Design* (Spon Press 2001) and *Regulating Design* (Wiley & Blackwell 2011), and author of *Disability and the City* (Sage Publishers 1996) and *Accessible Housing: Disability, Design, and Quality* (Routledge 2006). He is co-editor of *British Urban Policy* (Paul Chapman Publishing 1993; 2nd edn, Sage 1999), *Urban Renaissance* (Policy Press 2003), and *Regenerating London* (Taylor and Francis 2009). His background is in geography, planning, and urban studies, and he was previously professor of Geography at Royal Holloway University of London.

Jim Kemeny is Emeritus Professor of Sociology, Institute for Housing and Urban Research, Uppsala University. His research interests are in comparative housing; constructionism; corporatism and political sociology; the sociology of science. His main publications are *Housing and Social Theory* (Routledge 1992); *From Public Housing Housing to the Social Market* (Routledge 1995); and *Social*

Constructionism in Housing Research (Ashgate 2005) (co-edited with Keith Jacobs and Tony Manzi).

Loretta Lees is Professor of Human Geography at King's College London. Her research interests are in urban geography and urban policy. Relevant publications include: 'Policy (Re)turns: Urban Policy and Gentrification, Gentrification and Urban Policy', published in *Environment and Planning A* (2003); 'Critical Geography and the Opening Up of the Academy: Lessons from "Real Life" Attempts', in *Area* (1999); and the book *Researching Human Geography* (Oxford University Press 2002).

Tony Manzi is a Principal Lecturer in housing studies at the University of Westminster. He is co-editor (with Karen Lucas et al.) of *Social Sustainability in Urban Areas: Communities, Connectivity and the Urban Fabric* (Earthscan 2010), co-editor (with Jim Kemeny and Keith Jacobs) of *Social Constructionism in Housing Research* (Ashgate 2005), and co-author (with Nick Bailey et al.) of *Creating and Sustaining Mixed Income Communities: A Good Practice Guide* (Joseph Rowntree Foundation 2007). His main research interests are in social theory and housing management practice.

Pauline Marne has been a senior lecturer in the criminology department of Liverpool John Moores University since September 2005. Her research interests broadly encompass urban regeneration, exclusion and social harm as well as historical geographies of the city. She is also interested in the sociology and politics of knowledge production, and in the use of participatory research methods. She recently utilised the latter in research with young people in two communities exploring their everyday geographies, their identities, and their views on culture-led regeneration and Liverpool ECOC08.

Paul O'Hare is a Research Associate in the Centre for Urban Policy Studies, University of Manchester. His current research examines contemporary issues around urban resilience, particularly regarding crime, counter-terrorism and flooding. Previous research has involved the study of how civil society organisations engage with community or neighbourhood governance initiatives, and how locally based protest groups interact with spatial planning decision making

Gilles Pinson is Professor of Political Science at Sciences-Po Lyon (Université de Lyon) and research at TRIANGLE, a research centre specialised on political and economic actions, discourses and thoughts. His main research interests are urban policies and governance and comparative public policies. He recently published *Gouverner la ville par projet. Urbanisme et gouvernance des villes européennes* (Presses de Sciences Po 2009) and a chapter on 'France' in the forthcoming *Changing Government Relations in Europe. From Localism to Intergovernmentalism* (Michael Goldsmith and Edward Page [eds], Sage).

William Smith-Bowers is a Principal Lecturer in housing studies at the University of Westminster. His main research interests include social housing finance, gated residential developments and social research methods (including research ethics). He is co-author of *Temporary Housing: A Good Practice Guide* and has published a number of papers in academic journals including *Housing Studies* and the *European Journal of Housing Policy*.

Huw Thomas is a Reader in the School of City and Regional Planning, Cardiff University. His current research interests are values and professionalism, the operation of urban planning (with a particular focus on issues of equality and diversity), and research, education and ethics. Recent publications include two co-edited books (with F. Lo Piccolo) *Ethics and Planning Research* (Ashgate 2009); (with S. Pattison et al.) *Emerging Values in Health Care* (Jessica Kingsley 2010).

Preface

The commercialisation of university research and teaching has become paramount across the globe. This is occurring in a context in which governments seek to harness the skills of the academy to contribute to the enhancement of broader strategic goals relating to economic productivity, growth, and social well-being. It is no longer sufficient for universities to (re)produce knowledge as an 'end in itself' or as part of a process for individuals' self betterment. Rather, knowledge is increasingly defined as the means to an end: the production of product lines that can be sold to a diverse customer base. This is indicative of the knowledge business, or the universities' turn towards a new series of relationships with government, and private and third sector organisations. These relationships are characterised by the university sector seeking to enhance revenues through commercialising their services, and mimicking the behaviour and actions of corporate business organisations.

The book provides a critique of the knowledge business, and describes and evaluates its different manifestations in, and impacts on, the university sector. Its focus is the social sciences and, in particular, housing and urban studies. The chapters draw on a wide range of experiences, both in the UK and elsewhere, to illustrate the changing management of the academy, and the development, by university managers, of instruments or techniques of control to ensure that academics are disciplined in ways that are commensurate with achieving commercial goals. The chapters highlight the different ways in which the academy is being put to work for commercial gain, and they evaluate how far the public service ethos of the universities is coming apart in a context in which what is to be serviced is increasingly a private clientele defined by their 'ability to pay'. The book draws out some of the contradictions and tensions associated with these processes and highlights the implications for the academic labour process.

In bringing the book to publication, we are indebted to a number of people. Foremost, we would like to thank the contributors to the book for their willingness to be involved in the project, and for their responsiveness to the various deadlines that we set. We are particularly grateful to a team of referees that looked at each of the chapters, and provided useful comments and observations that fed into the reshaping of the book. We would also like to thank the original reviewers of the book proposal for their constructive comments, and to the editorial team at Ashgate, particularly Aimée Feenan, in helping in the editing of the manuscript. We are especially grateful to Sarah Fielder and Pauline Marne who provided helpful comments and support at various stages of the process.

Chris Allen and Rob Imrie, July 2010

Chapter 1

The Knowledge Business:
A Critical Introduction

Chris Allen and Rob Imrie

Introduction

The university is part of an ideological system that represents it as an 'ivory tower', somehow separate from the world that surrounds it. This separation and isolation from the social world provides the conditions in which scholarly work is said to be undertaken in an impartial and dispassionate way. It follows that the distinctive nature of academic knowledge is a consequence of its difference from the forms of knowing that are prevalent in the world that surrounds the university, but which, so it claimed, never intrudes into it. Forms of knowing that originate *within the social world* are thought to be characterised by passions, prejudices and political interests of those that inhabit it, while, conversely, the scholastic tradition is alleged to be one of disinterest, the pursuit of objectivity, and impartiality with regards to political view or interest.

However, this characterisation of scholarly production does not stand up to close scrutiny. For instance, medieval universities, such as Oxford and Cambridge, were less interested in the pursuit of knowledge than they were in the production of a cultivated aristocratic class whose privileged position was partly contingent on its ability to assert its cultural superiority. This was an aristocratic class that, for centuries, had been composed of *individuals* that engaged in competition for personal position within its own class hierarchy and that invested in the cultivation of their own cultural sophistication for these reasons (Elias 1972). The establishment of the medieval universities was indicative of a shift from *individualised strategies* of cultural investment to a *class strategy* designed to assert the cultural superiority of an aristocratic class threatened by the emergence of a new commercial class (Rait 1912; cf. Elias 1972). This is why the social organisation of everyday life within the medieval university, and its curriculum, was informed by the need to cultivate the dispositions of its members and not simply their knowledge (Rait 1912). Moreover, a consultation with the history of the London, Scottish and Civic Universities shows that the modern universities were no less problematic. They were established by, and partly to service the knowledge needs of, national and local state bureaucracies and business elites (see Bender 1988). Suffice it to say that these state and business elites were concerned to have an input into the content of teaching programmes rather than research, which guaranteed at least some level of academic freedom to researchers (see Allen and Marne, Chapter 6, this volume).

Nevertheless, the general point remains: Universities have always existed to service powerful and elite groups in society. What is significant about the contemporary context is the broadening and intensification of the ties between universities and the goals and objectives of corporate business organisations (see Standish 2005; Worthington and Hodgson 2005). The ties between universities and corporate organisations have intensified to such an extent over the last few decades that some commentators now refer to universities as sites of 'academic capitalism'. This term has been coined to indicate the level of cultural change that has taken place within universities: Universities have changed from being distinctive academic institutions that simply respond to the knowledge needs of the commercial world outside, to themselves becoming business organisations that have adopted the mentalities and practices of the corporate organisations they work with (see, for example, Deem 2001; Slaughter and Rhoades 2004; Allen and Marne, Chapter 6, this volume). In other words, the boundaries between universities and the business world have been eroded to such an extent that it is difficult to distinguish one from the other.

The pressures upon universities to become more business-like have arisen because they are being forced to diversify their income streams in order to assure their financial futures in an uncertain fiscal environment. Government is no longer a guarantor of financial support so part of the rationale for universities moving towards a business model is stimulated by their changing attitude towards the commercial ethos, which is no longer seen as something 'outside' of universities that should be engaged with but as something that universities need to become themselves. The most significant development in this regard concerns the way universities relate to their prime asset – the knowledge generated by academics. Contemporary universities tend to value and support the production of knowledge that can be sold on the market, and they are increasingly questioning knowledge that lacks commercial value. Thus knowledge is no longer being produced for its own sake, if ever it was. Universities are increasingly seeing knowledge as having an economic value that can be exploited in order to generate new revenue and funding streams. Foremost in this is the re-branding of knowledge production and other research activities as part of a product base to be sold onto the global market as, indeed, Peter Mandelson, the former Minister for Business, Innovation and Skills, has indicated: 'we will ... throw our weight behind UK universities looking to export their brands globally'.

This has all sorts of consequences, including a well documented trend towards activities that are narrowing universities' operations to little more than providing services to government and private sector corporate organisations. This is an implication of recent ministerial statements on the future of higher education in a range of countries, including by Peter Mandelson (2009) in the UK. He has suggested that government wishes to see 'more of the knowledge that is generated in UK universities [turned] into jobs and growth, especially by bringing businesses and universities together to collaborate'. Universities are seeking to commercialise their knowledge in multiple ways, for instance, by pursuing commercial 'contracts' to produce knowledge for government and business organisations, the development of 'short courses' aimed at government and business professionals, and through the proliferation of degree programmes aimed at high fee payers. This is being facilitated by organisational changes in the academy, including the development of infrastructure to enable academic entrepreneurship to take root as well as the appointment of business development managers and a raft of administrators to orchestrate and over see the process. As one of the raw materials in and through which knowledge is constructed, then, academics are increasingly being put to work in ways that seem far removed from the scholastic tradition described by writers such as Mills (1959), who emphasised the relative freedom and autonomy of academics to produce knowledge. Academic labour is increasingly 'sweated' and thus subject to control by managers who have recourse to techniques that seek to measure performance and discipline individuals into values and practices commensurate with the emergent enterprise culture.

The book has been written because there is a relative absence of literature that examines the relationships between universities, academics and the organisations that buy their knowledge, and that, in particular, examines the ways in which 'research funders' and the broader business environment are shaping research activities and outcomes within universities. The book seeks to explore some of the tensions and contradictions relating to the commodification of knowledge with a particular focus on the way knowledge is increasingly being produced 'under contract' to government and business organisations and within business-like university settings rather than within relatively autonomous academic environments. The remainder of the introductory chapter is presented in two parts which describe how the book addresses itself to these issues. First, we examine how university managers have constructed their institutions as knowledge businesses, and how they have suppressed critical discussion of the knowledge business in order to present their 'agendas for change' as self-evident. Second, we provide an outline of the chapters that make up the remainder of the book. These chapters deconstruct the knowledge business by exposing its various parts and elements to the type of critical scrutiny and discussion that has sadly been lacking in internal debates about the re-organisation and corporatisation of the university.

Constructing the Knowledge Business

Globalisation is a hegemonic discourse that, as such, constitutes the 'common sense' that frames political discussions about social and economic futures. What this common sense emphasises is a ubiquitous need for competitiveness, flexibility and innovation in order to succeed in the global market place. The need for such changes to take place within Universities – so that they become enterprising universities – is thus now a key agenda item. Yet the enterprising university is neither necessary nor inevitable because the 'global' and competitive pressures that have necessitated its' creation are not real or inevitable. At least this is the view of Bourdieu and Wacquant (2001).

Bourdieu and Wacquant claim that the discourse of globalisation forms part of a 'new planetary vulgate' in which the *choices* that have been made by political elites are presented in terms of *necessities* that cannot be avoided. For Bourdieu and Wacquant, then, globalisation is a language that was invented to justify political elites' voluntary surrender to global capital – which many of them form a part of – rather than a language that emerged to describe something that was happening outside of their control as, indeed, we are led to believe. Moreover the international circulation of globalisation discourse by, amongst others, academics, has helped to conceal its origins which, in turn, has enabled the political class to claim that globalisation and international competition constitute a factual reality that we must live with rather than reality that has been constructed and that can therefore be understood otherwise (see, Bourdieu and Wacquant 2001; cf. Latour and Woolgar 1979).

What is interesting here is the role that academics and, in particular, university managers, play in the circulation and promotion of these ideas. May (2005, 2007) argues that university managers are particularly culpable because they have been complicit in the political construction of organisation change – i.e. the commercialisation of the university – as a matter of necessity and thereby in the suppression of any meaningful discussion and dialogue about the future of the university. This is evident in the way in which university managers deem critical forms of knowledge that were once so axiomatic to their work as 'radical' social scientists to be idealistic and unrealistic in the context of their roles as managers where they are faced with the realities of the world in which they manage. The end result is the reconfiguration of the university in the image of the competitive world outside and, thereby, a neglect to consider what it might mean to be a university and an academic in the contemporary world.

This is why academics that made their name as critical or radical scholars have, as university managers, repositioned their institutions as enterprising universities that work with neo-liberal urban governors and the world of business in the pursuit of economic growth, but without exhibiting any signs of reflecting on what this might mean for the civic role of the university. What is even more fascinating about this is that the same university managers then deride academic criticism of such strategies as cynicism, which they juxtapose with their once standing preference for critique that, they claim, has necessarily been super ceded by a realistic acceptance that they are now required to work within the context of a neo-liberal hegemony which requires pragmatism. Curiously, this pragmatism too often involves an evangelical championing of neo-liberalising economic strategies that place the university at the heart of urban growth coalitions, thus legitimising urban elites' strategies to gentrify the cities within which they are located, rather than a reluctant accommodation that might place the university at a greater critical distance from such strategies.

The consequences for the university, and the academics that work within them, have been profound. Reconfiguring the university in the image of the competitive world outside has necessitated more than the strategic positioning of the university within urban growth coalitions, i.e. by positioning the university to service their needs for knowledge. It has also necessitated the creation of an entrepreneurial culture within universities. This has been achieved in various ways, for instance, by recruiting personnel from the worlds of neo-liberal government and private sector business to academic and academic management positions. Although university managers' capitulation to neo-liberal capitalism in the name of necessity has resulted in the suppression of discussions about what it means to be a university and a university academic, then, paradoxically, their recruitment practices have the opposite effect because they have opened up new discussions about the attributes ('entrepreneurial' etc.) of those that should be recruited to academic positions. In doing so, they raise the question of what is so distinctive about the academic if 'outsiders' from the worlds of government and business can undertake the role. But that is not all. University managers also hold their new recruits up as examples of what career academics need to become whilst also using them as a means of changing the culture of the university by, for instance, bestowing career rewards (e.g. promotion) on enterprising staff whilst withholding them from academic staff (see, for example, Delanty 2001).

The erosion of academic distinctiveness by university managers, who should arguably be tasked with protecting it, has opened up all sorts of opportunities for those whose primary interest is in making money rather than knowledge. For instance if we transport ourselves back 20 years, to around the time that we both entered the academy, universities and academics regarded their competition in the field of knowledge production to be other universities and academics. Thus we were located in the relatively autonomous and self-regulating world of social science. Nevertheless, we were also members of an academic world that was under pressure to adopt a greater business orientation towards its knowledge production. This business orientation had been pushed upon universities by Rothschild who, in the 1980s, devised a system of competition for research funding in which the client (e.g. government) invited contractors (e.g. universities) to compete for contracts to undertake research projects that had been specified by the client.

This increased emphasis on the allocation of research funds by competition, aligned with the erosion of academic distinctiveness, has opened up the field of knowledge production to new players. The last two decades have seen an explosion of private consultancies (some of which have been established by academics themselves) that now form part of the competition that universities face in the scramble for government and other research funds. Since these private consultancies are primarily motivated to make money rather than knowledge from government research, they have arguably had a negative effect on academic knowledge production. This is the view of Walters (2006) who argues that to be competitive in the brave new world of government and other forms of sponsored knowledge production, academics have had to behave more like consultants than academics and that, consequently, banal and uncritical research that lacks imagination and integrity is now prevailing within universities.

There is an irony to all of this. The university managers' whose actions have resulted in the erosion of academic distinctiveness by insisting on 'entrepreneurialism in everything we do' contribute, at the same time, to the re-assertion of the symbolic importance of the academy but by promoting the work of the consultants that they consecrate with academic titles rather than by promoting the academics that spend their entire working lives under their leadership. A good example of this is the increasing trend amongst university managers to make use of titles such as 'Visiting Professor' which they bestow upon 'consultants' that occupy important positions within governance networks and the private sector and that are therefore 'good for business', i.e. because they provide the university with a 'presence' within the world of government and business. So, the same consultants that erode academic distinctiveness by their very presence within the academy also take forms of symbolic capital from the academy which then enables them to make special claims for the status of their own practices of knowledge production – even though, as Walters (2006) warns us, their knowledge production practices might be anything but academic and might lack academic integrity. This brings us to the irony, which is that consultants' use of symbolic academic capital – their possession of which dilutes academic distinctiveness and credibility – is what enables them to contribute to the re-assertion of the importance of the academy by providing it with a presence in the world of government and business.

Deconstructing the Knowledge Business: An Outline of the Book

The origins of this book lie in an ESRC seminar series that sought to open up the knowledge business to scrutiny by focusing the critical attention of participants on specific aspects of it, namely, the social relations of contract research production in the fields of housing and urban studies. The seminars were based on discussions of original research papers, written by sociologists, geographers and political scientists that subjected the knowledge business of contract research to critical scrutiny from a range of disciplinary perspectives. Some of the papers that were presented appear as chapters in the book. These chapters provide critical examinations of how the commercialisation of the academic environment has influenced the way in which universities are conducting themselves in the worlds of government and business where research funds can be obtained; the way in which universities are internally re-organising themselves along business lines in order to maximise their institutional appeal to the worlds of government and business and thereby their ability to secure funds from them; the way in which universities recruit staff to management and academic positions that are becoming more business oriented; the way in which universities relate to, and manage, academics so that their staff are individually equipped to obtain research funds; the way in which they 'train' staff to execute their tasks as academic entrepreneurs; and the way in which academic staff undertake to engage in the business of knowledge production itself. In general terms, then, the chapters are concerned with two dimensions of the knowledge business. They are concerned with: (a) the management of the institutions that academic researchers work within; and (b) how this is changing the context within which academic knowledge production takes place and the changing nature of the academic labour process itself. The book is structured in such a way that it addresses itself directly to these two overarching dimensions. Part I of the book addresses the institutional politics of the knowledge business in urban research whereas Part II of the book addresses itself to the changing nature of the academic labour process in urban research. Part III provides some concluding contributions that critically reflect on the issues raised in parts I and II of the book.

Chapter 2, by Imrie, opens up the discussion of the institutional politics of contract research in Part I of the book by providing an overview of the pressures for a commercial approach to academic research. Imrie describes how the commodification of academic knowledge is not entirely new but, rather, must be considered in the light of long-standing and ongoing attempts by government to make the social sciences more 'relevant' to public policy and to public policy objectives, such as wealth creation and economic growth. Although these pressures have been applied for a long time they have not necessarily succeeded in penetrating the walls of the entire university as, indeed, Allen and Marne show in Chapter 4. Imrie nevertheless notes that a trend was set that has eventually culminated in the contemporary university being reinvented as a corporate organisation characterised by the adoption of organisational forms and practices more readily associated with private sector business. This is because the corporate university is now more explicitly involved in a knowledge business.

If academic work was conventionally undertaken in a context of academic freedom, which Imrie is sceptical about, then the knowledge business is very different. Imrie provides an insight into the process of commissioning and contracting of social research but, crucially, he notes that research sponsors, such as government departments, do not simply seek to exert a direct control over research by specifying research aims and the methods to be used. Rather, he shows how research production is subject to often subtle controls that work in a variety of different ways. One way in which he does this is with reference to the concept of 'epistemic communities'. Thus Imrie argues that the knowledge business is best understood as an epistemic community, by which he means it is a loosely constituted network of professionals that possess a shared set of values, a common way of seeing the world, and a common language for describing what they see. This provides the basis for the dominance of certain forms of knowing that is little understood, even amongst academics who are sometimes bemused at the failure to win the right to undertake policy research in the light of their academic status when, in fact, it is perfectly understandable when one considers the epistemic community to which they belong. What Imrie shows, then, is that typical academic representations of the knowledge business belie its complexity: it is not simply composed of research managers that tell reluctant academics what they can and cannot do. Conversely, Imrie shows that academics that win the right to undertake policy research tend to be members of the same epistemic communities as policy-makers and that, as such, they might be deemed what Walters (2006) calls co-conspirators in the policing of knowledge production. The key point, then, is that the institutional management of knowledge production is far more subtle than some commentators have suggested.

Kemeny undertakes a similar exercise to Imrie in Chapter 3, where he examines the case of research governance in Sweden. Sweden is an interesting case because it is a social democratic country that has refused to allow the forces of neo-liberalisation to intrude into the fields of housing and urban policy or into universities (see Kemeny 1995). At least this was the case until recently. Kemeny shows how the inspiration for recent neo-liberalisation of knowledge production in Sweden has, in part, come from Britain. This has seen the ending of 'core' funding for research in Sweden, that is, a situation where research funds are invested into permanent academic posts whose incumbents are 'free' to chose their own research topics. Kemeny shows that Sweden has also travelled down the road of creating a market for knowledge in which the client (i.e. government) specifies the knowledge to be produced by the contractor that wins, through a process of competition, the right to produce it. Kemeny (1996) has previously shown how this has resulted in the closing down of core funded research centres and their reconstitution in a different organisational form, so that they are more sensitive to the needs of this competitive market for knowledge. Kemeny's chapter in this volume shows how the marketisation process has extended out from attacks on individual institutions, such as research centres, to permeate the entire research infrastructure in Sweden. He shows the multifarious ways in which research in Sweden has come under 'political management'. Although Kemeny acknowledges that some parts of his analysis will inevitably be 'all too familiar to British researchers', his chapter stands out in the way it takes the analysis of the knowledge business onto a new and fascinating terrain. For Kemeny, the issues that confront us not only concern the political management of research and all that this entails, which he describes in detail. The issues that confront us should also concern the efficiency of the knowledge business. The greatest irony, in this respect, is that a system based on the principles of economy and efficiency is found to be bureaucratic, expensive and wasteful. Kemeny proves his case by providing an analysis of the number of working years that are required to operate the system of research commissioning in Sweden at any given time. The figures are truly staggering and raise all sorts of issues about the ethics of a process that services a huge bureaucracy whilst masquerading as a system that is anything but.

In Chapter 4, Allen and Marne build on Imrie and Kemeny's discussions of the politicisation of social science knowledge. Whereas Imrie and Kemeny make a general case about the political management and uses of knowledge production in Chapters 2 and 3, Allen and Marne provide an in-depth case study of how this happens. Their focus is on the issue of the public interest, which is a form of political rhetoric that is commonly used to justify and legitimise state policies that have invited opposition. For instance they show how regeneration programmes are commonly justified and legitimised by recourse to the rhetorical idea that they are in 'the public interest' – even though this is patently not the case. A key issue for them is that political elites are increasingly conscripting social scientists to the task of 'objectively' identifying the public interest in order to scientifically legitimise their political interpretation and use of it. Since these social scientists tend to be members of the same epistemic community as political elites and policy-makers they tend to work within the parameters of the policy-makers' worldview when producing an 'objective' knowledge of the public interest.

Unsurprisingly, the result is research that scientifically proves the policy-makers case that what they are proposing to do is, indeed, in the public interest even though, as Allen and Marne demonstrate, what is proposed often serves the political and economic interests of the powerful and is frequently manifestly against the interests of some members of the community, notably the poorest. Allen and Marne use this as an opportunity to raise questions about the ethics of the knowledge business that universities are involved in. They are particularly concerned that a social science commissioned by political elites is filling the discursive space that has been vacated by institutions that once, but now no longer effectively, represented the interests of the poorest in debates about issues such as 'the public interest', e.g. the Labour Party and Trade Unions. This is because the interests of the urban poor are now being represented through the lens of the powerful – aided and abetted by social science – rather than organisations that were created by, and to represent the interests of, the urban poor themselves.

In Chapter 5, Thomas articulates similar concerns to those outlined by Allen and Marne. Thomas tracks the relationship between the university and the city from inception to the contemporary context. The relationship is shown to be an intimate one, involving a lot of mutual back scratching for mutual benefit. This provides the background against which Thomas analyses the current relationship between Cardiff University and the political governors of the city. Urban governors see the city as an entity that needs to compete in the global marketplace for business and to cultivate an image that is consistent with this, whereas the university needs to be located in a city that is successful (in order to attract students) and to win business from the city council in the form of urban research. All of this pointed to one thing when Cardiff County Council commissioned Cardiff University to undertake a piece of research on the history of regeneration in the city with a view to the research being used to write a coffee table book that would mark 50 years of Cardiff as a capital city.

Although the corporate university and the city council might have shared the same interests in this project, Thomas points out that universities are internally differentiated and complex entities with divided loyalties – for example, to disciplines as well as the organisation. This means that academic research takes place in a problematic context. The research in this instance was undertaken by an academic Historian who chose to examine regeneration in the city from a critical distance, pointing out the successes, but also problems and issues too. The council took exception to the research that was undertaken, and refused to pay for it or to publish it. But that is not the end of the story. Thomas' main concern is with how members of his own academic department, within the university, reacted to this situation when the council returned to the university and asked if Thomas and his departmental colleagues in the planning discipline would undertake the work instead. Following internal discussions, some academics agreed to take on the work on behalf of the university – partly on the grounds that it provided access to data that would otherwise be unattainable and which they could use in future publications (see, Horowitz 1967; Walters 2003). Thomas disagreed with their decision on academic grounds. He outlines the reasons for his disagreement and his assessment of the consequences that followed from his academic colleagues' decision to accept the research commission from Cardiff County Council. One of these concerns relates to the status of academic knowledge. Thomas asks 'how are we to identify what counts as true academic knowledge if it is produced in different ways and contains different truths?' Why should we believe the academic account over and above accounts produced for funders if both accounts are based on selection – in the former case for a 'policy audience' and in the other for an 'academic audience'? In a nutshell, then, Thomas provides an important contribution to the debate because his chapter raises important questions about how the knowledge business renders the status of knowledge even more problematic than it might otherwise be.

This issue of the status of knowledge is also addressed by Allen and Marne in Chapter 6, which examines the governance of the enterprising university. They draw on ethnographic work undertaken within enterprising universities to show how academic managers are reconfiguring parts of the academy in the image of the business world that lies outside. They show how there is a worrying trend in which the enterprising university, and those that manage it, are increasingly seeking to distance themselves from the academic world. This not only results in a loss of academic distinctiveness but, also, university managerial rhetoric serves to denigrate academic practices of knowledge production which are represented as inferior to those that exist in the alleged dynamic world of business. This is why university managers at enterprising_university.co.uk seek, and celebrate, consecration from the business world in the form of the 'Business Woman of the Year' awards and so on.

What the chapter shows is that consecration works both ways between the academic and business worlds. One example is that the former award visiting positions to personnel from the latter if they are thought to be 'good for business', which affords the recipients enhanced reputations in the world of business and politics, whereas the latter confer status on the former by recognising their entrepreneurial qualities with awards from the world of business. The mutual back scratching can, of course, be shown to be little more than window dressing designed to elevate *some* knowledge managers and producers to a status that belies their true value. The reason why is obvious; corporate and consultancy research tends *in reality* towards the menial, uninteresting and uncritical even if those that produce it possess visiting academic titles (see Walters 2006) whereas academic managers with so-called 'entrepreneurial qualities' actually manage institutions that are wasteful in the way they invest in bureaucratic structures at the expense of knowledge production, as Allen and Marne point out. Like Kemeny, then, Allen and Marne present a version of the knowledge business that shows it to be everything it claims not to be.

The final chapter in Part I, by Gary Bridge, is less concerned with the way existing institutions of knowledge production – namely, the university – are being remodelled in the image of the markets they are seeking to serve. Bridge is more concerned with the new institutions that are being created to service the market for knowledge. His specific concern is with the creation of intermediary institutions that offer a bridge between the knowledge produced within universities and the world outside which, one must therefore presume, is hungry for this knowledge. In his chapter, Bridge provides an insight into the creation of the Centre for Neighbourhood Research (CNR) at the Universities of Glasgow and Bristol. This was an intermediary institution that constituted a part of the government's 'Evidence Network'. A key role for the CNR was to make maximum use of social science knowledge by ensuring that it was made available to policy-makers and practitioners in a useable form.

Bridge sees clear benefits in intermediaries such as the CNR. For instance, he is well aware that social scientists tend to concentrate their efforts on the production of new knowledge rather than the re-use of existing knowledge, since the former is more likely to attract attention, recognition and rewards to them as individuals. Bridge regards the value of CNR to be its focus on the under-rated and under-performed activity of bringing together existing knowledge in a way that is usable for policy-makers.[1] This focus on maximising the use of existing knowledge is valuable because it ensures that knowledge production leads to more than merely the enhancement of the reputations of individual researchers. It also ensures that policy-making is 'informed', even if what informs it might be deemed to be problematical. This brings us to another key point in Bridge's chapter.

Bridge is certainly aware of the problems of knowledge and, in particular, the problems of knowledge intermediation. He makes this case by focusing on the task of compiling 'systematic reviews' of existing evidence, since this was a defining feature of the work of CNR. The problem with systematic reviews, Bridge argues, is that they are based on a hierarchy of knowledge that treats quantifiable knowledge as superior to other forms of knowledge. Bridge discusses

---

1   The irony of this can be found in Chapter 6 where Allen and Marne describe a recruitment process at a research centre within enterprising university. They discuss how one academic sought to enhance his candidature by emphasising his ability to 'make more' of the research produced by the research centre by 'knitting it together' in an academic way, i.e. by relating it to debates in the social sciences. His candidature was denigrated by the panel for being too academic. Thus 'bringing together' research findings is only considered to be a valuable exercise if it undertaken in a particular way.

the philosophical problems of locating evidence within a hierarchy of knowledge and thereby questions the type of knowledge that ultimately informs policy-making as a result of the conduct of systematic reviews. Although there is value in knowledge intermediation, then, the manner in which it is undertaken in a policy context should be seen to be problematic.

This is not to suggest that Bridge is completely sceptical of the value of knowledge produced by intermediary organisations. Such organisations create an institutional space that allows a small number of academic researchers to task themselves with interacting with policy-makers. This institutional space facilitates relationship building and, as a consequence, mutual learning. Ultimately, intermediary institutional spaces provide the context within which academic researchers that have these relationships can be more critical of the dominant policy paradigm and that can open policy-makers' eyes to other ways of seeing and understanding what constitutes evidence. This is what encourages Bridge to make the claim that 'the positive elements of this more accessible interface to research is that it potentially opens up the range of positions from which urban policy problems are defined and viewed'.

Having addressed the institutional politics of the knowledge business in Part I of the book, Part II of the book turns the spotlight on the micro aspects of the knowledge business. It is essentially concerned with what goes on at the coalface where academic producers work at some distance from the university managers that seek to regulate their practices. The final part of Allen and Marne's chapter, on enterprising_university.co.uk, provided an initial insight into how the academic labour process has been affected by the importation of business principles into the university. For instance, they showed how the governance of academic practice, in the form of disciplinary mechanisms, such as timesheets, has shaped the subjectivities of those that are exposed to them. In a nutshell, the exposure of researchers' to market disciplines – for instance, by making them constantly aware of how they spend their time, how much time spent costs, and how this cost relates to the monetary value of 'research contracts' – ensures that researchers are acutely aware of the market context in which they work. So, in contrast to the chapters that discuss the corporatisation of the university 'from above', Allen and Marne show how business initiative also emerges 'from below'. This is evident in the way that academics at enterprising_university.co.uk, voluntarily undertook to change practices so that they were more in tune with the demands of their markets. Allen and Marne also show how these academics enthusiastically ceded their autonomy to the market, to which they outsourced roles such as peer-review. And whereas Imrie highlights *self-regulating individuals* whose academic practices conform to the demands of the market, Allen and Marne show that the enterprising university is a *self-regulating environment* in which the 'enterprising gaze' of enterprising researchers has a disciplining effect on other researchers. The suggestion here is that the enterprising university is governed by an entirely different set of business principles and disciplines to those that govern self-regulating academic environments, as the 'social studies of science' literature shows (Bourdieu 2004; Latour and Woolgar 1979; Kuhn 1970).

This is something that Manzi and Smith-Bowers take up in the first chapter in Part II of the book. Manzi and Smith-Bowers seek to understand the academic labour process in terms of the principles and commitments that underpin it. They divide academic labour, and the principles and commitments that are part of it, into three ideal types. These are activist, academic and consultancy driven labour processes. Manzi and Smith-Bowers suggest that activist driven housing research has a long history which can be traced back to the originating housing studies, undertaken in the nineteenth century, by Booth and Rowntree. These were concerned to uncover injustices, and to change social attitudes and social policies and practices. Manzi and Smith-Bowers suggest that activist driven housing research can be distinguished from academic housing studies which they term 'pure work' that is undertaken for the purposes of developing theory and knowledge. Kemeny's work on *Housing and Social Theory* (1992) is cited as a classic example of this type of work. Manzi and Smith-Bowers' third category of housing research is consultancy, and its distinguishing feature is that it is conceived, and undertaken, in partnership with policy-makers. Much more housing research undertaken within universities is taking the form of consultancy. However, Manzi and Smith-Bowers are quick to recognise, with Imrie, that there is diversity and complexity of contractual relationships between research funders and academics. They suggest that we can divide contractual relationships into a further three ideal types which are partnership, master-servant, and expert-innocent – each of which have their own implications for the academic labour process.

In a partnership model, the academic is recognised to possess knowledge that has a distinctive value. Whilst this might be taken to suggest that commodification of knowledge production has not entirely succeeded in eroding the distinctiveness of academics' knowledge, as we claimed above, we must remember that researchers will tend to be members of the same epistemic community as policy-makers and that it might be the trust that flows from this – rather than the expertise of the academic – that encourages policy-makers to value the input of academics in a partnership arrangement. Manzi and Smith-Bowers are clearly alive to this when they discuss how researchers, in partnership relationships, can be 'complicit handmaidens of government policy' that 'follow a political agenda set by politicians'. Manzi and Smith-Bowers proceed to discuss how the relationship between funders and academics can develop into a master-servant context when partnership ceases to run smoothly. This involves the research funder taking a much more directive role, to the extent that interference in the work of recalcitrant researchers is sanctioned. They cite various examples of this happening in housing research.

Manzi and Smith-Bowers' final category is the expert – innocent relationship that, as they acknowledge, is unusual. This is where the researcher is able, and allowed, to take control of knowledge production because the funder is inexperienced. Manzi and Smith-Bowers show that this does not simply involve the researcher taking control of the research process away from the funder. It also involves the researcher, as the expert, taking control of the research process away from society, or, social and civic interests that might wish to have a voice in the research process. For instance, researchers might refuse any input into the research process from outsiders, such as those people that are the subjects of the research that is being undertaken. Although this assertion of expertise might offer some comfort to those that worry about the erosion of academic distinctiveness, it is important to note that it actually says very little about the distinctive value of academic knowledge. Conversely, the assertion of expertise in this instance tells us more about the role of power, rather than knowledge, in the research process. Following arguments by Allen, Manzi and Smith-Bowers point out that the assertion of expertise *vis-à-vis* the subjects of research is often only possible because housing researchers are members of the same epistemic community as policy-makers ('the policy community') and that, as such, they use a language that is particular to this epistemic community and to which non-members do not have access. Non-members, in this instance, are those people that are the subjects of research, and upon whom research may impact, yet have no way of influencing the research process.

If there is one thing that stands out in Manzi and Smith-Bowers' chapter, it is a concern with the different ways in which research partnerships work, as well as the way they shape the academic labour process. The chapters that follow Manzi and Smith-Bowers build on this issue of partnership by addressing the manner in which the co-production of research is changing the nature of the academic labour process. The first of these chapters is by O'Hare, Coaffee and Hawkesworth and examines the co-production of research on counter terrorism. Their chapter shows that the academic labour process in co-produced research contrasts with that which characterises Mills' (1959) version of lone scholarship. Far from being preoccupied with 'the state of my problems' (Mills 1959), O'Hare, Coaffee and Hawkesworth provide a fascinating insight into how they were required to address a range of challenges and dilemmas that arose as a consequence of the political sensitivity of their work, as well as addressing themselves to the essence of their task – the production of knowledge for policy-makers. In doing so, they provide an account which recognises the problems and benefits of co-produced research which, they argue, should be valued because it provides access to elites and to insights that would otherwise be unattainable.

Although O'Hare, Coaffee and Hawkesworth acknowledge the benefits of co-produced research to be the access it provides to elites and to secret knowledge, they also acknowledge that this, in itself, does not justify the choice to undertake such research. For instance, one might recall that the same justifications were given by social scientists involved in Project Camelot which collapsed amid concerns that social scientists working for the US Army were being used to service military strategies to suppress insurrection in Latin America (see Horowitz 1967). Moreover, others have claimed that access to elites' lacks justification as a reason for undertaking co-produced research because, ultimately, the funder owns the knowledge that is produced and therefore access to it is severely restricted

(Walters 2003). This is particularly problematic because, as Allen and Marne's chapter on 'the public interest' shows, this suggests that policy-makers who claim to support knowledge production 'in the name of the people' are actually more concerned with restricting the same people from access to such knowledge which must therefore be seen as serving power rather than people.

Nonetheless, the value of O'Hare, Coaffee and Hawkesworth's chapter is that it provides a counter to these arguments by drawing on their own experiences as co-producers of research. They accept that there were restrictions placed on the production and use of knowledge in the context of their work on counter terrorism. For instance, they discuss how they were subject to 'Chatham House' rules[2] and about how their written work was subject to a censorial form of peer-review by their research funders. But they also seek to show that they were not, to quote Manzi and Smith-Bowers, merely 'handmaidens' of the state. Conversely, they provide us with an insight into the way they managed – through what they refer to as a process of 'compromise' – the challenges of undertaking research in a restricted context with a view to ensuring that they were allowed to produce and use knowledge as much as possible. The maxim here might be 'better that we learn something, than nothing at all'. Thus, they discuss how they deliberated about, but declined, the opportunity to achieve security clearance (which would have enabled them greater access to sensitive data) in the interests of ensuring that they could publish their work with as few restrictions as possible.

They also discuss how they developed a coping strategy by positioning themselves as 'critical friends' of their research sponsors, which involves a process of trust building and, as a consequence of this, greater openness between the parties. Thus they describe how this enabled them to blur the boundaries between themselves and their research sponsors which, in turn, opened up the possibility for a process of mutual learning. They argue that this provided them with feedback from the real world which enhanced their understanding and, thereby, the epistemic value of their work. Having said that, it should be noted that they are also aware of the limits that such a close relationship places on knowledge production because constant involvement in such relationships strips researchers of the opportunity to achieve the necessary level of estrangement from the field that may enable them to be more critical about what they learn from their 'friends' in the field. The problem with critical friendship, then, is that it is productive in one sense but also problematic from the point of view of achieving a critique of the powerful.

Although one can claim that commodification has resulted in the co-option of career social scientists to the service of the state, such claims were, until recently, less likely to be directed towards postgraduate research. This is why some academics

---

2   The Chatham House Rule is a rule that governs the confidentiality of the source of information received at a meeting. Since its refinement in 2002, the rule states: When a meeting, or part thereof, is held under the Chatham House Rule, participants are free to use the information received, but neither the identity nor the affiliation of the speaker(s), nor that of any other participant, may be revealed.

have previously been able to point out that critical research, in some fields of social science, has predominantly been undertaken by postgraduate researchers and published as PhD theses (Allen 2007). The chapter by Lees and Demeritt shows that this situation no longer prevails because the PhD has also been undergoing a process of commodification. This has resulted in a greater emphasis on research collaborations between universities and external organisations: Although PhD students continue to receive ESRC funding support to undertake postgraduate research, the aims and objectives of collaborative research are negotiated with an external organisation, such as a government department, which is expected to provide some funding to support the research study. The question is whether or not this is problematical.

Lees and Demeritt acknowledge the problems of collaborative research to be the amount of time and effort that partner organisations are required to invest in collaborative projects that may not be successful in securing funding for a PhD studentship. As far as the academic partner is concerned, collaborative research might also compromise recruitment exercises because they are undertaken in conjunction with co-sponsoring organisations and not simply academics. The result is that pressure may be exerted by the co-sponsor to ensure that recruits meet their needs, which means that new entrants into academia might be tending to come from the ranks of those that possess the skills, and whom are more disposed to the ethos of, the consultant rather than the academic. The implications of this are obvious if we return ourselves to the discussion at the beginning of this chapter: it contributes, potentially, to the ongoing erosion of academic distinctiveness *but for the wrong reasons*.

That said, Lees and Demeritt are, on balance, in favour of collaborative research despite its limitations. For instance, they suggest that it is one thing to say that collaborative research might be problematic for collaborating organisations that have large research programmes. But what about charitable organisations that only have a small research budget or even no research resources at all? Collaborative research presents such organisations with opportunities to produce knowledge that might be valuable to their ability to operate. Lees and Demeritt make their case in this regard with reference to the Peabody Trust, whose small research budget is necessarily focused on short-term concerns of immediate import. Collaborative research, with ESRC funding attached to it, enables such organisations to work on research projects that are longer term in their conception and that enable them to seek a more in-depth understanding of issues. This acknowledgement of the importance of collaborative research, especially to organisations that would otherwise not be players in the knowledge business, is evident in the way Lees and Demeritt's chapter provides an insiders' 'how to' guide on how to win and manage collaborative research funding.

If the chapter by Lees and Demeritt provides an insight into how the recruitment of postgraduate researchers is contributing to the accumulation of a body of academic staff with dispositions that are aligned to the market for knowledge, Cooper devotes her chapter to showing how these dispositions are subsequently cultivated to their maximum potential in post graduate research training programmes. Cooper writes as a postgraduate researcher that has participated in these training programmes. She provides an insight into the origins of the contemporary concern with postgraduate research training which can be located in a government concern with the 'quality' of social science. Cooper suggests that this concern with quality belies the governments' primary motivation to intervene in postgraduate training, which stems from its desire to ensure that social science research becomes more 'relevant' to the needs of policy-makers. This rationale, which conflates the quality of knowledge with its relevance to policy elites, is reason enough for us to be sceptical of the value of post graduate research training since quality is used as a justification for training programmes that are actually expected to produce researcher compliance. Cooper confirms why such suspicions might be founded. She discusses how the ESRC has sought to deliver its research training programmes through dedicated training centres, located within a small number of universities, because this makes them more amenable to the control of a government that is seeking to make them responsive to the market for knowledge.

Cooper shows how postgraduate training has been linked to the 'rational turn' in the social sciences, which involves providing postgraduate students 'with various calculative research techniques that enables them to extrapolate evidence from the research field and analyse them within a measurable framework. This analytical approach makes research findings not only relevant, but also useable within the field of social policy'. She also shows how training is designed to enable postgraduate researchers to communicate more effectively with the world outside (media, government etc.), which is different from a form of training that might equip students with knowledge of how to communicate within the field of social science itself. Cooper's chapter indicates that she is not impressed with this system of research training, or her experiences of it, because it results in the production of more compliant forms of knowledge on ever narrower terms.

If Cooper is concerned about the epistemic consequences of exposure to the market, then Pinson takes us down a different road. Unlike most analyses of the commodification of knowledge, which focus on its implications in terms of *what we come to know* about the social world, Pinson takes the analysis of its consequences wider than this by asking what its implications are for the future of the 'academic tribes' (i.e. members of disciplines) on which academic knowledge production is parasitic. He is concerned about the ability of academic tribes to defend themselves, and what they do, in the face of a form of academic managerialism that is seeking to restructure the internal workings of the university in the name of the neo-liberal world outside which, as we have seen, results in the academy becoming more and more indistinguishable from the business world outside (see also May 2005, 2007).

Pinson's argument is that the academy is a distinctive environment in the sense that it has conventionally been composed of individuals dedicated to the disinterested pursuit of knowledge. Recognition, value and reward have conventionally been accorded to those with scientific achievements and, as far as Pinson is concerned, rightly so. However, he uses his chapter to provide a discussion of how and why this is changing in France. He also uses his chapter to reflect on his experiences of working in a British university, in order to decipher the consequences of the changes that are happening within French universities. His conclusions are pessimistic: The commodification of knowledge, and exposure of academics to the market for knowledge, is producing a change of academic ethos and an unwelcome one at that.

Pinson argues that, conventionally, French academics shared a peculiar (i.e. disinterested) relation to the social world and that, moreover, their dedication to scientific achievement meant that they tended to live this ethos in private as well as public. The result was an academy that lived together as well as worked together, and an academy composed of individuals that collaborated rather than competed with each other. Pinson was shocked at what he found when he came to work at a British university in 2002. He found a set of individuals that were more concerned to enhance their market value, which is what brought career rewards at the enterprising university where he was located, than with scientific or scholarly achievement. Loyalty to the academic community, he says, had been replaced by a loyalty to the self. As such, he says that he found himself working with a group of academic researchers that were in competition with each other, and whose sense of common purpose had been destroyed.

Pinson is particularly concerned with the lack of collegiality in universities because he sees in it the erosion of the academic community as a consequence of what goes on *at the coal face* and not simply as a consequence of what happens *at the strategic level*, i.e. as a result of university managers' attempts to remodel the university in the image of the knowledge markets that it seeks to conquer. Pinson says he is worried about this because it is leaving the academic community fragmented and individualised and therefore incapable of defending itself and the principles upon which it is based. This is particularly problematic because it is occurring in the face of university managers' business strategies which are attacking the academic community in the name of the dynamism of the market and with scant regard for what is valuable about academic forms of knowledge production (see also, the chapter by Allen and Marne on the enterprising university in this volume).

Conclusion

While there might be a tendency amongst some academics to over idealise the academy (May 2005, 2007), the retort to this might be that university managers' and enterprising researchers themselves are equally culpable of idealising the market. What the various chapters of this book show is that neither position is particularly useful. Academic production, and the socio-institutional environment it is based on, might be problematic but, surely, the way to challenge its form, content, and relevance is through a considered debate and not simply by throwing it to the market. We hope this book provides insights that stimulate thinking about the future of knowledge production that take us beyond the idea that the problems of academic production can be resolved by continuing to commodify the resources of the universities. As the various chapters of this book show, this strategy has created more problems not less. The resolution of these problems or – rather, the consideration of alternatives – is the purpose of the concluding chapters that form Part III of the book. These chapters examine the case for reconstituting the university, and academic research, in ways that respect the broader public remit of the university which, for Castree, is a key institution of civil society that should support the conduct of democratic debate. A key problem with the knowledge business is that it is governed by powerful elites that are seeking answers that enable them to close debate down. As Castree, and others suggest, it is the responsibilities of academics and others, with vested interests in defending the public and democratic basis of society, to fight back against the erosion of the academy as part of a broader remit to protect the cornerstones of a liberal and open society.

PART I
The Institutional Politics of the Knowledge Business

Chapter 2

The Interrelationships between Contract Research and the Knowledge Business

Rob Imrie

Introduction

> Good government is thinking government ... rational thought is impossible without good evidence ... social science research is central to the development and evaluation of policy (David Blunkett, former United Kingdom Minister for Education 2000: 4).

Blunkett's statement identifies the importance of the social sciences to the art of government, particularly in supporting policy development and innovation. It reflects a broader debate about the role and *raison d'être* of the social sciences, and the ways in which they can be used to contribute to national government objectives, such as economic growth, personal well being, and quality of life. For Blunkett, and others, the relevance of the social sciences relates to their capacity to generate practical knowledge, or knowledge that is usable and useful (see Rappert 1999; Solesbury 2002; Willensky 2000). This is an objective of the UK research councils, with the Economic and Social Research Council (ERSC 2003: 1) noting that 'meeting the needs of the user' ought to be a defining feature of a relevant discipline, that is, one being put to work for the good of society. Here, the remit of knowledge production in the academe is not an end in itself, but a means to an end in which the latter is defined, so Blunkett (2000: 1) suggests, as evidence 'to determine what works and why'.

These pronouncements are not new or novel and reflect a perennial debate and disputations about the role of the academe, as sites of knowledge production, and their contribution to societal goals, such as the betterment of economy and society. In 1900, the President of the University of Illinois characterised the (traditional) universities role as a 'great civil service academy preparing the young men and women ... for the civil service of the state, the country, municipality, and township' (quoted in Veysey 1965: 73). Likewise, Walshok (2004: 4) notes that the academe ought to be 'the preserve of truth seeking ... characterized by standards of proof ... and a culture of informed discourse'. Others, such as Mannheim (1921: 12), define the point and purpose of knowledge (in the academe) as propagating 'critique of questionable political order', that can be used 'to open up new ways of seeing' (also, see Bourdieu 1998; Doohm 2005; Foucault 1977).

These (classic) re-statements of the academe and its *raison d'être* have, however, not gone unchallenged, as evidenced by Blunkett's (2000) pronouncements. A 'new utilitarianism' pervades the academe in which Government ministers, and others, increasingly identify the universities as sources of knowledge (production) that can contribute to providing the competencies and skills for the nation to participate in the modern, knowledge-based societies of the twenty-first century. The utilitarian approach in social science research has been re-stated by the former Chief Executive of the ESRC, Ian Diamond. He notes that the research councils are 'good at funding research relevant to the needs of business, charities, and government' (Diamond 2006a: 10). For Diamond (2006a: 10), the point of research is, first and foremost, to improve economic performance or, as he suggests, 'research councils have a big role in ensuring that the best ideas have the maximum chance of influencing economic development …'.

This conjures up the importance of the mediation of knowledge in society, in which the role of the academe is being pushed towards what Osborne (2002: 16) calls 'the formation of certain kinds of – vehicular, practical, usable, marketable – ideas' (also, see Bauman 1987). An outlet for this is the commercialisation or commodification of knowledge production, primarily through the context of consultancy through contract research. A Higher Education Funding Council (HEfCE 2008) report shows that UK universities made £288 million from research consultancy in 2006–2007, 19 per cent more than in the previous year. Birch (quoted in Shepherd 2006: 1), executive director for research and enterprise at Staffordshire University has noted that 'we have been on a mission for 3 years to generate more external income and diversify income sources. We have to become more in control of our own destiny'.

The commercialisation of academic research, and the rise of contract research between the academe and non-academic organisations, is, however, an under developed field of academic enquiry, particularly in relation to applied social sciences such as housing and urban studies (although, see Allen 2005; Imrie 1996). What writing there is about the contract research process is often prone to caricatures of it and research conducted through other routes, such as the research councils, usually by highlighting the negative features of the former relative to the positive features of the latter. Thus, contract research is seen, by some, as involving the academe in relationships that, potentially, dilute, and undermine, the pursuit of free enquiry and autonomous intellectual activity (May 2005). In contrast, non-contract research is sometimes presented as nurturing and protecting the autonomy and neutrality of intellectual activity, and, as a consequence, ensuring that the integrity of the knowledge production process is upheld (Merton 1957; Weiss 1990).

These versions of the research and knowledge production process are not without problems, and I develop the contention that the contract research process is a more complex phenomenon than presented in some accounts of it. In the chapter, I describe and evaluate the changing socio-political and institutional contexts related to academic research, and comment on the different ways in which contract relations may be influencing, and changing, the knowledge production process in universities. The discussion notes that there is much complexity of contract-types, and that there are no simple ways of characterising them or their impacts on knowledge production. Far from the relationship between academics and clients being a benign or a neutral process, as some suggest, I develop the observation, after Pal (1990), that the understanding about external funding of contract research in the academe ought to be framed with reference to, and discussion of, the relationships between knowledge and power, theory to practice, and ideas to action.

I relate such discussion to housing and urban research, with a focus, primarily, on the knowledge production process through the context of the central government department with responsibilities for the development and delivery of urban policy programmes. This organisation is the Department of Communities and Local Government (DCLG).[1] Referring to a mixture of secondary documents and publications produced by, and for, the DCLG, such as briefing notes, tender documents, and evaluation reports, I describe and evaluate the conceptual and categorical terms of reference of urban research, and their implications for the methodological and epistemological content of research programmes. I refer, in brief, to the role of inter and intra organisational structures and processes in influencing the social relations of (contract) knowledge production, and discuss what Beck calls 'non-knowledge', or those theories and ideas that are considered, by some clients, to be irrelevant and beyond the bounds of consideration as part of the substance and methods of contract research.

Knowledge, Power, and Contract Research

The role of research in the academe has been subject to much scrutiny and comment since the early twentieth century, and particularly after 1945 when the social sciences became a prominent part in government research programmes (Walker 1987). Literature describes the popularisation of the social sciences in the USA, the UK, and other developed countries, in a context whereby the expansion of government policy led to the demand, by governments, for more information about policy subjects, and evaluations about the outcomes and effectiveness of policy programmes. Social scientists were generally regarded as contributing to a technical and administrative process oriented towards, as Callaghan and Jennings (1983: 6) note, 'fitting of means to ends already given'. The popular understanding of academic-research contract relationships was that of the social scientist as

---

1 The DCLG defines itself as the government ministry that 'sets policy on local government, housing, urban regeneration, planning and fire and rescue. We have responsibility for all race equality and community cohesion related issues in England and for building regulations, fire safety and some housing issues in England and Wales' (see, http://www.communities.gov.uk/corporate/about/).

passive and an objective, value-neutral, actor, in which, as Walker (1987, 2000) suggests, ethical questions were rarely broached or asked.

A positivistic paradigm dominated in which the mentalities of government, in relation to social sciences, reinforced the limited use of interpretative forms of social scientific method and research design. Thus, particular ways of knowing were privileged, while others were often disregarded and seen, by some, as unlikely to contribute to the collection of the evidence base required by government. For instance, Donovan (2004) refers to the Clapham report (Clapham 1946), set up to review government support for research post-1945. It rejected public funding for social sciences until, as Donovan (2004: 22) says, 'it could replicate the methods of the natural sciences, match its achievements, and thereby similarly contribute to national wealth creation'. This set a trend that has been heightened in recent times, in which the governance of the social sciences is occurring within a context of scientific and technology policy that expects, as a minimum, (social scientific) research to contribute to national government objectives, particularly focused on wealth creation and economic competitiveness.

This is what some refer to as a 'new utilitarianism' in the social sciences. Intellectual activity is harnessed towards specific forms of problem solving or 'relevance', relating to the institutional requirements of funding or sponsoring organisations (see May 2005; Walker 1987, 2000). The popularisation of terms such as 'knowledge economy' and 'knowledge transfer' signify a shift in the perception and the role of the academe as a site of knowledge production, and the codification and commercialisation of knowledge has become centre-stage. Meadmore (1998: 32) characterises this trend as facilitating the development of the 'normalised' university, or institutions that are 'partially privatised, increasingly marketised and fiercely competitive, a shrine to economic rationalist ideals'. For Meadmore (1998), universities are being reinvented as corporate organisations, characterised by the adoption of organisational forms and practices more readily associated with private sector business.

Academics are encouraged to develop entrepreneurial dispositions, or ways of selling their skills and knowledge, with an emphasis on income generation. For instance, the HEFCE (2008: 1) have encouraged academics 'to increase their capability to respond to the needs of business, including companies of all sizes in the community'. The proliferation of demand for knowledge has encouraged a diverse market to emerge, including an increase in the numbers of 'think tanks' and consultants that, at first glance, appear to be what Plato called 'doxophers' or 'technicians of opinions who think themselves wise' (cited in Bourdieu 1998: 76). Bourdieu refers to the emergent consultocracy as part of the 'new intellectuals' who are, as Bourdieu (1998: 71) notes, 'engaged in the vague debates of a political philosophy without technical content, a social science reduced to journalistic commentary for election nights, and uncritical glossing of unscientific opinion polls'.

The new intellectuals embrace a 'can do' approach to research, characterised by 'working to order' in which, as Ozga (1998: 4) suggests, 'intellectual inquiry is replaced by the identification, pursuit and management of research effort'.

For academics, caught up in this, the rise of academic entrepreneurship is part of a context in which, so some claim, 'the free exchange of knowledge begins to be replaced by the alienation of intellectual property' (Marginson 1995: 19). This alienation, and possible estrangement, from aspects of the research process, is characterised, so some allege, by aspects of the contract process, in which academics' control over the form and content of the knowledge production process is not guaranteed (Allen 2005). The specification of substantive concepts and categories of research programmes may not necessarily be determined by academic contractors, and there are usually few guarantees, from clients, about the end uses of research findings.

Such observations provide fuel for those who regard contract research as undermining the sanctity of the academe, or those values that seek to uphold the principle of objectivism, that is, a critical openness to others and their views (see Sayer 2000). For Merton (1957), for instance, the values and actions of (academic) scientists were characterised by a commitment to communalism or the sharing of ideas, and the pursuit of truth by virtue of organised scepticism and the purging of personal views and values. The objective was to maintain distance from the research object, or to create a position of disinterest, in order to avoid the 'contamination of data'. As Merton (1957: 605) said, 'the scientist came to regard himself as independent of society and to consider science as a self validating enterprise, which was in society, but not of it'. For Merton (1957), the values and actions of the (academic) scientist were characterised by universalism, communalism, disinterestedness, and organised scepticism.

While one might doubt the extent to which such ideals have ever been replicated in social science research, whether by contract or not, they provide a point of reference to contrast with the emergent utilitarian ethic in the academe. They are based on a rationalistic conception of the knowledge process, in which the intellectual is conceived of as occupying a place of privilege that provides a context for thought, deliberation, and purposive reflection (all of which are denied to those outside of academia). Mannheim (1993: 74), for instance, conceives of the free-floating intellectual or those who propagate a controversial position 'on practical political problems facing human co-existence'. For Mannheim, a key characteristic of intellectual activity is normative critique that, as Doohm (2005: 271) suggests, seeks to destabilise 'the functioning of the plural public sphere'. Likewise, Adorno (1997: 413) notes that intellectual activity is about resisting the course of the world that, as he says, 'continues to hold a pistol to the head of human beings'.

For Bauman (1987), however, such resistance is unlikely or made difficult given the interpenetration of the market into public institutions and organisations. Bauman (1987: 134) characterises the traditional role of universities in relation to knowledge and its production as 'legislative', in which: 'being in control meant operating, without much challenge, the mechanisms transforming uncertainty into certainty, making decisions, pronouncing authoritative statements, segregating and classifying, imposing definitions upon reality'. Bauman (1987) suggests that this has changed with expertise increasingly vested in think tanks, government research units, and contract research organisations (such as those operated by the pharmaceuticals industry) (also, see Mirowski and Van Horn 2005). In a world in which knowledge is measured by its market value, universities can do no more than compete and collaborate with such providers of knowledge, offering their services as experts and interpreters, with little capacity to 'legislate' or fashion ideas or opinions.

Characterising the Contract Research Process

Much contract research is derived from a consumer-contractor principle that has its roots in a review of government sponsored research funding carried out in 1972 (Rothschild 1971). The Rothschild report (1971: para. 5) characterised the relationship as one whereby 'departments as customers define their requirements; contractors advice on the feasibility of meeting them and undertake the work; and the arrangements between them must ensure that the objectives remain obtainable within reasonable costs'. The approach outlined here has been described as the engineering model. Here, the researcher (or contractor) is at the service of the commissioning department who define the social issue or problem that is the object of research (see May 2005; Meadmore 1998; Walker 1987; Weiss 1990). The contractor is the instrument of the client or commissioning organisation, and expected to follow a prescribed course of action.

The Rothschild view of (contract) research was devised with the sciences in mind but it is applied to the social sciences and evident in tender documents produced by the DCLG and other organisations. It conceives of the (contract) research process as a series of linear stages, with clearly definable roles for the different actors involved in the process. It pre-supposes that the relationships between researchers and clients are akin to those who buy and sell goods in the market place. The researcher is dispassionate, and characterised by a moral distancing of research staff in relation to the use and application of research findings, once such findings have been sold on to the client. Other accounts of the contract process are more convincing, ranging from an interactive model, which conceives of the process as non linear and fashioned through complex social interactions between researchers and other actors, to enlightenment and political models, in which contract research is implicated in the production of knowledge as part of adversarial political decision making.

Such decision-making revolves around the production of knowledge as part of a political framework, and the contract research process as driven by complex social interactions between different actors. It is suggestive of a complexity of contract types and processes, that there is no single type of contract or contractual relationship or process that academic researchers enter into, but a variety of types. These are characterised by different funders or sponsors with contrasting rules relating to the conduct of research, usage of data, publication of findings, etc. For instance, research council projects may be instigated as part of a responsive mode, to encourage academics to apply for funding on a broad range of subject matter. In contrast, the subject matter of external contracts is usually tightly defined and specified; it is expected that researchers will 'work to order'. The types of contracts issued differ with research councils saying little about the substantive or methodological content of the research proposal. It is left largely to Principal Investigators discretion to define it.

The contrast is that external sponsors tend to draw up research specifications that, in Walker's (2000: 29) terms, reflect aspirations of organisations 'to commission a product tailored to their needs', but that, in doing so, limits 'the scope for creative design'. Walker (2000) refers to evaluations of New Deal for Communities in which, as he says, pilot and control areas were chosen before appointing contractors. There are contrasts in types of management structures, and controls or checks, on projects too. Research councils rarely specify how a project is to be managed, and they require no more than annual and end of project reports of progress and achievement. These may or may not be sent to external evaluators depending on the policy of particular research councils. In contrast, projects funded by external sponsors tend to be highly managed, and usually comprise a steering group and a series of milestones as targets to be achieved by specified dates.

A condition of research council funding is that applications are subject to scrutiny in relation to ethical issues. In contrast, external sponsors rarely raise ethical issues as part of contractual discussions or obligations, and rarely as one of the conditions for assessing a tender or awarding a contract. However, government and commercial organisations do not operate in an amoral context, in denial, necessarily, of ethical or moral issues in relation to the conduct of the research. In part, this is because universities have guidelines and checks about the scope of researchers' involvement in contract research, and some insist that project tenders be subject to ethical approval and scrutiny by internal university committees (see, for example, King's College 2009; Mello et al. 2005). Some clients and government organisations also produce guidelines about the conduct of projects, although there is limited knowledge of how far, and in what ways, they influence the contract research process.

For instance, a study of contract provisions that restrict researchers control over clinical trials shows much variation and little standardisation of approach or contract (Mello et al. 2005). Contracting organisations were divided in their responses to issues about data confidentiality, ownership, and dissemination. Recent evidence suggests some 'opening up' of corporate clients in response to accusations of excessive control over specification of contracts. In one case, Proctor and Gamble's response to accusations of preventing publication of data is the establishment of a 'bill of rights' governing its relationships with academic researchers. It states that 'our commitment is to maintain the highest standards of research integrity, sound science and open communication during the research process' (cited in Washburn 2005). Despite this, there is still some doubt as to what this statement means, and the data at the source of the controversy that led to the 'bill of rights' has not been released for analysis to the academic team that generated it.

The contrasts between research council and commercial or government contracts should not necessarily lead to a conclusion that one type is any better than another, or more likely to uphold specific research practices or values. The distinctions between research council and commercial/government contracts is, so some argue, more difficult to sustain given that the former is increasingly subject to the utility ethic, in which the social sciences have, arguably, been assigned a specific role by government. That is, they are to be deployed as a means to boost the scientific and innovative capabilities of UK sciences. As Diamond (2006b: 56) has said: 'there's no evidence that the government is not committed to the ten-year science framework. That's really good news, and our job is to make sure we've as effective and efficient as possible'. This implies that the broader science governance structures of social scientific research activity has led to, so Donovan (2004) argues, the creation of a 'social science in the service of science and technology', with implications for the form and content, even management, of research programmes.

It also seems likely, given the complexity of contract-types and contexts, that process and outcomes of contract research do not necessarily conform to popular caricatures. For instance, one of the fallacies of the contract research process is that it necessarily constrains or limits the autonomy of academic researchers and is implicated in the subjugation of academic freedom. This assumes that all contract research is the same, and works within similar moral frameworks and forms of authority. Yet, as Burchill (1990: 28) argues, some contract research can lead to 'a new and different kind of autonomization'. This may provide researchers with opportunities previous denied to them, or not easily facilitated outside of close contacts with client organisations. One obvious situation is access to data and information held by the client, or where the client is a gatekeeper to research subjects or sources of information.

The Conduct of (Contract) Social Research

One way of viewing, and seeking to evaluate, academic-research contract relations is based on the assumption that the moral authority of the academe is increasingly being subsumed by, and subject to, different types of ethical-moral practices stemming from commercial and non-academic sponsors. In particular, Krimsky (1995: 125), notes that the growth of relationships between academic and commercial development has 'resulted in a new public examination of the moral status of science'. It has lead to awkward, yet pertinent, questions being posed, such as, can academic researchers be trusted to uphold professional ethical standards of research conduct, and to what extent are commercial sponsors responsive to, and able to adhere by, ethical or professional codes of good research practice? Likewise, issues are raised in relation to the potential dilution of trust in academic or scientific practice, and the potential for distortion of research findings to fit sponsors' objectives.

These observations reflect, in part, an understanding that the scientific ideals held by Merton (1957), and others, are disappearing, although, as Mirowski and Van Horn (2005: 503) note, most accounts of the contract research process are 'long on anecdotal horror stories, but rather short on specifics'. However, the impact of commercial and contract and government sponsorship of research, on knowledge production, has been part of an intense debate since the mid-1960s. Then, the form and content of the social sciences, based on an idealised positivist and empiricist natural sciences, came into question, and was part of what Novick (1988) calls 'the epistemological revolution'. This 'revolution' was encouraged, in part, by a range of events and controversies relating to the use of social sciences by government and external contractors, and the observation that they were no more than a tool in the service of political interests.

Foremost was the controversy surrounding Project Camelot (PC), a US military sponsored project that started in 1964 and ended in disrepute in 1965. In the Cold War context of the period, it sought to explore the feasibility of producing a systems model that would enable prediction of social and political change in developing countries. However, by 1965, and US intervention in Vietnam, observers began to question the ethics of academic involvement in PC that was seen as 'social scientists serving power'. Horowitz (1967) characterised PC as the military 'hiring help' to legitimate its understanding of social change, in which concepts were pre-given and premises written into the contract signed by academic collaborators (see Beals 1969; Herman 1995; Solovey 2001). The significance of PC was the exposure to a broad audience of the role of knowledge brokerage in contract research, and the deep politicisation of the research process.

Mirowski and Van Horn (2005) refer to the modern regime of commercialised (social) science, characterised by changes in the conduct of research. For Mirowski and Van Horn (2005), five areas of change are important relating to treatment of human subjects, control of disclosures, subjection of research to commercialisation, redefinition of authorship, and re-engineering the goals of research. In relation to control of disclosures, a perennial observation is the publication of academic articles with undeclared interest, in which corporate sponsors who do not want their identities revealed have funded the research. Likewise, redefinition of authorship and the right to publish have been highlighted by a recent case, referred to above, involving Proctor and Gamble in which a Sheffield University academic Professor Aubrey Blumsohn had been complaining of scientific misconduct (see Washburn 2005). He claimed that the company had denied him access to key data and then tried to ghost write his analysis of it.

These episodes are not new or that rare, and Washburn (2005) notes that while university academics used to insist on running their own projects, this is now breaking down with much more direction from companies. This is indicative, in part, of clients sometimes being less interested in the (social) scientific basis of the evidence base, and much more interested in proving a particular point.

This may involve the re-engineering of research goals, as evidenced by Bell and Baverstock's (2006) account of radioactive waste policy in the UK. They note that the Committee on Radioactive Waste Management (CoRWM), a government committee set up in 2003 to advise on the disposal of nuclear waste stockpile, has been 'ditching science for public relations'. Bell and Baverstock (2005) suggest that CoRWM did not have the 'expertise to be an intelligent customer', did not listen to expert opinion and that, far from producing data to support a strong waste management policy, it did no 'more than provide shallow pointers'.

There are numerous other accounts of government organisations side-steeping unpalatable messages, or rejecting research findings that do not fit a pre-conception of what policy ought to be. Tooley (2001), for instance, notes that the former Labour government's drive to reduce class sizes, based on the assumption that smaller class sizes improves pupil attainment, is not borne out by the research evidence. Yet, as she suggests, 'there wasn't time to pursue what impact it might have but it was politically necessary – it went down well on the streets'. Much contract research is symptomatic of a culture pre-occupied with short-term outcomes; time for thinking about the substance of the subject, and related theory and concepts, is not encouraged. It is unlikely to ask 'first order' questions about principles and philosophy of method or substance, or to deploy much social science theory outside of the dominant subject, that is, economics.[2]

It is also well documented that sponsors may well refuse to publish or support findings that do not tie in with their corporate goals or objectives, or work against messages that they want to be associated with. In one instance, a research student, funded by an ESRC-CASE studentship, and sponsored by a charitable organisation, interviewed individuals identified by the sponsor as being able to provide authoritative views on the subject matter of the project (Vellani 2006). The sponsor agreed to publish the findings in their journal, but then retracted once the findings were known. The informants' views were counter to those held by the sponsor and the Chief Executive of the charity said that she felt the interviewees' views must have been misconstrued or misinterpreted by the student, despite counter evidence on tape recordings and transcripts. The student disputed the sponsor's interpretation of the process, but the outcome was that the results were not published.

Universities management are not unaware of the potential for conflict in contract research, and most have drawn up guidelines for procedure and practice that, at face value, provide mechanisms to protect the integrity of the (academic) research process (see Mello et al. 2006). For instance, King's College London's (2009: 1) policy for the acceptance of external research funding states that 'the independence of academic integrity of the conduct of the research and its results must not be compromised'. However, it is stipulated that 'researchers should be

---

2   As Cairncross (1195: 19) notes, it was during the Second World War that economists entered government service in large numbers and 'they left behind an expanding demand for economic advice from professional economists'.

sensitive to the views of other major sponsors on whom the College depends for research funds'. Likewise, a survey of contract research practices in Norway shows that a majority of survey respondents felt that their institutions upheld routines to ensure good practice. Despite this, few universities have a clear concept of (their) autonomy, organisationally and ideologically.

The research contract process is also implicated in what Seddon (1996) refers to as a transformative labour process, in which changes occur not only to the product, that is the knowledge produced, but also to the research staff. As Seddon (1996: 202) argues, 'the practice of research is also a learning labour process which contributes to the process of subject or self-formation'. In what ways does this happen, and with what implications for research staffs' biographies and identities? This is an empirical question for which little data exists. However, some insights, and suggestions, are provided by Allen's (2005) use of Foucault's concept of docility in which, as Allen suggests, the discipline of research funders is akin to the creation of the docile researcher. By this, Allen is arguing that academics' exposure to the managerial procedures and practices of contemporary research cultures serves to create 'docile academics' that, so Allen (2005: 995) suggests, become 'intuitively moulded to the needs of research funders and university managers'.

For Foucault (1977), for docility to appear institutions and actors and agents must be able to observe and record the bodies that they seek to control, and ensure the internalisation of the disciplinary individuality within the bodies being controlled. That is, discipline must come about without excessive force, but rather through careful observation, and moulding of the bodies into the correct form through this observation. In Allen's (2005) account, docility was created by a combination of the constant disciplinary gaze of funders, and his, self-acknowledged, unreflexive acceptance of them and the conditions of contract. Allen's account of his personal experiences is interesting yet it seems to underplay what Pal (1990) refers to as the points of resistance, or those contexts in which the researcher is able to influence the knowledge-production process (also, see Bourdieu 1998).

Epistemic Communities, Knowledge Production and the Understanding of Cities

The rest of the chapter considers the contract research process in relation to the development and propagation of knowledge about cities, with the focus, primarily, on projects sponsored by the DCLG. The DCLG is a central government spending department with responsibilities for the development of policy on 'local government, housing, urban regeneration, planning and fire and rescue' (at http:// www.communities.gov.uk/corporate/about/). Its overall budget for 2008–2009 was £34.3 billion, of which £31 million was allocated to fund commissioned research projects. The research function in the DCLG is part of its remit to evaluate policy programmes in order to satisfy, primarily, the Treasury's spending targets and government criteria relating to value-for-money. To understand the nature of contract research involving the DCLG, or any organisation, requires, therefore, a description and evaluation of the broader political and organisational relationships that define, and delimit, its terms of reference (see Allen 2005; Imrie 1996).

The DCLG's *raison d'être* is the development and implementation of policy, partly in relation to urban change. Its programme of research is derived from a process of internal consultation between analysts and policy customers, with the objective of generating evidence to fill gaps in knowledge to help policy development and delivery. Part of the consultation exercise may involve stakeholders, and use of knowledge networks including the DCLG's subject specific expert panels, select academics, consultants, and members of policy think tanks. The research programme is constrained in that it has to fit in with government's strategic priorities related to the DCLG's policy remit, and to evaluate targets set out in Public Service Agreements (PSA). Evaluation research of policy targets is a paramount feature of DGLG's research, and it is underpinned by a set of values that, as an interviewee from the DCLG said, revolve around terms that are rarely problematised but 'are taken at face value, including the nature of evidence, evidence-based policy, evaluation, and what works'.

The value bases of the DCLG may be understood, in part, with reference to the concept of epistemic communities (Chiwieroth 2007; Haas 1992). This refers to a network of professionals with shared values that are part of the propagation of a particular discourse or ways of seeing and understanding a specific subject matter. The network is based on a claim to possessing policy relevant knowledge relating to a substantive field. For Haas (1992: 3), the members of the network possess 'a common set of causal beliefs and shared notions of valid knowledge based on internally defined criteria for evaluation, common policy projects and shared normative commitments to a special research agenda'. This commitment, in the DCLG context, is characterised by the dominance of economics as the basis for the development and propagation of knowledge of urban issues. The recent history of the DCLG, and other government departments, is their employment of more economists as part of ongoing restructuring to ensure the supply of the evidence base.

For instance, in 2007 the DCLG underwent a Capability Review, a procedure introduced by the Prime Minister's Delivery Unit (2007: 2) to determine 'how well a department is placed to face the future'. It concluded that the policies of the DCLG needed to be more consistently based on the evidence, and identified this as most likely to occur by use of econometric techniques and related methods and modes of analysis. In line with this, there has been a restructuring of personnel including an increase in the numbers of analysts who are economists. The strategic posts in the DCLG, such as the Chief Analyst who directs the research programme, are occupied by individuals who are either economists or are predisposed towards economics as the subject base for research. This is part of the epistemic imperialism of economics in policy arenas. Chiwieroth (2007: 459) suggests that 'economists are an important conduit through which ideas diffuse and are implemented into policy', and, as an interviewee from the DCLG said, 'the ambition of the Permanent Secretary is for DCLG to be seen as an economics department' (also, see Babb 2001).[3]

The operations of the DCLG as an epistemic community are evident in the various procedures and processes relating to its commissioning of contract research. The department's research priorities are published annually in its analytical research programme (ARP, see DCLG 2009). For 2009–2010, the programme outlined and described 24 projects it wished to see being implemented, and external researchers were invited to write expressions of interest to carry out specific projects. Here the DCLG is operating through the context of process-based expertise, or the deployment of expert staff to conduct and facilitate the different elements of knowledge production and its dissemination (see Giddens 1982; Imrie 1996). The process is not necessarily linear or top down, and there is some evidence of complexity of interactions between key personnel, with the ARP representing a highly charged, and political, series of negotiations internal to the DCLG. As an interviewee from the DCLG said, 'it's a process that goes up and down and around for a while before it's finalized … and then it has to be agreed by ministers'.

Part of the DCLG's approach to knowledge building is also a turn towards applied behavioural change and behavioural economics to enable the department 'to deliver more successful interventions' (DCLG 2009: 2). An interviewee from the DCLG confirmed the epistemological privileging of such subject matter: 'projects do tend to favour a particular approach, which can be implicit or explicit'. The Treasury 'drivers of productivity' approach has provided a framework for several pieces of DCLG-led research on regional and urban economic performance and competitiveness. The 24 projects advertised in the 2009–2010 ARP are underpinned, without exception, by a subject-specific language and a terminology that conceives of the objects of study through the epistemological and conceptual lenses of neo-classical economics. Thus, the terminology that underpins the conceptual basis of projects refers to the importance of measuring the 'short and long run' and 'short run finance', and seeking to establish 'the direction and strength of causality'.

An implication is that projects come with concepts already in place that have potential to delimit the conceptual and categorical terms of reference of urban research. If this is so, what are the implications for the methodological and epistemological content of (DCLG) research programmes, and also the practical implementation of projects? For external researchers, the DCLG programme provides limited scope in utilising a broad range of research methods. Of the

---

3 The bias towards appointment of economists is evident in the DCLG's employment profile. Thus, in July 2009, individuals appointed at the senior grades, grades 3, 5, and 6, totalled 24 people, of whom ten were economists and nine were statisticians. Only five were social researchers or those with research expertise not grounded in economics. At grade 7, the proportions were similar: 15 individuals were economists, 22 statisticians, and 15 social researchers.

24 research projects advertised in the ARP, none are based, solely, on the use of qualitative techniques or research methods. All require the use of quantitative methods with, at best, a small number of projects using some qualitative methods as part of a mix. The emphasis on use of quantification is outlined in the ARP. It suggests projects should include 'robust and disaggregated metrics', 'the development of econometric models', and the application of 'quantitative methods and analysis suitable for establishing causality'.

This is not dissimilar to tender document notes, with one set, produced by the DCLG under its former departmental name, the Office for the Deputy Prime Minister (ODPM), suggesting that the successful contractor will provide a range of skills, including 'data handling and analysis; familiarity with census data … the use of different spatial levels; knowledge of evaluations …' (ODPM 2003: 4). Reference to such techniques is, in part, a claim to their importance in establishing the validity of research, a notion that is key to epistemic communities' (self) identities (Chiwieroth 2007; Haas 1992). Nothing is said in the OPDM document about qualitative research skills or dispositions, or ability to use ethnographic methods and techniques. This type of brief is not likely to encourage social scientists with such skills to tender, and becomes one of the bases by which an epistemic community reinforces its self identity, i.e. by the marginalisation of particular categories of researchers and methods of data collection and analysis.

Given the social organisation of policy-orientated research of the type evident in the DCLG, in what ways is it likely to impact on, and influence, the behaviour of academic researchers? Castles and Miller (2003: 23) note that the time lines of policy research will pressurise researchers into 'short-term empirical approaches without looking at historical or comparative dimensions' (also, see May 2005; Mirowski and Van Horn 2005; Sayad 1996; Weiss 1990). For Castles and Miller (2003), and others, the present and future focus of much policy research does not encourage engagement with historical matter, with the implication that the contexts underpinning the substance of policy may not necessarily by recognised nor centred in the research process (Sayad 1996). In other words, there is some likelihood that the complexities of the 'policy field' will not be specified in advance of the research, or feature as object or subject of the research itself.

Castles and Miller (2003) suggest that narrowly focused empirical research, which seeks to provide a response or answer to an immediate problem of government concern, is likely to accept the ways in which problems are framed and the terms of reference of a project brief. An implication is that researchers will accept government's characterisation of the phenomena of study and not, as a consequence, 'look for more fundamental causes, nor for more challenging solutions' (Castles and Miller 2003: 17). Such characterisations are constrained by the hierarchical nature of the research process, in which concepts, ideas, and methods stem, usually, from 'expert' views. One example is a DCLG (2008: 1) project on establishing acceptable environmental standards for local environmental quality that discounts involvement of research subjects at the outset. It requests researchers to use existing research on quality indicators and standards 'to help inform and identify factors' that relate 'to what people regard as important to the quality of where they live'.

This process is one whereby the DCLG's epistemic community may operate by excluding non professionals from research as part of an 'expert exercise'. It is closed off to scrutiny, beyond some chosen stakeholders, and projects appear as 'pre-packaged' with ready-made specifications (see Imrie 1996). This has potential to encourage engagement of researchers with no more than special interest groups or, as the DCLG's (2008: 1) research on environmental standards suggests, 'a large number of stakeholders and experts will be interested … it is critical that key stakeholders are engaged at the outset'. This is revealing about the hierarchical nature of the contract research process, in which the possibilities for local, non-professional, involvement in the research process may be foreclosed. Like much commissioned research, the research is 'about' people in places rather than 'with' people, so reducing the scope for seeking to understand urban phenomena through the context of local lives or specific ethnographies or biographies.

An outcome may be categorical closure or the delimiting of concepts, the effect of which is a reduced scope for knowledge production (see Adorno 1997; Bourdieu 1998; Weiss 1990). Sayad (1996: 23) provides some insights into this issue by suggesting that the ways in which some policy areas, such as immigration, are described and thought about by government officials is influenced by 'national or even nationalist categories' (also, see Castles and Miller 2003). For Sayad, these concepts and categories reflect dominant political discourses that naturalise the state and support and justify its policies and programmes, The role of the academe, as Sayad (1996: 11–12) intimates, ought to be counter-category, or, as he suggests in relation to his subject matter: 'to think about immigration is equivalent to question the state, to questioning its basic principles, which corresponds to denaturalise the categories the state has shaped, to 're-historicize the state'.

There are also matters relating to the substance of socio-political relations that are rendered sometimes inadmissible by commercial or government sponsors such as DCLG, and beyond the bounds of consideration as part of the substance and methods of many contract research programmes. For instance, Katznelson (1986: 311) suggests that all political and procedural systems have boundaries 'between that which is discussed and disputed and that which is not discussed and depicted'. This is one of the potential traits of an epistemic community and it suggests that the power of the unspoken, the silences, what Beck (1994: 174) refers to as 'non knowledge', are important as an analytical focus of enquiry. The non-knowledge syndrome is, in part, linked to the limited use of interpretative social sciences, or methods that are likely to destabilise common-sense understanding of phenomena and contribute, so Giddens (1982) argues, to conditions of uncertainty and ambivalence.

Conclusions

A recent statement by the Confederation of British Industry (2009) makes it clear that university researchers have obligations to use their skills for the greater economic and social well being of British citizens. As they suggest (CBI 2009: 38), university research is not sufficiently business focused: 'research must be strategically priced – or universities risk losing business investment'. This chimes with changes to the governance of British universities, with their absorption into a new ministry that, at face value, appears to be propagating higher education as an off-shoot of corporate business enterprise. As Peter Mandelson, former Secretary of State for Business, Innovation, and Skills (BIS) has stated, 'in equipping the UK for a post-recession global economy, higher education and adult skills will be not just important but decisive' (Mandelson 2009). These sentiments reflect, in part, a rapidly changing context in which, as May (2005: 193) suggests, 'the relative stability that was once thought to characterise universities is now much reduced'.

The reduction in stability is reflected by the re-orientation of much of the knowledge production process in universities towards contract research, and the encouragement, by university managers, of entrepreneurial behaviour and activities. This trend is likely to be intensified in the present context of global recession, with public sector finances much reduced, and onus on academics to contribute to universities' aspirations to develop their identities as global institutions. The scramble for cash is reflected in record grant applications to research councils and correspondingly high rejection rates, pushing the academe further towards alternative sources of funding. The implication is that external contract research will become more significant as part of the knowledge business of the academe. Such business is often orientated towards short-term, impact, outcomes, in which the expectations placed on academics, by both university managers and sponsors of research, is production of knowledge defined by its relevance to the organisational goals and needs of those paying for the contracts.

May (2005: 195) refers to the evolving context as one of 'the application of knowledge to the production of knowledge'. This characterisation is useful in capturing much of the context shaping the shift towards the commodification of the knowledge production process. This commodification, through the contract form, is, however, not reducible to a type or particularity, but is, as I have argued in the chapter, comprised of a complexity of contract-types and different possibilities. In some instances, the research may be no more than a legitimating exercise, or one of finding the evidence to fit the contract brief. In other instances, it may reflect genuine desire and commitment of research sponsors to advance understanding, and provide academics with scope to determine much of the form and content of the programme of research and its outcomes. In this respect, there is complexity in relation to contract research that reflects not only the diversity of sponsoring organisations and their needs, but also 'the university as a diverse site of knowledge production' (May 2005: 205).

For instance, in the DCLG example, while academics need to insert themselves into, and work through, an epistemic community, one ought not to conclude that contracts are 'closed off' to those who do not reflect the values and views of the organisation's members. There is porosity to, and complexity of, intra and inter organisational forms and dynamics. One helpful way to extend this understanding of organisational relations relating to contract research is provided by Irwin and Michael's (2003) notion of ethno-epistemic assemblages. This concept seeks to describe, and understand, organisational complexity by directing attention to the diffuse networks that organisations like the DCLG are embedded into, that is, a hybridity characterised by reflexive conduct and actions by actors. This is not to deny the partialities of much contract research, or the potentiality of self-seeking actions of actors in sponsoring organisations; rather, it is to highlight the often indeterminate nature of knowledge production through the context of contract research.

Such indeterminacy places onus on academic researchers to move beyond reductive characterisations of, and caricatures about, the contract research process, and to develop programmes of research and writing about the evolving contexts in ways whereby the complexity of contract types and processes is revealed. This is not just an academic exercise or something divorced from the lived experiences of the academe. It is in and through *those* lived experiences that the possibilities are provided for rich, first hand, accounts about, and explications of, contract processes, and their use, potentially, as part of a politics contesting what knowledge is being produced, for whom, and in what ways.

Acknowledgements

I would like to thank Chris Allen, Sarah Fielder, and Marian Hawkesworth for constructive comments on an earlier draft of the chapter. The chapter was only possible because of support from the Economic and Social Research Council (grant number ID 119248).

Chapter 3

The Political Economy of Contract Research

Jim Kemeny

Introduction

For the last 20 years Swedish government research policy has been to increasingly diverted from long-term independent research to short-term contract research. Sweden's Moderate-led bourgeois coalition government elected in 2006 is completing the task begun by the Moderate Bildt minority Government of 1991–1994 a task that was continued by the Social Democrat Governments of 1994–2006. This chapter examines the way in which successive Swedish governments have put in place political and bureaucratic structures of decision-making designed to organise government funding to control research so that it is tailored to meet the demands of political and economic interests.

The interweaving of politics and the government funding of social science research was highlighted in the 1960s by researchers such as Sjoberg (1967) and Thompson (1971), and, in the wake of the political furore over Project Camelot, by Horowitz (1967). Since then much has changed, including the spread of a form of research-funding that greatly increases the power of vested economic interests, governments, political parties and pressure groups to commandeer social science research for the attainment of political as well as economic ends (Etzkowitz and Leydesdorff 1997; Demeritt 2000; Mirowski and van Horn 2005).

Commercial interests almost certainly account for the lion's share of contract research in fields where large profits are to be made, such as pharmaceuticals, weapons, the construction industry and genetic manipulation. But there are many areas where profitability is low and among those who want to commission research other motives than profit maximisation often rule. One of these is politically-motivated contract research. Some of this is private, as part of the lobbying exercise of vested interests – attitude surveys, preference studies, demographic projections, consumption surveys etc. – but some is funded by whichever political party happens to be in power – centrally, at the state/county/regional level, or locally, or indeed by opposition parties, not to mention lobbying pressure groups of reformists, religious bodies, labour and trades associations and other organisations. Much of this kind of funding is aimed at providing or strengthening the ideological underpinnings of reform programmes of either left or right – in welfare, family policy, education, health, housing, environment etc. The attitude survey, keeping a finger on the pulse of the voters, as well as trying to influence the electorate by strategically released survey findings make such contract funding volatile and heavily dependent on short-term politics.

Etzkowitz and Leydesdorff (1997) refer to 'the triple helix of university-industry-government relations'. But the political management of research funding is an under-investigated grey area in the analysis of the social relations of contract research production, even though most work touches the political dimension or deals with it in general terms. There is also much more awareness in today's society of the importance of spin, media massage and positive publicity. Discourse is therefore central, best achieved by anchoring political decisions in legitimate scientific knowledge conducted by researchers in the university sector, organisations that had retained considerable public respect. Research is therefore a valuable tool in supporting political claims and counter-claims based on scientific (read 'objective') results. However, one might question the long-term viability of researchers increasingly become associated with the political views of the patrons whose research results they deliver. In the long run the respect given to universities as being independent, objective – and detached from vested interests – cannot but be undermined by an increasing dependence on contract funding.

Background to the Marketisation of Swedish University Research-Funding

Sweden is a post war late-comer to the use of the university sector as a targeted instrument to exercise political control over research. The traditional 'third way' view has been that of maintaining the autonomy of research through long-term funding that does not try to control in detail what is or is not researched or how or when. The Swedish reliance on the German university *docent* system – in which tenured posts are restricted to professorships – itself encouraged the exercise of grant-capture simply to help keep the large majority of untenured research staff in employment. Throughout the development of the welfare state during the long rule of Social Democratic governments reliance was placed on a parallel system of quangos in the form of research institutes employing permanent researchers.

The escalating involvement of universities in contract research is justified in terms of 'serving the community'. This sort of rhetoric is common as a way of referring to the political control of research. In Sweden 'serving the community' was a lofty ideal made legislatively explicit in the mid-1990s, expressed in terms of higher education institutions being required to 'collaborate with the surrounding society and inform it of their activities' (Högskolelagen 1996: 1392, my translation). Universities have come to refer to this as their 'third task' alongside higher education and research. However, it should be noted that under the ordinance 1 kap. 2 § 2 this task is not given equal status with teaching and research, so to call it a third task is to give it more prominence than it deserves. Rather it is more a self-chosen emphasis by senior university management that reflects their need to prioritise grant-capture as a way of supplementing dwindling general university funding and justifying the increasing pressure to hunt for grant-funding to fill the gap.

Governments, political parties, pressure groups, lobbyists, public relations agents etc. want access to research that supports their own or their clients' claims-making. They are therefore interested in commissioning research that does this, that provides the reasoned basis for their own political planning [*utredningar*] or that shows how policies might be implemented, or that conducts feasibility studies in which their own particular slant on dealing with a problem can be most effectively demonstrated and tested, or simply to lobby for their members. Political parties commission opinion polls frequently from commercial pollsters to publish the results at strategically-timed dates.

For example, in time for nearly every election year the Home-owners Society [*Villaägarnas Riksförbund*] have commissioned a survey that shows a high percentage of respondents want to own their homes. It is clear that one purpose of this is to make political parties aware of the potential strength of the home-ownership lobby during an election campaign. Similar political research is funded by many other vested interests, such as the Swedish Automobile Association [*Motormännens Riksförbund*] in their campaign against the six-month experimental Stockholm toll-charge system inspired by the London experiment, introduced in 2006 then made permanent. Another example is the survey commissioned by the Confederation of Swedish Enterprise [*Svenskt Näringslivet*] showing higher levels of parent-satisfaction with private schools than with public schools.[1]

Institutional Context

Quangos

Political research has always been undertaken in Sweden, just as in other countries. Until the early 1990s, research behind the development of the Swedish welfare system was strongly sectorised, with state investment concentrated in a number of research quangos entirely funded out of public finances. Significantly, the jewel in the crown of governmental research organisations was the Swedish University of Agricultural Sciences at Ultuna outside Uppsala funded by and answerable to the Minister for Agriculture. Research Institutes comprised the other units responsible for research into different aspects of welfare, some of which have since been themselves transformed. These include the Swedish National Institute for Building Research, abolished in 1995 by the Bildt bourgeois minority government (Kemeny 1996, 1997) and the National Institute for Working Life, abolished by the Reinfeldt government just weeks after it took office in 2006.

---

1   It is interesting to note from a discourse perspective that just as *private* schools in the UK are called *public* schools, so in Sweden, where the majority of private schools are run as public limited companies, they are called '*free* schools'.

The research done by these and other quangos laid the foundations for the postwar Swedish welfare state, and from the start were largely, if not entirely, financed by the funding of permanent posts rather than short-term project contracts. These quangos continue to play an important part. However, their funding has been increasingly dependent on grant-capture, as permanent posts have been progressively cut back, just as has been the case in the university sector.

Breaking the Mould: The Abolition of the Wage-Earners' Funds

The Wage-Earner's Funds were created by the Palme Government in the 1970s. They had originally been intended to give employees a degree of shareholding influence over company decision-making, though in their final form were watered down into a new kind of pension fund especially benefiting the employees of high-profit companies, as a means of rewarding efficient companies without breaking wage-bargaining solidarity (Engelen 2004).

An important impetus to the targeting of research funding was given by the decision by the Bildt Government (1991–1994) to abolish the Wage-Earners' Funds. Much of the share-capital was diverted and used to fund politically-controlled research. The original political decision was that the capital should simply be consumed and then the research trusts wound up. In fact, this clearly is not happening as the growth in value of these invested funds has so far been greater than annual expenditure, and the Social Democrat government that inherited the system entrenched it in its major 2001 reform of the contract research allocation system (see below). It may be that the temporary system introduced under the Bildt government that increased contract research funding was seen by the following minority government under the Social Democrats as fitting well with their plans to cut back on permanent funding and give them more control over research. The Government-controlled MISTRA – the Foundation for Strategic Environmental Research – is financed by such diverted Wage-earner funds with a total capital of SEK 3.6 billion of what were previously SEK 3 billion of Wage-Earners' Fund capital.

It must surely be one of the supreme ironies of Swedish working class history that the use of funds set up to give wage-earners a more secure old age is being used instead to finance short-term research employment of the most insecure kind.

Research Councils and their Political Governance

A radical and far-reaching reform of contract research funding was introduced in 2001, creating a new system of funding bodies with a new organisation and a new more uniform structure of decision-making. It would be tedious to provide a comprehensive catalogue of even the main research councils, both public and private. By way of indication, I briefly describe the best known of the three major research councils through which Government funding of contract research is organised: the Swedish Research Council [*Vetenskapsrådet*]. The research funding at its disposal is second only in size to state base-funding of research. The others, FORMAS (the Swedish Research Council for Environment, Agricultural Sciences and Spatial Planning), and FAS (the Swedish Council for Working Life & Social Research) are constructed along similar lines.

The Swedish Research Council with an annual budget of SEK 2 billion comprises an Executive Board [*Styrelsen*] and five Scientific Councils (Human and Social Sciences; Medicine; Natural Science and Technology; Educational Sciences; Research Infrastructures) as well a number of committees. The discipline-grouped Scientific Councils are responsible for processing grant applications, peer review management and the first filtering of proposals to be considered by the Board for a funding decision.

In 2006 the Executive Board comprised a core of five permanent members (of which only one was an academic) appointed directly by the government. The Chairman of the Board was a senior ex-politician: Bengt Westerberg, Leader of the Liberal Party 1983–1995, Deputy Prime Minister and Minister for Social Affairs in the Bildt Government of 1991–1994 (replaced by Björn von Sydow, the Social Democrat Minister of Defence, by the incoming Reinfeldt Government). The other Executive Board members were Pär Omling (General-Director of the Council, previously a physics professor at Lund University), Jane Cederqvist (a teenage olympic gold medalist who became a career administrator holding a number of politically-appointed senior government positions), Arne Wittlöv (ex-Deputy Chairman of Volvo) and Lena Andersson (author and media writer).

Besides this core of five government appointees, there were eight elected members, all senior researchers voted into membership of Council by national ballots of docents and professors. The permanent members, headed up by a senior ex-politician as chairman, provide the continuity in terms of central guidelines, precedents and the governing praxis. Researchers may comprise the majority, but the key decisions have clearly been in the hands of those whose experience and world-view is in politics, industry and the media.

This is a clever social construction. Because the Board is comprised of a majority of elected academic members, and is provided with a peer-review process of initial sorting of applications by the second-tier of the organisation – the five discipline-grouped Councils, it was possible for the Education and Research Minister to describe the political and policy priorities of the Science Research Council as being 'researcher-governed' [*forskarstyrd*]. In a short article entitled 'The Free search for knowledge by researchers is fundamental' (Östros 2004: n.p.), the minister deployed the word 'free' or 'freedom' no fewer than five times in a short six-paragraph statement.

It is instructive to compare this system of appointment with the much more centralised and less transparent system of appointment in the ESRC, the British equivalent of the Swedish Research Council as far as social science research is concerned. The government's influence over appointments is not just more comprehensive than its Swedish equivalent, it is total. *All* members of its governing body (Council) are appointed by government minister. And in this case it is not, as one might expect, the Minister responsible for research who appoints but the Minister for Trade and Industry.[2] Nor does the reach of politician influence end with such appointments. There are then further rewards available in the form of an honours system. Swedish prime ministers may not have life peerages to give away as rewards for loyal service but County Lieutenant-governorships and ambassadorships as well as breath-takingly generous pension agreements[3] are no less effective.

Bo Rothstein (2005), Professor of Political Science at Gothenburg University, does not mince words in his criticism of the reconstitution of Swedish contract research funding as an extension of the arm of government, describing it as 'a staggering blow to the independence of Swedish research'. He notes the irony of the fact that Bengt Westerberg, a previous leader of the Liberal Party which has always stood for defending civic freedoms, has become the government's poodle [*nyttig idiot*], heading up the Swedish Research Council in the task of creating more effective political control of Swedish social science research.

In another debate article, Rothstein (2006) criticises more directly the government appointment of the heads of research institutes and research councils funding research into what are for the Social Democrats politically sensitive areas such as EU policy (SIEPS – Swedish Institute for European Politics), labour policy (see National Institute for Working Life, above) and environmental policy (MISTRA, see above). The head is often chosen from among the holders of a social democratic party-political appointment such as an ex-minister, ambassador, under-secretary of state, or the general director of a public administrative bureaucracy such as Social Welfare [*Socialstyrelsen*]. Rothstein describes such nominees as 'Commissars' who exercise detailed control over what research is carried out and by whom, citing an example of funding from MISTRA (see above) in which he was personally involved as an applicant.

Another reform newly-introduced is to earmark funding for the creation of what are termed 'strong research environments' (Centres of Excellence), needed, it is argued, by a small country to maintain its leading position in research (a copycat version of the earlier British initiative). The way in which this reform has been

---

2   Currently the board comprises a majority of academics, though this may not indicate much. It would be instructive to see an analysis of the membership of the ruling body of the ESRC in terms of their politics, their holding of positions in business and public administration, and compare it to that of the Swedish Research Council. The power structure of research councils and how they operate is a remarkable *lacuna* in the study of contract research.

3   So-called 'parachute agreements' (*fallskärmsavtal* – common among the directors of large PLCs) give early retirement to senior politicians and politically-appointed senior administrators on what can only be described as gigantic pensions that can be SEK 1,000,000 a year or more. They regularly give rise to media storms that the government ignores as best it can.

constructed has been to only accept bids from the university Boards, reflecting the Social Democratic government's penchant for centralisation. Furthermore, they must be able to demonstrate that the bids they choose to be submitted to the Government in the name of the university are appropriate to each university's strategic research development plan (the upshot is that research groups are not permitted to make a bid except to the University Board, and then only if the Board requests such bids). The new Stockholm Environmental Institute is the most recent addition to this initiative.[4] This is further bolstered by the *Linnaeus Grants* as lesser boosts to an additional 20 centres.

Apart from the Government sector, Sweden also has a private sector of trusts specialising in funding contract research. The Bank of Sweden Tercentenary Foundation is one of the better known in the humanities. The Board of Trustees is made up primarily of two groups – academics and Members of Parliament (*Riksdag*). Its permanent members are made up of five Riksdag members, three academics and two administrators, plus the Chair (an academic) and Vice-Chair (a Riksdag member), chosen by the government but in consultation with the Bank of Sweden (some attempt is made to include representatives from all the larger political parties with seats in the *Riksdag*). The six 'Preparatory Committees' are made up of a majority of academics but include *Riksdag* members. So this private foundation mirrors the power structure of the government-controlled research councils. If anything it is even more politics-oriented, having a permanent governing body equally balanced between academics and politicians but with no elected academics and with no appointees outside of either parliament or academia.

The University Sector

Bo Rothstein has directed a sustained critique of the move from base funding to contract funding. In a debate article in *Dagens Nyheter*, Rothstein (2005) describes the 'long and grim list' of reforms introduced by the Social Democrats to increase government control and direction of research. These include replacing majority University Board membership of staff and students with government appointees, replacing staff and student election of the *rektor* (vice-chancellor) with a government appointee chosen by the Board, and increased power of University Boards to decide strategic research priorities.

Nor is this all. The Swedish university system in which only full professors have security of tenure with relatively generous time for research is based on the

---

4   The first ten-strong research environments of the Swedish Research Council have been chosen, between them to receive SEK 44 million every year over a five-year period. Only one is in the Humanities and Social Sciences, the Centre for Population Studies at Umeå University, to construct a demographic data base and this despite the Council's criticism of government underinvesting in these disciplines.

German *docent* model. Yet the old professorships are being phased out and in their place those employees with docent competence may apply for recognition of professor competence. Such new professorships are titles only, the posts remaining lectureships in their terms of employment and in their work conditions, being predominantly – usually 70 to 80 per cent – teaching posts and characterised by insecurity of tenure. Because Swedish labour laws are based on the 'first-in-last-out' principle, they offer strong protection to older employees. The result has been to discourage the mobility of labour, producing an ageing academic workforce, a high proportion spending their entire working lives from undergraduate to retirement in one department. The resultant inbreeding combined with the way this entrenches patronage and discourages new ideas, is reinforced by a high rate of unemployment among new entrants to the labour force, notably the young and immigrants. More important in this context, the growing teaching commitment acts as a stimulus to clutching at the straw of the only remaining route into research: grant-capture.

One of the first areas affected by the shift from funding posts to funding short-term research contracts has been graduate education, and especially the funding of doctoral studentships. The dramatic decline in the funding of doctoral studentships that allow graduate students to freely choose their research topic has involved a tightening of the selection process whereby the doctoral programme cannot be embarked on unless funding is available, if not in the increasingly rare traditionally-funded studentship then externally funded. Nor is it any longer sufficient to be able to claim or even demonstrate that the programme can be completed on personal savings, an inheritance, or the salary of a spouse or partner.

This has effectively meant that to become a graduate student increasingly requires joining the contract research application lottery in order to obtain grant funding. For most students, this means having a project already approved and finalised *before even applying for postgraduate studies.* The work to write and submit such research proposals diverts time and resources from undergraduate degrees, preferably a year or two in advance. This also means that students tend to be channelled into research that is of current interest to policy-makers rather than their own burning interest. They also have to find a senior member of staff who will act as their mentor and if possible be a joint-applicant for funding, as well as being prepared to supervise the project and the doctoral research.

The system also introduces extra work for the graduate student so financed. They are expected to complete their doctoral training parallel to their completion of the contract research: a double work-load that no account is taken of, as it is unrealistically assumed that the contract research and research for the dissertation, including writing the final research report to the contract funders and the writing of the dissertation are completely isometric and so involve no extra work.

Given these reforms that affect everyone from professors to undergraduates, plus the accumulating impact of cheese-slicer savings, in combination with the increase in grant-funded research made possible by the abolition of the Wage-earners' Funds, the government has been able to increasingly harness the universities to conduct research that is of interest to whatever party happens to be in power at the time. Some of the research institute quangos were simply transferred, lock, stock and barrel, to a university. A notable early example of this was the Swedish National Institute for Building Research, the social science divisions of which were reconstituted in 1995 as the Institute for Housing Research (later re-named the Institute for Housing and Urban Research) in the Faculty of Social Sciences at Uppsala University (for an analysis of this transfer see Kemeny 1996, 1997). The other half of that institute – the physical science divisions – was first transferred to the Royal Institute of Technology in Stockholm, but later reconstituted at Gävle College of Higher Education.

But the cheese-slicer policy towards the research sector has continued relentlessly, the rate of change greatly speeded up in the case of universities by the policy of the government to expand student numbers without a corresponding increase in general funding. Effectively, university staff have been forced more and more to apply for grants to fund their research or else find more and more of their research time taken up by teaching. And university departments have felt the growing pressure to increase their grant-capture or face the loss of posts as they fall vacant.

Yet while existing universities have been left underfunded, the government embarked on an ambitious and long-term increase in the number of universities. Despite the stagnation of state spending on research, the higher education system was expanded dramatically during the 1990s. In the decade 1991–2001 registered students increased by 62 per cent, doctoral students by 90 per cent, the creation of new universities increasing the number of universities from seven to 13, and the number of other higher education institutions with the right to examine doctoral candidates from five to nine (Swedish Research Council 2004: 9).[5]

The increase in the number of universities has not been decided by politically-motivated Government fiat as has been traditional in the UK. There has been no equivalent of the creation by the Conservative Government in the early 1960s of 'new' universities in the leafy suburbs of places like Essex, Warwick and Stirling, nor the following Labour Government's response of bestowing university status on the working class inner city polytechnics like Aston, Salford and Strathclyde – nor even of the mass-conversions of the remaining polytechnics to university status a generation ago by the stroke of a ministerial pen. Instead, the Swedish Government has instituted a public review process whereby higher education institutions may apply for university status to a standing review committee. Each higher education institution must demonstrate that it meets a minimum required standard of research activity in order to gain examination rights and access to research resources. By no means all applications are successful, though this has

---

5 This 172-page report, packed with statistics, comprises a sustained and devastating critique of the Government's under-investment in research, perhaps reflecting that its government-appointed Chairman is a senior Liberal Party statesman. It is particularly scathing about the neglect of the humanities and social sciences.

not stopped virtually every higher education institution from calling themselves 'university', there being no copyright on the word.

Consequences of the Increasing Marketisation of Research

The Political Roller Coaster of Research Funding

The above control mechanisms contribute to ensuring that research that is funded is both scientifically legitimated and of some relevance to governance. The relevance can be practical in relation to policy-implementation, or as evidence that can be cited in speeches to demonstrate that the government gives the issue high priority (whether it does or not is of course another matter), or simply research that is on topics of considerable current interest or that is politically correct, as well as, more transiently, that reacts to the latest media hype or moral panic.

Some recent research subjects that have been topical in Swedish social sciences contract research have been gender equality, male violence against women, 'honour murders',[6] ethnic integration, 'vulnerable urban areas' [*utsatta områden*],[7] the Holocaust, sustainability, 'the right to buy', care of the elderly, the social dimensions of IT, and the privatisation of welfare. Some of these, such as gender equality, the environment and ethnic integration have remained of interest to government throughout the Social Democratic period of office from 1994 to 2006 and continue to be so today. Others have emerged later (such as vulnerable urban areas, care of the elderly and the social dimensions of IT). Others, such as the privatisation of welfare, are on the back-burner though likely to rise rapidly in government esteem since the election of the bourgeois government in September 2006.

Still others have come and gone in a much shorter time-period. The right to buy (or rather convert non-profit rental housing into tenant-owner co-operatives [*bostadsrätt*], that was introduced by Stockholm City Council after the bourgeois parties won the city local election of 1998, resulted in a dramatic increase in interest. However, after the Social Democrats regained control of Stockholm in 2002 and cancelled the policy, interest all but disappeared. Research proposals on the impact of this policy submitted around the turn of the millennium were much more likely to be funded than those submitted only two years later. With new national and Stockholm City bourgeois administrations this particular roller

---

6   Murder or other violence by a male relative of a female, commonly a daughter or sister, who has dishonoured the family.

7   The word 'vulnerable' [*utsatt*] is used as a politically-correct label for indices of multiple disadvantage, poverty or deprivation (high unemployment, low educational attainment, low income, etc.), in this case signifying suburbs with a high percentage of immigrants.

coaster gathered speed again, only to come to a grinding halt in the wake of the financial crisis.

Of course, contract research in particular has always been responsive to shifts in government interest. But with the proportion of research that is driven by grant-funding increasing dramatically the difference between the crests and the troughs of the waves can be expected to increase, and the distance between crest-tops to shorten. This is perhaps less noticeable now than it could be as there have been remarkably few changes of Government in Sweden since the 1930s, the last two being in 1994 and 2006).[8]

Reactions

The Kaliber Survey

There has been growing concern over the impact of the major shift to contract funding and its political implications, in particularly for the independence of research. In spring 2006, Swedish Radio (P1) in *Kaliber*, a programme of investigative journalism, devoted a mini-series on the shift to contract research in universities. It took as its starting point the results of a questionnaire sent to all university professors based on over 2,000 replies, a response rate of 50 per cent. The programme was in two parts, the first on 14 May 2006 and the second part two weeks later, each with two repeat broadcasts.

The results make grim reading, though all too familiar to British researchers. Much of the programme was concerned with the way economically-powerful financiers have radically impacted on what is researched in universities as well as what results are produced, ranging from putting an acceptable 'spin' on the results to outright suppression of results that the commissioning company found not to its liking.

But for purposes of this chapter the political issue is of more immediate relevance. Half the respondents experienced their research as being politically-directed, but that 'political control' is rarely understood in narrow party-political terms. Again the kinds of political direction reported were wide, ranging from proposals being seen as politically incorrect to changes made (or insisted upon) to the final report by the commissioning public authority. When professors were asked if they would be prepared to address these issues on radio in the second programme many refused for fear of being seen as 'biting the hand that feeds them' and thereby alienating their grant-givers. The other even more striking result of this survey is that four out of five responding professors consider they spend an

---

8   British national politics have been even more stable, at least in the late postwar period, with only one change of government in the last 30 years. Local government is generally more unstable and so grant-funded local research is more vulnerable to political swings.

unreasonable amount of time applying for funding for their research (see below).[9]
The *Kaliber* programme made a major impact, calling forth a stream of protest and
bringing out the Minister responsible for research, Leif Pagrotsky, to defend the
system of research-grant funding.

Inefficiencies of the Make-Work System of Grant-Capture

The shift in research funding from the creation of permanent research positions
to annual or half-yearly rounds of competition for grants involves a carousel
of application submissions, assessment by panels of academics, and allocation
decisions by the senior administrators of grant-funding organisations, with a
rejection rate that can be as high as 90 per cent or more. This bureaucratisation
of research-funding generates a huge amount of make-work. The Principal of the
Higher Education College of Dalarna, Agneta Stark, in an article in *Tvärsnitt*,
a humanities and social sciences research magazine, calculated that in 2004 the
Swedish Research Council received 5,444 applications for a share of the total
sum of SEK 2 billion. She conservatively estimated the work to produce these
applications at the staggering total of 389 *working years*. This annual production
of nearly four centuries of work, was sent to 400 researchers to read and then write
their assessments, adding a further 28 working years. She estimated the salaries
of these 417 working years to be SEK 230 million, so consuming 10 per cent the
Swedish Research Council's total grant-allocation and consuming 20 per cent of
all social science research time (Stark 2004).[10]

But this is just the tip of the iceberg. To the yearly total of four centuries of
work must be added all the other applications to grant-giving bodies, both public
and private. The proportion of the total amount of university staff research time
invested in this process – and with a 90 per cent failure rate most of it is totally
or partially wasted – hardly bears contemplating. Agneta Stark questions the
creation and maintenance of these gigantic sorting bureaucracies, arguing that the
real sacrifice is not measured in how many centuries of research-time have to be
unproductively expended every year to keep the bureaucracy wheels grinding, but
the loss of all the research results that could have been produced instead, but that
no-one will ever see.

The increasingly competitive nature of funding also works to increase social
inequality. Magnusson and ten co-authors (2006) criticise the fact that none of the
20 Linnaeus Grants (see above) went to women (or, it might be added, to members
of ethnic minorities), reflecting the cumulative impact of social disadvantage from

---

9   A recent editorial in *Dagens Nyheter* on the *Kaliber* programme commented that in
12 years the proportion of contract-funded research to base-funded research has risen from
50 per cent to 70 per cent.

10   For comparison a report on the eight UK state research councils estimated the
annual cost of the review process to be nearly £200 million (Research Councils UK
2006: 3).

early childhood onwards. Somewhere a reasonable balance needs to be struck between secure base-funding and competitive contract funding. A Lund Professor of Literature went as far as to argue that 'to invest such a high proportion of research funds in Research Councils using gigantic bureaucratic "human-sorting systems" for application-procedures and grant-allocation decisions is itself a major threat to quality' (Hedling 2005, my translation).

Research Fraud

A quarter of a century ago, in a study of the US automobile dealership system, a symbolic interactionist coined the term 'criminogenic market structures' to describe the way some markets are socially constructed such that crime, fraud and misdemeanour become endemic (Faberman 1985). That this is a complex matter is well-illustrated by the widespread – not to say universal – use of doping in individual-based sport competitions that is not reflected in team sports such as soccer where top teams become public limited companies and where other kinds of fraud are found, especially involving big business, corruption and organised crime.

The same complexity applies to research fraud, which has increased in several countries in recent years, including Sweden, with a number of high-profile cases. As one professor in the *Kaliber* interview survey cited above puts it: 'sponsors don't buy research, they buy the results they want'. This, combined with growing vulnerability to insecurity of tenure, plus the placing of the responsibility onto the shoulders of the individual researcher rather than the employing institution together make a potent combination. Clearly the kind of criminogenic market that is produced will vary depending on what these pressures are, which in turn will be refracted by how research is organised in different countries, not to mention the leverage that political research patrons are able to command.

The Reinfeldt Government's Research Policies[11]

In the September 2006 General Election, despite the World pre-depression boom that in retrospect hauntingly echoes the 1920s, the social democratic government after 12 years in office lost in a clear swing to the right, resulting in the election of a four-party right wing coalition dominated by the Moderates, the Party occupying the most extreme right wing of the Riksdag. This is proving to be Sweden's most radical free market government in modern time, with huge tax reductions for the rich, major attacks on non-profit rental housing and large-scale privatisations of public companies, and of welfare, especially education and health. Its policy

---

11   A number of additional reforms are still being negotiated, too late to be finalised for this publication, including improving security of tenure. How this will work in practice remains as yet unclear.

in increasing contract research still further is by comparison modest, though only because their predecessors did most of the spade-work, and took most of the resulting criticism. Policy has been more to consolidate the privatisation of research already attained by facilitating a closer relationship between research and market interests.

A number of major initiatives are being introduced. Apart from the introduction of university student fees, that the previous government was considering, a research reform is already at the Bill stage of its legislative journey – significantly named 'A boost for research and innovation'.[12] This is a bundle of interlocking measures to encourage a closer relationship between universities and big business. The most important is the allocation of public funds to research by SEK 5 billion. The lion's share of this, 36 per cent (SEK 1,800 billion) is in the form of an entirely new kind of annually recurring third type of allocation to universities called 'strategic allocations', in addition to the two existing allocations of basic funding of university research via the faculties and the funding of research councils. This will give the government the power to define – and continuously redefine – what 'counts' as being 'strategic' – a significant increase in Big Brother Government. The other major change is organisational – funding 'innovation offices' at seven of the major research universities available to all research institutions and intended to 'assist the commercialisation of inventions and give advice on patenting and licensing'.

In addition to these measures, funds are earmarked for the private sector in the form of VAT-exemption for research funders and tax-exemption for donations to research, and to strengthen the economies of university holding companies devoted to commercial research. The whole tone of the measures in the Bill is to move away from what is patronisingly termed 'traditional curiosity research' in which 'problems are formulated by researchers themselves' [sic!][13] to referring to 'research-and-innovation' as if it were one word. This expression is enshrined in the title of the legislation and repeated mantra-like throughout its text, the press releases and in ministerial media articles. In addition, the texts are replete with words and expressions like 'usefulness', 'the commercial potential of research ideas', 'the early public risk-capital financing of ideas from academic research', 'seed-capital' and 'market potential'. Criticism of this approach have already begun (Rothstein 2008; Waluszewski et al. 2008; Svensson 2008).

Another looming tranche of reforms that appears to be copied from Finland, concerns making universities freestanding from the state, and a preliminary [*betänkande*] state investigation (SOU 2008: 104) called *Independent Universities* has been published evaluating what kind of organisational form would be most appropriate and with recommendations that will increase market dependence. The insistence that all research institutions be self-financing – the concept of

---

12   *Ett lyft för forskning och innovation*, Prop 2008/09:50 (Government Chancellery).

13   Lars Lejonborg (Minister for Universities and Research) 'Volvo's crisis shows the need for a new kind of research funding', *Dagens Nyheter*, 10 October 2008.

'Enterprise University plc' (Allen 2006; Marginson and Considine 2001; Mautner 2005) – is one that the Reinfeldt government is moving towards under the guise of 'freedom from big government'.

Conclusions

With the collapse of the Soviet Union and the end of European communism (*The Second Way*) Sweden's welfare system has been undergoing a process of degeneration. As a result, the Swedish model, itself drawing strongly from the Swedish Third Way[14] inspired by *der dritte weg* in interwar Germany has been increasingly undermined and neglected. Without an established Third Way discourse to nourish and give expression to policy, 'Planning' has become part of a discredited discourse that conjures up images of Gosplan.[15] Instead, 'The market' will deal with long-term maintenance in its usual efficient manner. This has to be understood in the context of Sweden's policy of armed neutrality as a small power in international politics. Contrary to what many Swedes like to believe, neutrality and *The Third Way* are most effective when the balance between the power blocs is even, as it was in the days of Hammarskjöld and Palme. At other times it means bending with the strongest wind, as with Germany in the early years of the Second World War, or, the US since the collapse of the Soviet Union which accelerated the spread of the influence of the neoliberal model in Sweden from Reaganomics via Thatcher-Blair marketisation. Key sectors of Sweden's welfare such as public health, housing and education have experienced falling standards and creeping privatisation (Kemeny 2005). It is therefore not surprising that this is also reflected in terms of the financing and organisation of research.

Acknowledgements

I would like to thank Chris Allen for his comments on an earlier draft of this chapter.

---

14   Since the collapse of the USSR, reference to the Swedish 'Third Way' between communism and capitalism is hardly ever made in Swedish politics.

15   The complete revamping of the Institute for Housing and Urban Research's own academic journal *Scandinavian Housing and Planning Research* that I was centrally concerned with in 1996 and its renaming as *Housing, Theory and Society* was, to my surprise, supported partly on the grounds that the word 'planning' was obsolete.

Chapter 4

In the Name of the People?:
The State, Social Science and the
'Public Interest' in Urban Regeneration

Chris Allen and Pauline Marne

Introduction

The idea of 'the public interest' was first used in the nineteenth century to justify state intervention in the operation of markets. The case for state intervention was made on the grounds that, in certain circumstances, the invisible hand of capitalism produced optimal outcomes but, also, sometimes undesirable outcomes and side-effects. This case was made by nineteenth century 'reformers' who had come to realise that the self-interested nature of market behaviour could generate social and economic costs as well as benefits that, moreover, were damaging to capitalism itself. A good example of this argument, that readers of this book might recognise, concerned the unregulated nature of housing provision in the industrialising city. An unregulated market in land use and housing provision had resulted in the mass building of slum dwellings, owned by private landlords who were free to operate as they pleased. The reformers thought that this unregulated system of housing provision had resulted in poor quality and overcrowded living conditions for the working class and that this was the cause of 'public health' problems that would ultimately damage labour productivity. It was this recognition of the social and economic costs of unregulated capitalism, by some members of the political class, which led to the emergence of the language of 'public interest'. That is to say, the reformers were able to justify state intervention on the grounds that it improved the lot of the population generally – in this instance, by providing better quality housing. Suffice it to say that the idea that state intervention was needed to protect the 'public interest' was a misnomer; it was also needed to sustain capitalism itself. Thus the idea of 'the public interest' is fairly ambiguous: Since its conscription into the lexicon of the political class in the nineteenth century, the idea has accumulated both progressive ('in the name of the people') and regressive ('in the interests of capital accumulation') connotations.

Notwithstanding the political uses and abuses of the term 'public interest', philosophers have attempted to provide the idea of 'the public interest' with substantive content (that is, by providing a definition of 'the public interest' that has clarity of meaning). However, their endeavours have proved to be problematic

so there remains no clear philosophical definition of the public interest that has
secured widespread agreement. From a philosophical point of view, then, there
remains a lack of clarity about what 'the public interest' means and what it
refers to. However, this does not mean that the term is redundant. Far from it.
The state and powerful urban interests continue to refer to the public interest in
order to justify policy interventions. Nevertheless, some things have changed in
this respect. The idea of 'the public interest' was used in the nineteenth century
to reign in some elements of the capitalist class (e.g. developers, landlords) in
order to protect capitalism from itself. Thus its negative effects were felt within
the capitalist class itself, whereas its positive effects were felt amongst the urban
poor. However, contemporary appeals to the public interest in the field of housing
and urban policy have been somewhat different. This is because contemporary
housing and urban policy is more concerned with boosting markets, than with
restraining them, because this is believed to provide a boost to the performance of
the urban economy in general. In the contemporary city, then, the idea of the public
interest has been mobilised to legitimise policies that facilitate the pillaging and
plundering of *inhabited* housing land from working class people and others (e.g.
small and alternative businesses) by development interests. The 'public interest'
justification given is that some parcels of land in the contemporary city can be
put to more productive use by development interests (as opposed to people) and
that select people must suffer the consequences of land use change if the overall
performance of the urban economy is to improve – which is said to be in the
interests of everyone. The benefits that accrue to these development (and other
powerful) interests as a result of policy interventions that facilitate the pillaging
of land is therefore obscured by the way urban elites promote the idea that their
activities are undertaken in the 'public interest' and 'in the name of the people'.

What is significant here is the role that universities and social science have
come to play in legitimising urban elites' use of 'the public interest'. This is because
changes in the Higher Education sector have resulted in its increasing exposure to
the market for knowledge (see Imrie, this volume). This has made it easier for
the state and powerful capitalist interests to 'buy' social science evidence which
'demonstrates' that what they propose *is* in the public interest. Thus social science
is increasingly being conscripted – through a commercial contractual relationship
with the state and other interests – to the task of 'identifying' the public interest
and legitimising policy interventions that service 'the public interest'. This brings
us to the rationale and purpose of this chapter.

If a realist philosophical concern with the public interest might be regarded as
superfluous, then a critical sociological one is perforce necessary. In other words,
understanding what 'the public interest' actually is (or might be) is arguably far
less important to us than understanding who defines it, how it is defined, how it
is used and in whose interests it is used. Moreover, an examination of the role
of social science, undertaken within the context of a commercial contractual
relation with the state and other agents, is axiomatic to any exercise that seeks
to understand how the public interest is defined and used. The reasons for this

should be obvious. Appeals to the 'public interest' are now routinely justified with reference to an 'evidence base' compiled by social scientists that willingly service the state (and other powerful interests) in this regard. The chapter addresses itself to this issue. Specifically, it is concerned with the manner in which the term 'the public interest' has been invoked to justify a whole range of policy interventions that have fundamentally reshaped the city of Liverpool over the last decade. We refer, in particular, to the programme of 'transformational regeneration' that has involved a radical programme of 'restructuring' of the housing and urban landscape in the city. We argue that interpretations of the public interest by the policy-making elite in Liverpool tend towards a deontological interpretation of it. So, political references to the public interest in Liverpool tend to be made in terms of the (undefined) 'we' that will benefit from transformational regeneration of the housing and urban landscape. For instance, the policy-making elite in Liverpool, and those who speak on behalf of this elite, continually refer to the benefits of transformational regeneration to 'the city' and 'the people of Liverpool'.

However, policy-making elites are also aware that such claims can – and need to – be substantiated and that social science has a contribution to make to the policy process in this regard. Accordingly, we also discuss how the state has conscripted social science to the task of establishing a more exact insight into the nature of the public interest. We show that social science tends to produce these insights for the state by establishing an aggregated insight into the public interest, i.e. by providing calculative insights into the 'we', e.g. by aggregating individual preferences for policy change into an 'objective' picture of the preference for policy change such as '80% in favour, 20% against'. Such an approach has been used to legitimise controversial regeneration initiatives in Liverpool. However, we argue that aggregative approaches are anything but objective. They are political. This is because social science understandings of the public interest are produced from positions in social and ideological space and can never, therefore, be objective. More specifically, we argue that a social science that has been conscripted by the state will tend to produce understandings of the public interest from the hegemonic position in social and ideological space occupied by the policy-makers that purchase it. This is because a social science that has been conscripted by the state tends to develop epistemic sympathies that conform to hegemonic policy paradigms (Allen 2009) as Hillyard et al. (2004) have previously suggested by arguing that ideas tend to conform to the power that finances their production rather than vice versa.

This provokes us to develop an alternative interpretation of the public interest which is based on the hermeneutical idea that an understanding of it – or, rather, the different perspectives of it – can only be generated through a dialogical process. What we are suggesting, then, is that an understanding of what is in the public interest can only be *resolved* through *political dialogue* between those with an interest in its realisation. It is not something that can be *objectively established* by social scientists that are tasked to *identify* it by the state, on the grounds that the state somehow embodies the public interest. This is not to say that social science does not have a role to play in identifying the public interest. In a political context where the institutions of the labour movement have either been weakened (e.g. trade unions) or transformed into vehicles for middle class interests (e.g. the labour party), working class people have been left without institutions that can effectively articulate their interests. We conclude the chapter by arguing for a hermeneutical social science that is 'genuinely public' (Castree 2006) in the way it engages with oppressed minorities to identify and articulate their interests rather than one that is servile to the state and the powerful interests that are parasitic on it to provide them with enhanced opportunities for capital accumulation.

Urban Policy, Social Science and 'the Public Interest'

Urban Policy and the Public Interest

Urban policy elites' appeal to of the idea of 'the public interest' suggests universalism and a homogeneous universalism at that (Campbell and Marshall 2000) where the rationale for urban policies and initiatives is said to be the enhancement of the well being of 'the city of X', 'the people of City X' and so on. This interpretation of the public interest tends towards what Box (2007) refers to as a deontological interpretation which emphasises shared values and that appeals to the 'we' feeling of community. Let us examine how this plays itself out in a contemporary urban policy context: The 'entrepreneurial turn' in urban governance has meant that the pursuit of urban economic growth (and not simply welfare service provision) now features heavily in urban policy-makers' minds. The logic that prevails here is that the benefits of urban economic growth will accrue to 'the people' and 'the city' in a variety of ways, most notably in terms of increasing employment opportunities for the people that live in the city and by bringing empty industrial buildings back into use thereby erasing scars from the urban landscape. We do not have to look very far to find numerous examples of these claims being made; they are present in the literature produced by almost every major urban regeneration initiative – Glasgow 1990; Manchester 2002; and Liverpool 08 and London 2012. But let us take Liverpool because it is the focus of this chapter. The architects of regeneration in Liverpool have made extensive appeals to the imagined 'we' that make up the city by suggesting that regeneration initiatives, such as the 'City of Culture' programme in 2008, have been pursued in the name of the people and for the benefit of the people:

> Liverpool won the 2008 race because people – our city's greatest asset – were at the heart of the bid and we want to ensure that everyone is given the opportunity to take part when Liverpool takes its curtain call before the eyes of the world in 2008. We are working closely with all our stakeholders – including cultural organisations, communities, creative industries, artists, schools and businesses – to help Liverpool shine on the world stage by delivering the best-ever European

Capital of Culture 2008. As a result, we hope to leave a lasting and positive legacy for the people of Liverpool, including more jobs, a stronger economy and a better place to live (source: http://www.liverpool08.com/about/).

There's a lot of hard work going on behind the scenes around legacy planning to make sure Liverpool benefits in the long-term from this brilliant year (source: http://www.nwda.co.uk/news--events/features/enhancing-quality-of-life/rave-reviews-liverpool-08.aspx).

2008 was a life-changing year for this city (Warren Bradley, Leader, Liverpool City Council, source: http://www.liverpool08.com/streets/Transition/index.asp).

This usage of the term public interest tends towards the rhetorical (Box 2007): Thus the 'City of Culture' programme in 2008 rhetorically appealed to interests of 'the people of Liverpool' and, as such, claimed it had been 'life-changing for the city' which had consequently 'benefited'. But the architects of urban regeneration have not simply relied on political rhetoric to appeal to the undefined 'we' that so clearly belies the social and economic divisions that ravage the city (Fainstein et al. 1992). Urban policy elites have, historically, also conscripted the 'expert' knowledge of planning and other professionals to the role of 'informing' decisions about 'the city' in the name of 'the public' that constitute the city:

> The rhetoric of serving the interests of *the public* is central to the folklore of planning and is enshrined in chartered object of the RTPI in the United Kingdom. For individual planners this overriding obligation is very much a taken-for-granted part of what it means to be a professional … a defining characteristic of the planner's claim to a distinctive professional expertise [is] the ability to be synoptic in an effort to arrive at wise and just policies and decisions taking all views and relevant information into account (Campbell and Marshall 2000: 306).

Now although urban professionals have a long history of serving 'the public interest' in the modern city, the entrance of social science to the heart of policy-making at local level *as a matter of epistemic necessity* is a much more recent phenomenon. So this is an important change that needs to be considered carefully.

Social Science and the Public Interest

Although links between modern universities and urban elites go back to the historical origins of many of these institutions, which lay in the nineteenth century and sometimes earlier, the utility of these links was originally realised in the curriculum that social scientists taught (Jones 1988; Rothblatt 1988; Phillipson 1988). Urban elites were concerned to ensure that teaching programmes were useful and relevant to the needs of the state, economy and society. However, they showed little or no interest in social science research which was undertaken in conditions of relative academic freedom where the pursuit of knowledge for its own sake, rather than its relevance to urban elites, was prioritised.

This is not to say that the national or local state has never shown an interest in social science research and its utility *until now* because it has. Moreover this interest has been growing since the mid-twentieth century, when governments began to take an ever greater interest in the political uses (and abuses) of social science research. Labour Governments, in particular, have shown a long-standing interest in the potential relevance of social science to public policy-making that dates back to the mid twentieth century. This interest was first apparent after the Second World War when a Labour Government was elected that contained strong Fabian influences; Fabianism emphasised the importance of developing a scientific understanding of society and in developing scientific informed solutions to social problems (Webb 1979). This Post-WWII Labour Government established the Clapham Committee to examine the need to expand the social sciences in order to enhance the capacity of universities to undertake research into the social and economic questions being posed by government at the time (Lee 1996). Although some of the key Clapham recommendations withered under the Conservative Governments that spanned the 1950s and early 1960s, the return of a Labour Government in 1964 witnessed the establishment of the Heyworth Committee which was formed to support the previously identified need for an expansion of the social sciences *that were socially useful and relevant*. Thus one striking feature

> ... of the Heyworth Committee Report [1965] was the instrumental view taken of social science and the focus on the use of research in policy-making. [Its] report speaks of the need for social scientists to work alongside administrators in identifying emerging problems and dealing with them (Lee 1996: 78).

Although this rhetoric of utility prevailed, it did not readily translate into the practice of social science. This is because the Social Science Research Council (SSRC) that was established at the recommendation of Heyworth took a liberal view of the social sciences, so a much wider range of research was commissioned than simply 'policy' or 'industry' relevant research (Lee 1996). In any case, the block grant system of university funding already provided social scientists with the time and resources to work on their own research problems within the course of their 'normal' duties (Hillyard and Sim 1996; Allen and Marne, this volume), which meant that they did not need to seek funding for 'policy relevant' research from the SSRC (Allen and Marne, this volume).[1]

---

1   Nevertheless, there is a long standing 'tradition' of social scientists undertaking research in the service of 'informing' policy-making, even when the policies they have sought to inform have been less than ethical (Horowitz 1967).

This situation changed with the election of the Thatcher government and, in particular, with the arrival of Keith Joseph as Secretary of State for Education and Science from 1981. Joseph was hostile to social science on the grounds that its value was questionable, so he established the Rothschild Enquiry into the SSRC in 1981. However, the enquiry did not have the desired effect. Rothschild was supportive of social science but, nevertheless, held the view that social research needed to be more directly useful to Government and Industry in order to enhance its value and status. To this end, he introduced formal procedures for commissioning SSRC research which were shaped according to the customer/contractor principle (Lee 1996). In this arrangement, the customer (i.e. the SSRC – an executive agency of government) produces a 'specification' that outlines the research that is useful to its requirements, whereas the contractor is the university academic that wins the competition (with other researchers) to undertake the work as specified by the customer. From Rothschild onwards, then, the content of social science research has increasingly been defined by policy-makers who have tasked it with serving 'the public interest' that they claim to embody

> ... The criteria of "good research" are "helpfulness" and a concern for its consequences; it is assumed that the policy-maker should control research in the public interest (Commission on the Social Sciences 2003: 73).

> The social sciences have a huge contribution to make to the economy, society and politics and to improve people's well being (AcSS/ESRC 2008: 3).

The 'good social scientist' is, then:

> ... in touch with government agendas, in tune with the realities of the political and policy-making environment (Commission on the Social Sciences 2003: 70).

The Private Uses of the Public Interest

A common perception is that the move towards an incentive system in which research is 'externally funded' by the state (or other, say, business interests) is problematic because normative conditions of 'academic freedom' are compromised. But this is erroneous because, as we indicated above, even a cursory consultation with the history of the university shows that it was captured as an institution, at the outset, by aristocratic interests (Rait 1912), business interests (Phillipson 1988, Rothblat 1988) and urban elites (Jones 1988). In any event, classic 'social studies of science' by the likes of Kuhn (1970) and Latour and Woolgar (1979) have shown that academics have never been entirely 'free' to define the content of their work even when they have been left alone to 'get on with things' on their own terms. This is because the scientific field, itself, has historically been organised in such a way that powerful interests *within it* have also been able to exert significant degrees of control over the type of research that has been undertaken and the type of research that has been published. This brings us to the issue of what is so different about the contemporary context of research production: What is different about the current context of research production is that the controls on research production are external *rather than internal* to the scientific field. So, why is this problematic?

If policy-makers can, as they claim, embody the public interest then the fact that social science is increasingly producing knowledge for those that can pay for it – whilst starving those who cannot pay for knowledge – would not be so problematic. But it makes no sociological sense to say such a thing. Generally speaking, sociology presumes the city to be divided and therefore studies it to understand the nature of the social and economic divisions that exist (e.g. between ruling and corporate elites and city dwellers); the manner in which ruling elites exercise power to maintain their social and economic position and thereby maintain inequalities; and the manner in which order is imposed on the conflicts that arise as a result of these social and economic inequalities (Fainstein et al. 1992; Harloe and Lebas 1981; Harloe 1977). This means that appeals to 'the public interest' by ruling elites obscures the nature of the (e.g. corporate) interests that urban policies represent and that social science is therefore being tasked to work for (Harloe and Lebas 1981; Harloe 1977).

The remainder of this chapter provides a material insight into how this abuse of the public interest occurs – and the role of social science in its occurrence – with reference to a case study of transformational regeneration in Liverpool. Our argument is as follows: Urban policy elites in Liverpool did not merely rely on rhetorical appeals to the public interest in order to justify regeneration programmes that serviced the interests of developers and middle class housing consumers whilst working against the interests of working class people in the city that vigorously opposed these regeneration programmes (Allen 2008). Urban policy elites in the city relied extensively on social science in order to 'demonstrate' that what they were doing was in 'the public interest': Social science was a powerful tool in the armoury of urban policy elites in the city because it enabled them to claim that what they were doing had 'emerged' from a series of 'independent' and 'objective' studies that had examined the regeneration context 'in the round' and that had resulted in a series of policy proposals that served 'the city' as a 'whole'. Yet our critical analysis of the production and use of social science knowledge of the regeneration context in Liverpool shows that this research has done *anything but* serve the interests of 'the people of Liverpool' or 'the city' as a whole. Conversely social science knowledge of the regeneration context in Liverpool has served the interests of powerful voices in the city (most notably those of developers) 'in the name of the people' whilst, ironically, legitimising the violation of the 'right to the city' of working class Liverpudlians (see also Harvey 2008). These are important points so let us examine our case study in detail.

The Problem of Social Science and the Public Interest in Liverpool

> There is no doubt that Liverpool has been transformed over the last decade …
> billions of pounds of investment has created a new city centre, better retail and
> leisure facilities such as Liverpool One and the Arena and Convention Centre
> (Warren Bradley, Leader, Liverpool City Council).

Liverpool has apparently undergone a dramatic transformation during the last decade. Moreover, this dramatic transformation has been undertaken in the name of 'the people of Liverpool'. This has certainly been the case for a wide variety of regeneration initiatives that have taken place in the city. One of these regeneration initiatives has necessitated the demolition of working class homes so that they can be replaced with 'modern and contemporary' houses that will attract 'service sector households that are influenced by a consumer society' (Nevin et al. 2001). Liverpool City Council has argued that such developments have been necessary to satisfy public interest in the city so let us briefly consider the nature of this claim.

Liverpool City Council (LCC) placed Compulsory Purchase Orders (CPO) on 'obsolete' working class homes in parts of inner Liverpool in 2006. LCCs argument is that some neighbourhoods in the city were suffering from 'housing market failure' because contemporary housing consumers did not wish to live in them. The stated purpose of the CPOs is to facilitate a redevelopment of the urban dwellingscape so that it is more 'exciting' and therefore attractive to knowledge workers that generate the economic growth which will benefit the city as a whole. Speaking about this initiative at Public Inquiry, the legal representatives of Liverpool City Council claimed the compulsory purchase orders were being made in the public interest:

> The compelling case in the public interest is overwhelmingly shown through
> the operation of national and development plan policy to seek to reverse the
> market failure in the Renewal Areas beginning with the Order Lands (Landmark
> Chambers 2006b: 40–1).

> Effective intervention is overdue and it is needed now. It is needed in the public
> interest, for the benefit of the people of Liverpool (Landmark Chambers 2006a:
> 28).

> The case in the public interest could not be more compelling (Landmark
> Chambers 2006b: 2).

The idea of the public interest mobilised by LCC is not simply rhetorical. Thus LCC does not simply appeal to an assumed 'we' that will benefit from its regeneration plans, which would constitute a deontological interpretation of the public interest. The significant thing here is that LCC has purchased social science evidence to show that what it proposes 'in the public interest' is 'evidence-based'. Thus when faced with opposition to its urban regeneration plans, which resulted in a Public Inquiry to decide whether the Compulsory Purchase Orders should be granted, LCC emphasised that it had commissioned eight reports from 'independent' researchers located at the Centre for Urban and Regional Studies, University of Birmingham in a four year period.

> The council's approach is evidence-based ... based on an immense base of research, evidence and policy debate. The issues with regard to the Liverpool housing market have been thoroughly investigated and analysed by the independent CURS, which produced 8 reports over the period 1999–2003 (Landmark Chambers 2006a: 20).

What is significant about this is that it enabled LCC to claim to the Public Inquiry that its interpretation of the Public Interest had been inductively derived from the 'evidence base' provided to them by these 'independent' researchers. These researchers appeared for LCC at the public inquiry where they emphasised the importance of their 'independent' and 'academic' status whilst arguing that the CPOs were necessary because the need for them was 'evidence-based' (Nevin 2006). The researchers claimed that they had unearthed 'evidence' that spoke about the need for demolition of 'obsolete' housing and its replacement with a better 'residential offer' which they interpreted to mean 'modern and contemporary' housing (Nevin et al. 2001; see also Cole and Nevin 2004). Moreover, the same researchers actually claimed that this was in the interest of the people that were losing their homes, through CPO, because their location in areas of 'housing market failure' meant that they were experiencing 'asset depreciation'.

> [T]he fact that 24 per cent of properties are situated in neighbourhoods experiencing acute decline has a significant negative impact upon the regeneration effort within the city. Within these areas individuals are seeing their major asset depreciate and experiencing negative wealth distribution (Lee and Nevin 2002: 50).

They also claimed that 'housing market failure' was having a negative *general impact* on 'the city' as a whole because it was inhibiting the inward movement of middle class knowledge workers (a claimed key source of economic growth) into the city – thus implying that the city 'as a whole' was suffering the consequences of 'housing market failure' and not just those experiencing 'asset depreciation'. The 'evidence-based' compulsory purchase and housing demolition policy was, therefore, presented as something that was being pursued 'in the public interest' which was assumed to cover the 'wider city' and all of the interests that existed within it (Nevin 2006).

Social Science and Official Interpretations of the Public Interest in Liverpool 08

So far we have seen that 'public interest' arguments, to legitimise urban regeneration policies in Liverpool, have been mobilised in two ways. First, political elites and their legal and public relations officials justify the need for regeneration programmes in the city by appealing to the interests of the imagined 'we' that comprise the city of Liverpool. In effect, then, they make deontological claims about the public interest in Liverpool. Second, they have sought to buttress these deontological interpretations of the public interest by using social science to establish statistical indications of the 'we' that will benefit from regeneration policies. Political elites have therefore drawn on social science to justify the making of rhetorical statements that represent policy change in the city 'in the name of the people'. The purpose of this is to provide independent and objective representations of the public interest which thereby becomes 'evidenced' and therefore 'evident'.

The problem here is the social science that informs the regeneration of the city is represented as 'independent'. It is said to speak the truth in a matter of fact way, thereby entitling its practitioners to speak of the 'evident' need for the compulsory purchase of houses in areas of market failure. However, the idea that social science is 'independent' and that it speaks an 'objective' truth about the situation in the city is fallacious. This is because such independent and objective interpretations of the 'we' that will benefit from regeneration masks the fact that the social scientific thinking that identifies the 'public interest' case for policy change is actually articulated from particular positions in social and ideological space and that it speaks to the interests of those that occupy these positions. Thus although 'independent' researchers working for LCC claimed that regeneration policies in the city had emerged in response to their social science which spoke an impartial truth (Nevin 2006) this simply masked the fact that their social science knowledge was produced within the parameters of a neo-liberal view of the performance of cities and their housing markets. Specifically, LCC had conceived and commissioned housing research – from sympathetic housing researchers – on the basic assumption that the market for houses in the city was a field of competition between houses and neighbourhoods. And since the research employed this basic assumption, it logically problematised houses and neighbourhoods that had become 'uncompetitive' in the field of competition between houses and neighbourhoods. However, the research also erroneously problematised houses and neighbourhoods that had become uncompetitive in the field of competition between houses and neighbourhoods because it was erroneously based on the hegemonic assumption that people living in these houses viewed their houses as financial 'assets' that were in competition, for equity growth, with houses in other neighbourhoods. But this was not necessarily the case, as we will now see.

Social Science and Aggregative Objectifications of the Public Interest

The social scientists that work for LCC, and who were tasked with providing scientific evidence that regeneration proposals were in the public interest, claimed that their social science spoke an impartial and objective truth about the public interest. For instance, at Public Inquiry, one of the architects of the housing demolition plans in the city claimed that this science was merely representing an aggregate picture of what people said about what they wanted to happen in the city. In other words, social science was merely providing an aggregate voice for people so, presumably, the voices of local people were speaking to the Public Inquiry through the apparatus of social science, i.e. through statistics and the like.

> Allen particularly takes issue with some of the wording of the CURS/ECOTEC research. The researchers are merely recording back to the reader, the aspirations, desires and prejudices of the thousands of people who we have contacted as part of this research and who form part of the housing market ... The simple fact which appears to escape Professor Allen is that the market is what it is, comprises people who are entitled to, and who have, their own wishes and aims ... Professor Allen obviously does not like what consumers have told us or how we have interpreted it (Nevin 2006b: 6–7).

What these people were *apparently* saying to the social scientists working for LCC was that they wanted housing demolition so that 'modern and contemporary' houses, that would be competitive in housing market terms, could be built in their place. There are two things to note about this. The first is that social science was being used, by the local state, to express an aggregate (that is to say, utilitarian) version of the public interest which, in Liverpool, was based on the claim that

> ... The public is a collection of separate, individual thinking units holding predetermined preferences ... [The public interest] consists of whatever the majority of the people want at a given time, a utilitarian calculation of measurable and additive individual positions (Box 2007: 587).

In Liverpool, then, the public interest is understood as an aggregation of the preferences of individual people who are assumed to be separate thinking units that speak for themselves and whose preferences are articulated by a social science that is able to aggregate these preferences into something that is statistically meaningful. For instance, LCC sought to convince the Planning Inspector who chaired the Inquiry that the case for the CPO of homes in parts of the city was in the public interest by drawing on social science to claim that

> ... A majority of respondents in Edge Hill (60.68%) and Holt (51.5%) indicated a preference for a new housing environment (Major 2008: 42).

Having accepted this aggregated interpretation of the public interest, presented through social science, the planning inspector was simply unable to accept alternative interpretations of the public interest. Although these social science findings were contested by resident groups opposed to housing demolition, then, the planning inspector dismissed this opposition on the grounds that they could not prove that their case was representative in the same way that social science was able to claim representativeness for its aggregated interpretation of the public interest:

> The fact that BEVEL [a resident group opposed to the housing demolition programme] does not represent the local community in any meaningful way has become even clearer at this inquiry ... in reality BEVEL is a tiny, *unrepresentative* and loosely knit group of people, who cannot claim to speak for more than a minute proportion of either the past or present community, the true voice of that community is clearly expressed in the written and oral evidence of ... Kensington Regeneration (Major 2008: 34).

The problem with this reliance on an aggregated interpretation of the public interest, provided by Kensington Regeneration but purchased from social scientists, is that it does not represent the aggregated preferences of 'the people' at all. Even a cursory examination of the questionnaires that were used to establish the public interest shows this to be the case. For instance, the inspector quotes the social science research, commissioned by LCC, which asked residents whether they wanted 'a new housing environment', but it did not ask them the more relevant question of whether they wanted housing demolitions. This was highlighted at Public Inquiry by the chair of BEVEL but to no avail:

> Are you aware that residents voted unanimously for regeneration when it started? ... Do you think we thought that meant losing our homes? (Elizabeth Pascoe, speaking at Public Inquiry, January 2008).

Indeed, far from representing an aggregated view of the public interest, the social science purchased by LCC actually suggests that there is a majority preference *against* housing demolition and that, far from representing the 'true voice of the community', the regeneration agencies in the city had actually alienated the community with their plans to demolish homes. Specifically, government sponsored research co-ordinated by Sheffield Hallam University, and undertaken by MORI, actually show that 51 per cent of the residents surveyed said they did not trust these regeneration agencies and that 70 per cent of residents said they had no influence on decisions affecting their area. It should come as no surprise, then, that only 22 per cent of residents agreed with the much more explicit (about housing demolition) statement that 'I want my neighbourhood largely cleared and redeveloped'. Far from representing the public interest in an unproblematic manner, then, the social science commissioned by LCC and national government actually raises serious issues about the ability of social science to speak in the public interest. As Engels has taught us many years ago, this is because 'independent' and 'impartial' claims to reconcile the conflicting interests within the capitalist city into a wider 'public interest' are designed to encourage and mislead us to believe in the impossible, namely, that these conflicting interests can be reconciled in the public interest:

> The very people who, from the "impartiality" of their superior standpoint, preach to the workers a socialism soaring high above their class interests and class struggles, and tending to reconcile in a higher humanity the interests of both the contending classes ... they are the worst enemies of the workers – wolves in sheep's clothing (Engels 1892: 26).

Social Science and the Public Interest as a Process

The state's preference for positivist approaches to research is well documented (see Bridge, this volume), as well as the acceptance of this situation by social scientists who argue the case for 'comprehensive empirical enquiry' and against anecdotes, single case studies and partial 'stories' (Martin 2001: 198). What we have, then, is a situation of mutual-dependency that serves to reinforce the status quo. On the one hand the local state needs social science in order to justify its claims that what it does is in the public interest but, crucially, it has a near monopoly position as a purchaser of social science. Therefore it is able to specify what type of social science it is prepared to buy. On the other hand, social scientists need state funding in order to undertake research. This means that social scientists have become 'service providers' to the state. Crucially, social scientists compete with each other for business from the state which means that there is an incentive to conform to the demands of the monopoly purchaser in order to 'win' business. Since those that win this business seek to produce 'satisfied clients' in order to secure 'repeat business' (Allen and Marne, this volume) they are able to establish long standing relationships with the state which results in their 'concerns', as social scientists, shifting from critical perspectives of local problems to a starting point that is intuitively sympathetic to the view of the policy elite that exercises power (Allen 2005; Allen 2009). This has certainly been the case in Liverpool where the social science architects of its regeneration policies have shifted from arguing that knowledge serves political power (Loftman and Nevin 1998) to the view that they are merely communicating to readers what ordinary people have told them during the multiple research projects that they were commissioned to undertake between 1999 and 2003 for Liverpool City Council and its institutional partners (Nevin 2006).

> The aggregative view is associated with social scientists who describe the world in the way they think is objective, keeping their distance from its meaning or the possibilities for change (Box 2007: 587).

What is particularly interesting here is the epistemic superiority that is assigned to social science aggregations of the public interest that, after all, emerge from the statistics and therefore 'speak for themselves'. Indeed the superiority that is assigned to the social science aggregations of the public interest is so taken for granted, by those that produce them for the state, that they are simply unable to comprehend any other way of understanding the public interest and how it may inform policy-making. For instance, the argument below is taken from a researcher that is well versed in working for the state and whom understands the public interest accordingly:

> The idea of replacing methodical approaches to understanding housing phenomena with selected opinions is unconvincing when placed in the context of policy-making or increasing our knowledge and understanding of social problems (Sprigings 2009, forthcoming).

The social science aggregated view of the public interest is, then, what serves to justify what the local state is able to do because it provides it with legitimacy – in the name of the people. However, the idea that social science speaks from a position of impartiality ('we are just relaying what people have told us') has always been regarded as problematic in the philosophy of knowledge and increasingly so in the contemporary social sciences which speak of the importance of understanding the social position from which knowledge is produced. Such critical thinking has also found its way into the political philosophy literature on the Public Interest which has become sceptical of social science approaches that aggregate consumer preferences because it represents

> ... The view of those who accept the status quo ... The politico-economic system that forms individual preferences is not questioned, because the aggregative view is epistemologically positivist, not normative; it accepts the given, the way things appear at present. The aggregative perspective can be attractive. It has about it the feeling of democracy because it valorises the majority view and seems consistent with the [British] penchant for individualism. It is amenable to quantification (Box 2007: 588).

The idea that researchers can establish the public interest by 'merely recording back to the reader, the aspirations, desires and prejudices of the thousands of people who we have contacted as part of this research' (Nevin 2006) is, then, naive because in such an

> ... aggregative view people [only] know what they have learned through the media or other sources of information and vote as individuals in accord with *what they think* are their interests (Box 2007: 592, emphasis added).

In other words, aggregative approaches to establishing the public interest in Anglo-American societies will tend to produce a neo-liberal interpretation of the public interest and not an 'objective' interpretation, as adherents to the aggregative approach might wish to think. What is clear in Liverpool, then, is that the social science research commissioned by LCC cannot possibly speak from a position of impartiality. It speaks from a political position. Moreover it speaks from a hegemonic neo-liberal political position that posits housing as an 'asset' that should be traded for the purposes of accumulating equity and therefore the market for houses as a field of competition for equity accumulation. It also speaks from a neo-liberal position that views housing in terms of the wider agenda of urban boosterism, which is the idea that the city needs to compete for business and that the benefits of this competitive behaviour accrue to the people of the city. So, a 'new housing environment' – indeed, an 'upgraded' urban environment in general – will attract new hi-tech business to locate into the city whereas the knowledge class that work in such industries will be tempted to live in the city rather than outside it. And the key beneficiaries of this are, of course, the developers that are provided with compulsory purchased land that is then passed onto them – for a token price – to enable them to develop a 'high value' dwellingscape.

However, the problem in Liverpool is not simply that superiority is assigned to the aggregative view of the public interest – for instance, at Public Inquiry into the compulsory purchase of homes where the planning inspector only accepted the aggregated interpretation of the public interest that had been produced by social scientists working under contract to LCC. Another problem is that political elites in the city, and the social scientists that were working for them, demonstrated contempt towards alternative interpretations of the public interest produced by residents because they were said to be based on 'selective' and 'selfish' interpretations of the public interest which, by definition, were inferior (see Sprigings 2009 quoted earlier for an example of this argument). Yet such an argument demonstrates an epistemic ignorance of the nature of the aggregative view which is equally selective because it articulates, and elevates, the interests of those that occupy positions of dominance in political and ideological space.

This brings us to the crux of the issue. Since social science cannot produce a definitive statement of the public interest – because it is a matter that can only be addressed through political debate and not by science – Box argues for a non-social scientific view of the public interest which is based on the hermeneutic principle of open dialogue in which social science should play a facilitative rather than directive role:

> The process view of the public interest regards individuals as participants in dialogue about what is in the public interest and what the public sector should do about it. Instead of packages of predetermined interests, individuals are perceived as people with interests who can learn from social interaction. In such interactions, they acquire new information about public issues and become aware of the perceptions and desires of others ... Common examples of the

process view of the public interest at work include citizens boards, commissions, committees, and neighbourhood groups (Box 2007: 588–9).

A process view of the public interest is much more challenging, as well as democratic, because it opens participants to a range of possible alternatives beyond the 'given' options ('a new housing environment?') that social scientists might present them with: 'what choices would people make if they were aware of a wide range of options including some that involve significant changes in existing political, economic, institutional and legal arrangements, if they did not think that existing arrangements were all that is possible?' (Box 2007: 592). Nevertheless, Box is pessimistic about such a view of the Public Interest prevailing because it would involve consideration of

> ... A list of possible alternative futures that can threaten entrenched economic and ideological interests ... Much of the knowledge of alternatives and possibilities for change already exists; the question is how to make it available to people who may find it useful ... discourse about the public interest is intended to permit open, relatively unconstrained consideration of [such] alternatives, potentially reducing violations of human dignity, pointless aggression, inequality and degradation of the physical environment, allowing people to choose to flourish in a peaceful, self-created setting (Box 2007: 594–5).

This raises two issues about the way in which wider interpretations of public interest were 'dealt with' in Liverpool in order to protect entrenched economic and ideological interests. First, superiority was assigned to interpretations of the public interest produced by social scientists working for LCC because they had used 'methods' to produce an 'aggregated' understanding of it. In contrast, interpretations of the public interest produced by residents were denigrated for being based on 'select opinions' that were 'self-interested' and therefore inappropriate because the issue at stake concerned 'the public interest' which LCC and the social scientists that worked for it claimed to be upholding.

> ... Several of the objections are *simply* that residents do not want to leave their homes and their communities (Green 2006: Appendix i).

But this is not simply about LCC's dismissal of residents' opposition to the compulsory purchase of their homes on the grounds that they were 'self-interested' and 'unrepresentative'. The residents' 'alternative plan' – which claimed to *properly* serve the public interest – was regarded as 'impractical' and therefore 'irrelevant' because it had been 'rejected by the authorities whose support and participation would be essential' (Major 2008: 35). However, although the residents' 'alternative plan' was ostensibly rejected by the Planning Inspector on *technical grounds* and thus for 'soundly expressed reasons' (i.e. the alternative plan was 'inadequate' because it had been drawn up by a group with no 'relevant experience') the alternative plan was actually dismissed on *political grounds* because it was 'utopian'. In other words, it simply did not fit with LCC's neo-liberal interpretation of the public interest which identified a need for 'transformational regeneration' and therefore a large scale programme of land assembly that would enable mass developers to create an entirely 'new' and 'exciting' urban landscape that would convey a positive view of the city to potential investors:

> The suggestion is that the sale of one house would provide the funds to refurbish two more. The idea requires a "community developer" ... The idea was rightly described as utopian. As was stated in paragraph 4.5.5, "*formulating a just and effective basis for this group is a nice problem, but one that is beyond our scope*" (Major 2008: 36–7).

Thus although the planning inspector argues in his report to the secretary of state that the alternative plans had not been properly consulted upon, there was no sense that this was a problem that could be rectified through a 'proper' process of consultation on the alternatives that were being proposed. Conversely, the lack of consultation is actually proposed as a reason for rejecting the alternative plan which was *actually* rejected because it provided an alternative ('utopian') choice that would require 'significant changes in existing political, economic, institutional and legal arrangements' (Box 2007: 592). This is why Crooks argues that such a defence of the 'existing' arrangement of political and economic power – by a social science whose claims to represent the public interest obscure the fact that such social science represents the interests of those that buy it – actually constitutes an affront to the public interest rather than its realisation:

> LCCs evidence to this Inquiry reveals a stunning lack of empathy, insight and imagination with respect to its citizens and the task of regeneration ... The people affected by these CPOs have a resilience, humility and simple dignity that LCC could learn much from. Their strengths, talents, hopes and fears are what make Liverpool a city of culture. To force these residents from their homes to make way for unknown, high income outsiders (and investors) amounts to little more than state sponsored gentrification. Far from being a compelling case, it is rather an affront to the public interest (Crookes 2006: 14–15).

Conclusions

This chapter has discussed the idea of the public interest and the way in which it has been used by urban policy elites to legitimise programmes of change that have actually served the interests of the powerful. However, the chapter had a more specific purpose. It examined how policy elites are increasingly conscripting social science to the task of providing an 'objective' understanding of the public interest in order to justify programmes of urban change. Although this might seem unproblematic on the surface, the chapter critically examined the claim that social science can produce such an objective interpretation of the public interest. It did this in two ways; with reference to debates in the philosophy of knowledge and with reference to a case study of regeneration in Liverpool. This enabled us to show how social science serves the interests of the customer that buys it rather than the wider public interest that it purports to serve. But the chapter was not simply concerned with the problematic nature of urban policy elites' (and the social scientists that work for them) interpretation of the public interest. The chapter also examined how urban policy elites 'dealt with' alternative (process) interpretations of the public interest in order to establish their own interpretation as the legitimate one.

Urban policy elites in Liverpool denigrated process interpretations of the public interest that residents groups produced through a process of open dialogue – rather than by using 'research methods'. However, our discussion of the process interpretation of the public interest showed that its advantage was that it does not make the naive claim that it can 'establish' a definitive definition of the public interest. On the contrary, it merely claims to 'open up' the range of issues that needs to be *considered* within the context of *democratic political debate* about 'the public interest' which cannot, therefore, be *identified* by an authoritarian *social science* that claims to speak the truth. So what are the implications of this? As things stand, social science interpretations of the public interest are filling the vacuum that has been left by the demise of the institutions (trade unions etc.) that represented the political interests of working class people in political debate. Moreover, social science is being commissioned to fill this vacuum by policy elites that seek to secure legitimacy and consent for the programmes of change that they seek to impose on disparately constituted, but nevertheless hostile, opposition to these programmes. The implications of this argument are obvious. It poses ethical questions about whether urban policy elites should 'buy' social science in order to legitimise their interpretation of the public interest because the rationale for such procurement of social science is so clearly political rather than epistemic. Thus although the social science that is procured might provide deontological clarity with regard to what is apparently in the public interest, this clarity will simply provide us with a clear view of what is in the interests of the status quo and preservation of the position of the powerful. Conversely, a genuinely democratic social science that is based on the hermeneutic principle of open dialogue necessitates recognition of a range of knowledge claims that should be discussed in such a way that interested parties are treated as participants in a dialogue about the public interest rather than the 'subjects' of 'research' into the public interest. In the absence of strong institutions, such as Trade Unions, that were previously able to articulate the voices of working class people, social science has a potential role to play in facilitating the articulation of these voices. This will necessitate a more democratic social science that is very different to the authoritarian type of social science that currently prevails, which makes its claim to epistemic authority on the grounds that it uses 'research methods' to develop its 'objective' insights into the public interest (Allen 2009b). In a democratic social science, ownership of the research process is taken out of the hands of research funders and researchers themselves so that it is constituted much more widely amongst participants in the research process in order to ensure that 'epistemic justice' prevails which requires

> ... the conferral of *credibility* upon knowledge claimants ... The process of credibility assessment may favour those groups who are already powerful or privileged in society ... Epistemic injustice occurs when the credibility that a person deserves to have does not correspond to the credibility they are actually afforded ... [We] need to consider a [broader] set of knowledge claims ... in order to make moral progress, that is, the putative knowledge of marginalised groups regarding the oppression and injustice they suffer (McConkey 2004: 199).

Such a democratisation of social science would threaten the interests of the powerful that have prevailed in Liverpool because they have been able to 'buy' an 'objective' social science interpretation of the public interest *which is actually nothing of the sort* because it has been articulated from within the parameters of the dominant neo-liberal political and economic view of the public interest that prevails in the city. In other words, it threatens the constitution of the knowledge business – which allows institutions with 'research budgets' to purchase the knowledge they need in order to legitimise their actions – as we know it.

Acknowledgements

We are indebted to the architects of 'the public interest' in Liverpool for providing us with some fabulous material that has enabled us to see the 'public interest' for what it is.

Chapter 5

Knowing the City: Local Coalitions, Knowledge and Research

Huw Thomas

Introduction

This chapter discusses some of the tensions associated with coming to know the city. There are many ways in which the city is experienced and understood; none are innocent of relations of power (Flyvbjerg 1998; Hubbard 2006: 44ff). Of particular interest in this chapter are understandings of the city that are deployed in policy frames (or policy discourses) which enjoy dominant or hegemonic status in particular cities.[1] Part of the way such policy discourses cement their popular legitimacy is through claims to a particular kind of rationality and objectivity; I suggest that it is in this context that university support – as guarantors of scholarly objectivity – can be helpful to those who would promote and sustain an hegemonic policy discourses in a particular place.

Links between universities and urban governance have a long history in Britain and elsewhere (Bender 1988). In the nineteenth-century, establishing a university, or university college, was regarded as an effective move in the civic competition engaged in by influential elements of the urban middle class in Britain and other industrialising nations. In the new industrial metropolises a university helped symbolise the significance of the town and especially its regional (or sub-regional) importance (Briggs 1963). As Jones (1988: 113) describes it in analysing the struggles to found university colleges in the great northern English cities of Leeds, Liverpool and Manchester:

> The merchants, manufacturers, and professional men of Manchester, Liverpool, or Leeds were united by financial, religious and other interests. They worked together to create institutions of local government and civic improvement. They also created an intellectual and artistic culture of which the civic colleges were an important, perhaps a culminating part.

Against this background, a certain historical closeness between universities and institutions of governance in their host towns and cities might be expected,

---

1   There may not be such policy discourses in every city; interest in this chapter is confined to the cases where they exist.

especially in places with tight-knit social networks for the local middle classes (Jones 1988: 108–115). As late as the mid-1990s a study of UK higher education found that in its case study universities (selected to provide variety) close to 50 per cent of governing bodies of universities were also members of other locality-related public bodies such as local authorities, National Health Service Trusts, or Urban Development Corporations (Bargh et al. 1996: 47). Yet the same study also found diversity among universities – in mission and governance.

Even in relation to a given institution there can be changes over time. For example, Shils (1988) records how relations between the University of Chicago and the city government changed as the demography and politics of the city changed. Moreover, universities have to be responsive – to varying degrees depending upon their mission – to pressures and expectations from well beyond the civic boundaries. This is perhaps especially obvious in centralised public university systems such as the UK's, but any university which seeks funding, students or esteem from sources beyond its immediate locality will feel similar pressures. Historically, the relationship between local authorities and universities has thus been diverse and complex.

This chapter concentrates on one aspect of university relations within urban governance: namely the way that the privileged capacity of the university to produce knowledge with a certain status offers opportunities for the insertion of the university within governance arrangements. Its argument proceeds in a number of stages.

The first section endorses analyses of urban governance which emphasise the significance of institutional co-operation and bargaining (often falling short of coalition formation or fully fledged urban regimes). In the UK, at least, local councils remain the most significant single organisation in the governance of their localities, albeit that they need to engage in co-operative activity with others to get things done. The chapter goes on to suggest that urban entrepreneurialism remains an accurate characterisation of the dominant approach to governance in many cities, especially those where social tensions associated with economic restructuring are politically salient (Harvey 1989). Entrepreneurialism and competitiveness in general has also taken a grip of higher education in Britain and beyond as part of a particularly crude application of new public management (Bundy 2004; Laffin 1998; Whiteley et al. 2008). The new political economy of higher education produces, and is sustained by, a set of dominant attitudes and practices – a mentality – which brings universities and urban governance into close ideological alignment. In these circumstances we might expect exploration (not necessarily self-consciously) by universities and local councils of the scope for collaboration which might be mutually beneficial. Yet, there are tensions in these relations, not least because universities have internal differences about what their priorities and objectives should be. This may limit what a university can 'deliver' in a partnership with external bodies.

The second section of the chapter provides a case study of how the pressures and opportunities explored in section one may play themselves out in a particular setting. It considers ways in which a university's being part of the institutional relations of local governance may have an impact on the nature of the knowledge produced (including what is not encouraged to be produced).

Urban Governance, University Governance

It is widely accepted that no single institution is in a position to act alone in order to get things done in cities (Stone 1989; Stoker and Young 1993). In relation to the UK, the institutional landscape of urban governance is probably more complex now than, say, 30 years ago, but as Imrie and Raco (1999, 2001) among others point out it is important not to exaggerate the changes at the cost of underestimating continuities. In particular, the elected local authority remains the single most important institution in the day-to-day governance of cities. Typically, it will be the lynch-pin in any significant activity aimed at promoting or boosting a city and its hinterland.

It is possible, also, to exaggerate (and misunderstand) the significance of the trend towards entrepreneurialism and competition between cities and regions. Harvey (1989) is persuasive in arguing that, in the face of economic restructuring which threatens the material underpinning of localities and their social relations, coalitions can form around the idea of defending a place, and these may draw support across classes and other social cleavages. Institutions which take themselves to symbolise the area/city will be prominent in these coalitions – city councils will be at the forefront usually, and local universities are also likely to play a part. But I share the scepticism of Lovering (1999) and others about some of the theorising which has legitimised competitive behaviour by regional development agencies and others claiming to promote an area's interests. Portraying the economic world as a competitive arena in which 'urban-regions', as much as firms, compete legitimises the activities of those institutions, individuals and groups with a material interest in promotional activity, and, more significantly those whose interests are served by emphasising social cohesion/solidarity rather than injustice, oppression and the necessity for reforming social relations. There are losers as well as winners in any social system and any set of policies intended to manage that system; those who can help legitimise any given system and set of interventions have much to offer those who wish to maintain that system, whether for their own benefit, from a lack of faith in alternatives or for a combination of both motives. Lovering's scepticism of the theorising of competitive behaviour between regions revolves around the theoretical poverty of much that is put forward as a framework and the lack of hard evidence for the entrepreneurial 'new regions' of Europe. This chapter on the other hand, considers the mechanisms and pressures which issue in flawed 'knowledge' of this kind.

Yet, whatever the limitations of the analysis underpinning the notion that the economic and general well-being of any locality depends on its being viewed as a competitive unit in an increasingly fluid world, there can be little doubt about the grip that the picture has on contemporary politics (Healey 2006). Establishing and sustaining competitiveness – with all its (politically expedient) ambiguity (Begg 2002; Hubbard 2006) – is the hegemonic political project in contemporary cities in the 'West'. Gordon and Buck (2005) argue that there is a 'new conventional wisdom' about how the economic world works which emphasises the significance of fostering competitive cities as part of successful economic policies. Hence agencies charged with urban governance strive to create conditions under which they believe their cities will be competitive.

The nature of institutional relations – like the nature of local politics in general – varies geographically. In relation to universities specifically, Deem (2001: 13) has shown how misleading it can be to ignore the 'continued importance of local as well as international and global factors in higher education'. As Harloe et al. (1990) and Warde (1988) argued persuasively, the historic differences in the social relations bound up with production and reproduction of the labour force will underpin differences in local politics. Not all, perhaps not many, cities will have a classic urban regime with its quite disciplined, persistent and focused coalition of interests (Stone 1989).

Yet there is little doubt that the attempt at creating coalitions and networks of actors (institutions, groups, individuals) whether for limited or more ambitious ends is widespread, even in cities with little history of successful mobilisation of this kind (Hubbard 2006). This is a consequence of two factors: the logic of the necessity/ideal of competitiveness, and often, pressure from national and international agencies that such co-operative behaviour be manifest (Lawless 1994).

Engagement in collective action is only required of those who have something to offer the more or less temporary coalition engaged in any given aspect of urban governance. Byrne (2001: 178) suggests that to be part of a regime you need 'control over resources seen as meaningful in relation to policy implementation'. It is this chapter's contention that an important resource that the university can offer is production of knowledge with a certain privileged status. Those with something to offer have then to be induced to take part – and, crudely, this means they need to get something out of it (Stoker and Mossberger 1994; Stone 2005). What that might be for universities will be discussed shortly.

Little has been said in the literature about the involvement of universities in city governance. Logan and Molotch (1987) argue that universities are likely to see advantages in urban growth, and thus to have an incentive for assisting growth coalitions, albeit as secondary players. That remark is made in the US context of a highly-differentiated higher-education sector, with many universities heavily dependent upon local catchments for their students. In the UK, higher education is becoming more differentiated, and universities vary significantly in their dependence upon regional, national and international catchments for students. A university like Leeds Metropolitan that sees advantages in sponsoring its city's professional rugby team is clearly targeting a relatively local market in so doing. Yet such a university will also invest heavily in international marketing. Yet it is arguable that to some extent all universities are – to use Cox and Mair's (1989) term – 'locally dependent'. For the governance of host cities is of significance to universities in a number of practical ways.

First, universities compete – with increasing sophistication and effort – for (good) students, both regionally, nationally and internationally. For the student-consumer, the host city is part of the university's 'offer'. A cursory examination of any commercial guide for would-be students confirms that the attractiveness and functionality of the host city are among the factors commented upon. The city's 'brand' helps market the university (Shepherd 2008). In addition, rather traditional town planning concerns such as the compactness and legibility of city and neighbourhood centres are among the things which can feature as plus or minus points. A reputation for night-life and excitement are among the things that urban governance can affect less easily. Community safety – and, crucially, public/press perceptions of it – are also important. In general, the image that a city has – nationally and internationally – can help or hinder (or be thought to help or hinder) university marketing. Secondly, the functioning of local labour, housing and land markets is of significance to universities. Universities need large numbers of lowly-paid service workers as cleaners, porters, catering staff and the like – these staff must be able to access the university relatively easily, often by public transport. These same staff need to have relatively low cost housing, as do university students. Finally, universities are major property owners and users, and often developers of new (often large) facilities too. As Adamson (1996: 136) points out, 'with the exception of the employment of staff, by far the largest element in a … [university's] … budget is estates management'. They bump up against the planning system quite regularly (140–142), and 'the estates director will need to have good working relationships with the chief planning officer and the housing director of the local authority …' (Adamson 1996: 151). For example, in Cardiff, over the last couple of years Cardiff University has developed two major buildings – one for its Optometry department, the other a block of flats for medical students – in the face of local resident opposition. In such circumstances, the resolve and support of the city council as planning authority can be invaluable.

It is a reasonable hypothesis, then, that universities will have a concern that the governance of their cities at the very least does not endanger aspects of labour and property markets that are of importance to them; in addition, they will wish to see their host city develop a positive image nationally and internationally. So, for example, we should not be surprised that of the sixteen Urban Regeneration Companies (URC) operating in UK cities in September 2009 which have a university, and for whom relevant information was available, eight have a representative of a local university on their boards.

Universities might have an incentive to be involved in urban governance, but what have they to offer the coalitions that Byrne and others have discussed? In part, their significance as employers and landowners earns them a place in discussions of policy (Cochrane 2007: 107–108). In addition, a university that has a good national and international reputation can help develop its host city's reputation;

stories about the successes of local universities are staples of the regional press. Shils's (1988: 212) assertion that 'A city without an important university is an incomplete city' has undoubted appeal to very many involved in urban governance in an era of competitive cities.

In addition, I suggest, the university's standing as the guardian and constructor of knowledge– the (ideological) notion of it as a supposedly neutral, objective commentator on the world as it is – still gives it a potentially important role in justifying and sustaining any given set of governance arrangements, whatever criticisms the notion has been under from social theorists and philosophers (Bender 2002: 152). For governance can work most effectively where consensual activity within shared frames of reference is the norm (Healey 2006). By a frame of reference we mean, in this context, a way of seeing and interpreting the world. A shared frame of reference can ease collective action among a coalition of interests, or partners needing to work together (Keith 2004); it can also help ensure the tacit support of a diffuse public which does not have the conceptual resources to frame or see the city and its problems in any other way. An example of the former is the way that a shared understanding of south Wales as a region suffering from the terminal decline of heavy and extractive industry, and needing to modernise, has welded actors across the political and class spectrum in a regional spatial coalition since the 1930s (Rees and Lambert 1981). An example of the latter is the way that Cardiff's docklands has been characterised as empty, 'ripe for revitalisation' and liminal – socially and ecologically – so that oppositional strategies for its redevelopment have been virtually impossible to generate (Cowell and Thomas 2002). In the context of urban governance, a vital task of such frames of reference is the delineation/construction of the city itself – i.e. the object of governance. So, in Cardiff's case, its capital city status is part of a hegemonic frame/discourse which has shaped the city's politics for at least 40 years (Coop and Thomas 2007).

The discussion up to this point has treated universities as cohesive and almost homogeneous entities. But of course, they are not. They are complex organisations, defined like any other by webs of social relations which reflect the history and tasks of the university, as well as the way its activities and personnel relate to the wider social world of which it is a part. For example, to understand universities as gendered organisations we would need to understand them as intimately connected to a wider social world; but to understand the particular nature of the gendering of any given university we also need to understand its particular structure, purpose, history, pressures and power relations. Universities will not relate to urban governance arrangements in any unitary manner therefore. References made above to university participation on URC boards highlight what the corporate management of universities (vice-chancellors and other senior executives) do. It is those elements in universities which are charged with maintaining external relations which support the increasingly significant corporate mission of the university (Clark 2001; Bundy 2004). We might expect these corporate divisions within a university to be especially sensitive, then, to the need for constructive relations with agencies of local governance. However, they are not (usually) the constructors of knowledge. Academics are the knowledge-makers. But academic departments do not exist in an organisational vacuum. First, they are subject to increasing pressures to be constructive corporate players, shaping departmental priorities and behaviour so that it is congruent with university priorities (Becher and Trowler 2001). For example, universities are regularly compared corporately, with rankings on teaching and research produced on the basis of aggregations of departmental rankings. So, an atmosphere develops in which thinking 'corporately' is valued by the 'centre'. On the other hand, departments remain responsive to disciplinary norms – to the values associated with their 'academic tribe' (Becher and Trowler 2001). In some disciplines – such as History – the dilemmas associated with undertaking research for a non-scholarly client, such as a company or government agency, remains live topics for debate (Johnes 2007). We might speculate that from the perspective of the corporate centre this kind of scholarly squeamishness may raise doubts about whether historians constitute a 'safe pair of hands' for certain kinds of contracts.

Moreover, there is a tradition of critical engagement by academics in their localities. Bender (2002: 155) reminds us of the strong Pragmatic tradition in the United States which links knowledge production to social progress (and often an associated critique of the status quo), but there are countless examples from other intellectual traditions, and various countries (e.g. Attili 2009; Dennis 1970, 1972; Hayter and Harvey 1993; Lo Piccolo 2009) as well as innumerable undocumented ones which show scholars engaging with the city around them. Because academic activists are often critical of the powers that be we can expect that this kind of involvement may be in tension with the university's corporate desire to maintain good working relations with powerful agencies of local governance.

In a less elevated sphere, departments cannot be indifferent to the urban context as discussed above – they are at the sharp end in recruitment of students (and staff) and so have an interest in the image of the city, as well as its functioning. Students need to be attracted, and then they need to remain happy, so that they are 'ambassadors' for the university (and, ultimately, happy, grateful alumni). The material reality and image of the city can come to have a particular significance for academic staff, therefore. Of course, these pressures and concerns operate differentially across a department – a head of department may come to see the urban context in a way which is very different from a researcher beginning her or his career.

The case study which follows – of urban governance and universities in Cardiff – examines how these pressures and claims on universities and their staff can play themselves out at university and departmental level. It focuses on the way the following factors inter-twine in helping to shape the specifically local relationships between universities and urban governance:

- differences in the characters and missions of universities;
- tensions within universities;
- differing interests of local councils and universities.

Its two key themes are:

- the ways that the mutual interests of university and local councils come to be recognised; and
- the way that production of knowledge can be implicated in this.

The University and City in Cardiff

This section adopts an historical approach to address the two themes set out above, each of which is dealt with in a sub-section. It highlights some key moments, and draws on secondary and primary sources.

The Shared Interests of the City's Political Elites and the University

The establishment of a university college in Cardiff in the late nineteenth century was an example of the kind of civic boosting mentioned earlier in this chapter. The proposed college was a government initiative, part of the growing political acknowledgement of Welsh distinctiveness, and Cardiff's borough council (it was not then a city) lobbied hard that it be located in what was then the largest town in Wales. In making a case, the civic fathers (the gendered term is used advisedly) painstakingly put together a coalition of support which crossed political and social divides (Chrimes 1983). A site was made available at the heart of the city's civic centre and whatever occasional hiccups there were in realising all promises, there was little doubt that the success of university college was central to the ambitions of governing elites in the city (Chrimes 1983).

Securing the college was part of a broad strategy to promote Cardiff as the premier town in Wales. Consistently pursued, and supported by all political factions from the late nineteenth century, this culminated in the grant of city-status in 1905 and capital city status in 1955 (Thomas 1999). In the mid-1960s the idea that the presence of a university bolstered the city's status was endorsed by the foremost town planner of the time, Colin Buchanan, in a major plan commissioned for the city by the national government. Buchanan's (1966) study envisaged university expansion in the city centre as part of a collection of civic buildings which symbolised the city's significance (Coop and Thomas 2007).

Buchanan took account of two university colleges, because by the late 1960s national plans for university expansion meant that Cardiff had this number of colleges: the original nineteenth century foundation, now University College Cardiff (UCC) and an ex-College of Advanced Technology now dubbed University of Wales Institute of Science and Technology (UWIST). Both were located in, and on the fringes of, the city centre in collections of scattered buildings, and both were being supported/encouraged to expand by their national funding body, the University Grants Commission (UGC). Buchanan envisaged the development of a university precinct which would have a clearer physical identity and would be part of Cardiff's symbolic and material functioning as capital city of Wales. The city council accepted this vision of Cardiff's future and was prepared to assist in its realisation.

A dramatic expression of this support was the council's compulsory purchase order (CPO) in 1970–1971 on a residential/ex-industrial area on the fringe of the civic centre that was earmarked for university expansion.[2] This was an area of nearly ten acres, containing 154 plots. The CPO was the culmination of a series of meetings over the previous years involving the council, both colleges and the UGC.[3] The colleges had expansion plans agreed with the UGC, subject to support from the local authority;[4] the city council agreed to pay 75 per cent of land acquisition costs as well as sponsoring the CPO under planning legislation, and being the applicant for the planning application that needed to run in parallel with the CPO. The minutes of the so-called quadripartite meetings, council meeting and associated correspondence make it clear, however, that the unanimity needed to promote and defend at public inquiry this major initiative was forged after much effort. University – council entente was (and is) not guaranteed on any given occasion. It was (and is) worked at, but against a background of the underlying considerations sketched earlier in this chapter.

In the case of the CPO for the university precinct, for example, UWIST was always a reluctant subscriber to the plan. Its principal's fulsome support of the CPO at the Public Inquiry was in marked contrast to attempts in the immediately preceding years to argue the merits of an out-of-town location for the institution. UWIST's council minuted its reservations about the idea of expansion in the centre of Cardiff, and there was public opposition from its own staff.[5] The overt reasons for the opposition were practical: there might not be enough room in the centre, and land and building costs were higher. UWIST supported its position with a planning consultants' report that it commissioned in the face of a study on university expansion in the city jointly funded by the city council and the UGC. The commissioning of such a report suggests that underlying UWIST reservations was the thought that its needs might be submerged by those of its older and more prestigious neighbour, which was – after all – twice its size.

2 'The City of Cardiff (Higher Education Precinct) Compulsory Purchase Order 1970'. Cardiff City Council papers relating to the Compulsory Purchase Order (CPO) and associated planning application, including a public inquiry into both, are held in the Glamorgan Record Office in Boxes BC/CRS/1/16 – BC/CRS/1/23.

3 There are records of quadripartite meetings on 25 September 1969, 16 January 1970, 27 May 1970, and 22 November 1971 (BC/CRS/1/16; BC/CRS/1/17 for the November 1971 meeting).

4 *City of Cardiff (Higher Education Precinct) Compulsory Purchase Order 1970. Statement of Reasons for the Council's Proposals* (BC/CRS/1/17).

5 Minutes of UWIST Council meeting, 6 March 1970 (BC/CRS/1/19). See also the confidential note for the City Council's counsel at the public inquiry written by UWIST's planning consultant, Dr Lynn Moseley (BC/CRS/1/19).

A general prickliness comes across in the documentary record.[6] However, the UGC was strongly in favour of both colleges staying in the centre, apparently for functional reasons; as was the city council, very much in the grip of the Buchanan vision for the city.[7] For its part, the city council had to be told pretty directly by the UGC that unless it contributed generously to site acquisition costs then UGC would not be funding any expansion in the city. It also had to bear considerable criticism of its CPO from residents who were affected and the local newspaper, which on this occasion portrayed the project as local resident underdogs fighting against a council/university behemoth.[8]

This episode demonstrates the way that shared interests between universities and local councils can be forged; but also that they *need* to be forged – these institutions may share interests, but they also have to respond to different constituencies and pressures which may create tensions at times. The quadripartite meetings of UGC, university colleges and the council were a recognition of these tensions and of the reality of shared interests.

In the event, the CPO was not confirmed by the national government in the form of the Secretary of State for Wales, and public expenditure constraints in the mid and later 1970s and thereafter reined in the more ambitious prospects for both universities (which, since the late 1980s, have been merged). University expansion has still occurred, and of necessity it has involved new development. Politically, an up-dated version of the Buchanan vision for the city remains hegemonic (Coop and Thomas 2007) and the council has generally been extremely supportive of university plans, often in the teeth of opposition from residents.

The Production of Knowledge

Shils's view that cities without a university are somehow incomplete is understood even by those who might take issue with it. For it trades on a commonly held idea that universities are part of a world that stretches beyond

---

6   See, for example, minutes of the UWIST council meeting of November 1970 where the council objected to UWIST'S librarian being given only observer status at a meeting between the UGC and University College Cardiff about a proposed new Arts library which might be shared between the two colleges; though as the minute conceded, 'it was understood that UWIST was in no way committed to the plan as yet' (BC/CRS/1/19).

7   That the coalition of 1970–1971 was the result of discipline and sanctions became obvious a few years later when UWIST negotiated a deal for a new campus over ten miles outside Cardiff in Cwmbran New Town.

8   The 15th July edition of the *South Wales Echo* printed a letter from the City Planning Officer, Ewart Parkinson, complaining that 'Your editorial policy is so set against the expansion of the university precinct ...'.

the city of which they are a part, a network of culture and learning which connects the host city to prestigious places in the wider world and owes nothing to parochial interests and intrigues. Universities may be major employers, and major customers, but their unique contribution to local networks of governance is as producers of knowledge. There may well be new modes of knowledge production (Hessels and van Lente 2008), but the idea of the university as the producer (and validator) of dispassionate, objective, and by implication generally incontestable, knowledge retains a strong grip on the public imagination.

In practice it is individuals and small groups within the university which produce knowledge, and historically these have been difficult to direct and manage (especially in the humanities and social sciences) and have guarded their discretion over what they research very jealously. As a result, the members of universities can have a variety of working relationships with local organisations: for example, some may do contract research for local organisations while their colleagues may use their skills and knowledge to develop critiques of local public policies. This has happened over the years in Cardiff (see, e.g. Alden et al. 1988; Guy and David 2004). Rarely, if ever, will such activities intrude into corporate relationships between the university and organisations such as the local council. On occasion, however, knowledge production may be caught up in these corporate webs. In Cardiff this happened on the demise of South Glamorgan County Council in 1996, with repercussions for a later project in 2003.

In the latter year, the School of City and Regional Planning was asked by the central administration of the university whether it was interested in doing some contract research for Cardiff Council. It involved researching the background to a coffee-table book on the recent history of 'regeneration' in the city. The book was intended to be part of the council's centenary celebrations of city status (and 50 years a capital city). The book would be written by a journalist, with academics providing the research (and this being noted in the publication itself). The advantages for the council are clear: the knowledge that would be constructed of the city would have the imprimatur of objectivity and neutrality which is associated with university scholarship, but precisely what was communicated would have been vetted prior to publication, and hence would not be allowed to embarrass any significant interests.

The significance of this way of organising matters became clear when a draft of the research contract linked the project to an earlier one. The earlier project involved an historian researching and writing a history of the South Glamorgan County Council (a body which existed from 1974–1996). The outcome of that project was a manuscript, the scholarship of which was well-enough regarded for it to be accepted by a university press (after peer-review), but the present Cardiff Council (which had inherited the responsibility for funding the project) seemed to be unhappy with some of the interpretations and also thought that it was potentially defamatory. As it was not more specific and the work drew on material that was not in the public domain the researcher was left with a Damocletian

Sword above his head should he pursue publication. He moved on to other projects and appointments. The university and council, meanwhile, had a rift to heal and it appeared that the new project was part of the process. A letter from the council told the earlier researcher that he would not be part of the new research.

There were debates within the School of City and Regional Planning over the ethics of taking on the work after the earlier researcher's attempts had been if not suppressed then frustrated. But, to the dismay of at least some people in the department, notably the author of this chapter, they took the commission. Thomas was privy to many of the internal discussions in relation to the second commission, and accounts of that episode rely on his memory, cross-checked by e-mails and other documentation if available. Inevitably, in relation to disputes of this kind there may be differences of memory, perception and interpretation among the participants. It should be said that the academics who eventually did the work spoke sympathetically of the historian involved in the earlier project. They insisted that any references to the earlier dispute between him and the university and council were deleted from the contract for the second commission. In this way, the two pieces of work would be, or *could* be portrayed as, independent (the first, superseded, draft of the contract explicitly stated that the payment for the history of regeneration would also settle the outstanding dispute over the first commissioned history). In addition, they insisted on the right to use any research findings from the commissioned work for other research. In particular, they intended to – and indeed, did – produce an 'academic' book about Cardiff (Hooper and Punter 2006). Both the researcher of the earlier project and Thomas were invited, separately, by the editors of the proposed academic book to contribute a chapter to that work. Both declined. Yet the unpublished manuscript history of South Glamorgan County Council is referenced in the book, which demonstrates just one of the many ways in which 'independence' is a term subject to many interpretations.

It is impossible to reach a universally-persuasive conclusion as to why the City and Regional Planners took on the commission, and for this chapter it is enough to say that no academic involved was interested in writing any kind of advertising copy for the city council. Yet the work was constrained: by the long history of university-council relations which must have affected the council's decision to approach *Cardiff* University and not some other institution, and the immediate circumstances of delivering to the council an output that served its arguably self-aggrandising purposes. In these circumstances, what kind of knowledge of the city did Cardiff University help produce?

Knowledge and the City

First, a few words about the journalist-written coffee table book which drew on the university research. One reviewer noted that 'it's hard to know who might want to buy a book that often reads like it's come directly from Cardiff Council's press office'. The book was, the review concluded, 'an uneasy blend of boosterism and half-hearted critique … neither enterprising nor creative: another lost opportunity to really explore the urban challenges we face' (Jones 2006: 102). How far beyond this did the academic output get?

In this chapter I am asking one question of the academic book that was produced, rather than reviewing it (for that, see e.g. Thomas 2008). The question is what kind of knowledge of the city did the book produce? The answer is that – to use a distinction and terminology of Nigel Thrift's (2008) – the book was, at best, 'innovative' rather than 'inventive' in that it produced knowledge that was 'more of the same', rather than a radical re-conceptualisation of the city. The subject discussed might be new (i.e. regeneration of Cardiff) but conceptually the book was conservative. In that respect it exemplified a trend that Thrift identifies of even top-ranked universities becoming increasingly similar to think-tanks in the kind of knowledge they produce. In this case it is suggested that the conservative outcome – discussed in more detail below – was directly related to the limitations imposed by the conditions under which the research was undertaken.

A few messages, or themes, emerge pretty clearly from the book. The first is that the boosterist rhetoric used to promote Cardiff is at best exaggerated, and at worst almost ridiculously false. Economically, Cardiff's performance over the last two decades has been pretty similar to many other British cities of its size. Explanations of economic changes in the city do not need to invoke supposedly unique attributes of the city (or its governance). Cardiff is simply a pleasant, if in some ways rather ordinary, British provincial city. The book does its best, therefore, to puncture the overblown rhetoric characteristic of entrepreneurial/ boosterist governance. Yet, while making this point, the book still reinforces one of the key elements of city-boosting: that the city is, in some fundamental sense, singular, that it (in this case, Cardiff) can be defined/known as a coherent entity. The very title of the book – *Capital Cardiff* – has this implication. This is reinforced by the choice of topics in the book, which in effect follow the construction of the boosterist rhetoric's categories of how Cardiff should be thought about and understood. The book is dominated by economic development (understood as paid employment) and physical development – largely in the city centre and Cardiff Bay. It is true there are individual chapters on parks, housing and culture, but there are two on Cardiff Bay, *the* major boosterist redevelopment project in the city in the last 20 years. There is little sense in the book of an everyday Cardiff, or *Cardiffs*, of diverse lives, and hence diverse Cardiffs that are experienced. It is an intervention in a debate about how best to run the city; but what we might mean by 'the city', and whether that construction contributes anything useful in relation to how we explain people's fortunes, is left unexamined. In part, this may simply be an example of a general academic conservatism in the way cities are understood; but in this case, to the extent the researchers were drawing on materials from the research project they had just undertaken then they had to use data generated within the boosterist framework of the research project's sponsors.

Another example of this conservatism is the way the book criticises the hierarchical, closed, nature of Cardiff's politics; but doesn't ask why such a political style has flourished in the city – how is it rooted and what does this tell us about the nature of social relations in the city and their potential for change? Moreover, many of the book's conclusions – especially in relation to politics and governance – are based on unattributed personal sources ('it is said', and so on); the book itself draws on and reinforces the political culture it ostensibly criticises.

These limitations arise from the book's genesis. The research project on which it draws was framed by a client which had no desire to question the hegemonic understanding of the city. While the book takes issue with some of the excesses of boosterism in Cardiff, as long as it relies on the research conducted under the auspices of the contract with the county council it will never have the basis to construct a radically different understanding of the city. The case study shows that there are limits to the way that intellectual fancy-footwork can resolve one of the more acute contradictions in the position of the contemporary entrepreneurial university. The university is valued as a player in local governance networks because of the common (ideological) perception that it provides truth untainted by interest or bias (a view which academics, it must be said, are not usually overly-anxious to dispel). But if local relationships are to remain cordial and constructive, the knowledge that the university is required to produce needs to be sensitive to power-relations in the city and to support the hegemonic policy discourse. In the case of Cardiff, central to the city's governance for many decades has been the idea of a city modernising through commercial redevelopment and regeneration of its central area (and extensions thereof) (Coop and Thomas 2007). This idea has associated with it a vision of the city's spatial organisation, and implicitly a hierarchy of claims on expenditure and other resources (e.g. officer and member time). The production of knowledge about redevelopment and physical regeneration in the city over 25 years serves to consolidate the significance of this approach to understanding Cardiff and its needs. Individual researchers may not subscribe to every detail of the discourse (and agenda) of local powers that be, but if they accept a research contract framed within that discourse the knowledge they produce will inevitably be constrained.

Typically, the direct producers of knowledge internalise the contradiction between the claim to produce disinterested knowledge and the need to keep a reasonable relationship with any agency active in local governance, but especially a local council, and act appropriately – with greater or lesser ease – in any given circumstance. On occasions on which the academic producers of knowledge fail to act appropriately then the division of labour within the university, in particular the distancing of corporate services from knowledge production, allows the university to both claim and disclaim ownership of knowledge: hence, disputed work on South Glamorgan County Council was – *de facto* – disclaimed by the university in its relationship with the city council yet claimed in relation to the researcher as an employee. Academic researchers themselves typically forestall the kinds of consequences that befell Cardiff's historical researcher by attempting to use the findings of contract research to both assist and undermine the client; that is, as a basis for consultancy and academic publications (e.g. Healey 1991). But as this case study shows, the contract research – framed as it is within particular sets of power-relations – constrains what can be concluded from it, even by a (sometime) radical researcher.

Another feature of the case study, which is in one sense mundane, but on reflection should be startling, is the casual approach that academics have to some of the knowledge they produce. The City and Regional Planning team appears to have been resigned to the fact that their work and name would be used by the council to produce a view of Cardiff's regeneration over the last twenty five years that was consistent with, and supportive of, the dominant political project in the city over that time, a project which has appeared to be largely regressive and exclusionary (Thomas 2003; Thomas and Imrie 1999). This was a price the researchers were willing to pay in order to write an alternative account – one they were more happy to identify with. But the obvious question for the reader of these works is why one is to be preferred, or privileged, over the other. Why should any reader believe that the inevitable selection of material and topics that underpins both works is more justifiable in one case than the other? After all, the involvement of the same team in each case might suggest that each provides solid knowledge of the city.

Conclusions

This chapter is not suggesting that universities, still less individual researchers, are poodles of urban coalitions or regimes. Given that knowledge is produced within social processes constituted by networks of social relations which can push and pull researchers in different directions, its claim is that the place of a university in local governance is one of the less examined elements in the constellation of social forces influencing the production of knowledge in universities. Yet there are reasons for thinking that this element might on occasion be an important influence, especially in relation to some kinds of social scientific research. Moreover, there is evidence that the contemporary focus in universities and local government on boosting of image, and promotion of place, has made more complex and heightened pressures on those researching the city. The chapter begins the task of exploring how the university's insertion in governance arrangements may generate tensions in knowledge production, and pre-dispositions to frame understandings of the city in certain ways. It alerts us to the way that the internal differentiation of the university – between corporate and disciplinary departments, especially – may also be a source of conflicting pressures. But it is no more than a beginning.

More needs to be known, for example, of the ways in which the different arenas in which the entrepreneurial stance of contemporary universities (at a corporate level) is taken up with claims of the university on researchers as employees, relate, in practice, to disciplinary and/or vocational norms. What new pressures are being placed on researchers as universities become apparently more adept at (and more interested in) imposing a corporate identity on a workforce that is notoriously individualistic?

Knowledge is produced for many purposes, and most knowledge of the city will not be conceptually ground-breaking, nor will it need to be. But all knowledge is produced within power-infused social relations which leave their mark on the output. And it is sensitivity to one set of such relations – those between universities and the complex of local governance- that this chapter has sought to increase. The role of universities in local governance needs to be researched far more, as even this preliminary excursion has suggested that greater awareness and reflexivity about it will change the nature of the knowledge of the urban that is produced.

Acknowledgements

I would like to thank Chris Allen and Rob Imrie for their comments on early drafts of this chapter. Martin Johnes was kind enough to discuss the background to some of the more recent events that the chapter recounts. He also commented on earlier drafts, though of course I take sole responsibility for the way the chapter has turned out. I am also grateful to the staff at the Glamorgan Record Office for their assistance in unearthing material on the 1970–1971 compulsory purchase order and planning application associated with the Higher Education Precinct in Cardiff.

Chapter 6

Entrepreneurial_research@enterprising-university.co.uk

Chris Allen and Pauline Marne

Introduction

There is a consensus of opinion that the context of academic knowledge production has been changing for some time (May 2005). Gibbons et al. (1994) have characterised the nature of this contextual change as a shift from Mode I to Mode II form of academic production. Mode I is said to consist of homogeneity of knowledge producers ('academics') located within the university. It is also characterised by a state funded system of knowledge production that is discipline based, e.g. sociology, psychology, history etc. (Jacob 2000). This state funding of academic knowledge production provides the practitioners of the academic disciplines (academics) with 'research time' which means that they are able to generate and address their own research problems (Mills 1959; Kemeny 1996). Their work is subjected to a 'quality control' regime based on anonymous peer review by other academics working in the same disciplinary field (Jacob 2000; Etzkowitz et al. 2000).

Mode II is characterised by an increase in 'teaching loads' and reductions in the state funding of academic research which, it follows, has created a concomitant pressure on academic researchers to seek 'external funding' to support their research (May 2005; Etzlowitz et al. 2000). Typical sources of 'external funding' for academics working in the social sciences are government departments, local authorities, welfare agencies, local businesses and so on. Academic researchers must now negotiate the content of their research with these 'external funders' or, more often, have the content of their research defined by external funders that 'invite' them to submit 'proposals' to undertake such programmes of research that have been previously defined by the funder (Jacob 2000). Quality control regimes differ from Mode I because accountability is to the external funder which judges research 'proposals' with reference to 'market principles'. The emphasis of 'quality control' is on the comparative advantages of 'competitive tenders' ('value for money'), the perceived 'reliability' of researchers (reputation for producing 'deliverables' on time), and the perceived 'policy orientation' of academic researchers (they should not be 'too academic') (Allen 2005). Steering groups 'keep an eye' on academic researchers to ensure their adherence to all of these 'market principles' of accountability (Allen 2005).

Now although the binary divide between Mode I and Mode II is not as clear cut as it might appear (Shove 2000), there has nevertheless been a significant shift in the context of academic production (May 2005). Social science is increasingly becoming a 'knowledge business', in which academics and institutions are involved in 'competitive tendering' for research work and also securing their 'position' in the market for 'sponsored research' (Allen 2005). The issue for this chapter concerns *whether* and *how* this shift has informed analyses of contemporary academic knowledge production. We suggest that two points are pertinent in this respect. First, the accounts of academic knowledge production that have emerged since the 1970s give the impression that the conditions of academic production have not changed at all. Reading these accounts one is left with the misleading impression that academic production continues to take place within the enclosed social world of the academy that Gibbons et al. (1994) refer to as Mode I. This is unsatisfactory when the majority of 'applied' social research is undertaken in a Mode II context and therefore funded by, and conducted under contract to, a range of government departments, quasi-government institutions and business organisations (Kemeny 1992; Clapham 1997). Second, analyses of academic knowledge production that have been undertaken in a Mode II context provide limiting insights into the nature of the 'knowledge business'. Specifically, they tend to focus on the nature of the relationships between individual researchers or research teams and the research commissioner (Allen 2005). But the product of academic labour is not simply defined by the relationships that academic researchers have with the organisations that commission their work. They also work for universities, and this also has a bearing on the labour process. Little work has been undertaken on how the universities that academic researchers work within influence the context of academic knowledge production (see Harding et al. 2007 for an exception).

This chapter seeks to fill that gap by analysing the social organisation of research labour within enterprising-university.co.uk. Enterprising-university.co.uk is the name that we have attributed to a fictional university that possesses the structure and characteristics of the 'newer' universities where we have worked. The chapter is based on our experience, and knowledge accumulated as a result, of working within enterprising-university.co.uk. Our ability to write about enterprising-university.co.uk has been facilitated by our long-standing curiosity with how universities work. The empirical material that is used in the chapter was collected in a number of ways. First, the material has been generated using participant observation of the labour process, and its institutional organisation, within 'newer' universities. Notes and records of these observations were maintained for analysis at the end of the fieldwork. Second, empirical material has been sourced from the universities where we undertook participant observation in the form of written material available through web sites, official documentation, publicity material, and various forms of correspondence from 'the university' to its employees and relevant others. Third, other material made its way into the chapter as a result of 'memory recall' during the process of writing.

Perspectives on Academic Knowledge Production

One of the best descriptions of 'intellectual craftsmanship' in what might be termed a Mode I context has been provided by C. Wright Mills (1959) who suggests that social scientists should always have *their own* plans which are logged in a special file on 'the state of *my problems*'. This file contains

> ... personal notes, excerpts from books, bibliographical items and outlines of projects ... All this involves the taking of notes. You will have to acquire the habit of taking a large volume of notes from any book you read ... The first step in translating experience ... of your own life, into the intellectual sphere, is to give it [theoretical] form (Mills 1959: 198–9).

Although the subsequent corpus of work on the social relations of academic knowledge production takes issue with Mills' rather personal view of the research endeavour it does nevertheless, qua Mills, represent the academy as a self-regulating world. Although the subsequent literature is sceptical of Mills' idea that academics can make personal choices about what they research, it nevertheless suggests that academic labour takes place within a relatively enclosed world where the problem of what we need to know is defined by academics themselves. For instance, Kuhn (1970) provides a fascinating discussion of the self-regulating nature of 'normal science' which is constituted on the existence of hegemonic paradigms, and their powerful protagonists, who evaluate research solely in terms of its potential contribution to the hegemonic paradigm. Researchers that are responsible for the successful elaboration of the paradigm will find their reputations enhanced whereas, conversely, 'failure to achieve a solution [within the context of a paradigm] discredits the scientist not the theory' (Kuhn 1970: 80). Latour and Woolgar (1979) similarly analyse scientific knowledge production as a relatively closed and self-regulating field of activity that is driven by – amongst other things – the desire of academic researchers to secure credibility within the scientific field. Latour and Woolgar's scientists take account of fluctuations in the scientific market (for knowledge) and invest their credibility where it is likely to be most rewarding – grasping and dropping theories as circumstances demand. Successful investment means that other scientists show interest in their work and listen to them with greater attention, thereby enabling their progression to the ranks of the elite that regulate and valorise the field (Latour and Woolgar 1979).

Since Kuhn (1970) and Woolgar and Latour (1979) wrote about the social relations of knowledge production *in the natural and physical sciences*, an increasing number of social scientists have turned the 'critical gaze' of social science upon their own practices of *social scientific* knowledge production. The purpose of this has been to develop a more 'reflexive' social science that problematises positivist, empiricist and realist tendencies to 'bracket' researchers out of the picture since this would suggest that social scientists and their research subjects were *not* embedded in a field of power relations when, of course, they

are. For some social researchers this has translated into a concern with the intersubjective relations of knowledge production in the fieldwork context (Cealey-
Harrison and Hood-Williams 1998; Davis 2000; Coffey 1999; Behr 1996; Van
Mannen, 1988; Okely 1996). An increasing number of social researchers are
now writing about themselves as active contributors to the process of knowledge
production (Stack 1972; Charmaz and Mitchell 1997; Bell 2001; Birch and Miller
2000; Hubbard et al. 2001; Atkinson and Silverman 1997). Other social scientists
have been concerned with the *objective relations* of knowledge production, that
is, the ontological relation between 'being' and consciousness that precedes the
fieldwork context (Heidegger 1962, 1978). These social scientists are variously
concerned with the 'habitus', 'standpoint' or 'natural attitudes' that social
scientists unconsciously adopt towards the social world as a consequence of their
privileged position ('being') within it and that, as a taken-for-granted point of
view, places limits on their ability to be 'reflexive' about knowledge production.
For example, Bourdieu (2000) demonstrated a long-standing interest in the
tendency for social researchers' to misrecognise the institutional conditions in
which their 'natural attitude' of reflexivity is formed (i.e. at a social and temporal
distance from practice) as universal rather than particular to the privileged context
in which social science is conducted. He argued that this results in the unconscious
production of a 'scholarly view' of the social world that, as reflexive, is different
to the practical view which tends to be immersed within – rather than formed at a
critical distance from – the demands of the social world. Sociologists such as Hill-
Collins (1990) and Harding (1991) have developed a similar idea of 'standpoint
epistemology' which is based on the idea that consciousness is a product of being-
in-the-world and that knowledge about particular groups of people, therefore, can
only be legitimately produced by those whose 'being-in-the-world' is as a member
of those social groups (see Skeggs 2001 for a fuller outline of this argument).

Such literatures on academic knowledge production are fascinating, but
they give the misleading impression that academic production continues to
take place within a relatively closed and self-regulating context of academic
production that Gibbons et al. (1994) describe as Mode I. Yet the contemporary
context of knowledge production is characterised by an increasing emphasis
on the 'commodification of knowledge' and an intolerance of 'curiosity driven'
knowledge production which is now deemed to be indulgent (Gibbons et al. 1994;
Rappert 1999). This increasing emphasis on the commodification of knowledge
is partly the result of an increasingly parsimonious University funding regime
(see below) and concomitant and dramatic expansion in the volume of 'contract
research' which is now the main source of financial support for research (Kemeny
1992, 1996; Clapham 1997; Jacob and Hellstrom 2000). Thus Jacob and Hellstrom
(2000) refer to the emergence of a 'commissioning model' of social research in
which 'funders', such as government and industry, define the research task and
then outsource it to academics who have been only too willing to do it in order to
access resources to continue undertaking research. The success of this strategy is
evident in the field of housing and urban research which is overwhelmingly funded

by, and conducted under contract to, a range of government and quasi-government institutions as well as charitable organisations (Kemeny 1992; Clapham 1997).

The 'commissioning model' of social research, and commodification of knowledge more generally, is seen to present threats to the critical capacity of the academy (May 2005). The exact nature of the threat to the critical capacity of the academic has been described in a variety of different ways. First, some accounts of Mode II production present a Hobbesian view of its consequences for the critical capacity of scholarly production. This is based on the notion that there has been a transfer of power from one party to another; academics have 'lost' the 'academic freedom' to define the content of their research whereas government and industry are increasingly telling them what to do. Of course, this still leaves researchers with the scope to challenge their research funders and therefore to attempt to shape research within the context of the projects that they are 'commissioned' to undertake. However the claim is that they seldom do since this would simply 'bite the hand that feeds'. This is not surprising when the majority of academic researchers that undertake it (i.e. 96 per cent: Allen Collinson 2004) tend to be employed on fixed-term contracts that are tied, in one way or another, to the funding received from the commissioning body. Indeed Oliver (1996), Barnes (1996) and Goodley and Moore (2000) argue that even principal investigators that are on secure contracts tend to 'kow tow' to funders because they are 'career academics' ('positional intellectuals') that have 'other interests'. These 'other interests' are tied to the 'income generation' pressures that academic institutions impose on social scientists as a condition for career advancement which therefore undermines their willingness to challenge funders (Allen 2005; Delanty 2001). This has led Oliver to claim that 'career academics' tend to 'to sell out to the highest bidder' (1996: 167–8). So although it is important to note that some researchers have documented their struggles to mitigate what they regard as the pernicious influence and questionable conduct of some research funders there are relatively few such accounts of contract research (Harrison 2006).

Second, some scholars have presented Foucauldian and negotiated order views of the consequences of Mode II knowledge production. For instance, Allen (2005) has written about how a career of 'constant exposure' to the disciplinary gaze of research funders can create 'docile' social scientists that develop a way of doing things that is effortlessly attuned to the needs of research funders. Since Allen's (2005) social scientists uncritically absorb, over time, the funders view of the research problem they gradually lose sight of the state of their own problems. A variation on this theme can be found in 'negotiated order' perspectives which emphasise how scholars struggle to manage the multiple, and often conflicting, identities that are required to be successful in Mode II where being known, and valued, across a range of 'user' communities is now a key currency. The need for academic investment therefore extends far beyond the sealed academic field that Latour and Woolgar (1979) describe as typical of Mode I. For example, Shove (2000) describes the need for academic researchers to inhabit multiple (academic, policy, practice, commercial) worlds and to manage a whole portfolio of investments in those worlds so that they secure credit within them. This is achieved by becoming cognisant with the preoccupations of the other actors involved in these worlds but, in doing so, avoiding becoming 'docile' in the way Allen (2005) describes. Shove (2000) certainly believes this to be possible and argues that academics that have developed successful strategies of portfolio management have been able to retain 'greater degrees of control' over their research strategies. However, their inability to fully direct their research endeavours in the way Mills (1959) describes still leaves them compromised. Thus Hobbesian, Foucauldian and 'negotiated order' perspectives of Mode II present a picture of social scientists whose freedom for manoeuvre has been restricted (at best) and outright violated (at worst).

The Enterprising University and the Knowledge Business

Accounts of the social relations of knowledge production in Mode II are valuable but currently limiting. One of the limits of these accounts, to which the remainder of this chapter is addressed, concerns their substantive focus. Accounts of knowledge production in Mode I are immersed in concerns with the social relations between researchers in the academic field whereas Mode II accounts are concerned with the social relations between researchers and research funders. But where does the Mode II university fit into this picture? Although some accounts discuss how the 'income generation' pressures that Mode II universities place on academics (as a condition for 'career advancement') has better enabled research funders to impose themselves on academic researchers (see Oliver 1996; Delanty 2001; Allen 2001, 2005) little else has been said about how the Mode II university has shaped academic knowledge production (see also Fuller 2001, who has previously argued that studies of higher education and studies in the sociology of knowledge have largely ignored each other). Yet understanding the social organisation of the Mode II University is critical, notably because the 'external pressures' that govern academic knowledge production do not simply seep through the walls of the University and into academic practice. Conversely, the governance of research within the university matters. This is the focus of the remainder of the chapter.

The Business of enterprising-university.co.uk

The enterprising university is not simply concerned to use its funding allocation from the state to provide 'education' and 'research'. The enterprising university is a competitive animal that is concerned to establish a position in the market for knowledge (education, research and consultancy) in order to maximise and secure its income. This means that it must make itself 'relevant to' and 'engaged with' institutions (government, business etc.) that are its potential 'partners' – and thus sources of income – with whom it will work to generate business opportunities of mutual benefit. The enterprising-university.co.uk is, then, a pro-active institution that is:

> *Actively involved* in regional partnership initiatives supporting and promoting social and economic growth and regeneration … Our commitment to supporting wealth creation through enterprise and knowledge transfer.

> [A]n upsurge in confidence and investment is reshaping both the city's economic profile and whole swathes of its city-scape … We're proud to be playing a part in that success story, but we know there is much more to be done.

Since enterprising-university.co.uk is 'engaged' in partnership initiatives that promote regional economic growth it defines its 'successes' and 'achievements' in 'business terms' (numbers of 'customers', 'turnover', 'capital investment', 'growth', etc.). And since it is a 'business', enterprising-university.co.uk seeks to align and associate itself with the 'business community' with whom it enters into 'research partnerships' ('multi-national companies as our partners') but, interestingly, it makes no mention of 'partnerships' with Research Councils that fund academic research. Consider, for instance, the way in which enterprising-university.co.uk describes itself in the 'statement of purpose' cited below:

> A *progressive* and *dynamic* modern university with more than 28,000 students, over 3,000 staff and a *turnover* of £150 million, Enterprising-University.co.uk doesn't stand still. The university has an ambitious positioning for *growth strategy*, which includes *capital investment* of over £140 m over the next decade. We count multi-national companies, government agencies and local businesses as partners or clients for our research.

The interesting thing about enterprising-university.co.uk is not simply its embrace of research partnerships with 'multi-national companies, government agencies and local businesses'. Perhaps even more interesting is the way in which enterprising-university.co.uk actually seeks to distance itself from the 'academic community' and 'academic research' which it actually denigrates as somehow 'less focused' and 'less professional' than the entrepreneurial alternative that it embraces ('business solutions, not ivory towers'):

> *Our service* to business and industry clients and partners is all about *applied* creativity and innovation – business solutions, not ivory towers. Near-market and high tech research, R&D partnerships and applied consultancy are all great strengths and *our social and economic research is no less focused and professional*.

The tendency of enterprising-university.co.uk to celebrate its 'business achievements' in this very public way is indicative of its valorisation of symbolism and presentation since this is what enables it to appeal to a 'mass market' of potential students and business partners. Although some lecturers at enterprising-university. co.uk *commonly* share offices with up to eight other full-time lecturers, then, and despite high staff: student ratios that leave these lecturers with little time for research, enterprising-university.co.uk has made investments in making symbolic 'statements' such as building a multi-million pound 'new entrance' to replace an entrance far more 'functional' than these lecturers' offices, i.e. the old 'entrance doors' to the 'main building' opened and shut perfectly well so that students and staff could enter and leave the building. The point is this. Enterprising-university. co.uk is less interested in the functionality of its buildings than their symbolic importance. So, when its staff made suggestions about the design of a new building to enhance the quality of the interaction between academics and students, they were told that what really mattered was that the new building had a 'wow factor'. The purpose of the 'new entrance' and new buildings at enterprising-university. co.uk, then, is to symbolise the 'self-confidence' of the university even if the lecturers working behind the scenes do so in the most appalling conditions and under the most extreme stress:

> The Vice Chancellor [was] joined by around 80 guests to mark the opening of the multi-million entrance, which is expected to welcome thousands of people each day. Professor Brown said the entrance reflected "the modern face of enterprising-university.co.uk. It is a *symbol* of how much we have changed; from the time we were a small technical college and then a Polytechnic, to the *proud* and *self-confident* University of today" … Public areas will be used for displays and exhibitions (Press Release).

This brings us to another important point. The ultimate recognition for those that aspire to be recognised, and whom recognise no other criterion of legitimacy than recognition by those whom they recognise, is the level of recognition that is accorded to them by dominant groups in their field that have the power to consecrate and recognise their involvement in the field as legitimate (Bourdieu 1993). The ultimate recognition for enterprising-university.co.uk came when the Vice Chancellor of enterprising-university.co.uk was nominated for 'Business Woman of the Year' by a panel representing 'a cross section of industry'. This recognition was celebrated with the issue of a press release that emphasised how enterprising-university.co.uk was seen to be a part of the 'broad cross section of 'industry' within its city:

> [The Vice Chancellor of] Enterprising-University.co.uk has been short-listed for the Businesswoman of the Year award. She is one of six finalists *representing a broad cross section of industry* … She has been the driving force in refocusing the mission and position of the university, securing its future academic and financial health in an increasingly volatile and competitive environment. Her initiatives include … The development of the enterprise initiative and its contribution to the

wealth creation central to the successful regeneration of [the city] ... The other finalists are: Julia Willoughby, founder of Willoughby PR; Elizabeth Millett, Chief Executive of City Centre Company; Anne O'Meara, Head of Property and Planning at the Birmingham Office of Hammond Suddards Edge; hairdressing salon owner Karen Woolgar from Nottinghamshire and hotel owner Louise Potter from Buxton ... The Businesswoman of the year will have demonstrated *exceptional business skills.* She will have made a significant contribution to the financial success and performance *of her company,* whether managing a subsidiary or particular area of a large organisation, or setting up and running her own business. The judging criteria will reflect the different skills, abilities and influences of both entrepreneur and senior manager.

However, this 'picture of health' could not be further from the truth. The enterprising university is often a clumsy institution that is perpetually and pragmatically lurching from one financial crisis to another. The historical reasons for this are due to the gradual erosion of its funding base. Between 1981–1982 and 1983–1984, there was a 13 per cent reduction in the grant given to higher education which, it was estimated, would lead to a loss of between £130 million and £180 million to the higher education sector (Stewart 1989). Moreover, the expansion of student numbers in the 1990s was accompanied by a tightened public financing regime, meaning that the unit of resource (total public funding divided by number of full time students) actually fell year-on-year (Ross 2003: 66; Scott 1995). Giddens (2002) argues that funding per student has fallen significantly, by 29 per cent in real terms between 1976 and 1989 and by an additional 38 per cent between 1989 and 1999. This has resulted in an increase in staff: student ratios – with the average student:staff ratio of 9:1 in 1980 increasing to 13:1 in 1990 and to 17:1 by 1999 and with a ratio of 30:1 imminent in some universities. In effect, the average class sizes in universities have doubled in the last 20 years (Greenaway and Haynes 2003: 154) and will have likely trebled in the next few years in some universities. The pressure has been at its most acute in the newer universities (i.e. ex-polytechnics) that have bore the brunt of the expansion in student numbers (Leathwood and O'Connell 2003) in a context when funding per student has been falling significantly.

Reductions in funding per student, in a context of expansion, have placed academics under contradictory pressures in the new universities. On the one hand, they are being placed under pressure to engage in 'income generation' from other sources (notably consultancy) to cover 'funding gaps', yet they have had less time in which to do this following expansions in student numbers and increases in staff:student ratios. The consequences of this are notable in the outcomes of the Research Assessment Exercise which has seen the 'red brick' universities perform 'better' in research terms which has, of course, resulted in a further concentration of academic research funding within these established sites of knowledge production (Sharp and Coleman 2005; see also DFES 2003). It is instructive to note, nevertheless, that the newer universities are not being excluded from participation in *research per se.* They are simply being marginalised in the competition for *academic research funding* (Bekhradnia 2001) and, as such, impelled to engage in a distinctive form of research (e.g. consultancies with local authorities and local businesses). This means that the newer universities often find themselves operating in particular 'research fields' with their main competition being other consultants rather than necessarily red brick universities. This can be seen in the diversity of funding sources that now sustain the newer universities, which were almost entirely publicly financed in the 1960s but that now attract one third of their income from 'indirect funds' such as research consultancy and other forms of 'business' (Greenaway and Haynes 2003: 150). Indeed, at enterprising-university.co.uk the 'largest single source of income for the university comes from contract research' (Research and Enterprise Office 2004).

The Institutional Organisation of enterprising-university.co.uk

Since enterprising-university.co.uk is compelled to operate in a contingent funding environment, it is increasingly hostile to the conduct of 'curiosity driven' research because it tends to be unfunded or funded by Research Councils: 'curiosity driven research has no strategic value to the university' (Vice Chancellor). A key reason for this hostility is that, until recently, research councils have not paid 'overhead' costs to universities, i.e. research councils have conventionally provided funding for 'staff time' to undertake research but they have not provided finance to cover the 'overhead' costs – such as the rental costs of office space – of undertaking research. For this reason enterprising-university.co.uk has sought to avoid undertaking any (or, at best, too much) work for research councils and other funders, such as Joseph Rowntree Foundation, that have conventionally refused to pay 'overhead' costs. Conversely, the priority for enterprising-university.co.uk has been to engage in 'consultancy' activities for research funders (government departments, industry partners) that pay 'good rates' which include overhead costs. This is recognised in the 'corporate plan' at enterprising-university.co.uk which emphasises the need to 'diversify the revenue base' by increasing 'third stream income', which is the currently fashionable term for 'consultancy'.

> The corporate plan has given a sharp focus and direction – and degree of urgency – to the enterprise agenda … The drivers for its development were two fold; the need to diversify our revenue base and the increasing importance the government through the funding bodies has been placing on the so-called third mission (Research and Enterprise Office 2004).

Thus,

... [An] encouragement of applied research in the form of contract research or consultancy, the so called "third leg" or "third mission" of university goals (Research and Enterprise Office 2004).

This need to organise enterprising-university.co.uk so that it can maximise its ability to 'generate income' from consultancy activities has resulted in the abolition of the 'Research Office'. The limitation of the 'Research Office' is that it is the product of a Mode I research environment; it is essentially a *bureaucratic office* that provides *administrative support* to researchers within the university. The creation of the 'Research and Enterprise Office' out of the ashes of the 'Research Office' has provided enterprising-university.co.uk with a much more proactive 'Business Exchange'. The commercial activities of this 'Business Exchange' have been supported by funding to enable it to invest in and 'employ business development managers with *solid private sector pedigrees*, and so engender a further cultural shift towards the '*can do*' approach of the twenty first century' (Research and Enterprise Office 2004). The need for business development managers with 'solid private sector pedigree' is deemed to be necessary to ensure that enterprising-university.co.uk realises 'the economic value of our intellectual capital, skills and facilities' in order to facilitate its 'financial sustainability' (Research and Enterprise Office 2004).

Cultural_change@enterprising-university.co.uk

What is clear from the above is that the creation of the Research and Enterprise Office and employment of 'business managers' with 'solid private sector pedigree' is necessary because Mode I researchers with 'solid academic pedigree' are thought to produce 'curiosity driven' knowledge without properly thinking about its application, relevance and therefore economic value. Worse still, researchers with 'solid academic pedigree' are also thought to have a 'can't do' attitude when it comes to enterprise. The role of the Research and Enterprise Office and its 'business managers', then, is to achieve a cultural shift within the university by embedding an 'enterprise culture' in 'everything that it does'

> *Our* Research and Enterprise Office aims to redefine the concept of enterprise in education. Its mission is to embed an *enterprise culture in everything the university does*, benefiting students, clients and partners in new and unusual ways ... The Research and Enterprise Office is not just a building, but something much more significant – it represents a state of mind.

This mission to create 'entrepreneurial scholars' has been pursued in a plethora of ways and through a variety of mechanisms that have redefined the role of the university and the academics within it. First, since 'traditional' universities with 'solid academic pedigree' are thought to breed 'can't do' researchers, enterprising-university.co.uk has engaged in concerted attempts 'to commercialise from our research base [by] send[ing] academics into industry to help companies solve problems, and bring[ing] that experience back into the university to ensure teaching and research benefits from the latest business experience'. This is the role of the so-called 'Knowledge Exchange' which has a 'corporate aim' to:

> ... encourage academics to work with and understand the needs of industry and to encourage businesses – especially but not exclusively to Small to Medium Size Enterprises (SMEs) – in the region to work with and understand the benefits of collaborating with academia (Research and Enterprise Office 2004).

The purpose of this 'strategic engagement' with 'industry' is to 'liberate' scholars from their 'ivory towers' and expose them to the 'dynamism' of the 'real world' of business[1] in the hope that industry will work upon and through them and, ultimately, reinvent them in the image of the 'enterprise culture'. Second, enterprise-university.co.uk has tried to breed an entrepreneurial culture of 'grant grabbing' within the university through the:

> ... active encouragements of visits from external funding bodies. The main aim of these visits, facilitated by the Enterprise Centre, are *to enhance interest in external funding* and to *inform academic staff on how to apply for funding* and the review processes involved (Research and Enterprise Office 2004).

The type of organisations that visit under such schemes are the multi-national companies that enterprising-university.co.uk counts amongst its 'business partners' and that also provide it with a recruiting ground for senior academic positions such as Pro Vice Chancellor (see below). Securing funding from multi-national companies is important to enterprising-university.co.uk because it seeks to present itself as a 'world class' institution as if the scale of funding somehow equates to the quality of its research activity. Third, enterprising-University.co.uk also devises and runs its own 'staff development' courses to ensure that its academic staff are equipped to reap the 'benefits' of these 'industry visits' and thereby sustain the 'university's evolving *enterprise culture* through increasing the breadth and practical skills and expertise of staff in dealing with external clients'. These courses are delivered through the Research and Enterprise Office and are aimed at 'developing the skills which have been identified as critical to enhancing enterprising-university.co.uk research and business development successes'. The staff development includes courses on topics such as 'Enterprising Teaching', 'Writing Research Proposals' and 'Networking for the Terrified'. At the time of writing the first draft of this chapter, one of us was in receipt of an email from a 'Business Improvement Manager' from the 'Business Transformation Services'

---

1   This begs the question, of course, of where the dividing line lies between the so-called 'real world' and the apparently 'non-real world'.

section of the University[2] inviting us to a course that would improve our 'project management' skills and thereby help us to deliver projects *to budget and time*. Moreover, publicity material produced by enterprising-university.co.uk suggests that these courses have been a resounding success because they have produced a new breed of 'bright eyed' entrepreneurial researchers

> I was asked to give a speech on entrepreneurship at enterprising-university.co.uk, expecting a few dozen at best. I was astonished to find more than 250 note-taking enthusiasts in the audience. After the lecture I found myself pummelled with questions from bright-eyed students, and professors, for more than two hours afterwards. Having visited around 90 universities in the UK, I can honestly say I've not encountered such a degree of determination as I did at enterprising-university.co.uk (Marcus Gibson, *Financial Times*, quoted in EC FTY).

Consecration by the Financial Times! How satisfying for an institution that seeks to secure its legitimacy as a 'business partner' via recognition from its 'business partners' and the like. However, despite the plethora of courses on offer, neither of us have been invited to take a course on how to 'be academic' within the new enterprise culture, or that recognises the importance of purpose (i.e. *what* academics do and *why*) over process (i.e. *how* to be a successful 'project manager').[3] Moreover, we are not aware of any such course existing within enterprising-university.co.uk. Thus although enterprising-university.co.uk operates a 'promising researcher scheme', the purpose of this is not to facilitate 'intellectual craftsmanship' (cf. Mills 1959) but, conversely, to 'to enhance their profile *in preparation* for applying for external funding'. Research only matters at enterprising-university.co.uk if it attracts 'external funding'.

Despite all of this 'stimulating' activity at enterprising-university.co.uk, it has a problem because less than 20 per cent of its academics are deemed to be 'research active'.[4] However, this lack of entrepreneurial research activity should not be seen as surprising. Foucault (1977) points out that power only works itself upon and through people when it is omnipresent *and* meaningful to them, whereupon it has disciplinary effects. For example, Allen (2005) notes how the disciplinary effect of 'publication talk' emanated from its omnipresence (in gossip) and significance (career progression) in the lives of scholars that wanted to succeed in the university

---

2   We have only just discovered that enterprising-university.co.uk has a 'Business Transformation Services' (whatever that is) section!

3   Enterprising-university.co.uk only tends to concern itself with issues of *purpose* periodically, for instance, prior to an RAE exercise when it needs to devise a coherent narrative for the RAE submission.

4   Although there were 250 staff in attendance at a speech on 'entrepreneurialism', there appears to be little interest beyond this audience which, the photograph of the event suggests, was primarily drawn form outside of the university anyway – unless academics have suddenly taken to wearing three piece suits!

department he describes. The initiatives described above have been ineffective because they only intrude into the lives of some of the staff, some of the time. Moreover, staff at enterprising-university.co.uk are given little incentive to submit to the so-called 'enterprise culture' within the university because such effort is not rewarded in its pay scales. Curiously, enterprising-university.co.uk rewards the assumption of management and administration tasks with salary increases *but not* involvement in research activity. This point was made by a senior manager at enterprising-university.co.uk. The exact words of this senior manager were that 'we do not pay you for sitting in your office doing research and writing. You have to have a recognised management or administration role'. Far from being the 'dynamic' research institution, then, enterprising-university.co.uk is actually a 'top-heavy' institution that has invested heavily in the proliferation of its management and administration, as well as projects of symbolic import such as the multi-million pound entrance that nobody wanted other than the Vice Chancellor and a 'management group' that is drawn from the private sector using 'recruitment agencies' that specialise in 'head hunting' across the business sector to enable universities to 'look outside academe for private sector expertise'.

The Centre for Contract Research

CCR is a 'stand alone' research centre within enterprising-university.co.uk, that is, an autonomous entity that is institutionally separate from academic departments where teaching takes place. CCR was established to facilitate the 'income generating' activities of academics that were previously engaged in limited forms of 'income generation' within the context of their normal academic roles, which included teaching and administrative duties *within academic departments*. The establishment of CCR provided these academics with institutional context that protected them from the teaching and administrative duties that distracted them from involvement in income generation, thereby maximising the time available to them for enterprising activities. Moreover CCR is a self-financing research centre that obtains its income exclusively through 'research and consultancy' and, moreover, has 'been successful in niche markets … Combining a range of income generating activities that are built on the interests, knowledge and expertise of staff' (CCR Publicity material). Self-financing involves a level of 'income generation' that covers staff salaries and 'overhead costs', i.e. the *costs of running the centre*, e.g. buildings, facilities, administration staff. However this 'overhead charge' is centrally imposed and so is calculated to include the *costs of running the university* rather than simply the research centre. Thus the centre 'generates income' that contributes to the burgeoning management and administration costs of enterprising-university.co.uk. But that is not all. CCR is also provided with a 'surplus target' which is, in effect, a 'profit target' that is set over and above the income level that it is required to generate in order to meet its own and university costs. This surplus (profit) target is usually set at about 25 per cent of CCR's annual income.

This surplus (profit) element is then used by enterprising-university.co.uk for 'investment' purposes with recent examples of investment being the construction of its 'new entrance' and creation of a 'research and enterprise office'.

CCR charges 'clients' a 'daily rate' for using the labour of its research staff. At the time of writing the first draft of this chapter in 2007, 'day rates' varied from about £950 per day (usually Professors) to £350 per day (research assistants). It is worth noting that research staff 'charged out' at these 'day rates' are the very people that are not eligible for financial rewards within the remuneration system which rewards management and administration and not research, and whom are therefore inexpensive for the University to employ when compared to similar staff in other institutions.

When submitting 'research proposals' to 'clients', enterprising-university. co.uk requires CCR staff to identify the 'surplus element' that will be generated from their 'project' on an internal administrative form. Researchers within CCR are also required to identify the number of days of staff time that will be charged to the client in order to 'deliver' the project. The amount of time that these researchers actually spend working on individual projects is then monitored using 'time sheets'. These are documents that researchers are required to complete at the end of each calendar month identifying how each half day in the month was spent. Time sheet data allows CCR to calculate its profit and loss situation by identifying the +/- relationship between time charged to the 'client' and time actually used to 'deliver' the project. A crude example of how this works is as follows: If CCR charges 100 days of staff time to a 'client' to undertake a project, yet only uses 75 days of staff time to 'deliver' the project, it has generated a profit that is equivalent to the sum that it has charged the client for that 25 days of staff time.

The nature of the financial regime that governs CCR means that it is actively engaged in a very specific ('niche') market for research and consultancy; its clients are predominantly government and quasi-government institutions and business organisations that are prepared to pay good 'day rates'. It tends to shy away from working *too much* for research councils and charitable bodies because they are reluctant to pay its 'day rates'. Indeed CCR has even set a limit on the amount of work that it will undertake for such funders. This is usually set at about 10 per cent of overall income although this 10 per cent limit is pragmatically enforced depending on the state of the market for research and consultancy and therefore balance of 'opportunities' that are open to CCR.

Staff-Recruitment@enterprising-university_ccr.co.uk

The nature of the financial regime that regulates CCR has a huge influence on staff recruitment exercises. Recruitment exercises at CCR are often preceded by discussions about 'who' would be suitable for the available post. During one of these discussions, one of us raised the importance of 'writing' with the assumption that this would be interpreted in academic terms, i.e. that CCR should seek candidates with the ability to engage in scholarly publication. This elicited a response that emphasised the necessity to prioritise 'income generation' and that reduced 'writing' to a 'skill' (i.e. the ability to explain data) rather than an aspect of 'intellectual craftsmanship'. The response suggested that 'the absolute key' was 'income generation' and that successful candidates were 'in any event bound to have good writing skills if they have secured adequate income'.

Advertisements for senior staffing positions within CCR emphasise how a prerequisite for appointment is the capability for 'income generation', although this is *now* not unusual for most academic appointments. What is unusual is the level of emphasis that CCR gives to 'income generation' and, more importantly, the 'entrepreneurial characteristics' of applicants for posts. This was clearly evident during participant observations of recruitment exercises. Whereas our experience of sitting on interview panels for *teaching posts within academic departments at some institutions* suggests that the 'income generation' issue is 'touched upon', the issue of income generation pervades the entirety of interviews for senior posts at CCR. Participant observation of one particular interview panel at CCR is instructive in this regard. Candidates were asked six questions. Only one of these questions was explicitly addressed to academic concerns and, even then, this question was asked in an instrumental manner (i.e. it was oriented to the RAE 'target' of 'which four publications will you bring'?) rather than in terms that would elicit an understanding of the nature of the candidates' 'intellectual craftsmanship'. The other five interview questions were:

- What kind of senior researcher are we getting? (Responses to this question were judged according to the priority that was given to income generation, as we indicate below).
- What do you think it is like to work in a contract research centre?
- What have been your past funding sources and where do you think future opportunities for securing funding lie?
- Have your previous research contracts been delivered on time and to the satisfaction of clients?
- Provide an example of your involvement in 'staff development' on a research project or more generally.

The successful candidates were those that oriented their answers towards 'income generation' by reference to their past successes in the market for research consultancy *and* by demonstrating their understanding of future opportunities in the market for contract research and consultancy. The unsuccessful candidates either did not have a sufficient record of income generation *or* left the interview panel 'entirely unconvinced' about their 'answers to questions about future research funding opportunities' as this reflective account of the deliberations of one interview panel indicate

… It was obvious that "ACADEMIC X" did not fit into CCR. However, it was incredible how, once that point was made, some people on the panel jumped in with gusto to denigrate his candidacy. The external on the panel [who was from business-university.co.uk] was scathing about his pitch to want to come to make more academic use of existing research findings by academically knitting things together in the centre. The personnel person then reduced the issue to one of "personal characteristics" by saying that "he doesn't seem to be in a rush to do anything, not exactly dynamic is he". Yet this is an academic that, in my opinion, has written some of the best academic papers in his field during the last 10 years. One of my internal colleagues referred to his "completely unconvincing answers to the questions about research funding". So here was an extremely good scholar that had just not fully appreciated the context that he was in or the institution that he was pitching himself to work in: a contract research centre. He was a proper scholar that just did not fit into the CCR model, which was much more entrepreneurial. This clearly excluded him from the job. But the interesting thing about it was not only the way that the job was set up with an entrepreneurial agenda in mind, and thereby excluded traditional scholars. It was the intolerance shown towards this 'old school' form of scholarship. It's all about financial performance now (how much money can you make, and how can you help us to hit our targets?). There is no space for reflection in this model, which was evident in the disdain that the external demonstrated towards his pitch to come and "make more" of the wealth of CCR research.

Thus CCR does not (cannot) recruit its researchers from among the ranks of researchers with 'solid academic pedigree', i.e. those that are involved in scholarly production that is not externally funded, or that is externally funded but by institutions within the academic field rather than those within the more profitable market for contract research and consultancy. CCR tends to recruit researchers that possess entrepreneurial dispositions that have been developed as a result of following career trajectories that have exposed them to the 'disciplines' of contract research and consultancy. That is to say, CCR tends to employ researchers with subjectivities that have been produced by, and that are therefore oriented to, the demands of the field of contract research production and consultancy rather than the academic field of production.

Working (in) the Field of Contract Research Production

The demands of the relatively closed and self-regulating field of academic production have been outlined by a number of writers such as Latour and Woolgar (1979). Success is predicated on the ability of researchers to make 'investments' in research that is valorised by those in the academic field that have the power to consecrate, e.g. through the peer review process which determines who gets research council funding and what gets published. The key to making successful investments in the academic field is to undertake research on 'problems' that are 'current' in the academic field and that is informed by paradigms that are dominant in the academic field (Kuhn 1970). Accordingly, researchers tend to orient their work towards the 'state of the problems' that preoccupy researchers in the academic field since this is what will influence their ability to attract scholarly funding to further their own work (Kuhn 1970).

Bourdieu (1993) refers to closed and self-regulating fields of activity – of the type described by Kuhn – as 'restricted' fields of production. This is because knowledge production in closed and self-regulating fields of activity is oriented towards other knowledge producers and therefore relatively autonomous of the demands of outside influences. In other words, closed and self-regulating fields, such as the academic field, obey the logic of their own 'internal economy'. He contrasts this with 'large scale' fields of production that obey the imperatives of 'open competition' and the objective of 'conquest of the mass market' (Bourdieu 1993). The large-scale field of knowledge production is a mass market that operates as an 'open economy' where knowledge production is oriented to a wide range of 'clients' or 'users' and not, simply, other knowledge producers. Importantly, knowledge producers can only 'capture' the mass market by engaging in competition with other knowledge producers (other academics, private consultants). Knowledge producers engage in competitive behaviour by demonstrating their 'credentials' to 'potential clients' (government departments, local authorities etc.) that seek to commission research on the 'state of *their* problems' by researchers that understand *their business* and not simply *the academic business.* Two points are pertinent in this respect.

First, when the dispositions of researchers are in harmony with the demands of the large scale field of knowledge production, the task of 'appealing' to clients on an everyday level can be an *effortless accomplishment.* This certainly appeared to be the case at CCR where researchers were able to effortlessly communicate with funders in a way that other researchers, with more scholarly dispositions, simply cannot. For example, we have been struck by the way CCR researchers instinctively referred to 'literature reviews' (an academic term that we have used for the entirety of our careers) as the 'evidence base' (a term that had never occurred to us but which clearly appeals to funders of contract research and consultancy). Incidentally, this contrasts with our experiences of an_other-enterprising-university.co.uk where senior academic staff with subjectivities that had been formed as a result of exposure to the demands of the academic field, rather than the field of large scale knowledge production, had requested a half-day seminar on how to communicate with funders of contract research and consultancy. Second, when the dispositions of researchers are in harmony with the demands of the field of large scale knowledge production they are also cognisant of the more *labourious investments* that need to be made to maintain their appeal with funders of contract research and consultancy. This is certainly true of CCR where copious amounts of labour have been invested in the presentation and content of 'tender documents' which are both 'slick' and 'professional'. For example,

CCR tender documents routinely include sections on 'quality assurance' which provide a 'guarantee of quality'.

Furthermore, although CCR has high levels of 'repeat business' with 'clients' such as government departments, it also recognises that competition for the 'profitable business' of government and industry research is intensifying, especially as other knowledge producers (e.g. new consultancies, think tanks, and university research centres) have been entering the mass market for knowledge production. It is within this context that senior CCR staff that embodied the entrepreneurial culture of enterprising-university.co.uk recognised the need to make other labourious investments to secure its position in the mass market for knowledge. These researchers undertook a review of CCR research, consultancy and marketing activities. One element of this review involved an analysis of marketing activities to ascertain whether these activities were comprehensive enough to 'capture' and therefore achieve a 'conquest' of the mass market for knowledge production. This review identified the 'niche' that CCR occupies in relation to its market competition, which was identified as 'other parts of the university sector *and the private sector*', i.e. consultancies. Following the conclusion of the review, its architects recommended that CCR undertake the following initiatives:

- Promotional activities that are highly *tailored to our client base* (e.g. mail-outs).
- More personalised contact to discuss clients' research strategies and *how CCR could contribute.*
- *Anticipating client needs* and focusing contact around a small number of issues.
- *Identifying potential clients* where we are not on 'tender lists'.
- Maintaining links with existing clients on a regular basis and exploring the possibilities of 'research partnerships'. More regular contact would also help CCR to keep up to date with staff changes or changes in organisational/ strategic direction.
- More detailed and regular *analysis of our market*, e.g. share of income from different sources, levels of new/repeat business; range of projects (size/ funder); *profitability by client.*
- *Advertising* in industry magazines.
- Introduction of a common format for all tender documents, presentations and reports with the purpose being to improve the visual presentation of all reports.
- Introduction of post-project client feedback and interviews. These should involve a questionnaire or telephone interview and should not be undertaken by someone from the project team.
- Media coverage. Project managers to consider issuing press releases or making direct media contact as reports are published.
- The seminar series forms a *key part of CCR's marketing activities.*

The interesting thing here is that senior researchers within CCR were fully cognisant with its market situation, as well as the demands of the market for large scale knowledge production, and therefore able to 'read' and respond to this 'correctly', i.e. according to the principles that govern the field of large scale knowledge production. This cognisance of the mass market for knowledge is developed in such intricate detail that CCR researchers are acutely aware of the economic profits that can be secured from participation in different parts of it, e.g. 'share of income from different sources', 'profitability by client' etc. Thus 'research successes' at enterprising-university.co.uk tend to be defined in terms of 'winning contracts' which are primarily valued for their monetary worth. This is evident in the way 'winning a new contract' is celebrated, that is, by emphasising the monetary value of the contract but seldom how it relates to the 'state of our problems' (cf. Mills 1959).

> I received confirmation last night that we were successful in our bid for the X study (circa £50,000). Fingers crossed for more of the same next year!

> After much too-ing and fro-ing Funder A have finally confirmed that they would like us to undertake a survey of A, B and C in their area for them. The project is worth £44k as they have agreed to pay for a postal survey in addition to the work costed in our original proposal.

> Good news. We've been informed by the Funder B that we're now the preferred bidder for this contract. This means that subject to agreeing contractual terms and conditions that we will be awarded the contract. The major change Funder B have asked for is for a substantial reduction in the budget (to just over £800k). The project will nevertheless run over 5 years and is a major strategic project.

Perhaps the most revealing discussion occurred when CCR successfully secured a major government contract.

> Addressing All Staff: If you have not already heard we have been successful with [Stage 2 of PROJECT Y] … Amazingly they have gone with exactly the sum we outlined in the bid … We can work on the plausible assumption that the real figure is more like £15 million … When we take into account [the first contract] and indeed some work prior to that the overall value of [PROJECT Y] work to enterprising-university.co.uk is now about £30m. I am pretty sure this is the largest public policy evaluation ever commissioned in the UK. And Faculty Finance informs me that [the first contract] made 24% surplus [i.e. profit] on net income … Trebles all around.

> Response from Senior Member of Staff #1: This is absolutely fantastic news and all credit to you for delivering [the first contract] to time and budget with some to spare!

Response from Senior Member of Staff #2: Many, many congratulations! I hope
I can buy you at least one of the trebles! This really is a great achievement and
we should milk it for publicity.

This tendency also pervades the discussions of 'new contracts' that take place at
weekly 'team meetings' which primarily function to discuss 'tender opportunities',
where the value of research contracts is routinely discussed in terms of their
monetary value ('How much is that worth?'). A successful project is defined as one
that has been delivered to budget and on time according to time sheet information,
and that has produced 'satisfied clients' thereby enhancing further opportunities
for income generation. Sometimes discussion relates to issues of research content.
However insofar as these discussion of new projects relate to the 'state of our
problems' this concerns the way in which the research problems that are being
addressed relate to 'policy agendas' and therefore the extent to which new research
projects 'position' CCR for further 'income generation' opportunities in that area of
work. Although references are occasionally made to the need to develop 'different
ways of seeing things', then, this tends to be in relation to 'policy debates' (for the
purposes of 'positioning' CCR with the funders of its research and consultancy
activities) rather than via contributions to debates in the social sciences.

What this shows is that the contrast between Mills (1959) description of
'intellectual craftsmanship' and the entrepreneurial approach to research within
CCR could not be more striking. But that is not all. The entrepreneurial approach to
research within CCR also contrasts sharply with E.P. Thompson's (1970) account
of academics' response to the introduction of business principles at 'Warwick
University Limited'. Thompson's (1970) account of academic life at Warwick in
the 1960s describes how academic staff were 'outraged' by the unprecedented
influence that the 'business ethos' had achieved at that university. It is interesting,
then, that this account of the conduct of the knowledge business within CCR has
shown something very different.

Senior researchers within CCR have been proactive in identifying the need to
develop entrepreneurial initiatives (such as the development of 'marketing strategies)
reflecting the enterprising dispositions of its researchers whose subjectivities have
been developed as a consequence of exposure to the 'disciplines' of the mass
market for research and consultancy. These subjectivities are comfortably aligned
with the demands of the enterprising university and, moreover, co-exist in harmony
with the demands of the mass market for contract research and consultancy, even
enabling the researchers that possess them to 'anticipate' the demands that the mass
market will make on them in the future. But that, too, is not all. CCR researchers
also recognise the need to cede academic autonomy to 'stakeholders' in the mass
market for contract research and consultancy; thus research funders are asked
to conduct the 'peer-review' function ('post-project client feedback') which, of
course, reflects the ethos of enterprising-university.co.uk whose 'focus is firmly
on customer satisfaction'. All that said, it is easy to understand how the imposition
of 'industrialists' with 'solid private sector pedigree' in senior management

positions and the endless production of expensive and glossy leaflets describing the 'achievements' of the 'Research and Enterprise Office' have met with little controversy or opposition within enterprising-university.co.uk.

Scholarship and the 'Entrepreneurial Gaze'

The dominance of an entrepreneurial culture within enterprising-university. co.uk and CCR is not only interesting in its own terms, that is, for the way it speaks about the form of research is produced. It is also interesting because the predominance of this culture has marginalised scholarly work despite the attempts of a small number of academics to raise the profile of such work within the collective consciousness of CCR – against the express wishes of enterprising-university.co.uk which officially states that 'contract research and consultancy probably offer more scope for knowledge transfer and income generation than does pure research'. What is interesting here are the ongoing problems that those engaged in scholarly production encounter within the institutional environment of enterprising-university.co.uk.

The requirement to complete monthly 'timesheets', which enables CCR to identify the 'profit margin' ('surplus element') produced by each unit of research labour, allows all research labour to be judged with reference to the demands of its business culture.[5] And in the CCR business environment that subjects each unit of research labour to the 'inspecting gaze' of timesheets, a culture has developed in which researchers themselves (and not simply the institution they work for) maintain a 'watchful eye' on the 'fiscal position' and therefore on the profitability of the labour that is being invested by staff across the board. This is experienced as problematic by researchers that seek to spend some of their time engaged in scholarly production because their activities are considered to be 'loss making' or otherwise 'unproductive'.[6] These productivity judgements are legitimised by drawing on the timesheet and profit and loss information that circulates within the centre. Moreover, the business like nature of these productivity judgements prevails despite some senior academics' attempts to negate them by rhetorically valorising academic production in staff meetings. This is because such rhetoric is compromised by the routine discussions that take place in the same meetings

---

5   Indeed, this business culture is all that most of the junior researchers at CCR have ever known, which means that their subjectivities have been developed with reference to it and nothing else.

6   It should be said that this point of view is highly contentious because these activities generate symbolic profits, such as enhanced 'academic reputation' that policy funders value because it 'adds weight' to their research which means, of course, that it enhances the capacity for 'income generation'. It is also contentious because the RAE funding that it generates is administered at University level and is not recognised or calculated as part of the 'income generated' by CCR.

about the 'bottom line', which necessitates an acknowledgement of the financial consequences of engaging in scholarly production as opposed to contract research production which enterprising-university.co.uk calculates to be more profitable within its narrowly focused financial regime.

This frequent reduction of contract research production to its lowest common denominator (e.g. income levels, profit, loss etc) has resulted in a form of everyday 'business talk' that has had much the same – albeit opposite – effect to that described by Allen (2005) who referred to the disciplinary effects of 'publication talk' in an academic department. Furthermore, CCR researchers that seek to spend some time engaged in scholarly production cite how the effects of this form of 'business talk' are multiplied by the 'open plan' format of the office since this facilitates the 'inspecting gaze' (cf. Foucault 1977) of the entrepreneurial researchers.[7] One researcher that engaged in scholarly production at CCR has cited to us how s/he often interprets apparently innocent questions (such as 'What are you working on?', 'What are you up to?') with reference to the 'entrepreneurial judgement' that is likely to be placed on scholarly production. S/he also revealed that s/he sometimes had a tendency to conceal participation in scholarly production for fear that it would be deemed to be 'unproductive'. Such is the strength of the entrepreneurial culture within enterprising-university.co.uk that those with an academic dispositions, and involved in scholarly production, sometimes find it necessary to lie about what they are sometimes doing.

Conclusion

No matter how many times its VC is nominated 'business person of the year', enterprising-university.co.uk is not the 'dynamic' business institution that it purports to be. It is, rather, a pragmatic organisation that is driven by concerns to remain financially viable in a 'hostile funding environment'. This chapter has shown that this creates contradictions that, ultimately, have a fundamental impact on research undertaken within enterprising universities. First, since enterprising universities prefer to operate in the mass market for research and consultancy they are required to appeal to those that fund such activity (government, business etc.). This has resulted in the fetishism with symbolic investments (such as the multi-million pound new entrance) that 'speak to' a series of wider publics that have this power to fund the enterprising university, notably, the 'world of business'. It has also resulted in a series of investments in managerial and bureaucratic structures, such as the Research and Enterprise Office and senior staff with 'solid private

---

7   Interestingly, these entrepreneurial researchers use their 'inspecting gaze' to take an interest in the 'productivity' of the activities of research staff within the open plan office, which contrasts with the concerns of staff working in mainstream academic departments who tend to be more concerned with 'balanced workloads'.

sector pedigree', that have the dispositions do the *actual talking* to the world of business on behalf of the academics that they seek to mould in their own image.

Second, these investments in symbolic buildings, senior management and bureaucratic structures are costly and therefore worsen the financial plight of the enterprising university – unless they produce a 'pay-off'. Although academic researchers are responsible for delivering this 'pay-off', unfortunately, conventional academic research 'does not pay'. Thus academics have been required to reorient their activities towards 'consultancy and contract research' under the guidance of the 'research and enterprise office' and other senior managers with solid private sector credentials: 'contract research and consultancy probably offer more scope for knowledge transfer and income generation than does pure research'. This consultancy and contract research activity is regulated by a whole new surveillance apparatus (timesheets etc.) that measures inputs in relation to income and therefore the overall profitability of its research activity. This surveillance apparatus produces the context within which existing and future research staff are subjected to the entrepreneurial judgement which, through its disciplinary effects, breeds an entrepreneurial culture at 'ground level' that is relatively self-regulating. This is evident in the way that initiatives such as 'profit and loss reviews' and 'marketing strategies' originate from research staff themselves rather than university managers.

Acknowledgements

We would like to thank Rob Imrie, Jim Kemeny and Steve Tombs for their very helpful comments on an earlier draft of this chapter.

Chapter 7
Knowledge Intermediaries and Evidence-Based Policy

Gary Bridge

Introduction

Debates about the relationship of academic research to policy and politics are long-standing. In more recent times for instance, at the height of the influence of Marxism in the social sciences in the late 1970s, the debate was about whether academics did research funded by government departments or charities at all. The risks of ideological compromise were often seen as too great. More recently still there have been discussions on the policy relevance of academic research (for example in geography Martin 2001; Imrie 2004). The Evidence-Based Policy initiative reveals some desire from Government to use the results of research much more in assessing policy directions. At the same time academic funders such as the Economic and Social Research Council (ESRC) have become rather more instrumental (Solesbury 2002) in their orientation – to social science knowledge contributing to UK PLC and the value of the research to 'end users'. Alongside this it must be acknowledged that there have been substantial changes in universities that mean that accounting and workload management systems dictate that research activity is more and more synonymous with funded research. The implications here for lone scholarship, for unfunded research, or, in the UK case, individual scholarship beyond QR money from the Research Assessment Exercise (RAE), is likely to be severely compromised. These concerns have been heightened by a call for direct assessments of the economic value of research as part the new research evaluation system in the UK, the REF. So the questions we face are not just about the social relations of different forms of contract research production between funders and academics but the dominance of that form of research production as the form of valued research within universities – thereby implicating the social relations of university hiring, promotions, competitive study leave systems and the rest.

In this chapter I shall focus my comments on the idea of the knowledge intermediary systematising the results of academic and other research to present as evidence for policy-makers. Knowledge intermediary roles can be found across a range of interventions, including certain academics or academic groups being funded to assess the quality and implications of other research in their field (through systematic reviews and the like) for the benefit of policy-makers, through to research funders (such as the Joseph Rowntree Foundation) hiring consultants to disseminate the 'key messages' from their research programmes. These intermediaries have the role of brokering the knowledge produced elsewhere. This emphasis on dissemination is also tied to the fact that knowledge production in many areas of policy have been resolved in favour of quantitative evidence that is at the same time more amenable to secondary analysis and assessment. The role of knowledge intermediary has been growing rapidly in social sciences in the last ten years. In this chapter I shall refer to the example of the Centre for Neighbourhood Research as an academic grouping which had a knowledge intermediary role as a way of reflecting on these wider currents in knowledge production and dissemination.

The Centre for Neighbourhood Research

The Centre for Neighbourhood Research was one of a number of topic-specific nodes established in March 2001 as part of the UK Economic and Social Research Council's Evidence-based Policy and Practice Network (later called the Evidence Network). It was a collaboration between researchers at the Department of Urban Studies, University of Glasgow and the Centre for Urban Studies, School for Policy Studies, University of Bristol. It must be stressed at the outset that this was not a large core funded ESRC Centre in the conventional sense. The £427,000 over four years funded part FTEs (up to 50 per cent) of researchers' time with some administrative and secretarial support time in both centres. CNR aimed to advance theoretical and empirical understanding of neighbourhoods and neighbourhood change. It provided a resource for other researchers and policy-makers working in this field through and assessment of existing evidence.

Listed Activities

- Creation of a web site www.neighbourhoodcentre.org.uk to provide online papers and various form of support to the research and policy community.
- Systematic and other reviews of existing evidence dealing with important questions for neighbourhood and regeneration policies.
- Conceptual and methodological papers.
- Focused analyses of existing large data sets.
- The development of a neighbourhood question bank which brought together questions on neighbourhood issues from a range of official panel and other surveys (discussed below).
- A series of small conferences on policy-relevant issues for academics, policy-makers and practitioners. From 2001–2005 CNR organised ten conferences over one or two days in either Bristol or Glasgow. Around 800 people attended these events averaging 70 per event in Glasgow and 100 in Bristol. There was a mixed audience of academic researchers,

consultants, practitioners and policy-makers from central government departments and public agencies. Issues covered were: gentrification; crime and the neighbourhood; gated communities; health; education and the neighbourhood; anti-social behaviour; community cohesion and multi-ethnic neighbourhoods; children and the neighbourhood; securing urban renaissance: policing, crime and disorder.

Knowledge Production and Distribution

The CNR website provided access to the Neighbourhood Question Bank, CNR papers and the latest CNR news. On average the CNR website attracted 2,000 unique visitors per month from some 30 countries including Australia, Canada, Netherlands, Israel, Lithuania, Malaysia, Taiwan, Indonesia and China. Electronic feedback and face-to-face contact via conferences and workshops demonstrated that the website was used by graduate researchers, policy-makers in the UK and elsewhere, practitioners at local and national levels and the academic community.

The neighbourhood question bank was launched in December 2001 and displayed neighbourhood related questions that had been asked in major UK national and sub-national surveys since 1990. Users were able to determine their own search criteria online and search specific or multiple surveys by keyword, date and geographical coverage. The results of each search displays the methodology related to the selected neighbourhood questions, the most recent findings, how frequently the question is asked and links to other online survey resources. The development of NQB was a major undertaking for CNR both technically and in resource terms. The NQB was a resource for gathering research evidence for writing or review purposes and to identify suitable neighbourhood related questions, with national comparable results, for use in local surveys. CNR established a network of 500 associates who received electronic updates about CNR work.

Position within the Politics of Knowledge

One of the issues was to what extent the work done by CNR was strongly influenced by other agendas. One set of influences was that of the Evidence Network itself and the agenda to 'bring social science research much nearer to the decision making process' (Evidence Network website). The ESRC initiative (£3m over three years) had in turn been prompted by the New Labour Government's desire to use social science evidence much more to inform policy. Nevertheless the network was not set up as to deal comprehensively with social policy or the generic policy process (although papers were produced on the policy process and the nature of evidence). The nodes themselves dealt with quite discrete areas of policy and so the network was quite loosely structured. There were no specified topics or interventions. Within this, for the neighbourhood centre there was the structuring environment of New Labour's agenda on poor neighbourhoods and the problems of social exclusion and strategies of regeneration. Part of the structuring environment of CNR relates here to the topics chosen for systematic review. Some of this was framed by New Labour (and previous administrations) understandable concerns with poor neighbourhoods and issues of social exclusion. Combined with this was an idea that poor neighbourhoods contained implicit forms of social capital that could be released by Government intervention (via the Neighbourhood Renewal Unit/Social Exclusion Unit). Other interested parties were charities (such as the Joseph Rowntree Foundation) as well as urban regeneration groups and neighbourhood groups themselves. The looseness of the network as well as the diversity of the interested parties actually meant that the intellectual remit of the Centre could be fairly independent. The way the Centre was positioned (in the bid for funds and the work conducted) was to occupy a critical position that looked at neighbourhood dynamics, particularly of poorer neighbourhoods, but in the context of neighbourhood processes overall. CNR in its bid situated itself in relation to this agenda by arguing that to understand the dynamics of poor neighbourhoods it was necessary to get a better grip on how other types of neighbourhood functioned to be able to judge what might be expected from poor neighbourhoods. A broader range of evidence was required. So CNR online papers looked at gentrification and gated communities, as well as social capital and health and other issues more usually associated with neighbourhood studies.

CNR was also keen to critique the comfortable idea of neighbourhood interaction that suggested ideas of community in a more traditional sense behind the Government's agenda. The choices of systematic review were made by the academic members of CNR themselves, often aligning with long-standing research interests (such as in gentrification for three of the members) or as an outcome of other funded research projects (raising the interesting question of the multiple relations of the contract research environment in capitalising on knowledge) as well as free standing reviews that were seen to reflect key issues of the moment (such as e neighbourhoods). In all this there was no sense of a direct obligation to answer specific policy requirements or to be supportive of particular agendas. For example, the reviews on gentrification were quite critical (especially over the issue of displacement of working class residents) as it related to the Government's urban renaissance agenda. This latitude resulted from the loose and heterogeneous nature of the Evidence Network, involving nine nodes on different topics such health and social services, children, procedures of evaluation as well as the multi-disciplinary nature of the researchers involved. It proved very difficult in terms of time and money to get additional collaboration between the nodes of the network. So the network could not, in reality, be part of some comprehensive coherent and coordinated initiative to get social science research findings systematically into policy arenas. Also because CNR was part of this larger initiative to help provide systematic evidence it was not required to address any specific policy intervention but in fact was able to provide a critical background to policy.

The Evidence Base

The evidence-based policy initiative (though not necessarily the Evidence-based Policy network) tends to favour a form of strong positivism in the understanding of knowledge, that may seem naïve in the face of more recent poststructuralist and other critiques of the relationship between power and knowledge. This is highlighted by assumptions in the evidence base approach that social science knowledge in the form of evidence is somehow detachable and neutral, hard and objective. But such a stance of seeming scientific disinterest seems to contradict somewhat the more ambivalent ways in which politicians actually use evidence, with the precision of quantitative analysis being deployed by policy-makers in strongly discursive ways (the 'killer statistic') and, alternatively, the disparagement of qualitative analysis in some senses reflecting the danger of the 'killer quote' that conveys a situation in ways detrimental to the direction of policy. Evidence inevitably becomes discourse.

In its earliest formulation of the evidence base initiative there seemed to be an implication that the weight of evidence would strongly influence policy, although most observers seem to prefer the term evidence-informed policy. Whatever the degree of weight evidence was supposed to have, giving policy-makers a systematic review of the evidence as well as some judgement of the quality of the evidence was seen as important. Systematic reviews divide into meta-analysis and narrative reviews. Meta-analysis involves comparison of interventions through data processing and is concerned only with numerical outcomes (and will not be dealt with here). Narrative reviews seek to preserve some discussion of process in each project reviewed and having a more explanatory material (Pawson 2001a). Systematic reviews try to answer a clear question by finding, describing and evaluating all published, and if possible, unpublished research on a topic (Atkinson 2002: 3). The work that CNR was engaged on was narrative review. This involved specifying the search systems and search terms used to find material, including the grey literature, the process of selection of the papers reviewed and the time period over which they were sampled.

All systematic reviews are premised on a hierarchy of evidence that follows the medical model. It places experimental design in the form of randomised control trials at the top of a methodological hierarchy. Next in the hierarchy are quantitative analyses based on simple random sampling, then based on non-probability sampling and finally qualitative research. This way of organising evidence, and what counts as good evidence, is of course open to critique on a number of levels. There are philosophical criticisms of the idea of linear causality and the adaptation of naturalistic models into the social world. Furthermore even if we do accept naturalistic models they do not necessarily lead to a world of certainty and evidentiary clarity. Even within science (which the hierarchy of evidence model seems to privilege) much of the activity and the reporting of results is part of a wider discussion and debate on the interpretation of those results. So in science as much as social science there is ongoing discussion of what the evidence 'says'.

This is taking no account of wider discussions (from Kuhn's 1962 landmark book onwards) of the funding and reputational constraints about what counts as evidence or has the financial backing to be discovered as such in the first place.

Evidence is part of an ongoing discourse that includes different forms of analysis and interpretation. Evidence is equally as capable of promoting dissensus as consensus. This raises the issue that systematic reviews are not systematic in the sense that they do not use professional judgement to assess the interpretations of other professionals and the basis for that judgement. Being systematic about the categorisation of data (according to a framework that is open to dispute) will not arbitrate in this sense. Part of this should involve the primary purpose that the evidence is serving. In the academic context often it is to pursue a specific line of reasoning or experiment – in conventional scientific terms testing an hypothesis. The hypothesis is rarely likely to be the same specification of the problem that a policy-makers interest in the issue would call up. One example is in the use of quantitative data. Policy-makers favour as evidence quantitative evidence, which in turn puts economics in a privileged position within the social sciences in terms of type of evidence, techniques of evidence testing and form of knowledge it produces. Yet the primary motivation within the discipline of economics is not to pursue evidence that conforms to social policy issues (even if that is one of the motivations) but rather but to produce evidence that (hopefully) supports an equilibrium model. Economists gain their reputations and are able to publish in the highest ranked journals based on their ability to produce evidence that fits, refines an existing model or helps confirm a new model. Orthodox neoclassical economics has an incentive structure that involves producing evidence that fits a model that is a mechanical representation of the social world (involving ideas of linear causality). This informs the specification of the problem and its motivation, the nature of the variables to be considered, as well as the judgement of what can stand as those variables, the choice of technique to test the variables (or proxies) and the degree to which these are seen as tractable. All this may mean that the evidence produced and the way it is produced (and what is excluded) may or may not have a good bearing on the problems that policy users specify or the problems to which they want to apply the evidence. This issue obtains even where the study is expressly conducted and funded by Government. That is not to say that useful evidence and analysis are not presented by economists and econometricians it is to say that there are different incentives driving the formulation, analysis and presentation of data between academics and policy-makers which can be more or less consistent at different times. The point here is that a systematic review of evidence should take in the context of argument and the work that the evidence is doing within the intellectual context of the study being reviewed. There are different disciplinary contexts across social sciences and through to the various natural sciences.

This leads to a consideration of the distinctions between quantitative and qualitative methods and their characteristics in terms of validity and reliability. These are differently expressed, rather than being superior or inferior relative to quantitative method, as the hierarchy of evidence model assumes. The hierarchy of evidence model puts experimental data at the top of the hierarchy (in the way that medical research or drug tests use of randomised control trial involving the test group and a control group). Even if this method were the most desirable there are very few situations in social policy and social science research that lend themselves to the natural experiment approach. This is because the social world is inherently too complex and interrelated to be able to single out variables in the way needed or because the procedures needed to 'set up' an experimental situation are simply unethical. Quantitative evidence based on random sampling is next in the hierarchy and probably the type of evidence most often used in policy. Knowing how much there is of, for instance, poverty or unemployment is of course hugely important (although even these measures are often hotly disputed). But that does not necessarily put quantitative data used to measure relationships between variables in a superior position to qualitative evidence. Again the question is what is it that you want to know and what is the purpose of the evidence? As has been often rehearsed, but often still too little understood in policy circles, qualitative data has a different purpose to quantitative evidence but is no less rigorous, valid or reliable. Reliability applies in the way that qualitative methods are conducted and the consistency of analysis (for instance in the thematic coding of transcripts). Whereas quantitative methods work by statistical inference to achieve generalisability from samples, qualitative evidence achieves this through logical inference from techniques that iteratively and exhaustively interrogate the data and present a logical case for the dimensions of the data identified.

Politicians are in fact well rehearsed in the use of both quantitative and qualitative data and of the roles of both, for instance, in their use of survey polling prior to elections but also in the use of focus groups to identify underlying worldviews and motivations for the political attitudes identified in key segments of the population. So any review of the evidence should not be based on a hierarchy that is founded on an idea that knowledge is somehow separate and categorised according to an idea of science that itself is outdated (in terms of treating the natural world in mechanistic terms). Rather a review of evidence for policy and practice should be driven by an identification of the problems you want to address and the evidence that is most relevant to that (be it qualitative or quantitative). The hierarchy of evidence should work in terms of the conceptual and empirical relevance to the question.

The last point relates to a larger issue of the status of knowledge in all this. There is an assumption that knowledge is somehow just sitting there, apart, and ready to be used in different ways – that it is neutral and detachable and usable – but usable in some narrow instrumental sense. This relates to wider philosophical issues about what the pragmatist philosopher John Dewey claimed as the 'spectator theory of knowledge' and its 'quest for certainty' (Dewey 1929, 1930). Dewey criticised traditional philosophy for assuming its separateness and ability to reflect on other forms of knowledge and also its quest for foundational certainty. In a similar vein the knowledge produced by social science is not separate and disinterested but produced in ongoing arguments, hypotheses and ways of seeing the world. In science this interestedness meets other critiques in an ongoing discussion of the nature of the world but many of the ways that knowledge is produced is through experiment and trial and error and through forms of action in the world. Social scientific knowledge is infused with interests and power (as Foucault so persuasively argued). For pragmatists like Dewey all concepts are essentially contested and the main way of knowing the world is by acting in it. By these lights what gets defined as a problem focuses subsequent effort and enhances the possibilities for a solution. This suggests that a collaborative relationship between policy-makers and researchers, coming to an agreement over problems that need addressing, rather than researchers being the auditors of some form of countable currency called evidence that they supply to policy-makers. The latter kind of relationship would put the researcher in a subservient role and is one that, in some senses, can work to undermine the critical capacities of the academy.

Communicative and collaborative problem solving can be suggested in the historical example of Hull House. Hull House was a property in the poor inner city Italian American neighbourhood of Chicago occupied by middle class professionals at the end of the nineteenth century and early twentieth century. Led by Jane Addams Hull House was bought with the intention of putting professionals skills at the disposal of this poor immigrant neighbourhood. Hull House combined the skills of the professionals living there with the research knowledge of academics at the University of Chicago (including John Dewey), the residents of the neighbourhood as well as, increasingly over the time, city officials and policy-makers. The purpose of the establishment was to help improve the lives of the poor inhabitants of the neighbourhood. The activities of the House were practical (including literacy training, art and music classes, sport) as well as providing much needed services (such as a crèche for working mothers). Apartments were bought to house those in tied accommodation being made homeless if they lost their jobs. The approach to many of the problems was experimental involving trial and error. For example, the Cooperative Coal Association operated for three years in helping to provide people with fuel but failed because of the overly generous disbursement of coal. Addams had an idea of 'civic housekeeping' (Addams 1968) which reversed traditional divisions between private and public issues by making private experience an issue of public policy. One such was her witnessing the grime on the curtains of an immigrant apartment and making this a public issue over the effects of pollution from the nearby factory. Academic evidence, as well as philosophical thought, were current in Hull House and used regularly to serve the purpose of improving the lives of neighbourhood residents. This is an example of how action, evidence, academia, policy and practice came together, not always harmoniously, to improve lives and in the process change policy. Settlement houses like Hull House were established in most major US cities and formed much of the basis for the constructed of the Federal welfare state in that country.

The Presentation of Evidence

Returning to evidence-based policy, as well as the question of the degree of negotiation and contestation in knowledge production there is a further issue of the reporting conventions of academic papers in different disciplines having an impact on the systematic review. The details of the methods, and especially the analyses, are not necessarily reported in papers in the social sciences outside economics, or at least not in every paper that relates to a research project. Conducting systematic reviews of neighbourhood evidence judged by the standard of a hierarchy of evidence was very difficult given the lack of conventions for reporting these issues. There are perhaps lessons here for social science practice is terms of reporting the provenance of the data in the papers themselves. Quality judgements are more often made in terms of the reputation of the researcher, or the quality of the journal in which the work is reported. With peer review a lot about the basis of the evidence is (rightly I would say) taken on trust (it is assumed to have been dealt with in the peer review process). But that is also because the data do not 'speak for themselves' and because what is at issue is the theoretical perspective and quality of the argument as much as the data. That also begs a number of questions. One is that the evidence-base seems to relate only to empirical findings. This is an idea of the academic community supplying the unbiased, accurate and robust empirical findings in accessible form to a non-specialist audience that can then inform and be interpreted by the policy-maker, or used as evidentiary weight to help the policy-maker decide (certainly that's what the hierarchy of knowledge implies). This relates to Solesbury's (2001) point about knowledge being useful and useable. In fact in most social science research the findings, interpretations and argument are much more closely bound together. This also links to the nature of the evidence available in social science.

There is perhaps a presumption in the Evidence Network and Government that there is some vast untapped bank of evidence to inform issues that the Government faces. From experience of conducting systematic reviews reported here (ones that include the grey literature) the bank of evidence is patchy, in part because research funding (especially at full cost) is so rationed that often the empirical evidence is perforce limited. As has been argued, it is also because research is conceptually and not descriptively driven. Academic reputations are not founded on the production of new data per se but on data that relate to specific (and hopefully novel) sets of arguments (or conform to models in the case of economics, discussed earlier). I think this accounts for why archived secondary data from previous research projects are so under-used in social science generally. In the production of new knowledge the emphasis has been on new conceptual approaches accompanied by new data (from primary research). There is a tension between using existing data and sustaining a novel argument. This again explains the relative success of econometrics in the evidence-based world (aside from the privileging of quantitative analysis) because econometricians need data (especially from large panel surveys, or preferably natural experiments). However their primary reputational kudos does not result from the substantive findings per se (although they may be very committed to the substantive problem) but on what the data does for their refinement of a highly regarded model or, even better, for producing a new model. 'Institutional factors' come very low on the list of priorities here.

Knowledge Intermediaries

The aspirations of evidence-based policy research put the systematic reviewers in the position of a knowledge intermediary in a number of critical ways: first as critical interpreters of others' research (and their own!) and secondly by reputation or profile and thirdly reputation in the policy area to which the research relates.

1. Critical Interpreter – conducting systematic reviews puts the reviewer in an uncertain position regarding the research of other academics in the field. This is especially so in social sciences outside economics because the criteria of reporting of research and therefore the judgements on that research are not simply based on empirical findings and methodology. One example from CNR is Rowland Atkinson's (2002) attempt to put some numbers on the extent of working class displacement that is caused by gentrification. In data terms that review revealed a wide range of methods and data sources (official, primary, quantitative and qualitative) from different countries that meant that the data was patchy and did not easily cohere. Nevertheless it did at least result in Atkinson being able to state that the weight of research findings point to displacement being a significant negative element of gentrification. But the discussion of displacement in gentrification is also a theoretical and political one which the evidence will not sway one way or the other. What is the reviewer meant to do in this case – ignore theoretical argument in the interests of something equivalent to traditional conceptions of value-free research from positivism – or do they simply lay out the different positions for other researchers/policy to make judgements on – or is part of their critical/moral role to make a judgement on the persuasiveness of the competing explanations – and what how does that relate to evidence as conceived in the policy realm?

2. Profile – Setting up a Centre for Neighbourhood Research, with a question bank and online publications immediately gives you a profile in the policy and practitioner fields, that is in some senses separate from any reputation that may (or may not) exist because of your work in the academic field. There are a range of interested parties that can start to make requests and claims based on your profile. Some of this is positive in the sense of making academic research more available to other parties. However it is easy for assumptions to be made about expertise and indeed interest in the policy area that is beyond a centre members interests and expertise. CNR was inundated with requests for opinion and information from a range of

Government departments, local authorities, regeneration units, community groups, some of which had to declined either because they were not in the field of interest or expertise, or because there was insufficient time or funded support to deal with all these information requests. This may suggest there is a great need for knowledge transfer to other groups. There is a large unmet demand for data that is significant and could be addressed. However this also risks compromising the academics research and review agenda. There is a danger of being diverted by other agendas or treated as a quasi-consultancy or information support service. CNR was also approached by a number of think tanks and policy units wanting summary judgements on the state of neighbourhoods. Individual members made their own ethical choices about which of these they pursued and which they did not. The positive elements of this more accessible interface to research is that it potentially opens up the range of positions from which urban policy problems are defined and viewed.

3. Reputation, or the politics of visibility at least, can have positive effects – This was shown to some degree in CNR with the series of seminars that were held on neighbourhood issues and which drew in an academic, policy-maker and policy-practitioner audience. This revealed that some of the time each of these constituencies was talking to and within their own worlds, but there were moments and points of connection and the particular position that CNR had in the policy/academic world, facilitated this interaction. Here I think there is scope to break down the instrumentalisation of knowledge and to cross domains of understanding by helping practitioners to think beyond institutional imperatives and by helping academic researchers grasp the dilemmas of practitioners and the communities they are involved with. There might be scope here for the academic to play a much more critical role, rather than being experts in research or evaluators of initiatives. There is also the potential to open up the definition and critical assessment of policy problems in a process that is much more open to negotiation and interpretation than previous arguments (Gibbons et al. 1994) that suggest that policy-makers rather than academics are more and more defining the problems. It also gives the potential for a greater range of input on knowledge problems and away from the favoured few (academics and/or policy-makers) who have the minister's ear (Peck 1999; Banks and Mackian 2000).

A further issue in the capitalising on knowledge as knowledge intermediaries via systematic reviews is a dislocation between the value placed on reviews as part of the translation of research into use-able intelligence for policy formulation or evaluation and the value of these reviews within the academy itself. One blunt measurement of this is the UK context is that systematic reviews, although quite labour intensive, are not returnable for the purposes of the Research Assessment Exercise. Whilst that may or may not matter in for the researchers themselves, it did pose a dilemma for ESRC whose main aim is to support world class social science research. The practical response within CNR, given a fairly open brief, was to align systematic reviews as far as possible to existing research strengths within the Centre or to future research plans. Research for charities or Government departments, whilst being more focused on specific policy questions, is often translatable in this way. But in many cases it is not so easily re-positioned and this poses continuing dilemmas in terms of personnel and expertise and research profiles for policy oriented departments, but is being felt increasingly across higher education institutions, as many of the contributions to this volume have indicated. In terms of 'core business' it might make more sense for systematic reviews to be the domain of Government research departments rather than the academy. Having said that, I think that the systematic reviews conducted in CNR were found to be of use to, and as much used by, other academic researchers, as policy-makers. They point at least to the under-utilisation of secondary data, especially in archived form from other individual projects, but the intellectual reasons for this I have outlined already.

Some Reflections on Knowledge and the Evidence Base

If Government is seeking to incorporate the findings of social science into consideration of policy, then it would be useful to communicate how social science has gone through a series of philosophical developments (such as post structuralism) and that these have critical importance in how we understand knowledge and evidence. This cannot be dismissed as the latest bout of scepticism and withdrawal from the world by social science. Many of these philosophical developments take the nature of knowledge and evidence, its use-ability and relationship to power as the central problematic. It is misleading in many ways to try to separate, as the debate in geography for instance seems to have done, 'relevant' research from the cultural turn. It might also be limiting to focus, as Government research seems to do more and more (when research budgets are cut), on the evidence base provided by econometric analysis (coming as it does out of a discipline that is the least enquiring in social science into its epistemological base). Evidence comes as part of a discourse and problematic. For example poststructuralist claims for deconstruction and understanding the relationship between knowledge and power in the way that Foucault analysed the state and social science and other professional knowledge, can be important in providing a critical check on assumptions about and use of knowledge without disabling the policy process altogether.

There are several aspects to this. First there is what Lyotard has called the 'mercantilisation of knowledge – knowledge in the form of an informational commodity indispensable to productive power' (Loytard 1984: 106). He goes on:

> The old principle that the acquisition of knowledge is in dissociable from the
> training (Bildung) of minds, or even of individuals, is becoming obsolete and will

become even more so. The relationship of the suppliers and users of knowledge to the knowledge they supply and use is now tending, and will increasingly tend, to assume the form already taken by the relationship of commodity producers and consumers to the commodities they consume and the produce – that is the form of value. Knowledge is and will be produced in order to be sold, it is and will be consumed in order to be valorised in new production: in both cases the goal is exchange. Knowledge ceases to be an end in itself, it loses its "use value" (Lyotard 1984: 5).

There are very obvious indications of this commodification of knowledge in terms of the cash value of ideas – in the way that knowledge is both an economic commodity in itself (the knowledge economy) or in the way that knowledge enhances economic performance and human capital. It can be seen in the distinction between the value of a university education being measured in terms of returns to learning (the salary gain as a result of having a degree) as opposed to engendering a sense of critical autonomy as a result of the university experience. There is a danger that with scoping exercises and hierarchies of evidence this systematic treatment becomes one of audit or knowledge accountancy, rather than a critical account of knowledge and indeed how you account for knowledge in terms of claims for its legitimacy. At the same time that there is a flattening of knowledge and a withdrawal of critical engagement there is the understanding that knowledge is structured by power. That is why Derrida's deconstruction of binaries and Foucault's understanding of power discourse are important not least as a critical corrective to the use of language and its citational power. There might be all kinds of evidence in support of, or against 'empowerment' or 'social capital' for instance, but these terms have complex genealogies that give them discursive power in policy terms.

In a simplistic sense, policy-makers more than anyone, know the discursive power of the problem defining statistic or the killer quotation has for a political agenda or for launching a policy initiative. Nor is evidence something inert and separate from validity, in the sense not just of validity and reliability of method but claims to validity in political discourse. In this sense I think the debate should be widened to include the claims to validity that the evidence is assuming. This is not to dissolve into a discursive relativity but rather more in a Habermasian frame (Habermas 1984, 1987), could be seen as a recursive discussion between policy-makers, academia and practitioners in terms how policy problems are constructed, what empirical data and theoretical arguments weigh most persuasively on those problems and then questioning the validity claims of these arguments. This is evidence that is communicatively achieved, not instrumentally translated between knowledge spheres. Policy interventions are conceived in this way not as mechanisms but organisms. The use of evidence is not a quest for certainty to get the right mechanism to apply to the problem but an ongoing intelligence that involves improvisation and experimentation as well as implementation (Dewey 1958, 1930, 1929). Evidence here will involve the self-critical judgements (claims to validity) of academics, civil servants and practitioners and 'the public', and the acknowledgements of their interests in particular fields of knowledge and power (Bourdieu 1990) rather than the simple application of expertise (however much it is or is not drawn from empirical evidence in social science).

The focus on the evidence base through contract research as a key input to policy has the potential to open up discussion of the policy but there are also implicit pressures that close it down. The idea of evidence has a foreshortening effect in terms of the legitimacy of evidence arrived at through justification. Evidence is not its own justification in this sense. Treating knowledge as evidence to be exchanged has a flattening effect on the evidence itself, which is treated instrumentally and weighed as units of account. That process tends to render both the knowledge provider (the contracted researcher) and the knowledge receiver (the contracting government department) passive in relation to the knowledge. Evidence without argument has a numbing effect in this sense. It reduces the capacity of researchers to provide critical accounts of the research and the nature of the contract reduces the policy community's accountability for the way that the knowledge is used – how was the evidence used and what are the consequences of its use? Some of the difficulties here might be assuaged by a stronger notion of evaluation. Contractual relations tend to be fragmented in this sense. There is the contract issued for the researchers to do the primary research, or the secondary analysis or the systematic reviews and separate contracts to other researchers to conduct evaluations of particular policy initiatives. It might be useful to think of extending the time horizons of appraisal to include provision of evidence and evaluation of its use and effectiveness in a real form of meta-analysis. It might also be productive to expand the constituency of appraisal to involve not just the experts (academic researchers, policy professionals) but policy users – the citizen groups to which policy is aimed. Here the criteria of judgement will not be the nature of the evidence (much of which might be highly specialised) but the bearing that the use of the evidence has for policy (as Dewey [1927] argued) – the bearing of the consequential use of evidence. Archon Fung (2004) is arguing for something analogous in his idea of evaluation as a form of democratic deliberation.

The evidence-based policy initiative in many senses conflicts with the pragmatic 'what works' agenda. The idea of social science evidence as an accurate measurement of the problem and as in some value-free way informing policy deliberations is at odds with pragmatism in its deeper philosophical idea of knowledge as action (for example Dewey 1958) tested in pluralist communication for its validity. This requires a much more radically democratic and open set of relationships within Government, within universities and between the two.

Acknowledgements

With thanks to the Economic and Social Research Council who funded CNR and the wider evidence-based policy network. I'm also grateful to Chris Allen and Rob Imrie for their really helpful feedback on this chapter.

PART II
Entrepreneurialism and the Academic Labour Process

Chapter 8

Partnership, Servitude or Expert Scholarship? The Academic Labour Process in Contract Housing Research

Tony Manzi and Bill Smith-Bowers

Introduction

An examination of research activity necessarily raises fundamental issues in relation to higher education institutions. Are universities primarily teaching institutions or should they give priority to research activity? What role should consultancy or contract research play as opposed to 'pure' academic research? These questions have become especially pertinent within the 'new' universities, which is where most housing research centres are located. Moreover these questions have particular resonance to academic housing researchers because 'housing studies' has generally been seen as an applied subject that has been tasked with understanding housing problems and providing policy responses to them. Thus housing studies has struggled to assert itself in academic terms and, thus, to carve out an intellectual space for itself within the academy

> … Housing has become something of an intellectual ghetto: in developing a distinct profile it has cut itself off from the debates and discussions in other academic disciplines (Robertson and McLaughlin 1996: 27).

The purpose of this chapter is to consider the social practice of housing research. The chapter begins by establishing the context for the development of housing research in new universities and considers the role of housing scholarship, identifying three main 'communities of practice' (Wenger 1988). The chapter then outlines the social relations of contract housing research. Specifically, we argue that the academic labour process in contract housing research is the result of an interaction of various competing demands an increasingly commercial environment. The labour process is ultimately shaped through a process of negotiation that produces varying arrangements for the conduct of social research, categorised as processes of partnership, servitude or expert scholarship. The chapter concludes by considering the implications of a contract housing research culture.

Managerialism, Professionalism and Housing Research
in the New Universities

The UK 'new' universities emerged from former polytechnics granted university status in the *Further and Higher Education Act 1992*. These institutions aimed to recruit students interested in learning 'practical' subjects and generally offered vocational programmes as part of a government attempt to extend the opportunities of higher education to lower-income and less-qualified groups. However, they were often seen as 'second-tier' or lower status institutions due to reduced admissions criteria and in their concentration on vocational education. As Glennerster (2007) comments they were often seen as 'cheaper and more teaching-based universities' (138).

Nevertheless, the new universities contributed to a significant increase of UK higher education; the 1992 Act resulted in the creation of 30 new institutions (from former polytechnics) with total student numbers (in further and higher education) increasing from just over 1m in 1994 to 2.5m by 2007 (HESA, live statistics online). This increase was in line with government targets to ensure 50 per cent of young people attended university. The new universities were developed as part of the alleged contribution of university education to national economic growth and productivity as well as marking what King and Nash (2001) term the end of the application of 'liberal humanist principles' such as university freedom and 'knowledge for its own sake' (88).

At the same time new corporatised universities practiced a 'more managerial approach to governance' (*Times Higher Education*, 31/8/07) as well as paying greater attention to developing key skills or competencies that would feed economic growth and prosperity; an approach further encouraged in the Leitch (HM Treasury 2006) and Egan Reports (ODPM 2004). The adoption of corporate styles of governance and management was reflected in mission statements and mottos, such as at the University of ('Forward Thinking') Westminster:

> to provide high quality higher education and research in both national and
> international contexts for the intellectual, social and professional development
> of the individual and for the economic and cultural enrichment of London and wider
> communities (http://www.westminster.ac.uk/about/key-facts, accessed 10/11/09).

The extension of corporate managerialism has led to extensive criticism at the growing orientation of universities towards the private sector resulting in a 'colonisation of academia by the market' (Mautner 2005) involving commodification and the subjection of research to commercial pressures. This 'marketisation of the higher education landscape' (Mautner 2005) was viewed as a threat to core principles of disinterestedness, objectivity and independence, involving a blurring of boundaries between universities and the for-profit sector. Hence writers have warned of the drift in a new knowledge economy towards 'academic' or 'knowledge capitalism' (Slaughter and Leslie 1997; Burton Jones 1999). Academic study has been transformed by a discourse dominated by 'industrialised language', where 'understanding' is replaced by 'competence' and 'knowledge' by 'information' (Coffield and Williamson 1997: 1).

The consequence is that new universities in particular have been increasingly encouraged to view themselves as commercial institutions, valued primarily for their contribution to economic prosperity and socio-economic productivity. This approach was typified by the distinction drawn by the former UK Education Secretary David Blunkett (2000: para. 87) between the 'entrepreneurial' and 'do-nothing' university; the implication being that a university committed to traditional principles of knowledge for its own sake should not survive in a brave new modernised world of New Labour education policy. The combination of reducing grant levels, increased competition and pressure to increase student numbers has therefore resulted in a focus on external sources of funding (Harloe and Perry 2004: 217).

This process of marketisation has had a significant impact on housing education and research. The 1990s expansion of higher education coincided with a considerable increase in the provision of housing research and educational programmes; growth saw the delivery of housing programmes heavily concentrated in new universities – nine out of 14 institutions offering postgraduate professionally accredited courses are post 1992 universities, all of these nine based in England (CIH 2008). In addition the content of housing education programmes was strongly influenced by demands of the professional body (the Chartered Institute of Housing – CIH) with professional qualifications and corporate membership expectations incorporated into the curricula of new universities, rather than being separately administered through the CIH. These professional requirements have created significant tensions between training and education and academic knowledge and practical skills. Relations between the CIH and education institutions have become increasingly strained as a result of these pressures (see for example, Cole n.d.).

Housing research centres have increasingly been forced to rely on external sources of income in order to supplement student numbers (which are under threat from accelerated competition between education institutions). These centres in the new universities have embraced a corporate discourse; as illustrated in the mission statement of the Centre for Regional and Housing Research (CRESR) at Sheffield Hallam University:

> We pride ourselves on combining academic rigour and sector expertise tailored
> to the individual needs of our diverse client base; whilst remaining competitive,
> flexible and business focused (http://www.shu.ac.uk/research/cresr/, accessed
> 11/10/09).

This emphasis on professionalism and practical application has culminated in a high reliance on consultancy and contract research, with policy relevance seen as a key source of legitimisation for research activity (Thomas 2005: 241); this professional ethos has important implications for the conduct of housing research.

First, housing study is in danger of losing its critical edge due to the strong correlation between practice and academia, where 'research is a commodity; a product that can be bought from a variety of suppliers' (Robertson 2008: 15). Similarly, Ian Cole (n.d.) has criticised the 'drift of housing courses towards an uncritical concern with 'practice relevance' as a guiding principle' (1). Housing courses have become 'dominated by the concern to equip practitioners with an appropriate armoury of skills for survival, rather than to open up new avenues for inquiry, controversy and analysis' (2). The consequence is that housing education and research is seen as a 'servant of the housing profession and the wider policy community' (Robertson 2008: 33–34).

The relationship between academia and practice is mirrored by the relationship between policy-making and research. Thus a 'system of social relationships in which housing research is procured and produced is also one where political agendas have created a close correspondence between research projects and the needs of policymaking' (Atkinson and Jacobs 2008: 13). This symbiotic link between policy-makers and researchers has resulted in a culture where 'housing research rarely challenges the constraints in which housing policy operates' (Robertson 2008: 33–34).

A second problem is that 'the sort of institutional structures that support the working lives of public intellectuals are under assault and ... there is too much complacency and conformism on the part of academic researchers' (Marston 2008: 179). Universities are seen to be driven by a 'narrow instrumentalism' (Thomas 2005: 242) in their focus on performance measurement and target setting and this has had a detrimental impact on the quality of academic scholarship by imposing a managerial agenda rather than one driven by the demands of intellectual enquiry. This managerial agenda is exacerbated by financial pressures which have made training officers in housing organisations more eager to ensure that courses met the perceived needs of their employees, rather than developing a broader appreciation of housing issues and ideas' (Cole n.d. 7).

A third difficulty with the shift towards a contract research culture is that ethical issues tend to be understated through 'the conflation of the norms and values of a practice with the instrumental norms and rationality associated with its institutional expression' (Lo Piccolo and Thomas 2008: 14). One of the clear dangers of a reliance on evidence-based policy is that research studies can in contrast be reduced to 'policy-based evidence' (Lovering 1999); where research studies are utilised to provide *post hoc* rationalisations of policy positions determined by funding agencies. As a consequence 'conventional social science has ruthlessly removed ethical ideas as improper objects of knowledge claims' (Marston 2008: 181). In order to evaluate these criticisms, the next section will distinguish between the different approaches to housing research.

Communities of Housing Practice: Activists, Academics and Consultants

A number of significant distinctions can be identified in the role and scope of housing research activity. Whilst Jones and Seelig (2004) distinguish between 'engineering' (problem-oriented), 'engagement' (critical) and 'enlightenment' (sceptical and reflexive) models, we prefer to use the terms *activists*, *academics* and *consultants* to identify the main 'communities of practice' (Wenger 1988) engaged in housing research and to reflect the tensions between politics, scholarship and entrepreneurship within new universities. Whilst such typologies can be simplistic and may fail to 'provide a sufficient account of the complexity of power relations within research communities of the discourses that inform choices and strategies' (Atkinson and Jacobs 2008: 2), we argue that they can illustrate some important tendencies in housing policy. Clearly these categories can overlap but they do help to inform the way that housing research operates.

An Activist Model of Housing Research

An 'activist' approach represents the historically dominant approach to housing study, taking the form of 'action research' or studies undertaken as part of a planned programme of social change. These studies involve applied work aiming to uncovering injustices, to change social attitudes or social practices. Dating back to the time of Charles Booth and influenced by the Fabian model of public administration, these studies used scientific, rigorous, mainly quantitative data to enable the development of effective social reforms to be undertaken. The main original housing research groups were described as 'spiritually embedded in the intellectual wing of the Labour movement' (Donnison and Stephens 2003: 250) and produced primarily empirical studies, based on a strong body of social science research in the positivist tradition; early examples include Young and Wilmott's (1957) examination of family and kinship in East London; Townsend's (1967) 'rediscovery' of poverty or Donnison's *The Government of Housing* (1967).

The Fabian activist model found a contrasting voice in the 1980s, influenced by neo-liberal economics (Friedman 1990) and public choice theory (Niskanen 1973). These studies severely criticised the state sector (Coleman 1985) and enthusiastically embraced the emphasis upon creating a 'property-owning democracy' (Saunders 1990). These kinds of ideologically influenced studies bemoaned the impact of regulation (Albon and Stafford 1987) and warned about the emergence of a 'dependency culture' in welfare policy (Marsland 1996).

However, activist housing research has tended be based around the themes of equality, redistribution and empowerment (see for example Holmes 2003), seeking to promote the aims of marginalised communities, such as gypsy and traveller groups (Richardson 2006). Since the end of the twentieth century considerable research has focused on community involvement in line with government policies to reform housing practice. Efforts at engendering resident involvement (Taylor 2003) have been influential in shaping approaches to contemporary housing policy.

These approaches have assisted in developing improvements to housing practice or in wider welfare reform (Power and Houghton 2007). Such applied research comprises original investigation to acquire new knowledge but that is directed specifically towards a practical aim, seeking a relationship where the purpose of housing research is that of speaking 'uncensored truth to power' (Donnison and Stephens 2003: 248).

'Academic' Approaches to Housing Study

Academic scholarship constitutes what is sometimes termed 'basic' or 'pure' research, comprising experimental or theoretical work to acquire new knowledge. The work is undertaken for its own sake and has no particular application or use (Durning 2004). Interestingly many of the most influential studies have been conducted by writers whose discipline was in political science or sociology rather than housing *per se*; for example, Rex and Moore's (1967) concept of 'housing classes'; Dunleavy's (1981) discussion of neo-pluralism or Ball's (1986) conceptualisation of 'structures of housing provision' which have helped refocus analysis of housing policy.

Occasionally involving econometric and statistical analyses; these kinds of studies can be said to entail understanding rather than prescription. They tend to take a technical form and may contain considerable complexity. These kinds of study are concerned with the formation of models to understand the behaviour of markets or the outcomes of subsidy systems (for example, Maclennan and Williams 1990) or discussions of the economic causes of social segregation (Meen et al. 2005). Often commissioned by government agencies (for example Holmans' (1995) discussion of housing need) these studies have again been highly empirical, primarily quantitative and based on detailed statistical analysis.

An alternative (and more recent) approach to academic housing research has used social theory and Jim Kemeny's work has been particularly influential here (see for example Kemeny 1992, 1995, Kemeny and Lowe 1998). This sociological trend has seen the emergence of qualitative, ethnographic studies, often influenced by symbolic interactionism. Such research often takes the form of case study analysis, the objective of which is to provide a detailed picture of social practices within a specific spatial locale. These ethnographic studies have become increasingly important in shaping an understanding of the social processes inherent in the production and consumption of housing. For example Watson and Austerberry's (1986) examination of homelessness from a feminist perspective, using interviews to explore the experience of a group of women. Foucauldian social science has been used to: analyse the meaning of home (Gurney 1999a and b); to critique initiatives such as 'foyer' schemes (Allen 2001a and b) or to reflect on culture and council housing (Ravetz 2001).

Since the 1980s contemporary housing studies has attempted to delineate a more explicit theoretical basis, with a range of conceptual approaches such as: theorising approaches to comparative housing (Kemeny and Lowe 1998); using social constructionism (Jacobs et al. 2005); and applying discourse analysis (Hastings 2002; Marston 2004), game theory (Garside 2000), new institutionalism (Mullins et al. 2001) and rational choice models (Boyne et al. 2003). Whilst such approaches have begun to enter the discourse of housing research, these perspectives are somewhat embryonic and generally under-developed. One criticism has been a lack of critical and reflective commentary on the practice of housing research. For example Marston (2008) charges that housing academics are guilty of a 'flight from responsibility and an inability to engage in anything more than a "spectator role" in processes of social change' (179).

Housing and Consultancy Research

The above two categories comprise what have sometimes been terms 'Mode 1' studies, based upon traditional disciplinary scholarship. In contrast 'Mode 2' studies are based around 'problem-oriented and team based' research (Gibbons et al. 1994) and these have come to dominate the contemporary research agenda in housing as in other areas of 'the knowledge economy' (Harding et al. 2007). Mode 2 research conforms to 'knowing how' rather than the 'knowing what' of traditional scholarship and provides the basis of meaningful 'knowledge transfer' (Levin 2007). This Mode 2 category, which we term 'consultancy', prioritises the relation with professional work, attempts to formulate practical solutions to policy issues and aims to develop research partnerships with policy-makers and practitioners.

Consultancy research involves the deployment of existing knowledge for the resolution of specific problems by a client, increasingly within a quasi-commercial context. This category of housing research provides a dominant modus operandi for many housing research centres in new universities, providing significant funding opportunities and shaping resource distribution within an environment where other sources of funding are increasingly constrained.

An emphasis on professionalism in housing research has helped to focus attention on revenue-raising activities and fostered a culture wherein research is viewed largely in economic terms. Contract research studies can be conducted to evaluate government policy (Stephens et al. 2005), to promote good practice (Bailey et al. 2006) or to develop policy instruments and problem-solving models to assist practitioners (Burns and Taylor 2000).

As noted above, the growth of consultancy research reflects the dominance of new managerialism in UK universities (Deem et al. 2008). Based on a model of academic entrepreneurship, consultancy-based approaches are representative of a pragmatic turn in housing study or a 'new utilitarianism' (see Imrie, this volume) typifying the commodification of knowledge wherein research agenda are determined by the clients or funding agencies rather than academic institutions. New universities are therefore indicative of the shift from the model of a liberal university where knowledge is neutral and academic staff have autonomy, towards an 'economic' model where research activity is valued for its use and its role in the delivery of tax payer investment in 'human capital' and its outputs; an institutional culture wherein truth is intertwined with 'usefulness' (Hammersley 1995: 152).

Clearly the above communities of practice overlap, but what they illustrate is the changing nature of housing research activity wherein judgements depend not merely on formulating appropriate research questions, based on academic curiosity, but also on commercial, institutional priorities and the requirements of funding agencies. It seems increasingly common for housing research institutions in new universities to establish themselves as profit centres and commercial consultancies, competing for research contracts from government, voluntary agencies or private sector sources. Having established the three main communities of practice involved in housing scholarship, the next section outlines how these different social relations operate, by reference to contract research within a new university environment.

The Social Relations of Contract Housing Research Production

The standard view of contract research is that power largely resides with funding agencies and research commissioners. This can take what Allen (2005) terms either a 'Hobbesian' (hierarchical) model of power or a more dynamic and diffused 'Foucauldian' approach. Within the former social relations in the research process operate according to a linear model; power flows from client and limited autonomy is offered to the contractor. In the latter researchers are subject to the 'disciplinary gaze' of funders and are guilty of supplicating themselves through self-censorship in order to gain future research contracts. Such insights can illuminate important features of urban policy research and in particular the way in which evaluation according to 'value for money' criteria ignores other more qualitative dimensions of urban policy. However, such a view ignores the potential for researchers and resident communities themselves to influence the collection of data, the interpretation of findings and research conclusions. In contrast, seen from a social constructionist paradigm, power is dispersed and discontinuous; social research is therefore subject to continual bargaining and negotiation. Relationships can be characterised more accurately as subject to transformation over the period of a contract, rather than fixed in passive or docile modes of operation.

Our analysis suggests that the research process involves a reciprocal relationship; power is not linear and researchers are themselves capable of exercising substantial autonomy as indeed are research subjects. For example Routledge (2004) argues that those being researched can chose whether to participate, to grant interviews, to conduct dialogue and the method of communication; they can therefore exert a measure of power over the 'construction of the parameters and dynamics of collaboration (85). Similarly, O'Brien's et al.'s (2008) discussion of education research found a 'complex struggle between research funders, "stakeholders", researchers and the researched' (371) and this struggle illustrates a variety of potential relationships which can provide 'spaces for resistance' (376). The rules of the game are flexible and not subject to immutable power; they rely on the starting positions of the parties in the research commission process, previous experience, pressure to produce a certain type of outcome and the extent of bargaining and negotiation available. These rules can be applied differentially not simply to the collection of research material, but also its interpretation and dissemination.

We argue that the social relations of housing research can be typified by a threefold classification which we term: 'Partner/collegiate', 'servant/master' or 'expert/innocent'. Table 8.1 (below) outlines this classification of the social relations of housing research production. Experience of contract research demonstrates that all of the above classifications have been utilised at different points in time and we discuss these processes in more detail in the following sections.

Table 8.1 The social relations of contract housing research

Position of Researcher	Power	Relationship	Possible commissioning agency	Position of client
Partner	Reciprocal	'Tell us what you find (and we will disseminate it)'	Large charity	Collegiate
Servant	Hierarchical	'We tell you what we want you to say'	Central Government	Master
Expert	Asymmetrical	'Tell us what you want to say'	Voluntary sector organisation (e.g. Small housing association/RSL)	Innocent

The Partner/Collegiate Relationship

A partner/collegiate relationship operates in circumstances where the contract research is based upon a common endeavour of knowledge seeking. This represents an idealised form of social relationship, wherein both parties have equivalent objectives and are committed to a goal of truth-seeking. In this model there may be relatively stringent monitoring of the contract, but the relationship proceeds on the basis that the contractor possesses considerable expertise and therefore the terms of reference have some flexibility. These contracts are often considered as 'high status' research projects. They can involve substantial resources and supposedly 'elite' institutions are the main beneficiaries, with named academics in the field often seen as having a head start in terms of winning bids. Traditionally these institutions would have comprised 'old' (Russell Group) universities but increasingly active housing research centres in new universities have developed significant experience and expertise in contract research. Power relations are based upon a principle of reciprocity with each party gaining from the encounter. Advisory groups tend to be consultative rather than instructive and the terms of the contract are dependent on the negotiating power of the different parties. The dissemination of the research findings is largely controlled by the client but the relationship tends to be defined in terms of collegiality.

Contracts undertaken in a spirit of collective endeavour may be rarely acknowledged, but often represent initial objectives; both parties are likely to lay claim to a relationship based on mutual goals; the contract researcher is seen as an objective party, hired on the basis of research expertise and the client is obliged to publish research findings regardless of its wider implications. Research conclusions may be either positive or negative but the client will not generally seek to restrict wider academic publication. However, research contracts may often begin with such idealised statements but over time, once the implications of research findings become clear, the client may be reluctant to allow publication of results and wider dissemination of findings. For example the implicit threat to prevent further contracts being awarded may be evident from (normally informal) comments made to the researchers. Significantly this kind of relationship rarely invites comment. It is only when the relationship is seen as asymmetrical that academics feel there is a need to pass judgment about the costs and benefits of the research relationship.

Partnership arrangements between academic institutions and the policy process are demonstrated by largely uncritical discussions of vague and temporally fashionable concepts such as 'Third Way' or 'stakeholder' housing policies (Brown 1999), 'sustainable communities' (Kearns and Turok 2004), 'community cohesion' (Blackaby 2004) and 'mixed community' initiatives (Bailey et al. 2006). Many of these studies are commissioned and written due to economic imperatives with the purpose of providing advice and guidance to governments, promoting good practice and providing recommendations to housing agencies to develop specific policy initiatives. Government emphasis on 'evidence-based policy and practice' serves to legitimate the activity of raising funding through research activity and moving away from 'investigator-led research' (Davies et al. 2000).

This reciprocity carries considerable ethical implications. Social relations between practitioners, policy-makers are viewed as interdependent and there is considerable goal congruence about what each will achieve from the research relationship. The research process is viewed as a relatively straightforward fact-gathering exercise, with findings presented to the client at the end of the process in the form of a report (the form of which has been jointly agreed). However, such a positivist model of the research process ignores the scope for selective data-collection for interpretation (and misinterpretation) of findings and the eventual dissemination of data. Seeing the research relationship as largely unproblematic is both simplistic and politically naïve. Researchers can become complicit in presenting policies in neutral and 'seemingly 'objective terms. The independence supposedly conferred by objective and rigorous analysis can be used in order to legitimate what may otherwise have been a highly contentious set of policies. The potential for 'speaking truth to power' is significantly reduced in situations where academics appear to be complicit handmaidens of government policy. The use of academic research to justify restrictions on eligibility in the Housing Act 1996 (Anderson et al. 1993) provides one example of the way in which government has used research for its own ends, developing policy regardless of the conclusions of those studies. Academics can follow a political agenda set by politicians and it is important that they retain their independence and a clear ethical sense of their responsibilities.

The Servant/Master Relationship

A more common representation of the social research relationship is that power is held by a client, through the control of resources. Bids are invited from interested parties (contractors) and winning bids are then offered a contract, with varying funds attached. These types of contracts can be categorised as a *master* and servant relationship, with researchers placed in a largely submissive position. There is little room for manoeuvre in the terms of the contract, advisory groups are appointed to ensure strict adherence to the initial terms of reference, and there are rigid deadlines for completion and sanctions for non-performance. Publication is strictly controlled by the commissioning agency, including ownership of the research findings. For example Karn et al.'s (1985) influential study of owner occupation reflected a traditional set of power relations between central government and academic researchers. As the authors commented:

> Permission to publish other articles or address seminars even after the final report was submitted was refused on the grounds that it would be inappropriate to disclose findings which had not received ministerial approval (8–9).

Moreover after much delay, on publication the researchers complained that 'though we have been given permission to publish, we are still hedged about with constraints … we are not allowed to make any further alterations to it without restarting a lengthy approval process' (9). The authors felt that their study lacked much of its force as they were 'not allowed to name any financial institutions' (9).

This example illustrated a classic master/servant relationship with strong control exercised by ministers and civil servants due to concerns about the political implications of the findings. This relationship was more fully explored in Allen's (2005) analysis, which uses a model of power influenced by Foucault (1977) to demonstrate how exposure to a 'disciplinary gaze' results in a relationship characterised by 'docility'; the research process is thereby intuitively and uncritically oriented to satisfying the demands and needs of funding institutions. Here the disciplinary process is self-sustaining; rather than being imposed from outside (by policy-makers) academics exercise self-restraint in the selection of data to analyse, interpretations of findings and conclusions which serve inevitably assist the agenda of practitioners and politicians.

The resulting absence of critical thinking has important ethical implications. For example Slater (2006) has complained about the lack of critical perspectives in gentrification research. Quoting Wacquant (2004) in the US, researchers who wish

> ... to address public officials are said to submit to severe censorship by reformulating their work according to technocratic categories that ensure this work will have neither purchase nor any effect on reality ... American politicians never invoke social research except when it supports the direction they want to go in any way for reasons of political expediency; in all other cases, they trample it shamelessly (Wacquant 2004: 99, cited in Slater 2006: 751).

Within a UK context these processes are apparent within research on 'social mix'; such policies have been insufficiently questioned for their impact. Hence, as Slater suggests, 'gentrification' has become a 'dirty word' in urban policy research: 'it is very difficult to secure research funding from an urban policy outlet to assess the implications of an urban policy designed to entice middle-class residents into working class neighbourhoods' (Slater 2006: 751).

The pressures on academic researchers are not unique to housing and these debates have been more widely considered in relation to planning theory and practice (see for example, Durning 2004). Healey's (1991) discussion of the implications of resisting government pressures to produce favourable interpretations of research findings illustrates the tensions contained within differing views of the roles and purposes of research activity. As a consequence, writing reflexively about funding agencies is seen as a 'risky business' (O'Brien et al. 2008) due to the fear of incurring the wrath of paymasters and reducing the likelihood of being awarded future research contracts. The power exercised by research funders is expressed by Mautner (2005) in the comment: 'The hand that feeds is less likely to be bitten' (97). Clearly, such pressures have influenced decisions about the research process and practices in new universities have responded to commercial rather than academic imperatives in situations where research centres are almost entirely dependent on continued funding streams from commissioning agencies.

The Expert/Innocent Relationship

The final category is one where the contractor obtains almost full control of the contract. This is not an orthodox relationship as the client still employs the contractor. However, the contractor may possess such specialist information that the client is unable (or unwilling) to exercise significant control over the conduct of the research. The researcher can therefore adopt a strong position as *master* of the contract, asserting their academic expertise and dictating how the terms of reference may change over the course of the project. An example of such research (conducted by the authors) was a study commissioned by a small housing association; the position of the latter could be characterised by innocence and naivety and consequently there was considerable flexibility in terms of the delivery and management of the research process.

Few researchers would admit to a relationship based on expertise over innocence, as it suggests a level of arrogance, presenting the client as naïve and to some extent ignorant. However, this kind of approach may be evident where the researchers are highly skilled, high status (often within a team including internationally recognised experts) and the client has considerable inexperience. In these circumstances the researcher will have considerable autonomy in the ability to determine the parameters of research, the general methodological approach and the publication of findings. Small organisations which commission small-scale projects will be likely to fall under this category. The central point is that researchers are able to exercise considerable autonomy, within certain constraints.

The ethical implications of an assumption of academic expertise are that research subjects have tended to be placed at the lowest level of a hierarchy of research. For example, Imrie (1996) has criticised researchers for ignoring communities and criticises the use of what he terms 'foundationalist' models of research, which are dependent on 'coercive values' and which claim legitimacy 'by recourse to the purity of objectivity' (1462). The subsequent research is 'intertwined with a politics of exclusion' (ibid.) as it treats consumers as passive recipients of research activity. Imrie complains of a research process that neglects self-reflexive commentary and fails to consider the extent to which research 'may be politicised and value laden (thus partial and biased)' (ibid.). Writers on planning research have also commented on the need for researchers to undertake work as part of a 'political practice' (Lo Piccolo and Thomas 2008). Hence research studies can be used as an aid to either the empowerment or further exclusion of marginalised communities and academics can exert considerable power through their position as expert scholars and independent commentators (see for example the discussion in Cloke et al. 2000).

The Housing Market Renewal Initiative (HMRI) represents one area where academics have played an influential role in the formulation and production of expert knowledge in order to influence policy outcomes. For example Mullins and Murie (2006) comment that this initiative was a 'relatively unusual' example of evidence-based policy-making 'triggered by evidence that challenged long-held assumptions' producing a 'stream of research and consistent lobbying' by housing professionals (267–268). The eventual policy proposed bore a strong relation to the research recommendations and because it had not been commissioned by government 'it was more likely to challenge predilections than legitimate convictions' (269). Whilst Mullins and Murie argue that it is important not to overemphasise the role of academic research (as effective interest group lobbying underpinned the policy change) it does illustrate the way in which academic research can have considerable impact in policy.

Taking this argument further, Allen (2008) argues that intellectuals can assume the role of 'academic nobility' (180) speaking with particular authority about issues (such as gentrification) to the extent that their voices deny legitimacy to marginalised working-class residents. For Allen, a middle-class academic nobility lacks 'the ability to be reflexive about the ontological status of its own positionality since this is what impedes it from achieving insights into working-class experience ... *in its own terms*' (182, emphasis in original). This 'epistemological elitism' and 'methodological totalitarianism' (ibid.) is a reflection of academics occupying a privileged expert status. Allen (2009) argues:

> Housing researchers seem to have become increasingly reflexive about the phenomena they are concerned with. However, there is little evidence that housing researchers have become more reflexive about the *grounds of their own practices of knowledge gathering and production* (54, emphasis in original).

For writers such as Allen, 'housing researchers routinely speak for powerful housing interests in a legitimate language to which working class people are denied access' (2009: 26) and moreover they objectify, sanitise, neutralise and euphemise working class experiences of pain and dispossession (ibid.). These types of criticism have proved contentious but they illustrate both the dangers of too close a relationship with government policy and in assuming a moral high ground in policy discussions. Whilst academics are trained to think critically, their propensity for self-criticism tends to be more limited. This role of expert scholarship is therefore an important feature of the social relations of housing research.

Conclusions

The categorisations that we offer illustrate the wide variety of roles that housing researchers can occupy as a community of practice; this community is not a homogeneous one and the roles vary according to the relationships between clients, contractors and research subjects. Nevertheless, what seems clear is that a number of influences have assumed particular significance since the 1990s and have affected social practice of housing research in new universities. First, the impact of funding institutions has enabled increased resource dependency; work follows the money (providing an 'economic' model of universities). This commercial imperative has affected the production of research, the agenda of research centres and the research questions considered.

Second the emphasis on policy relevance (and 'evidence-based research') means that studies have tended towards the atheoretical and unreflective. Whilst academic research still flourishes, this approach is increasingly threatened by an unwillingness to criticise core constituencies and a concern about jeopardising future research partnerships.

A third implication of the contract culture in housing research is that ethical issues have tended to be ignored in housing research studies. The absence of original thinking and critical, reflexive research in housing studies is most noticeable in terms of an absence of reflection on methods and on ethics. Even those writers who have written about housing in philosophical terms (such as King 2003) have generally not engaged in detailed discussion of ethical considerations. Furthermore, the main national and European housing research groups (Housing Studies Association and European Network of Housing Research) have historically issued little ethical guidance for researchers.

'Reflexivity' in housing research needs to involve more than simply being conscious about methods used, but rather adopting a critical approach throughout the research process, including a critical focus on the research methods utilised and their consequences for participants. What we want to suggest here is that within housing studies there needs to be a more direct articulation of standards in the conduct of housing research, to promote the academic autonomy of researchers in the discipline. Such statements are needed in order to create an environment in which ethical controversies are aired to better inform housing studies research practice. The docility of researchers is as much the ethical responsibility of housing researchers as it is the result of the complex patterns of power relationship that can be used to define the research relationships of contractor and researcher. Thus the question of the docile researcher can be reformulated as that of an ethically underdeveloped researcher. Instead of seeing this as a position in power relationship we need to ask if housing research education is lacking in the development of the ethical training of researchers. Contract research offers both opportunities and threats but the costs and benefits of this approach to housing study need to be carefully measured. The various social relations indicate dynamics of the academic labour process and the scope for power relations to be exercised by different stakeholders in the research relationship.

Given the increasing importance of contract research it is curious that there has not been more discussion of the emergence of an entrepreneurial culture in housing studies. In contrast, this chapter suggests that perhaps it is not so strange, given the lack of confidence in housing studies presenting itself as a distinctive discipline. This lack of confidence has led to a strong policy orientation and dependence on funding institutions and following a government-led agenda within new universities – researchers have tended to follow prevailing trends rather than being in the forefront of thinking about housing questions. One of the dangers is that housing researchers could be losing the skills and curiosity driven attitudes associated with investigator led research.

Acknowledgement

The authors would like to thank Rob Imrie and Chris Allen for their helpful comments on an earlier draft of this chapter.

Chapter 9

Managing Sensitive Social Relations in Planning Policy Research: Co-Production and Critical Friendship in the Enterprising University[1]

Paul O'Hare, Jon Coaffee and Marian Hawkesworth

Introduction

Collaborative or co-produced research is an increasingly prominent feature of the contemporary university. In engaging with such types of research, researchers can occupy a privileged location at the interface between theory and practice. Not only can such relations bring funding, employment and knowledge production, but the synergies generated, it is proposed, offers potentially illuminating insights into critical and challenging issues. Moreover, in a more practical sense, the support of actors who operate in spheres of policy or practice can 'open doors' into otherwise impenetrable worlds or can facilitate access to hitherto unreachable elites. Beyond these benefits, such co-produced research trajectories can serve to undermine the long-standing and often pejorative allegation that the academy is an 'Ivory Tower' – the (often unfair) assertions that the contemporary university is the domain of disconnected and often elitist individuals who conduct research in isolation and with little regard for the potential impact it may have upon wider society.

Yet, despite the varied benefits that such approaches can bring, a number of serious challenges may also arise. For instance, in contrast to critiques of the 'Ivory tower' model of operation, it is suggested that knowledge co-production and intense collaborations with agencies and actors external to research institutions may moderate critical thought, and ultimately erode the autonomy of academia. It is with these issues, and the trade-offs and the compromises that must be negotiated in their resolution, with which this chapter is concerned. We reflect upon our own research experiences of a project which focused upon the impact of counter-terrorism initiatives on the built environment. This project – funded by three of the main UK research councils and supported by governmental partners

1   An earlier version of this chapter has been published as O'Hare, P., Coaffee, J. and Hawkesworth, M. (2010) 'Managing Sensitive Relations in Co-Produced Planning Research', *Public Money and Management*, 30(4), pp 243–250.

– has, as well as providing manifold opportunities to work in novel and innovative ways, generated a number of critical issues for the researchers.[2] Through reflection upon our own experience of researching national security concerns, and their impacts upon spatial planning practice, we discuss a range of these challenges, the concerns that they raise for academia today, and more generically, for the condition of the research environment of the contemporary university. In doing so, we outline the emergence of critical tensions within our own study with respect to both its conceptual direction and its practical and ethical conduct. The chapter concludes by detailing how we developed a coping strategy for these challenges; namely an attempt to negotiate a 'critical friendship' with those that sponsor and consume our research in order to try and retain our 'academic independence'.

Collaboration in the Contemporary University

Traditionally, the role of the university has partly been viewed as that of a counterbalance to the state, and as having a historical role in promoting free thinking and the unfettered development of ideas and knowledge (for a discussion see, for example, Becher and Kogan 1992, Henkel 2007; Karran 2009). However, this historic position has, for many decades, been eroded as modern universities have become increasingly entrepreneurial and connected to – or possibly led by – an array of political agendas. In addition to the development of external connections to policy and professional communities, such 'entrepreneurialism' has also involved the introduction of internal models of organisational effectiveness. This has included strategic management of the delivery of outputs, and the implementation of regimes to monitor, evaluate and to ultimately improve academic performance against a range of markers established by the Government and funding bodies.

Against this broader context, it is now widely proposed that university researchers have an *essential* role to play in the delivery knowledge transfer and exchange (KTE) (see, for instance, Mowery and Shane 2002). KTE initiatives have been identified by institutions to be increasingly essential in generating revenue, and also in providing partnerships that support intellectual insight and technological innovation. Indeed, the extent to which now so-called 'entrepreneurial' universities actively pursue greater interaction with funders and sponsors has led to it being described by some as a 'second revolution' in the core activity of higher education institutions (Etzkowitz 1998, 2001). At the same time, and going some way to illustrate the reach of this 'revolution', today great emphasis is placed by higher education institutions on commercial spin-offs, business incubation and efforts to harness and protect intellectual property. These practices are being described in some quarters as the 'capitalisation' (Etzkowitz et al. 1998) or commercialisation

---

2 This project ran between October 2007 and April 2010 and involved over 100 qualitative interviews with key stakeholders and a variety of focus groups and workshops with professional planners, architects, local government officials and policy-makers.

of research, and ultimately of knowledge (for a more detailed discussion, see Gibbons et al. 1994). Elsewhere, by extension, it is asserted that such interaction and knowledge exchange underpins economic competitiveness and growth (Etzkowitz 1998, 2002; Imrie 2010, amongst many others).

Such efforts are not entirely new. Indeed, even a cursory glance at the early history and subsequent development of many of the 'red-brick' or Russell Group of universities in the United Kingdom uncover close links with the industrial or commercial cores of cities and regions. However, there is little doubt that the pressure for both institutions and individual researchers to become more 'outward facing' – more engaged with the 'real world' through closer co-operation with non-academic actors – has become compelling in recent years. In the pursuit of these aspirations, the co-production or collaborative production of knowledge with external partners has thus ascended to be a *fundamental* goal of universities. Many departments and research centres have been attracted to potentially lucrative relationships with commercial, governmental and voluntary sectors. Such collaborations are often heralded as being intensely policy relevant, theoretically helping redress some of the most critical challenges facing twenty-first century society. Illustrating this point the current Research Council UK over-arching research strategy has prioritised a number of key areas for research including, nanotechnology, climate change, as well as global insecurity and the threat from international terrorism.[3] At the same time, and underwriting these efforts, UK Research Councils now actively promote knowledge transfer and dissemination as central to research outputs:

> As the public bodies charged with investing tax payers money in science and research, the Research Councils take very seriously their responsibilities in making the outputs from this research publicly available – not just to other researchers, but also to potential users in business, Government and the public sector, and also to the public.[4]

Higher education institutions themselves frequently publicise details of such collaborative arrangements, with relationships advertised by universities and with partnerships and evidence of knowledge exchange and transfer highlighted on websites and promotional material.

Despite their support at various tiers of higher education establishments and Government, such initiatives, the aforementioned trajectories of entrepreneurial universities, and, more fundamentally, the forces that belie them, are not without critique. As mentioned earlier, entrepreneurial activities bring a series of restrictions that directly conflict with aspirations to permit more open, public access to data. For example, the results and findings of even *publicly* funded research of intense *public* interest are often published in subscription journals aimed at fellow academics

---

3   http://www.rcuk.ac.uk/research/default.htm, accessed 30 July 2009.

4   http://www.rcuk.ac.uk/research/outputs/default.htm, accessed 30 July 2009.

as opposed to professionals, practitioners and policy-makers. Under these circumstances, access to knowledge essentially becomes exclusive – available only to those who can afford the often expensive tariffs levied by publishers and copy-right owners, or those in the advantageous position of being affiliated to well-resourced research institutions. In some cases the obligations placed upon researchers are legally binding, particularly in circumstances where work has a commercial value, can be patented or perhaps when results are especially sensitive or potentially harmful to research subjects or sponsors. Simultaneously, however, researchers are frequently critiqued for treating 'the field' or 'the researched' as an infinite resource there to be harvested without any reciprocal arrangements and without any form of 'payback'. As one of our own research participants noted during a routine research interview: 'we are used to people coming in and asking us questions in relation to our work, but quite often we don't see the end results of that … which is sometimes a bit annoying!'

Developing a Collaborative Research Strategy

Overall, the *production* and *application* of knowledge has become 'inextricably intertwined', with new relationships emerging between institutions, industry and governmental agencies (Etzkowitz 1994: 384), with ever more emphasis placed upon building links between 'the University' and external entities. Co-produced collaborative research, in particular that drawing upon multi-disciplinary perspectives, potentially offers unique insights into the interface between theory, academia and practice. By extension, in a methodological sense, co-production can also often guarantee access to otherwise elusive research partners or subjects.

The current pressures for the co-production of knowledge arise from the convergence of a number of forces including the necessity to generate further income for institutions and to create research positions. Further there is a perceived need to unite efforts to address some of the most pressing challenges facing contemporary society, and to demonstrate knowledge transfer and exchange; or, as it is now called, to create 'impact'.

Critically, both the practical tensions and the wider conceptual debate surrounding the virtues or otherwise of collaborative academic research can be delineated into a rough dichotomy There is an argument that calls for academics to descend from the escapist 'Ivory Tower' and to engage with research with practical benefits and policy transferability. But there is a competing view that academic research should remain 'pure' or abstract – ideally above political and societal debate and direct application, and most certainly free from external influence.

These strategies, initiated from higher education institutions, funders, and from co-producers themselves, are illustrated by the expanding body of academic research on these very such activities, becoming something of a cottage industry for university business schools amongst other departments. Much of the, by now, vast range of academic literature pertaining to this field tend to focus on how knowledge production and transfer can be promoted and accelerated (see, for example, Agrawal 2001, O'Shea et al. 2005, Siegel et al. 2007), thus both further *implicitly* supporting co-operative and symbiotic research efforts.

However, in spite of the widely celebrated added value of co-produced research and knowledge, collaboration can bring too immense challenges both pertaining to the practical arrangements for conducting research and, in a more general sense, to the autonomous principles of academia. In short, whilst the activities of academics and of academia may have been re-orientated toward more entrepreneurial activity, serious concern exists regarding conflicts of interest between those involved in the production of knowledge, and also between the expectations and standards of co-producing partners (Etzkowitz et al. 1998).

In the next section, against the aforementioned backdrop of increasing pressure from universities to generate revenue and to connect to policy-makers and practitioners, we discuss how a spatial planning-related research project, jointly funded by three of the main UK research councils and supported by a governmental partner, as well as providing the opportunity to work in innovative ways and often to great effect, created a range of fundamental challenges for academics and university-based researchers.

Rather than concentrating on the by now well-charted and complex challenges that arise in attempts to foster knowledge transfer, exchange and uptake, the chapter discusses how obligations placed upon research teams by funders (who press for *tangible*, practical outputs) and from academia (to produce *critiques* on policy and practice), lead to a series of compromises in the research process, and ultimately in terms of research outputs. Drawing upon the reflections and observations of the authors, we analyse our encounters with these tensions. We reflect upon our own study (detailed in the next section) across a series of themes, including the conceptual basis and ethical direction of the research, issues arising from its methodological practicalities, and also tensions encountered when engaging with professional users such as town planners and architects. The chapter concludes by indicating how we adapted our own practice to negotiate these challenges; namely an attempt to become 'critical friends' to those that sponsor and consume our research outputs. Of course, these considerations are not unique for sensitive fields of inquiry, though they are undoubtedly accentuated by them. As such, we propose that many of the assertions made here are applicable across a range of research co-productions.

Research Background to the Resilient Design Project

The United Kingdom Government, like many others across the world, are currently identifying how the risk of terrorism, and the potentially devastating effects it may visit upon public spaces and those that use them, can be mitigated. It is acknowledged that such threats in the context of the UK are not unprecedented. However, more recently, the Government has reassessed the extent of the terrorist threat against critical national infrastructure[5] as well as 'everyday spaces' – namely 'crowded public places' (see, for example, Smith 2007) based upon an evolving terrorist *modus operandi* (HM Government, 2006). So, whilst specific targets such as embassies, military installations and key national infrastructure remain at high risk, a distinctive feature of current threats is that 'they often deliberately strike at ordinary people going about their lives' (HM Government 2006: para. 35).

Illustrating this development, and highlighting the diversity in the types of 'crowded' places that are increasingly identified at risk, the National Counter-terrorism Security Office (NaCTSO) has produced a suite of guides for various use classifications, including bars, and clubs, shopping centres, stadia and arenas, visitor attractions, cinemas and theatres, hotels, restaurants, commercial centres, and centres of education and health provision[6]. Such spaces must, a range of state actors including the Home Office and the Security Services claim, be protected, or at least designed and constructed in such a way that the most serious implications of a strike will be mitigated. In other words, crowded places must become 'resilient'.

Planners and other built environment professionals have a crucial role to play in the pursuit of this goal. As part of this effort, the Government is updating their principal crime prevention and the planning system guidance (often called Crime Prevention through Environmental Design) (ODPM and Home Office 2004) through the addition of a 'counter-terrorism appendix'. This will not be prescriptive or legally binding in any real sense, but it is intended along with a range of other issues and factors increasingly pertinent to contemporary society and for which built environment professionals – especially planners – are increasingly encouraged to help alleviate. Such planning praxis has been facilitated by the development of professional nation-wide courses for built environment professionals, which arguably entails persuading architects, designers, planners and others into the practical pursuit of the Government's counter-terrorism agenda[7]. There is, for instance, concern that such professionals (and by extension we as academics and researchers conducting work in this area) become complicit in political agendas, essentially becoming responsible for protecting crowded places and other vulnerable public spaces that people use as part of their everyday lives.

At the same time, and in support of this development, Counter-Terrorism Security Advisers (CTSAs) have been deployed (via police constabularies) to

---

5   Identified by the UK's Centre for the Protection of National Infrastructure to regard facilities, systems, sites and networks pertaining to nine essential services: communications; emergency services; energy; finance; food; government; health; transport; and water.

6   See http://www.nactso.gov.uk/crowdedplaces.php.

7   During the course of our research we were asked to advise the security services on the spatial planning implications of countering terrorism against crowded spaces. This advice helped guide the development of the national training schemes.

provide advice regarding current threat assessments and to help identify places that are deemed to be most at risk from attack. Ultimately, CTSAs aim to offer guidance to front line planning officers (often through the use of already existing mechanisms used by force architectural liaison/crime prevention officers) regarding how places may be designed, constructed, and managed in order to better withstand any potential attack.

The Resilient Design Project as Co-Production

Despite the government's increased emphasis on this issue, and the commensurate expansion of CTSAs and affiliated support systems, such initiatives pose a range of practical challenges for built environment professionals and for other stakeholders holding an interest in this agenda. In an attempt to address these difficulties, and to help the many varied actors that potentially hold a stake in, (or whose own activities will be affected by) this new agenda, various branches of the State's Security Service (such as the Centre for the Protection of National Infrastructure and the Home Office) and Policing (such as the Association of Chief Police Officers and NaCTSO) have increasingly sought to engage with academia in order to assist them in research and development and in the drafting and implementation of policy. It is to this issue that the authors now turn.

Research into issues and concerns pertaining to national security – particularly state initiated counter-terrorism strategies – has expanded greatly in recent years. Although much is still undertaken in 'secret' by an ever-expanding array of state institutions and security agencies, there are many opportunities for academic researchers from public higher education institutions to have an input. However, the aforementioned challenges of co-production are heightened when dealing with certain statutory institutions and agents, such as the security services or others who have responsibilities connected with public safety. Such actors are, for obvious reasons, averse to disclosure and public scrutiny, which itself creates a range of challenges for research methodologies. Moreover, there are long-standing and deep rooted concerns that any such engagement with such powerful actors ultimately risks merely contributing to their hegemonic control.

The engagement of non-state actors in security policy-making is by no means a new enterprise, and it is not without critique. To take just one illustrative example, in January 1961 the outgoing United States President, Dwight D. Eisenhower, used his final broadcast to the nation to introduce the concept of the 'Military Industrial Complex', using it to caution against the 'unwarranted influence' of the private sector in the militarisation of the nation. He continued to warn:

> We must never let the weight of this combination endanger our liberties or democratic processes. We should take nothing for granted. Only an alert and knowledgeable citizenry can compel the proper meshing of the huge industrial and military machinery of defense with our peaceful methods and goals, so that security and liberty may prosper together.

Over the last decade, catalysed by the attacks of 11 September 2001, from other terrorist attacks across the world, and through war in Iraq and Afghanistan, the idea that security-related corporations can reap benefits (primarily financial in nature, but also in terms of power) from the effects of hazards and conflict has gained prominence. The role of the private sector in homeland security and the effective 'marketisation of fear' are reinforced by such events (Coaffee 2003). As Mike Davis (2001) noted in reaction to the events of 11 September 2001, the military and security firms [are] rushing to exploit the nation's 'nervous breakdown'. Naomi Klein, in her recent book *The Shock Doctrine* (2008), has characterised such developments as composing part of a 'disaster capitalism complex'.

There are associated critiques when the impact of such trends, particularly the outsourcing of research, are applied to contemporary higher education institutions and research establishments. Universities are well known to have been at the vanguard of developing for the military, either directly for combat use (for example ballistic, surveillance and sensor technologies) or for other applications (such as the well documented sensory deprivation experiments which have been adapted for interrogation and/or torture). These very such developments were charted by Eisenhower in his aforementioned address when he highlighted how technological innovation, often conducted in research institutions at the behest of the Federal Government, underpinned the *Military Industrial Complex*. The 'free university' he noted, 'historically the fountainhead of free ideas and scientific discovery, has experienced a revolution in the conduct of research'. He added: 'Partly because of the huge costs involved, a government contract becomes virtually a substitute for intellectual curiosity'.

The methodological challenges of sensitive research in fields such as security have received academic attention over recent decades within the social sciences (see, for instance, Lee and Rezetti 1990; Lee 1993). These studies have shown that the sensitive nature of a research topic can lead to a departure from the 'textbook portrayal of ideal research practice' (Brewer 1993: 127). Those researching sensitive topics must be more attuned to their ethical responsibilities to research participants than they would be in the study of more innocuous topics. Lee (1993), for example, further proposed that 'sensitivity' can affect all aspects of a research project from the formulation of a problem through to the eventual dissemination of results.

Studies into national security are, of course, a particularly sensitive area of inquiry. Lee and Renzetti (1993: 5) as 'one that potentially poses for those involved a substantial threat, the emergence of which renders problematic for the researcher and/or the researched the collection, holding, and/or dissemination of data'. Moreover, sensitive and ethical issues can be particularly pertinent when studying elite networks and policy communities (see, for instance Bogner et al.). As Hertz and Imber (1995: viii) observed, 'few social researchers study elites because elites are by their very nature difficult to penetrate'. This is in part due to the powerful nature of elites, permitting them to resist potentially intrusive or exposing social analysis. As Raco (1999: 274) noted with specific relation to undertaking work on urban governance elites:

> Researching institutions of government has long been a difficult issue for social researchers ... research that sought to uncover elites and identify influences over decision-making processes came up against a series of barriers in terms of access and accessibility.

Yet, whilst much of the work undertaken on methods for sensitive research has focused on the ethical implications for participants or researchers, much less attention has been focused, until recently, on issues surrounding the processes of knowledge co-production between academia and communities of practice and policy. It is with this theme that this chapter is particularly interested.

The 'Resilient Design' project was funded by several bodies including three UK Research Councils,[8] and the Centre for the Protection of National Infrastructure (CPNI). The project was established to investigate the delicate and often contentious balance between the *effective* and *acceptable* design of counter-terrorism features for crowded places. Combining the efforts of academics and researchers at four United Kingdom universities, the project team worked in partnership with other public bodies including the Office of Rail Regulation and the National Counter Terrorism Security Office (NaCTSO). By extension, the study entailed consultation with a host of professional organisations such as the Royal Institute of British Architects, the Royal Town Planning Institute, the Commission for Architecture and the Built Environment, as well as range of local authority stakeholders from two case study cities in the north of England, including local planning authorities and local resilience forums. The research ultimately aimed to develop a supportive decision-making framework of use to a wide-range of stakeholders – particularly spatial planners. From a managerial perspective, a project Advisory Group, consisting of invited academics, interested civil servants, as well as with representatives from the sponsors, was established to provide strategic oversight and to act as a sounding board for team members. As it evolved, the research entailed collaboration and KTE that extended beyond the achievement of joint funding for the project and beyond the formal outputs agreed at the outset. It included contributions to the development and monitoring of training initiatives for built environment professionals and commentary upon policy and practice.

The remainder of the chapter turns attention to some of the main challenges and concerns we faced whilst conducting our own collaborative and co-produced research. We look at various critical moments over the course of the research process – from the original commissioning of the study, through the conduction of

---

8   The Engineering and Physical Sciences Research Council (EPSRC), the Economic and Social Research Council (ESRC), and the Arts and Humanities Research Council (AHRC).

empirical work, to issues regarding the dissemination of findings. Ultimately, we critique our own experience of a range of tensions associated with co-produced research.

Walking the 'Tightrope' of Collaboration

The project involved a number of knowledge co-productions; namely intra-academy relationships (inter-institutional and multi-disciplinary working with a Project including ten researchers from a range of expertise), between academia and policy arenas, and between academia and communities of practice. Beyond these individual strands of co-production, further issues arose regarding the *collective* management of co-productions; that is, the tensions and strains that at times one interaction placed upon another. Although elements of discussion touch upon aspects of all these relationships, in this chapter, we concentrate upon challenges arising from our relationship with governmental (policy-making) sponsors of the research.

Setting the Research Agenda: Implications for Researchers

As is implied throughout much of the literature that deals with knowledge transfer and collaboration in research efforts, perhaps the most dominant benefit accrued from co-produced research is the depth to which such studies are frequently, from the outset, presented with precise, topical (and often emerging) and identifiable outputs. Through such activities, researchers are presented opportunities to conduct research with policy relevance and which is of undoubted use to practitioners – in other words, to have 'impact'. In our case the funding for the research was awarded during a Research Councils UK 'Ideas Factory' or 'Sandpit'. Since the early 2000s such events have been periodically organised in response to major concerns facing society and policy-makers. These 'grand research challenges' emerge in a variety of ways, although this usually involves dialogue between politicians, policy-makers and selected experts, including academics. Ultimately, these events aim to generate research projects that address specific problems over several days by drawing together academics from a wide range of subject areas and policy communities in an attempt to ensure that research proposals are simultaneously inter-disciplinary and user relevant.

With specific reference to our own 'Ideas Factory' experience, in response to the 'crisis' posed by the threat of domestic and international terrorism, and by extension, the potential threat that such fear causes for national security, academia and researchers were asked to help frame problems, to provide a context for contemporary perils, and to build an evidence base for action will eventually provide a measure of redress.

It is critical to note the inherent anticipatory nature of such research processes and how this 'future gazing' increasingly underwrites policy innovation. The

UK Government's employment of 'foresighting' for an array of current issues (for example obesity, climate change, energy management, national security, etc.) where policy trajectories are predetermined by Government experts, with academics often used to confirm existing assumptions, is testimony to this.[9] The increasing worry is that polemics are not encouraged and academics may be reduced to functionaries where their labour is under the control of research councils with a range of beneficiaries (clients). Here the process of knowledgeability may be seen as not that dissimilar from the deskilling operations Braverman (1974) identifies in describing the degradation of work and management control.

From the perspective of research sponsors, engagement with academia is heralded as evidence of openness and transparency, supposedly lending rigour and critique to policy interventions. It is also quite clear that engagement with such research exposes researchers to multiple nodes of accountability. Such activity on the part of the state can itself be projected as being responsive: in our research, part of an attempt to reassert accountability and to combat the threats caused by terrorism – or at least to be seen to be taking action. It becomes, therefore, part of the strategy of the state to be seen to be in control – or to project the image of being able to afford protection to citizens.[10]

More generally, this type of research funding process (Ideas Factory) poses a number of contentious questions including who in a co-producing relationship is the knowledge producer, and who establishes an agenda for research? Without care, and by consequence of the potentially reactive fashion by which this and similar such research is undertaken, academics may fall into the risk of merely serving to post-rationalise existing and emerging practice or may be cornered into providing further legitimacy (or to provide a knowledge base or intellectual legitimacy) for contentious state intervention.

Taken to an extreme, co-produced research can, in effect, become viewed in some quarters as coalition building – or as being the conscription of researchers – to serve the ends of the state. Rather, therefore, than providing a critique of state policy, a conventional role for the academy, there is a risk that such research complements or underwrites predetermined practice. This also leads to broader concerns that the state could be subversively contracting-out its responsibilities by providing research 'opportunities' to willing researchers. For these and similar reasons, some individuals have been reticent to apply for certain types of security-related funding. For this reason, others have publicly boycotted similar security-related calls, seeing them merely as attempts to appropriate legitimacy for the state, becoming,

---

9   This is also increasingly true of many professions. For example, RIBA Building Future Studies aims to visualise and hypothesise the uncertainties of the future city exploring how architecture might resolve landscapes of conflict associated with terrorism, wars, climate change, flooding, population growth and other volatile threats.

10   For a further discussion of this, and a further insight into our research findings, see Coaffee et al. 2009.

as it were, 'conscientious objectors.' For instance in 2007 the Association of Social Anthropologists (ASA) advised its members to boycott a call for funding from the UK Research Councils and the Foreign and Commonwealth Office on *New Security Challenges and Radicalisation* as, in their view, it amounted to a recruitment of anthropologists for state spying and anti-terror activities.

There is, more broadly, an overarching risk that co-produced studies may be subjected to an almost inevitable 'pull' into external agendas, not least due to the sustained engagement entailed with co-producing partners. There is too a potential blurring of boundaries between the researcher and the researched, but this should not infer that it is impossible to resist excessive influence from external agencies. Although there may be a considerable degree of direction provided for a co-produced project, research agendas need not be excessively rigid. Therefore, a key role in working collaboratively – or as 'critical friends' – is the ability to negotiate clear independence.

Methodological Privileges and Limitations

Co-production, often through collaborative research efforts, can bring many privileges for the academic researcher. As detailed, it not only leads to a pre-determined set of objectives, often with a 'real-world' benefit or with practical and policy implications, but it also brings a treasured practical asset – access to information, to informants (some of whom are often considered to be elites in various fields of policy and practice) and case studies. The advantages of co-production and collaboration is particularly obvious when conducting research into national security policy, when the construction of trusting relationships can provide a much desired 'key' to unlock hitherto closed doors. Beyond *opening* doors, co-production may keep doors propped open through the development of long-standing commitments (or even friendships) or through more formal reciprocal agreements.

Direction and advice for teams embarking on perhaps daunting research projects is often welcomed, given that the selection of subjects can in itself be a time consuming and trying activity. Moreover, such access can frequently assume something of a reinforcing quality in that sponsors, and even some interviewees, can vouch for the reliability of the research team, leading to a snowballing of contacts and information. They can also help place information into broader contexts, limiting the risk that details may be misinterpreted by acting as a useful sounding board for emerging ideas and conclusions.

In our case, we were given access to members of the security services and their informal networks as a result of the project, as well as contact with an array of senior policy-makers across government and professional/user networks. As part of this, we were offered the opportunity to apply for 'security clearance' in order to access classified information. However, this was declined as on balance, we felt such a status could have seriously infringed our ability to disseminate our research findings (see latter discussion).

But such access also brings a range of obligations, some of which may place limitations on the autonomy of the research team. Researchers with considerable 'proximity' to subjects – who are at the same time research partners – can be prone to deeper restrictions. Other researchers, often using 'deep' ethnographic techniques (such as sociologists and anthropologists), have reflected upon how, within controlled places (such as prisons), researchers may be 'subject to unique controls, taboos and restrictions' (see Cohen and Taylor 1977: 67–86). With regard to our project, on more than one occasion critical meetings have been held when proceedings were 'off the record' or under the 'Chatham House' rule. This 'Rule' primarily concerns the dissemination of information after an event when there is the mutual understanding that participants *may* use the information mindful that 'nothing should be done to identify, either explicitly or implicitly, who said what'.[11] We were also compelled to undergo a University ethical approval process during which principal researchers were asked to justify the research approach, explain any ethical issues that may arise or sensitive methodologies that may have to be employed.

Beyond these restrictions, it is noted that there are cultural differences between academic and corporate (or, for that matter, other environments) that create barriers in traversing sectoral divides (Buchbinder and Newson 1985). In our case this often became evident when discussing issues of publication and the dissemination of research outputs. It is to this aspect of research practice that we now turn.

Limitations on Research Dissemination

Building upon the assertions made in the former section, we have identified the dissemination of research findings as a further 'moment' that is especially prone to interdictions on the part of co-producers. The current compulsion in UK academe to either 'publish or perish' means that all but a handful of academics *must* disseminate findings at conferences and through peer-reviewed journal articles. Dissemination activity is, in many respects, the linchpin of the profession. Publication is a critical method of asserting ideas and promoting research findings and it provides the nexus between academic knowledge and practice and policy. It would also be remiss to deny the fact that publication is the basis upon which individuals can progress their careers.

The academy has long cherished its role of knowledge production and many are increasingly disseminating knowledge to wider society, either to policy-makers, practitioners or to the community at large. The principles of

---

11   See http://www.chathamhouse.org.uk/about/chathamhouserule/.

dissemination are based upon openness and the ability to distribute findings with transparency.

The relationships and contacts, and to a certain extent credibility and insight induced through collaborative arrangements, may solicit further avenues for dissemination – in the professional press, or in an alternative discipline's journals. But the writing of research 'results' poses significant practical and conceptual challenges to *any* researcher; publication cannot take place with impunity. Moreover, whilst co-production can provide 'real world' feedback through interactions with policy and practice communities, sustained co-production can generate further restrictions upon dissemination. Given the pressures upon co-producing researchers to generate material with practical application, or in terms of the entrepreneurial university, to stimulate outputs with broader or even commercial appeal, dissemination strategies, and the information that is itself distributed, may face impediments.

Issues of timescales of output are commonly encountered in co-produced research. In our own experience policy-makers have requested 'results' immediately which conflicted with the due process of conventional academic outputs that must undergo peer review, but also that benefit from a period of critical reflection. For instance, it is acknowledged by some researchers – particularly those consumed by intense methods such as ethnography – that a 'task of estrangement' from fieldwork must be undertaken before findings are written, otherwise there is the risk that research becomes something of a 'plot rehearsal': 'recounting "what happened" without imposing a coherent thematic or analytic framework' (Hammersley and Atkinson 1983: 212–13). However, given the long-term and potentially intense interaction underlying co-produced research, such estrangement may not in fact be practical.

More generally, publication of any research can involve something of a loss of control – both for research subjects and for researchers. Those that have been studied surrender ownership and therefore also command of the 'afterlife' of their valued and usually guarded information. It has been further asserted, even if estrangement and distance in practical terms has seemingly been attained between the field and researchers, the dissemination of knowledge is dynamic; a form of disclosing something of ourselves – 'we dis-close and dis-cover our ideas and judgments and even ourselves as we write' (Badley 2009: 217). Publication potentially threatens the public or private self-image of those who have been studied (Wallis 1977). At the same time, on the part of the researcher, insights and opinions slip out of their hands and into public – or at least quasi-public – domains, and may be mobilised or criticised in justification or support of one or another contending party (ibid.).

In our case, information that may have perceived national security implications or risks, was reviewed in advance by partners in line with negotiated agreements with the sponsors whereby potentially sensitive material would be reviewed in advance by partners. This, although slowing up the publication process to a degree, did not in our case lead to any change in material put forward for publication: indeed further reflective comments from sponsors, it could be argued, as an extra peer review mechanism. We were, though, acutely aware that the need to adhere to such obligations can contradict the academic norms of openness and lead to fear on the part of researchers that trust could be betrayed (see, for example, Louis and Anderson 1998).

In our research these tensions became particularly pertinent when dealing with the media. Given the topicality of our research, which began at the same time as major Government policy developments regarding counter terrorism and national security, there was an expectation to actively engage with the media in order to demonstrate how our respective institutions were at the 'cutting edge' of contemporary research practice. Pressure was also exerted in order to demonstrate the effectiveness of the University's knowledge transfer and exchange polices.

When dealing with the media we employed a degree of *self-censorship*. During the course of our research we were given information 'off the record' and in confidence and we realised such agreements – however informal – had to be respected and treated with caution. In all instances we asked media representatives for the questions and topics of discussion to be raised in advance. Frequently, however, media interviews were declined as the planned questions sought examples from practice that we were not sanctioned to give, or could, we were warned, have potentially caused security breaches. We were further advised by our sponsors that even those examples of counter-terrorism interventions that were already in the public realm should not be mentioned as it would 'advertise' these sites to would-be attackers.

These challenges became particularly apparent when engaging in KTE with 'user communities' and policy-makers; in our case practising built environment professionals such as planners, architects, urban designers and developers, and their professional bodies such as the Royal Town Planning Institute, as well as a host of civil society groups concerned with issues of public access, disability and heritage. Such engagement can clearly present opportunities as well as dilemmas for researchers. For example interaction permitted us to generate research outputs which were grounded in everyday experience. But this also posed a serious validation question for our research: How do we enter a range of complicated socio-political relationships all of which have their own vested interests in what we produce? Moreover, with particularly sensitive subjects such as terrorism and national security, how could we be sure that representatives of organisations were reflecting the views of that organisation rather than their own personal views? Indeed, should we expect large associations to speak with 'one voice'? And if this is not the case, how do we reconcile this with the requirement to produce research outputs that are potentially diverse professions?

The vast range of views elicited when interviewing a large cohort of built environment professionals regarding the appropriateness of the State's agenda for 'designing in' counter-terrorism features to the built environment caused us to revisit our research objectives and attempt to convey disparate viewpoints in subsequent research outputs. In many cases, views differed significantly from those of our sponsors. Whilst the Centre for the Protection of National Infrastructure and the National Counter Terrorism Security Office encouraged architects and planners to consider counter-terrorism in the design of new and re-design of existing building and spaces, influential architects were engaging in a media campaign to 'discredit' this agenda (see Booth 2008).

For example, in light of a 2007 review of counter-terrorism policy, it was noted by the Prime Minister, that there would be an expanded role for planners, architects and designers to encourage them to 'design-in' protective security measures to new buildings, including safe areas, traffic control measures and the use of blast-resistant materials (Brown 2007). In a statement coinciding with the review, the Prime Minister's spokesperson also indicated that the announcements would prepare 'the public for the possibility that they may start to see some changes to the physical layout of buildings where people gather' (HM Government 2007). Nevertheless, leading architects accused the government of cultivating a 'culture of fear' and curtailing innovative design when in their view the threat of terrorism, compared to everyday risks was 'minuscule' (Taylor 2008: 17). Others still questioned whether '… planners, designers and developers [had] unwillingly become players in the anti-terrorism game' (Regan 2006: 22).

In summary, therefore, a further major tension becomes clear from co-produced research – between the long-standing principles of free and open dissemination of research articles within academic circles, and the challenging and sometimes contractually binding limits concerning the disclosure and dissemination of perhaps sensitive information. Such tensions are both practical and ethical in nature. As suggested, the publication of data and results leads to an increase in exposure, which in itself can be a double-edged sword. Sponsors are naturally reticent to distribute material that will breach their own relationships painstakingly built on trust, or that may help form useful material for those with malign intent. It is quite understandable, that sponsors attempt to limit the extent of information that is disseminated, sometimes through a degree of censorship on the part of sponsors or collaborative partners. Beyond this, as we have illustrated through our reflections here, there may occasionally be a degree of self-censorship or self-regulatory practice on the part of researchers – for fear of offending acquaintances made in the field, of jeopardising access to restricted aspects of practice or policy-makers, or in our case, of placing the safety and security (and increasingly the commercial and reputational attributes) of case studies in peril.

Critical Friendship as a Strategy for Research Co-Production

As discussed in some detail, until recently many research Universities have avoided transferring knowledge, but they have been catalysed into this activity by both a contraction of direct forms of state funding and greater awareness of opportunities for the practical application of academic knowledge (Etzkowitz et al. 1998). As Universities have become increasingly entrepreneurial and outward facing in their research aspirations, so the opportunities and temptations for the co-production of knowledge have become broader. In essence, there is the now widespread acceptance throughout academia that in order to avoid isolation, to counter reduced funding streams and to avoid the long-standing critique of universities as Ivory Towers, there *must* be engagement with practitioners and policy-makers.

Whilst KTE is increasingly upheld as an indicator of an effective academy, 'transfer' and 'exchange' is problematic to identify and quantify. Co-production of research through collaborative research strategies can help address this. Sustainable relations may be formed that can then be used to demonstrate interchange between academia and policy. The practical and policy value of research can be highlighted and used for the support for other work. For this reason, and the more practical reasons outlined thus far, co-production is likely to become even more common in the future. The town planning discipline is not immune from such pressures. However, as we have outlined, such co-production has diminished the traditional standing of independent academic endeavour and constrained the capacity of academic staff to pursue what might be deemed to be 'necessary' research.

We have provided an overview of several of the most pressing challenges that emerge in projects involving a significant degree of collaboration or that aspire to co-produce knowledge. We have detailed how, through obligations placed upon research teams by funders who press for tangible, practical outputs, and from academia, to produce critical commentary on policy and practice, research may be compromised. Underwriting concerns regarding the current state of academic integrity, there is debate regarding the appropriateness of such research with accusations that those involved in this type of study may become co-opted; that their outputs can be appropriated to serve the ends of the state.

We have little doubt, and can say from our own experience, that co-production presents many opportunities. Yet despite its increasing allure, it is, along with aspects of KTE, viewed by some academics with scepticism – even cynicism. Although this stretches beyond the confines of our particular project, and may be applicable to any of the plethora of research sponsors engaged with the contemporary university, managing research concerned with 'sensitive' topics inevitably involves negotiating relationships with state sponsors, raising notable questions regarding the independence of the academy. There is an irony, for instance, that co-production, whilst bringing access to a huge amount of material that would not otherwise be available, subjects researchers to a range of restrictions that would not normally be encountered. By consequence, co-production and the insight it generates may be subject to imposed – or even self-imposed – constraints. More broadly, there is the implication that any form of external funding will bring undue influence to external collaborators that do not have academic values as their primary concern.

Although the term co-production implies a degree of equality regarding the development of an overall research strategy, in practice this is a negotiated, and therefore fluid process involving research teams, sponsors and any advisory group that might be established. As has been stated, knowledge production is not static but dynamic (see Gibbons et al. 1994). Therefore, any such study is frequently underwritten by a range of concerns and compromises that need to be carefully balanced. Whilst undertaking co-produced research we should be aware of the comments of the academic planner, Bent Flyvbjerg, who warns us that the process of producing knowledge and the fate of projects in terms of desirable outcomes can be strongly influenced by the mechanics of power and rationality: '… power often ignores or designs knowledge at its convenience' (2001: 143). At the same time, all research data, we are reminded, is not collected but is generated (see May, 2002) through complicated researcher/subject interactions. Clearly, partners – or more appropriately, co-producers – often approach a project with certain motives, and may pursue pre-determined agendas. Indeed, it is unlikely to be in the best interests of any commissioner to fund or otherwise support research that *automatically* assumes an antagonistic stance to those of the organisation's core vision. And, as we have illustrated throughout this chapter, there is the threat that researchers may become 'guilty by association' by being bound within other policies authored by the state. In short, there are fears that some co-producers may become co-conspirators in the pursuit of certain agendas. These trends can, via the seemingly benign processes of co-operation and collaboration, risk researchers becoming encompassed by regimes of co-option. As a profession, academia is quite rightly pre-disposed to critique rather than co-operate, particularly with those traditionally viewed as power-holders. Its fiercely and rightfully defended independence may be threatened if arrangements are not entered with a degree of caution.

With these challenges and tensions in mind, as co-production becomes ever more sought after in the university sector we need to negotiate challenging relationships in order to both gain and retain access to research events and subjects and to meet the (often contractual) requirements of funders and partners. The coping strategy that we adopted was something as a promoter of mutual learning; in helping develop a better understanding among stakeholders of the multiple viewpoints surrounding a particular issue. This model of the 'critical friend', drawn from public policy literature (Rallis and Rossman 2000), blurs the borders between the act of research and those being researched. Here, the traditional power relationship between researcher and the researched made more equitable, with each recognising the contribution the other can make to the research process (see, for example, Coaffee and Diamond 2008). The 'critical friend' draws attention to the good practices that are in operation and any lessons that could be learned through honest critique.

In policy-related research, university researchers are often employed as evaluators and retain a distance from the sponsors. We would argue that developing 'critical friendship' is a more engaged role than that of the evaluator. In essence, the researcher is not an external judge but tries to act with an independent voice, holding a mirror to those involved in subjects, and helping them reflect upon their own practice. The critical friend – must also be a storyteller and present opinions for scrutiny. As Coaffee and Diamond (2008: 95) note:

> It is not only important to have the skills necessary to represent competing narratives, but also to identify themes and questions which challenge particular narratives.

Ideally, the negotiation of critical friend status should be held at the outset of research to help resolve (as far as possible) issues before the study gets underway, and to outline the expectation of co-producers at the earliest opportunity.

Our recent experience of working with and co-producing knowledge with policy-makers has been rewarding, yet immensely challenging. For all partners it has been a steep learning curve, involving fundamental challenges to the cultures of universities, users, and policy communities. Each co-producer has a preferred or traditional way of working with their associated timescales, the outputs that are required, and procedures that must be implemented to deal with sensitive information. As co-produced research becomes more the norm than the exception, these cultural impediments will lessen. But equally, the ethical challenges, particularly those regarding the overall independence of research, will become more pressing.

Chapter 10

Collaborative Postgraduate Research in a Contract Research Culture

Loretta Lees and David Demeritt

Introduction

There is a long-standing tension running through UK science policy between the desire to promote 'world-class' science and the desire to harness that research to serve the immediate interests of economic growth and policy formation. Ministers frequently deny any contradictions between these two goals of science policy with a sort of 'both/and' rhetoric rivalling that of even the most ardent post-structural feminists, but the tension remains nonetheless. For instance even as the then Prime Minister (Blair 2002) was praising the RAE for having 'fostered excellence and driven up the quality of research in universities', reviews conducted for HM Treasury (Lambert, 2003) and for HEFCE (Roberts 2003) were complaining that the academically-dominated RAE tended not to recognise, and even actively to discourage, what Lord Roberts (para. 72) called 'enterprise activity'.

One way UK policy-makers have sought to square this circle is through policies designed to encourage greater collaboration between universities and various 'end users' of research. It was one of the major recommendations of the Major Government's White Paper on science and technology policy, *Realising Our Potential* (HMSO 1993: 4), that:

> ... steps should be taken which, on the basis of other countries' experience, will help harness strength in science and engineering to the creation of wealth in the United Kingdom by bringing it [the publicly funded university science base] into closer and more systematic contact with those responsible for industrial and commercial decisions.

Recent Labour governments have taken up that challenge with even greater enthusiasm. The Treasury's 2003 *Lambert Review of Business-University Collaboration* is simply one in a long line of recent Government reports promoting collaboration as a means of increasing the relevance for, dissemination to, and up-take by so-called 'end users' of university research. As implied by the title of the UK Government's strategy for science, engineering and technology, *Investing in Innovation* (HM Treasury 2002), the uses and users of university research are largely imagined as private sector ones. Indeed, Lambert was concerned solely with research collaboration with business, while among the major recommendations of Sir Gareth Roberts' (2002) report for the Treasury, *SET for Success: The Supply of People with Science, Technology, Engineering and Mathematics Skills*, was that the government do more both to 'encourage research collaboration between businesses and HEIs [higher education institutions]' (recommendation 6.6) and ensure that 'the research be business-led and focused on commercially-oriented R&D' (recommendation 6.7).

To that end, the government has inaugurated a series of so-called 'third stream' funding initiatives that complement traditional streams of university funding for teaching and for research by focusing in particular on knowledge transfer. For instance, in 2005–2006, the Higher Education Innovation Fund (HEIF) spent £90 million to 'provide pump-priming resources for technology transfer, entrepreneurship training, corporate spin-outs and seed venture funding' (HM Treasury 2002: para. 0.15), while Lord Sainsbury's (2007) *Review of Government's Science and Innovation Policies* called for additional funding for such third stream activities and for Research Councils, the primary funders of basic research, to be given firm targets for knowledge transfer activity and for collaboration with business through Knowledge Transfer Partnerships.

Economic recession, far from diminishing these ambitions for science, has redoubled government determination to 'developing [science] as a key element of our path to recovery'. In his Romane lecture at Oxford University, propitiously entitled 'Science and our economic future', Prime Minister Gordon Brown (2009) called for 'a new partnership between science and industry – supported by record Government investment in science' (cf. Demeritt 2010).

Such reforms are part of a wider – and widely debated – transformation of the political and cultural economy of university research. With public funding for universities increasingly scarce, critics fear that short-term commercial pressures, either to generate research spin-outs or to recruit student-customers to new teaching factories, may compromise the spirit of academic freedom or even lead to the death of the university as a place of critical inquiry (Bok 2003; Readings 1996). Others complain that the increasingly strategic orientation of government research funding squeezes out curiosity driven scholarship (e.g. British Academy 2004). Acknowledging concerns about the methods, but not the aims of these reforms, Prime Minister Brown (2009) explained there are:

> ... questions about how we can best focus on areas with significant growth opportunities in the coming decades. The debate about how science can help us out of the downturn is a crucial one. And we should be looking constantly at how to develop clear competitive advantages which will directly help the future British economy. This does not mean compromising on fundamental research. But it will ... mean working with scientists and those funding research to both identify potential priorities and then ensure that the research base works as much as possible to support them.

In this chapter we consider this wider tension between research quality and relevance by focusing on the particular case of the Research Councils' Co-operative Awards in Science and Engineering (CASE) studentship programme (cf. Demeritt and Lees 2005). Created in response to the 1993 *Realising Our Potential*, White Paper, CASE involves universities collaborating with non-academic bodies in the sponsorship, supervision, and management of a PhD student research project. Building on its success, the ESRC has since embarked on similarly structured programmes for postgraduate research sponsored by various government departments (i.e. ODPM, Department of Transport, DEFRA, DfES) and devolved administrations (i.e. The Welsh Assembly, Scottish Executive). Drawing on our own personal experiences supervising four ESRC-CASE and two ESRC-ODPM studentships (see Table 10.1) as well as informal discussions with others involved in similar projects, we reflect here on the process of conducting collaborative research through the CASE and related programmes and the implications of those social contexts for the academic labour process and for what research gets done and how.

Table 10.1 List of ESRC-CASE and ESRC-ODPM projects

1. CASE partner The Peabody Trust, project title: Young People, Place and Urban Regeneration: The Case of the King's Cross Ten Estates

2. CASE partner The Peabody Trust, project title: Putting Urban Sustainability into Practice: An Ethnographic Study of Residents' Experiences of the Beddington Zero Energy Development (BedZED) in Greater London

3. CASE partner Arup Transport Planning, project title: The 'Walkable City': The Dimensions of Walking and Overlapping Walks of Life

4. CASE partner Johnson & Johnson, project title: Ethics, Ethical Review, and the Practice of Medical Research

5. ESRC-ODPM studentship, project title: High Rise Living in London: Towards an Urban Renaissance?

6. ESRC-ODPM studentship, project title: Planning at the Coalface: Local Authority Planners, Planning Reform, and the New Public Management

Initiating Collaborative Projects

For the purposes of our present discussion, the most important difference between ESRC-CASE and the various government-department sponsored ESRC studentship programmes modelled after it has to do with the process of initiating a research project. In the case of government-department sponsored studentship programmes, the ESRC and the sponsoring department have already worked out the financial and other terms of reference for the studentship. In this respect the relationship is much more like contract research than truly collaborative research in which both parties define the research agenda together. With the funding allocated and the broad terms of reference already defined, all that is left for the collaborating academic to do is to submit an application when the calls for tender are issued. In practice, the terms of reference for government-department funded studentship programmes with the ESRC have been quite broad, leaving considerable scope for the academic partner to define a project that contributes not just to the sponsor but also advances academic knowledge. Also, unlike normal contract research, decisions about which bids will be funded are made by an academic peer review panel taking advice from the sponsoring government department.

By contrast, with ESRC-CASE the academic must be entrepreneurial and take the lead in initiating the collaborative project, though this also means that there is considerably more scope for the academic partner to define the project. This can mean a foot in the door for critical research when that door is being shut elsewhere. Since ESRC-CASE awards are made to HEI-based academics, ESRC (2004) considers it 'the responsibility of CASE recognised academic outlets to take the lead in seeking non-academic partners to take forward discussions on likely projects to submit'. In practice, this also means that the academic is responsible not just for lining up collaborators, but also for writing the actual proposal and recruiting a student to complete it. For academics with existing relationships with non-academic organisations, the CASE programme provides an opportunity to deepen those collaborative relationships. The ESRC also hopes that the CASE programme will encourage academics to develop new collaborative links with non-academic partners, though this is rather more difficult. This was the advice from ESRC (2007a) regarding the 2007 ESRC-CASE studentship competition:

> There is a tendency for non-academic organisations to collaborate with universities and individuals they know, so university departments with previous collaborative experience with an organization are well placed to develop new areas of collaboration. Where there is no previous collaboration between the partners it will be important to find out what research issues are important to potential partners, and to use this knowledge to frame project proposals. Irrespective of whether there has been previous collaboration or not, a non-academic organization may still need to be "tempted" to participate in a collaborative project. Some of the methods employed include:
>
> - identifying current "hot" topics and then contacting external organizations which you think may be interested;
> - external organizations working with academics to develop projects of common interest;
> - students (both current students in a department and those totally new to a department) developing a project which is then submitted to a relevant external organization for support;

- a follow-on to student project work in a company (both at undergraduate and Masters level) where a good relationship has developed between the student, the company and the academic department.

The vision here is of an 'entrepreneurial academic' actively promoting knowledge transfer to somewhat reluctant non-academic customers. In the good practice guide provided by the ESRC (Bell and Read 1998: para. 3.8), academics are enjoined to '"sell" the benefits of collaboration to non-academic organisations', while here, in its 2007 guidance, the ESRC (2007a) warns that potential partners need to be 'tempted' to participate in a collaborative project. Of course, unlike some Research Councils, ESRC does not restrict CASE collaborators to the private sector whose sense of what Bell and Read (1998: para. 3.5) term the 'pay-offs' of research collaboration is more likely to be short-term, instrumental, and narrowly economic in nature. Indeed recognising that the public and voluntary sector are more likely to be interested in collaborating on ESRC-CASE studentships (see Demeritt and Lees 2005, who show that the public/voluntary sector is by far the dominant collaborator on ESRC CASE), ESRC (2007a) is quite explicit about the benefits of collaboration for public- and voluntary-sector organisations:

- The opportunity to access key expertise that may not exist within the company or which may not be cost effective to develop in-house.
- An opportunity to test the value of collaborative research for a relatively modest outlay.
- The ability to fund valuable but not necessarily the highest priority research, for which an economic case for doing the work in house would be difficult.
- Providing future researchers/potential employees with 'real life' experience of situations outside academia whereby academics have a better understanding of the public/voluntary sector and employees have improved research skills.
- Developing the skills and careers of staff (www.esrcsocietytoday.ac.uk/ ESRCInfoCentre/opportunities/postgraduate/pgtraining).

Nevertheless, the reliance of the ESRC on a rhetoric of 'selling' collaboration betrays a commercial sensibility that is thoroughly in keeping with the overarching emphasis of government policy on 'strengthening UK competitiveness and wealth creation through partnerships between academia and business' (ESRC 2003: 19). But this narrowly instrumental way of thinking about the motivations to engage in collaborative research goes beyond mere rhetoric. To encourage academics to engage in such activity, the ESRC (2004) reminds them that 'the success rate in the CASE competition ... has been significantly higher than in the standard research studentship competition'. The result of this has been many more submissions (in the 2008 competition there were 193 applications and 69 awards, in 2009 there were 246 applications considered and only 47 awards) and thus more intense competition and more annoyance from organisations who have invested time in the setting up of these collaborations but not received funding. Furthermore, ESRC also requires the collaborating partner not only to contribute to the student's stipend but also to pay the collaborating department an equal sum of money to help for the additional staff and other costs, relative to a normal ESRC studentship, of overseeing collaborative studentships.

While such financial incentives are certainly welcome to cash strapped social scientists, there are also dangers in gearing the CASE programme too closely to them. Given the effort involved, the risk that at the end of it all the ESRC will refuse to fund a CASE proposal, and the relatively meagre financial compensation to the academic supervisor, which often disappears into general HEI or departmental coffers without tangibly benefiting the actual award holder, the temptation is for the kind of 'entrepreneurial academic' idealised by Research Councils in their discussion of knowledge transfer, either to 'sell' the CASE research on a personally remunerating consultancy basis or as a straight research contract for which it is possible to charge much higher levels of overhead.

We are aware of several collaborative studentship projects at King's where social scientists have preferred to go the contract research route rather than CASE both because there is more money in it for the HEI and because it circumvents ESRC restrictions – and scrutiny – about the nature of the project, the training required, and the timeframe for initiating and completing it. In another instance a potential CASE collaborator decided that it was less time consuming and not much less money simply to pay the fees of an employee of theirs who wanted to do a PhD with us.

Particularly for large private sector organisations with established Research and Development departments, authorizing the expenditure of the relatively small sums involved in CASE research projects involves the same process as much larger sums. Why ask for £4,000 a year over three years, when it is just as much trouble to ask for £40,000 or £400,000? Indeed, sometimes requests for larger sums of research money are regarded as more credible, as evidence that the researcher is serious and professional, than those for the much smaller sums involved in CASE projects.

This was certainly the reaction from Arup when it was first approached about participating in a CASE project. At the initial meeting with that firm, undertaken in their newly designed office building over lattes in one of their new open plan coffee/eating areas, the initial comment was 'this seems like a lot of hassle for a very small amount of money – what's in it for us?' But then even that small amount of money became a discussion piece: 'You tell me why I should give *you* this money? We get graduate students from the Harvard Design School wanting to do projects with us, so why should we give it to you?'

Initiating a CASE project requires considerable time and effort from the academic, as well as the non-academic partner. But despite the warnings from Lambert (2003: para. 1.12) that the low level of demand for university research from outside organisations is the primary obstacle to fostering more widespread research collaboration, the ESRC does not seem to have given much thought to how to encourage more interest from business. Apart from the brief guidance outlined above given to academics about how *they* might sell CASE collaboration to potential collaborators, the dirty and time consuming work of promoting and setting up research collaboration is left to academics with relatively little support from the Research Councils.

It is not uncommon, in our experience working with a number of different organisations, for an initial letter of approach from an academic, even one carefully targeted at an appropriate contact within an organisation, to pass across a number of different desks before a meeting ever materialises. Successful proposals often have a 'high level champion' within the non-academic organisation who sees its potential and helps steer it through the organisation. Although the Peabody Trust employs a number of housing and policy analysts who recognise the value of research, research is not a core activity for the Trust. Approaches to engage in CASE collaborations are often low on the agenda for organisations and their employees busy with other activities.

Furthermore, high profile organisations like the Peabody Trust, Arup and Johnson & Johnson are regularly approached about all sorts of collaborative projects. The proposals that stand out are those that reflect an understanding of the needs and nature of the particular organisation but this in of itself may not be enough. In the case of Arup, although the proposal for collaborative research had reached the relevant director's desk and was steered to the research interests of the company, it was only when a relative of the academic who had written the letter spoke in person to the director to ask if he had received the proposal that a meeting was organised. Personal contacts are extremely useful. Demeritt was able to secure the collaboration of Johnson & Johnson thanks to the intervention of another colleague who had sat on an editorial board with the company's vice-president for European Affairs and who brokered the approach to Johnson & Johnson.

An initial face-to-face meeting between the academic and representative of the non-academic partner is just the beginning of what can sometimes be quite protracted negotiations over the nature of the research to be undertaken and the respective roles of the individuals involved. The two CASE projects that the authors were involved in with the Peabody Trust were winnowed out of a number of potential ideas initially proposed by Loretta Lees in a letter of approach to Dickon Robinson (the then Director of Development at the Peabody Trust). While some were not of interest to Peabody, others, for instance about the demand for key worker housing in London, were so pressing that the Trust could not afford to wait around for several years for a PhD project to generate some insights. Similarly the vice-president at Johnson & Johnson asked King's to pitch a number of potential project ideas. Eventually both the Peabody Trust and Johnson & Johnson agreed on two ideas for ESRC proposals each, only three of which were eventually funded.

Given the potential mismatches between the temporal imperatives and decision-making cycle of non-academic organisations and the annual deadline for

ESRC-CASE proposals, CASE projects tend to address questions of a long term and strategic nature rather than of day-to-day operational significance. In the case of the Peabody Trust, its own research programme is tied to its business plan and responds to external drivers, such as changes in policy or legislation. Accordingly, CASE collaboration provided an opportunity to address some questions at greater length and depth than would ordinarily have been possible for the Trust's own in-house research staff whom it would be difficult to dedicate to a research project that would not show results for several years.

Despite the necessarily somewhat more long term and blue-skies nature of CASE studentship research projects relative to contract and consultancy research, a common sticking point in negotiations is the balance between addressing the often very specific research needs of particular organisations and answering a question of more general import. CASE projects involve negotiating two distinct, if often related, tensions: between basic and applied research and between empirically specificity and theoretical generalisation. While questions of IPR may also be involved in such negotiations, in our experience 'ownership', in the narrow sense of property rights over the usage and commercial licensing of research results, is not, at least in the social sciences, the issue so much as questions of confidentiality and data protection, as well as the more general sense of control over the nature and conduct of the research project. In this context it is important to hammer out a mutual understanding, both of the organisation's potential demands for commercial confidentiality and of the academic expectations about publication. Such matters are often embodied in a formal letter of understanding stipulating financial terms of payment as well as mutual responsibilities and the like, which the ESRC requires as an annex to any CASE application.

Recruiting Research Students

Once an ESRC studentship award has been made, the next task is to select a suitable student for the project. Whereas it is the tradition in the natural and physical sciences for PhD students to complete research projects entirely designed for them by their supervisors, in the social sciences students often want and expect to design projects for themselves. Accordingly it can sometimes be difficult to recruit a student to an ESRC CASE or ODPM project, particularly a very specialised one. The much stricter requirement introduced in 2004 about the prior completion of an ESRC recognised research training master's degree has only made matters worse. Partly in recognition of these difficulties as well as of the additional challenges of having to satisfy both the academic demands of a PhD studentship and the requirements of the non-academic partner, CASE students are paid an additional contribution (in 2009 a minimum of £2,000) by the collaborating organisation above and beyond the standard ESRC studentship stipend, while ODPM students received the highest remuneration of any social science studentship.

Nevertheless there are still recruitment difficulties. Despite advertising nationally for the Johnson & Johnson project, only four (relatively poor) applicants applied and the project had to be deferred for a year until a suitably qualified candidate could be found. The ESRC acknowledges that 'institutions find this [recruitment] more difficult with research projects and that we do have unfilled [CASE] places each year', though it does not collect systematic data to monitor the scale of the problem (personal communication, Christine Deane, ESRC, 22 March 2004).

Another potential hurdle can be the different approaches to candidate selection taken by the academic and non-academic partners. Our experience in this regard has been quite diverse. In the case of the government-department sponsored studentships, recruitment is usually left to the University, which is responsible for finding and nominating a student for the award, in much the same way as a quota studentship. In this respect, the relationship is more like contract than collaborative research. The government department provides the funds and sets the terms and conditions for the project, but then leaves it up to the university to do the recruitment. With the CASE studentship programme, the structure allows for more of a collaborative, rather than contractual agent-principal type relationship, though not all partners are keen to involve themselves as full partners. Whereas we have found some non-academic collaborators happy to leave recruitment almost entirely to the university, others have wanted to be much more centrally involved. In the interviewing for the Arup CASE studentship the academic was looking for someone with a good geography background and with good quantitative and qualitative skills, whilst the collaborative partner from Arup was looking for someone with high computational and quantitative skills only. The final decision on the successful candidate as such was the result of quite intense negotiation.

Conducting CASE Research Collaboratively

Having recruited a student, further negotiations are often required to tailor the initial CASE proposal, written for the ESRC by the academic supervisor in collaboration with the non-academic partner, to the needs and interests of the particular student. The ESRC recommends that at this stage a new formal contract between the student, supervisor, and non-academic partner should be drawn up so as to prevent misunderstanding (Bell and Read 1998: para. 7.2). While good communication of mutual expectations is clearly required, in our experience such a degree of formality risks setting an evolving research project in stone at too early a stage. Furthermore, anything smacking of a formal contractual agreement between an HEI and another organisation also invites the intervention and oversight of organisational lawyers and HEI technology transfer departments. Not only can their involvement greatly multiply (and thus complicate) the number of parties to any agreement, it can also transform a relationship based on trust and mutual understanding into an inappropriate set of contractual requirements that must be fulfilled regardless of how the student's research ultimately develops. It is better, in our view, to ensure that procedures are in place to keep all parties abreast and involved in decisions about the conduct and broad research aims, rather than seeking to stipulate in formal contractual terms research methods and outcomes in any fine detail.

Flexibility is important because, as with all research, there are inevitably changes to a CASE project as it unfolds from proposal to finished PhD. Whereas the Johnson & Johnson project began as a study of how private sector scientists were responding to new European requirements for ethical review of their biomedical research, the project evolved quite substantially as the student has shaped it to shape her own interests in the ethics and ethos of scientific commercialism. Fortunately, the sponsor at Johnson & Johnson always saw the project as a wider contribution to understanding the ethical challenges facing the industry as whole rather than a narrow study designed to advance the particular interests of the firm. Thus there was room for the project to shift as the student's interests developed. But that is not always the case.

A similar process of evolution took place with the Peabody Trust CASE project on the King's Cross Ten Estates in London. The proposal had originally been geared around the question of whether and how revamping the physical fabric of the Ten Estates (ten ex-local authority estates that had been taken over by the Peabody Trust) abated anti-social behaviour by youth. That question reflected the interest of the academic supervisor in questions of public space and public order while offering the Peabody Trust a way of evaluating some specific policy interventions. However, as the research student's involvement in the project deepened, she transformed it into a more general study of the geographies of young people and fear on the estates. Though of less immediate use to the Peabody Trust, in terms of evaluating their redevelopment strategy for the Ten Estates, the Trust were happy to go along with this changing shift in direction because it still provided their estate management teams with some more general insights into the understandings and experiences of youth, who are often ignored in formal consultations about estate redevelopment policy and yet crucial to the success of those same policies.

By contrast, the Peabody Trust had much more specific expectations for and, consequently, a much greater level of active involvement in, the other CASE project on residents' experiences of the Peabody Trust's Beddington Zero Energy Development (BedZED) in Sutton. This high profile project has attracted a lot of media attention for its innovative and environmentally-friendly design features, and more recently, for cost over-runs and for charges that the Peabody Trust's involvement in a development in which roughly half of the units were for sale at full market value was a distraction from its core social housing mission (e.g. Beveridge 2004). Given how much BedZED involved experimental or previously untested design features, the Trust knew that it would need an independent evaluation of what worked and what didn't, both to satisfy external curiosity and to provide a basis for deciding which features might be mainstreamed to other Peabody estates and building projects. Within the context of those overarching goals, there was still room for the research student to exercise considerable discretion in deciding to focus, in particular, on the mobility of BedZED residents and the success of the car club and other facilities for sustainable transport provided as part of the development.

While completing any PhD involves the student steadily growing into and exercising more independent control over the direction of his or her research project, the process is somewhat more complicated in a CASE project because of the larger number of parties involved. Having written the initial proposal, the supervisor can find it difficult to let go and to allow the student the space to develop the project as s/he sees fit. Likewise the non-academic collaborator also has expectations about the project that need to be taken into consideration, though given the fact that their financial contribution to the project is small relative to the public contributions from the ESRC for tuition fees and stipend and the Funding Council for supervisory and teaching fees paid direct to HEIs for each PhD student, the collaborator's demands should never be absolute. There can also be problems if there is a fall out between the student (and/or academic supervisor) and the organisation; we know of two cases of this elsewhere where this has caused both access and IPR problems.

To ensure that the evolving project fulfils the needs of the non-academic collaborator and in turn receives the support required to those ends, it is important for the student and the academic supervisor to have a clear point of contact within the non-academic collaborating organisation. Ideally this person will know the organisation well and can pull in favours or otherwise persuade others that their involvement in the project is beneficial. At the Peabody Trust, Dickon Robinson, the then Director of Development at the Trust, helped set the academic objectives for both projects, while Elanor Warwick the then Research Manager played a key role in facilitating access to facilities, resources, and personnel required for the research. Indeed, one unexpected benefit of both CASE projects for the Trust was that the cross-departmental nature helped improve communication and working relationships between parts of the organisation that would otherwise have had much less fruitful contact. The BedZED research, in particular, would have been all but impossible without the Research Manager Elanor Warwick's help lining up contacts within the Trust and its collaborators in the BedZED project, as well as in coordinating the residents' surveys required for the CASE project with the Trust's regular procedures for securing feedback from residents. Particularly for projects that involve studying the non-academic organisation itself, the prospect of facilitated access and support is one of the greatest advantages of collaborative research. The experience at the Peabody Trust also suggests that the collaborating supervisors within the organisation need to recognise that they may have to do some work to build such relationships within their own organisations.

The relationship with ODPM was much more distant despite the fact that there were administrative layers in place. Professor Ade Kearns oversaw the ESRC ODPM studentship programme, organising an introductory meeting at ODPM for all studentship holders and their supervisors at the beginning of each academic year, organising themed seminars for ODPM students to meet up with other ODPM students and to present their research, and liaising with students in the production of reports for, and published by, ODPM. Each student was also allocated a specific ODPM co-supervisor, whom they were supposed to meet with on a fairly regular basis. But in reality, especially if that person was quite senior in ODPM, the meetings were few and far between. Quite understandably meetings with ministers took precedence for some of these ODPM co-supervisors.

The roles and power relations involved in a collaborative studentship project study can be complex. In practice, the CASE research student can often serve as the bridge between academic supervisors based at the HEI and collaborators at the non-academic organisation (see Macmillan and Scott 2003). Such a situation has the potential to create misunderstandings unless there is also good mutual understanding between the two (or more) academic and non-academic supervisors. There are also the relationships between the researchers and their research subjects. These are much more complex and potentially contested in collaborative research into the internal operation of the collaborator's own organisation (e.g. the CASE project on Peabody's Ten Estates) than those involved when collaborating in the study of third parties, in which both the academic and the non-academic collaborating organisation stand in the same position as outsiders relative to their research subjects. In the King's Cross Ten Estates project, the research student found that Peabody-employed youth workers were sometimes reluctant to speak to her because they were afraid that she would report back to Peabody's head office, while for some residents it was precisely the opportunity to 'send a message' back that made opening up to her in interviews attractive. Likewise in the study of BedZED, the research student's role as a researcher working with but independent from the Peabody Trust had to be continually negotiated in the context of a complex and increasingly fraught set of relationships among the architects, developers, various Peabody representatives and departments, and residents. At times access to informants was facilitated by stressing her affiliation with the Peabody Trust, while at others emphasising her independence made residents, in particular, more willing to disclose their concerns.

Such negotiations are not unique to CASE projects, but issues of positionality, as well as ethical considerations about informed consent and the confidentiality of informants' disclosures, are particularly important for CASE researchers working with but independent from their non-academic collaborators. A key issue for Elanor Warwick and Dickon Robinson on behalf of the Peabody Trust in both projects was the responsibility for data protection, and the ongoing responsibility of confidentiality for residents. By contrast, the research students both found that while their ethical obligations *vis-à-vis* residents were relatively clear-cut the more sensitive confidentiality issues arose when their informants were Peabody employees or contractors. On the one hand, such informants often had important insights that would be of real interest and value to Elanor Warwick and Dickon Robinson on behalf of the Peabody Trust, but on the other, the research students had to be careful in disclosing what they had learned from informants within the Trust to protect their informants' identities. As Harwood and Moon (2003) describe, collaborative researchers sometimes find themselves with conflicting loyalties to their informants and their research collaborators. In turn there are also questions about academic responsibilities to make research findings available to the research community and other publics at large. While the organisation's desire to defer publication so as to protect commercial or organisational confidentiality is probably the more common bone of contention, in the case of the BedZED study, the Peabody Trust had to resist the temptation to respond to critics of the project by disclosing some of the research student's preliminary research findings so as not to 'scoop' her yet to be completed PhD thesis. Elanor Warwick recalls needing to be very firm within the Peabody Trust about this – particularly as there were regular enquiries from other students wanting to use BedZED as a case study for their research.

Given current ESRC policy, the time consuming demands of doing collaborative research can be costly both for HEIs and students alike. In addition to writing their PhD theses, many CASE and ODPM students are involved in writing reports and other forms of dissemination for the collaborating body (the research council pays for the production of knowledge but not its dissemination). Because of the very different audiences involved for such materials, such work is typically additional to that of writing a PhD, which CASE and ODPM students are expected to complete in three years (or four if they can afford the unfunded fourth year). Delays in completing construction and moving residents into BedZED threw the research student's initial research plans off schedule, while further delays resulted from the need to coordinate her questionnaire surveys of residents with those conducted by the Peabody Trust and by the developers, so as to minimise intrusion on residents. Ultimately these delays made it impossible for her to submit her PhD in the three years of funding allotted by the ESRC. This is hardly unusual. Unpublished data provided by ESRC indicates that only 69 per cent of ESRC-CASE students starting between 1997 and 1999 managed to submit within four years, a rate about 5 per cent lower than that for standard ESRC studentships over the same period (ESRC, 2003: 100–101). For HEIs, there is a risk that getting heavily involved in the sort of collaborative research that the ESRC and the Government hope to encourage may end up costing them dearly if it makes it harder to meet the Research Council's on-time submission rate target. For research students, there is the risk of substantial financial hardship with the ESRC only providing three years of stipend support, despite the fact that the median time taken by full-time PhD students in the UK is 4.25 years (Millichope 2001). Whereas the Research Councils cut off stipend funding to PhD students after three years, the Funding Councils actually provide HEIs with three and a half years of supervisory funding for each full-time PhD student. The Roberts Review (2002: para. 4.62) recently recommended that the Research Councils extend the duration of studentship funding at least as far so as to 'reflect the "real" length of the three year PhD'.

As Roberts (2002: para. 4.63) notes a longer PhD would allow for more ambitious research projects as well as providing students time to disseminate their results. For instance, the Peabody Trust dearly wanted to see some further guidance notes and workshops for staff coming out of the two CASE projects they collaborated with, but the funding arrangements left no time for such activities, which would need to be negotiated as separate outputs from the requirements agreed initially. Perversely, if the CASE and ODPM programmes succeed in their objective of encouraging the employment of PhD students outside the academy, dissemination through academic and other publication is even less likely, given the current imperatives to submit the PhD thesis as quickly as possible.

Conclusion: Collaborating through CASE

With its focus on the transfer of discrete knowledge, often in the reified form of technology, official science policy has tended to ignore the actual process of collaborative research, except as it influences claims to intellectual property. By contrast, in this chapter, we have suggested that it is also important to consider the *process* as much as the substantive products of collaborative research. First of all those results depend upon the process through which they emerge.

But more importantly, 'results', for all their utility, are neither the only reason to engage in collaborative research nor the only outcome likely to flow from it. Often the most important and lasting effects of collaborative research are not the discrete research findings whose ownership and commercial exploitation are the subject of so much attention in policy circles (e.g. Lambert 2003), but the new roles and relationships that can emerge through the process of engaging in collaborative research. Feminists, for instance, have long emphasised that the intersubjective processes of trust building, mutual understanding, and social learning involved in doing research can be as important for participants as the substantive results (Maguire 1987).

The collaborative studentship programmes we discuss (albeit briefly) in this chapter are a good example of this. Unlike conventional forms of contract research, which are concerned solely with the production of a discrete research 'product', CASE also involves a training element. In addition to the substantive research supported by the CASE programme, the university and non-academic partner also collaborate in the training of a PhD student. In this way the Research Councils hope to encourage 'both knowledge and skills transfer and career mobility' (ESRC 2003: 105). This emphasis on the production of labour is very much in keeping with the wider emphasis of government science policy on economic productivity and the role of research training in delivering it (Demeritt 2004). But it also problematises the simplistic idea of knowledge transfer at the centre of science policy. Instead of being a one-way process of knowledge transfer *from* universities downstream to the world beyond, the collaborative research programmes we discuss here provide opportunities to open up those fixed identities and to encourage more two-way traffic in ideas as well as in skills and personnel between universities and other collaborating organisations. Unfortunately the narrow focus on outcomes and results, common both to government science policy discourse about knowledge transfer and to academic debates about relevance and activism, tends to ignore and thus devalue these intangible effects.

Acknowledgements

Thanks to those specific individuals involved in the ESRC CASE and ESRC ODPM projects discussed here: Juan Alayo (formerly of Arup), Scott Ratzan (Johnson & Johnson), Eamon Mythen and Sarah Fielder (ODPM, now DCLG), Dickon Robinson (formerly of Peabody Trust) and Elanor Warwick (formerly of Peabody Trust, now at CABE), and to the postgraduate students – Richard Baxter, Nina Brown, Ben Clifford, Sam Elvy, Kerry Holden and Jennie Middleton.

Chapter 11

Cultivating the Business Researcher: A Biographical Account of Postgraduate Educational Research Training

Vickie Cooper

Introduction

Over the past ten years the production of knowledge and commodification of knowledge has been a major debate in academia. The economy of knowledge is carving new and shaping pre-existing sets of professional relations within academia: where some universities focus on and forge relations on a global scale, other universities must 'rethink and rework curricula and pedagogies' in order to compete' (Marginson 2000: 26). More and more universities are making courses and programmes relevant to labour market conditions (Olssen and Peters 2005: 328), and research governing committees are becoming increasingly responsive to their research *users* expressing a commitment to 'research models' and 'evidence-based outcomes' (Solesbury 2001; Hamersley 2005). This is not a professional frame of conduct that academia can stand outside of, but conversely, the very nature of contract-research renders academics not only instruments of the knowledge economy but, by and large, they are also the producers of its effects.

It is fair to say that given this level of restructuring, there is some concern brewing in academic circles and, as a postgraduate student, I also share that concern. This chapter will discuss the ways in which parallel shifts are occurring within postgraduate research training and social science research. Premised on a biographical account of my own experience as an ESRC 1+3 student researcher, this chapter is a critical reflection of my Masters and PhD research training, provided by ESRC certified universities, to learn the 'tricks of the trade'.

Where recent studies of universities have applied concepts of new managerialism to modes of working (Deem 1998 and 2001), and explored how the knowledge economy impacts upon research strategies (Marginson and Considine 2000), this chapter situates postgraduate training within these broader critical discussions of the university enterprise. Drawing upon real examples of 'innovative' research methods training, evidence-based research skills training and communication skills, this chapter argues that recent developments in postgraduate training are aligning the spatial and conceptual relations between academia and public policy, with the intent to bridge the gap between these two parties. The crux of the argument is that social science research training is largely shaped by the current political emphasis on evidence-based research and the research economy. However, it should be noted from the outset, that this chapter acknowledges that researchers up and down the academic hierarchy have always been shaped by the structures that fund them, the contracts that bind them and the authorities that regulate them. Researchers and their outcomes are products of the knowledge that pre-dates them and of their socio-economic milieu. As Fuller (2003) succinctly puts it, 'ideas are not things we think with, but things that think us' (quoted in Fuller 2004: 464). Rather, what this chapter aims to do is unravel the wider socio-political context of postgraduate training in academia and situate it within the broader discussions around the enterprise university (Marginson and Considine 2000).

Historical Context

Research training at postgraduate level is not a new phenomenon: masters degrees and post-doctoral degrees, known as 'research degrees' (British Academy 1961), have traditionally involved 'reading for a research degree', with a dissertation produced at the end of the masters degree or a research study produced at the end of a doctorate degree. The practice of reading for a research degree has fuelled pedagogic debates as to whether reading for a research degree is sufficient training in order to become a qualified researcher. The general consensus, since the 1960s to date, has been that graduate students are too ill-equipped to move straight from their graduate degree to a doctorate degree: ideally, students ought to have some research training, prior to embarking on a doctorate degree (British Academy 1961; ESRC 2001). Some suggest that a Masters in research is a necessary qualification prior to undertaking a full-time or part-time doctorate degree because it equips students with the necessary investigative skills, research methods skills, and transferable skills (Green and Powell 2005). As well as prepare students prior to their doctorate degrees, MRes degrees also prepare them for their industrial research career outside of academia (ESRC 2005). However, there is an anxiety that reading for a research degree, at masters level, leaves students bereft of any applicable and transferable skills to carry into their post doctorate degree, or carry into the research industry (British Academy 1961).

Attaining the right educational policy in research degree training is tricky. On the one hand the university must cater to the needs and expectations of the students; however, it must do so in a way that it does not infringe upon the students' pursuit of freedom of thought and intellectual development. According to a survey by the National Postgraduate Committee, the two most popular reasons for undertaking postgraduate studies are the freedom to study in a particular subject of interest and to enhance one's career prospects (Groves 2002).[1] However, the pursuit of

---

1   This survey was carried out across 17 different universities in the UK and included 982 postgraduate students.

intellectual knowledge through research is largely an autonomous endeavour, whereby isolation is endemic (Johnson et al. 2000; Mason and McKenna 1995). According to Lovitts (2001), universities that do not live up to postgraduates' expectations and fail to facilitate intellectual forums, results in high levels of attrition. A sound educational policy, therefore, should facilitate *critical* learning environments that support freedom of thought. However, in order to prevent attrition, research degrees should also facilitate *active* learning environments that enable students to become more actively involved within their research 'area.

Social Science Research Training

Since the 1990s, '[R]esearch training has become a hallmark of doctoral work in the social sciences during the 1990s' (Burgess 2000: Foreword). State intervention has helped to accelerate the rate at which universities have reformed their research training commitments. In 1997, the Quality Assurance for Higher Education (QAA) was established to independently monitor and quantify the standard of education offered on master's and doctorate degrees in universities (Wilkinson 2005: 19). In 1998, Charles Clarke published his main findings around social science research and found that 'two thirds of them were poor quality', with the main issue being that research has 'often been conducted almost entirely independent of the policy and the political framework' (8). Clarke argued that the main focus of '[R]esearch should provide the evidence base to inform and contribute to the decision making process' (ibid.). In a separate analysis of research, Tooley (1998) argued that 'considerable sums of public money are being pumped into research of dubious quality and little value' (quoted in Hammersley 2005: 318). The problem with social science research then, according to Tooley and Clarke, was not so much about what the research outcomes were saying, as to what they were not saying. The failure to consider public policy, coupled with a lack of practical outcomes, left public policy bereft of any real understanding of how it could improve upon its current practice and decision-making. Altogether, these critiques about social research and quality of education raised some concern about social science research training at postgraduate level: where social science research failed to generate valuable knowledge for social policy, educational research training became the main vehicle to reform social science research in the future.

To remedy the shortcomings of social science research, the New Labour government proposed policy reforms to educational research training and called for more university resources to be spent on designing social science research training programmes. The DfEE-sponsored Hillage Report suggested that research needed to be more policy and practice relevant; practitioners and politicians must take more notice of the evidence (Hammersley 2005). In 2001, the Economic and Social Research Council (ESRC) developed 'postgraduate training guidelines' to 'help improve the quality of research training in UK social science' (ESRC 2005: Foreword). In 2001, ESRC highlighted that masters in research was a 'necessary precursor to any recognized three-year doctoral programme' (Green and Powell 2005: 25). It is now 'common place for PhD study to be preceded by a Masters programme' (ibid. 9).[2] In essence, ESRC have tried to manage the problem that debilitated academic research for so long: it has echoed the need for universities to offer sound educational research training programmes with the view to make future social science research more policy relevant. It has given universities a new perspective, new pedagogic objectives and new methods of recruiting ESRC postgraduate students (ibid.). For universities to be to be awarded ESRC research grants, they must also show a commitment to postgraduate research training that coincides with ESRC's postgraduate guidelines.

The development of new and innovative techniques of research training has become a major undertaking for universities across the UK. However, such an undertaking implies major changes made to pedagogic practice. For example, ESRC encourage universities to identify and evidence 'innovative teaching platforms' in accordance with ESRC guidelines:

> [T]hese *Guidelines* now urge the need for continuous innovation, even after recognition has been obtained, both in terms of new platforms for the delivery of training and also the provision of training in new and emerging research methods (ESRC 2005: Foreword).

In failing to meet the demands for 'new and emerging research methods', universities will be 'unlikely to meet the standard of provision for recognition from 2005 onwards' (ibid.). This also means zero sum funding and none of the academic prestige that ESRC certification can offer and, given the reality that universities have to maximise prestige and profit, universities cannot afford to miss out on the prestige that ESRC certification offers; the economic gain, high intake of postgraduate students and attracting other policy research grants (Marginson and Considine 2000: 136).

Masters in Research Training

ESRC accredited universities have designed and installed Masters in research degrees (MRes) in order to formally train postgraduates in social science research methods. MRes degrees are different to Masters in Art (MA) or Masters in Science (MSc): where MA and MSc degrees are taught courses that focus on specialist subject areas, MRes degrees include a large component of research methods training, comprising at least 50 per cent of an overall degree course, and supporting taught

---

2   However, it is important to note that masters programmes as a precursor to doctorate came into fruition prior to 2001. In 1995/1996 there were 23 universities offering postgraduate research degrees, funded by various other research councils (Green and Powell 2005: 25).

courses (Roberts 2002: 113; Green and Powell 2005). Applied Social Sciences, Sociology, Social Work, Social Anthropology, Criminology, History, Health and Social Care, Management and Business Studies, Urban/Housing Studies and Psychology are but some of the subject areas offering MRes degrees. Admittedly, no two universities offer identical MRes degree programmes as each university will differ depending on their core teaching resources and expertise. However,

> [ESRC] place a clear emphasis on generic training in research methods to enable all social science researchers to understand and use essential qualitative and quantitative techniques appropriately (ESRC Postgraduate Training Guidelines 2005).

An ESRC 1+3 quota award scholar, I was funded by ESRC to undertake my MRes and post doctorate study over a four year period at an ESRC certified university department. Below is a biographical account of my experience of research training as an ESRC MRes and PhD student.

ESRC quota applicants must design a clear outline of their research proposal, prior to embarking on their masters and post doctorate study.[3] This research proposal will have a significant bearing upon the master's dissertation and should also feed into the doctorate proposal. On the one hand, having a proposal prior to entrance enables the student to remain focused within their research objectives. However, and on the other hand, Scott (2005) argues that it is problematic to expect student applicants to know their precise area of research they wish to study, before they have studied their subject area at postgraduate level. This method of application limits academic manoeuvre within one's research area as it forces students to focus on one area.

When I embarked upon the idea to do my Masters and PhD, my main concern was funding. After carrying out extensive research on possible funding avenues provided by ESRC, I realised that my funding prospects relied upon how well my own research proposal coincided with ESRC's research 'thematic properties' (ESRC 2000). Thematic properties comprise a number of gaps in social research and policy based research. These include social stability and exclusion, governance and citizenship, lifecourse, lifestyles and health, work and organisations and knowledge communication. According to ESRC, in 2004, the overall proportion of the ESRC's budget which was allocated to themes was approximately 65 per cent (ibid.). Given the biased weight on thematic properties, I decided to engineer my research proposal around these themes, specifically to boost my chances of being funded. I realised that mimicking these thematic properties could limit the scope and shape of my future research analysis, as

---

3　Where quota ESRC students must develop their own research proposal, ESRC CASE students are selected to carry out a study based on a research proposal pre-designed by the university and social policy organisation.

mentioned above; however, I kept the research themes broad, allowing myself enough room for manoeuvre. I incorporated themes; such as citizenship and social exclusion, social inclusion, reflexive modernisation, New Labour governance and third way politics.

Fortunately, this approach gained results and I was accepted on the ESRC 1+3 quota award. I immediately embarked upon my MRes training at an ESRC certified university department where all social science research training was organised and managed by the university's social science 'graduate school'. Graduate schools have come into their own significance within universities since 1995 and, by 2004 graduate schools were seen to be central to the management and education of postgraduates in universities across the UK (Green and Powell 2005). During my MRes degree, the graduate school was composed of a wide range of disciplinary subject areas such as social psychology, sociology, social and economic history, politics, housing studies and anthropology. The main educational research skills taught were quantitative and qualitative methods. The research methods training modules were held in the evening and the specialist subject modules were taught within a consolidated teaching model of teaching. This involved consolidating a 10 credit module into a two day teaching timetable. Reasons for holding modules in the evening and within a consolidated timetable are twofold. Scott (2005) argues that the demand to include research training taught courses, in addition to specialist taught courses has reduced the time available for university departments to focus on the specialist area of teaching. The university I attended organised evening classes so that it could deliver their methods training modules to full-time and part-time students, and consolidated their specialist subject programme so they could deliver it to full-time students and professional students on day-release, simultaneously. While the quality of learning within this particular framework is questionable, it is a common approach to managing diversity within a competitive market environment. According to Marginson and Considine (2000: 49) 'universities must do whatever is necessary to retain the flow of revenues and to maximize institutional prestige'. Le grand (1991) also argues that organisations that are 'best equipped to enter the market' leaves a 'grim' future for those organisations who cannot compete (quoted in Taylor and Hogget 1994: 188–9). Universities that can generate economies of scale, adhere to official teaching guidelines as well as manage diversity, in turn, help to restructure the environment in which all institutions operate' (Marginson and Considine 2000: 178).

Acquiring the prestige of ESRC certification and managing the extra pressures that that can bring – such as developing 'innovative' teaching platforms, addressing diverse needs and generating economies of scale – have wider implications for the critical learner and their experience within the research training enterprise. From my own perspective, teaching in the evening, and teaching specialist subjects over a two day period, failed to facilitate any critical engagement amongst the student cohort. During the evening classes we were tired and during the two day consolidated specialist modules we were mentally exhausted.[4] It was rapid and functional: we had little time left to critically reflect upon what we were learning, and it lacked the time and space necessary to develop peer learning. While degree programmes such as these come as a rational response to the economic and competitive market environment, they can appear irrational as students struggle to make sense of a their own learning experience.

During the research methods training, quantitative methods training was more arduous than qualitative methods training. As the Spring School of Oxford put it, '[F]or those who are not mathematically trained, reading statistics textbooks can be a daunting prospect' (2009). Quantitative research training comprised the building and analysing regression models using Statistical Package for the Social Sciences (SPSS). I sat on two quantitative modules and produced two extensive SPSS assignments. Having no prior experience of SPSS and, in the event of relapse, my colleague and I pinned the signs 'greater than' (>), 'less than' (<) and 'equal to' (=) our notice board, above our computers.[5] Our self-disciplinary tactics worked and we passed both quantitative modules. I learned how variables and data within regression models can be omitted and manipulated – in the same way as qualitative data – to achieve the right 'fit' (Kuhn 1970). This experience reaffirmed my scepticism about knowledge produced by statistical packages and, thus, my scepticism remains unimpaired. However, I can see its merits on my Curriculum Vitae. Much later in my academic career, during an interview for an Associate Lecturer post, my interview panel asked if I would consider teaching SPSS to first year sociology students. I politely declined. Qualitative methods training during my MRes degree bore less significance than quantitative methods training. Although we were assessed on *two* quantitative research methods assignments, we were only assessed on *one* qualitative research assignment. We learned about and were assessed on the philosophical underpinnings of qualitative methods: ethnography, participant observation, interview techniques, focus groups and data analysis were all included in the training.

Based on this research training experience and doctorate training, two key things became apparent to me. The first is that ESRC social science training has professionalised research degrees whereby their use-value within the research industry is increasingly monitored and addressed in the actual research skills training itself. The second point is that ESRC research training degrees directly correspond to the 'rational turn' towards the evidence-based research culture (Hammersley 2005). These two points are not mutually exclusive. Over the past ten years, the university research economy has witnessed a 'rational turn' whereby

---

4   I was later invited back to lecture on this department's consolidated module and it is with this experience I can confirm that consolidated modules are exhausting, both for lecturers *and* students.

5   For much hilarity, I swapped my colleague's 'greater than' (>) and 'less than' (<) signs around and laughed as she became confused by this backwards order.

the value of research is measured against its usefulness to social policy; its ability to inform policy decision making and impact upon policy change (ibid.). Solesbury (2001) also calls this 'the utilitarian turn in research' (p. 2): to make a difference to the social world, '[R]esearch must not just be useful, but useable' (ibid. 5). I argue that this rational turn to evidence-based research is evident in social science research training within the university itself. It soon became apparent to me that the flexibility that once enabled the becoming and growth of the research object towards the end must now be elucidated at the beginning. ESRC's prerequisite for a research proposal, prior to commencing the research training and ESRC's preference for quantifiable methods training is indicative of the desire to know where the research is leading, prior to the end. The research training at master's level provides postgraduate students with various calculative research techniques that enables them to extrapolate 'evidence' from the research field and analyse them within a measurable framework. This analytical approach purportedly makes research findings not only relevant, but also 'useable' within the field of social policy (Clarke 1998; Roberts 2001). Social science postgraduate researchers are being stripped of their *raison d'être* and of their critical convictions that once brought them into academia. These convictions are being replaced with new calculative duties: a quantitative tool kit that enhances the efficacy of their research output and makes them more suitably apt for the research industry and the research economy more generally.

Doctorate Research Training

During my doctorate study, efforts were made variously by my university department and ESRC training centres to train doctorate students in research and communication skills. Since 1999, ESRC has spent a concerted amount of effort and money towards mobilising doctorate students from across the UK to meet and communicate their issues with other doctorate students, and communicate their research ideas and research evidence to a social policy audience. These research events are hosted by regional ESRC training centres. ESRC currently fund ten training centres: the University of Manchester, University of Plymouth, University of Bristol, Lancaster University and Cardiff University are to name but a few of these centres.[6] Research training centres play a key role in professionalising research degrees. In neo-liberal market economies, universities see research training centres as useful economic agents because they are more 'responsive to outside agents and market forces, than are traditional structures' (Marginson and Considine 2000: 161). They are selected and funded by the government and ESRC to control the research priorities of universities. In many respects, research centres 'are a means of securing top-down control' (ibid. 160–1). Training centers reflect

---

6   ESRC training outlets can be funded up to a maximum of £100,000 over three years (esrc.ac.uk).

an identity that is neither academic ivory tower nor business, but acts as a mediator between the two: they perform the role of 'independent' trainers that can equip researchers with the necessary academic tool-kit to use data in a way that can improve the immediate policy environment. In essence, they reproduce a research mandate that is active, responsive and useable.

As part of the eligibility criteria, training centres must include collaborative and comparative research training, as well as encourage a greater 'use of ESRC-funded datasets' and 'skills for maximizing impact beyond academia' (ESRC 2009).[7] In 2007, the Centre for Census and Survey Research (CCSR), at the University of Manchester, trained ESRC postgraduates on how to make complex data more applicable, measurable and transferable to the field of social policy. It facilitated workshops on how to manage research methods in practice and, using mixed methods and data coding practices, it also taught doctorate students how to apply research techniques and data sets to social policy. Inter alia, workshops included, 'qualitative management research: a guide to training needs and resources', 'methods and tools to support interactive ethnographic fieldwork', 'surveys, social capital and social networks', 'hands-on workshop on occupational coding', 'mixed-methods: identifying the issues' and 'research design workshop'.

As well as training centres, the ESRC also set up a forum called, 'the Evidence Network'. The Evidence Network was set up in 1999 to support ESRC's 'commitment to make research not just useful, but useable' (Solesbury 2001: 5). It was set up as a response to a decision in 1999 by the Economic and Social Research Council that a major initiative was needed to bring social science research much nearer to the decision making process (http://evidencenetwork.org/mission. html).[8] In 2007, the Evidence Network held a four-day PhD summer school called 'evidence and policy: making research count in public policy' (ibid.). Inter alia, workshops included 'communicating research to policy and practice'; 'policy transfer: learning from overseas experience' and 'successful tendering – familiarize researchers with the varieties of tendering procedures'. In addition to the evidence network forum, ESRC also organise a 'research methods festival' every two years, lasting three days. In 2006, it attracted approximately one thousand postgraduate social science researchers from across the UK. The aims and objectives of this research event were:

- To provide a concentrated event that brings the research methods programme to the key target communities.

---

7   According to Solesbury (2001), too much money has been spent on new and primary research projects, as opposed to the 'cumulation and re-use of past research results' (5).

8   This statement was originally published on the website www.evidencenetwork. org/mission.html, however, people now trying to access www.evidencenetwork.org are instantly redirected to the Kings College of London website. According to the Evidence Network Newsletter, February 2009, this problem is currently being resolved, and in the meantime have created a shortcut: www.kcl.ac.uk/evidencenetwork.

- To provide a vehicle for linking together other ESRC methods-related initiatives.
- To disseminate good current practice from the best examples of social research to the research community (http://www.ccsr.ac.uk/methods/ festival/; http://springschool.politics.ox.ac.uk).

The juxtaposition of quantifiable research methods training and the research mandate to make research outcomes more policy relevant is timely. With the quantifiable capacity to untie knotted data and latterly produce evidence-based outcomes in a measurable manner, trainee researchers are expected to carry social science research from the academic field, to the social policy field. However, the goal to make research more 'useful and useable' to policy and practice is only half complete without a consortium of research training centres to operate as independent trainers.

Research training centres and research festivals also train doctorate students in how to manage conceptual knowledge and data knowledge. Wallace and Wray (2006) – also authors of the book *Critical Reading and Writing for Postgraduates* – train students on how to manage their knowledge into three categories: theoretical knowledge, practical knowledge and research knowledge.

In Australia, Fink (2006) suggests that the knowledge produced within traditional doctorates is different to the knowledge produced under the professional doctorates, also known as 'ProfDocs' (ibid.). Where traditional doctorates produce knowledge about 'truths', ProfDocs however, purportedly produce knowledge that is more performative (ibid. 37). Here knowledge is considered performative because it is produced within the context of workplace sites and can contribute to 'improvements in the workplace' (Usher 2002, quoted in Fink 2006: 37). Not dissimilar to the ESRC, therefore, the impetus to train ESRC doctorate students on knowledge management and communication skills is fundamentally rooted in professionalisation of the researcher within the research economy. Communication and knowledge management are significant components within research training because different forms of knowledge production can significantly impact on the research economy as a whole. Displaying a correlative fit between the research concept and research data is necessary for postgraduate researchers to strategically refine their slippery conceptual framework within knowable and measurable outcomes: how to produce knowledge as outcomes, use knowledge to improve the research context and stimulate communication between universities and social policy environments are all core elements of ESRC research training.

However, the application of research knowledge also involves steering local level activity between policy organisations and university departments: facilitating partnerships that enable postgraduate researchers to know their end users. In 1998 Clarke suggested that, in order to curb poor quality research, '[R]esearchers should seek more effective ways to find out what research users need' (6). Similarly Solesbury (2001) also highlighted that:

Competition from the commercial research and consultancy sector has brought home to academic researchers the importance of conducting and communicating research in ways that 'users' (often actually clients who are footing the bill) find helpful (5).

Postgraduate researchers are not exempt from this research mandate: ESRC funded doctorate programmes forge partnerships between their postgraduate research aims and social policy research needs. From principle strategy officers, policy decision-makers, to ground floor workers, social policy and charity organisations take a more proactive role in doctorate training. For example, ESRC CASE doctorate students must share their study time between the university and their research placement, equally. Where ESRC quota scholars commence their research activity in the second year of their three year study period, ESRC CASE doctorate students are positioned in their research placement at the beginning of their doctorate study. This set of relations between the postgraduate researcher and social policy organisations is indicative of the empowered role that social policy now plays within academic enterprise, where they are more active and greater embedded in the research concept, design and output. The 'part-formed progeny' between academia and social policy is a cardinal feature of social science research in the UK, whereby 'public actors seek new forms of influence over both what is done and how it done' (Marginson and Considine 2000: 20). Now that the doctorate students have an identifiable other – a research user – they acquire an end vision as to whom their research is useful for and how it will be used.

On the one hand, such a partnership enables the unity of slippery conceptual frameworks on the academic level to meet the needs of the research users in public policy. However, on the other hand, ESRC is arranging a contested marriage between postgraduate researchers and public policy actors in the attempt to remedy the gap that once stifled evidence-based outcomes. Borrowing from Du Gay and Salaman (1992), this partnership between the researcher and public policy is quintessentially similar to the supplier/customer relationship: where universities fulfil their legal and ethical role as research suppliers, social policy and charity organisations fulfil their funding role as consumers of research activity:

> Defining internal organizational relations as if they were customer/supplier relations means replacing bureaucratic regulation and stability with the constant uncertainties of the market, and thus requiring enterprise from employees. This discourse has fundamental implications for management attempts to define working practices and relations and, ultimately, has impact on the conduct and identities of employees (Du Gay and Salaman 1992: 615).

Conclusion

Research training since 1999 has installed scrupulous measures over postgraduate work. Gone are the days of the social researcher as the 'bricoleur' or the 'Jack of all trades' (Levi-Strauss 1966: 17), the trainee postgraduate researcher must expel such nostalgic ideals altogether, for the researcher's spade and shovel is increasingly being replaced with a chainsaw and pick-axe. With unremitting demands to display a correlative fit between their research concept, object and evidence, master's and doctorate students are under a constant gaze from ESRC and the university to make the concept – data to become more visible and useable. Trainee researchers must act faster, reflect less, communicate to a wider audience, and for validity, display not one but multiple research techniques. Contrary to the myth then, postgraduate students are not procrastinators. If the quality of research and productivity of social science research was previously contested, this new economy of innovative master's and doctorate research training is decidedly more suitably apt for the 'professional researcher' of the future (Roberts 2002).

Postgraduate research training can be seen as an extension of the research economy that now governs most universities. MRes degree qualification is a highly desirable research qualification, both within academia and within the research industry. Seen as a professional qualification in the eyes of the research employer and/or contractor, an MRes carries prestige and status as it exudes an image of professionalism within the research economy (Olssen and Peters 2005). ESRC research training does not simply address poor quality research outcomes but also aims to reconcile spatial and conceptual gaps between academia and public policy. It recognizes the value of social policy research needs and the delivery of evidence-based results for facilitating strong relations between university and social policy and through its robust system of research training, ESRC is currently cultivating a cohort of professional researchers who can respond to and directly feed into the needs of their end users and research consumers.

Chapter 12

The Knowledge Business and the Neo-Managerialisation of Research and Academia in France

Gilles Pinson

What we need is to thatcherise France – Franck Tapiro (Nicolas Sarkozy's spin doctor, 31 January 2007).

Is research only a matter of resources and posts? So how do you explain that, with a higher research budget than Great Britain and nearly 15% more titular researchers than our English friends, France lags behind them in terms of scientific production? You'll have to explain it to me! More titular researchers, less publications and ... sorry, I don't want to be unpleasant ... but with a comparable budget, a French researcher publishes 30 to 50% less than his British counterpart – Nicolas Sarkozy (speech about the national strategy on research and innovation, 22 January 2009).

The greatest favour that can be done to sociology is probably to prevent from asking it anything – Pierre Bourdieu (inaugural lesson, Collège de France, 23 April 1982).

Introduction

French people like to see their country as the last bulwark against the tyranny of neoliberalism. They think their country does well to resist the tide of commodification induced by globalisation and the domination of Anglo-Saxon market-friendly visions of the world. The higher education and research system is seen as an essential feature of this 'French exception'. Higher education is free in France and anybody in possession of a 'baccalauréat' can have access to it. Research is conducted inside large public research institutions populated with researchers enjoying a civil servant status. Research is supposed to be one of the key missions of the 'Colbertist State' (Mustar and Larédo 2002), a form of state intervention considered to be in the public interest.

This conception and organisation of the higher education and research system is now under serious threat. Since the election of Nicolas Sarkozy as president in 2007, the right-wing government has made the reform of the system in accordance with neoliberal and neo-managerial precepts one of its priorities. The explicit

objectives of the reform are the adaptation of the university and research system
to the needs of the so-called 'Knowledge society', the reduction of the autonomy
of the academic community and the bureaucratic steering of higher education
and research activities. This trend is not new. We will see that a decisive turn has
been taken in the late 1990s when the left-wing government discretely decided to
introduce new principles, such as a closer link between public research and higher
education on the one hand, and business on the other hand. French actors have also
played a key role in the 'Bologna process' that is guiding the transformation of the
European system of research and higher education in line with the precepts set and
diffused by institutions such as the World Bank, the IMF and UNESCO. What is
new with Sarkozy is that for the first time in France a government publicly assumes
a neoliberal and neo-managerial orientation of the reforms, and those reforms
attack the heart of the system – universities and the government funded research
organisation, the Centre National de la Recherche Scientifique (CNRS) – while
creating new institutions to overcome the obstacles imposed by the existing ones.

   In writing this analysis, a decision has been made not to separate the evolution
and reforms of the higher education and research systems, since both are
inextricably linked and targeted by the same reforms. The first part of the chapter
consists of a presentation of the French system of research and higher education.
This preliminary section is essential since the historical forms of organisation of the
academic system shaped its evolution and the reforms that targeted it. We will see
that one of the peculiarities of the French situation is the precocity and recurrence
of State interventions to adapt the system to its proper needs. But for a long time,
those interventions consisted in adding layers to the existing system rather than
attacking its core principles and organisations. In the second part, we will see
that it is precisely this peculiarity that has been questioned from the mid-1990s
onwards. Until this period, policy-makers and politicians never really questioned
the autonomy of academia and its corporatist forms of self-governance. What is
new with the ideology of the 'knowledge economy' is that it paradoxically drove
the government to attack those almost millenary principles. In the last part, we will
try to identify how those reforms may change the academic ethos and practices.
For this, experience will be drawn from one year spent in British academia, where
experimentation in neoliberal and neo-managerial reforms have predated those in
France.

A Brief History of the French Research System

Even if supranational institutions tend to have an increasing influence on the
way national academia and research systems are evolving, it would be a mistake
to downplay the national specificities of research systems. As Shinn puts it,
'denationalisation does not eclipse the national component of the organisation
and funding devices of research and universities' (2002: 29). In this field as in
others, it is important to take into account inertia and path dependence. As far as

relationships between research and universities, on the one hand, and State, civil societies and economic interests on the other hand are concerned, the notion of 'national innovation systems' forged by Richard Nelson (Nelson 1993), is still very helpful.

The French national innovation system has been historically characterised by two main features: first, the congenital weakness of the institutions that elsewhere embody research and scholarship: the universities; second, the strong and recurrent intervention of the central State to reorganise the research and higher education system. This intervention was justified by the weakness of the universities but also tended to worsen it. This importance of the role played by the State drove Mustar and Laredo (2002) to define the French innovation system as 'Colbertist'.

Strong State, Weak Universities

The will to reorganise and to orientate scientific research is not only a recent habit of the French central State. It actually occurred much earlier in France due to two French peculiarities: the weakness of universities and the early rise of an interventionist State. The weakness of the universities became a French peculiarity under the 'Ancient Regime' (Musselin 2001). French universities fell quite early under the control of the Catholic Church and became places which reproduced an official knowledge rather than being cradles of the scientific spirit (Charle and Verger 2007). French Universities were specialised in the education of specialists –mainly lawyers, theologians and physicians- and their activities were submitted to the censorship of the Church and the State. But the centralising and reinforcing French State soon started to see in the conservative and bigoted stance of the universities an obstacle to its power and influence and started to create or to promote the development of scholar institutions released from the corset of scholastic and ecclesiastic orthodoxy. In 1530, Francis I created the 'Collège Royal' – then 'Collège de France', home of Michel Foucault and Pierre Bourdieu-where Greek and Hebrew were taught while they were prohibited in Sorbonne. The seventeenth century, the Enlightenment century, saw the generalisation of this model. Thus while the Universities were resistant to the development of the scientific approaches, the central State sponsored them. Royal academies were created often by the recognition and funding of the activities of scholar societies. These academies enjoyed privileges and franchises that enabled them to overcome censorship. With the parlours and scholars societies, they became the cradles of the modern secular scientific culture.

After being seen as obstacles to the development of sciences and techniques by the Monarchy, the Universities were seen as remains of the Ancient Regime by the Revolutionaries. They were consequently dismantled. The Consulate and the First Empire (1799–1815) recreated them but placed them under the strict control of the central State. Napoleon I also launched a process that then proved very harmful for the universities. Eager to develop engineering and applied research in order to backup the national military forces and economic development, he created engineering schools, the most famous and prestigious one being the Ecole Polytechnique, that provided the basis of the development of the system of the 'Grandes écoles'. This system is formed of very selective higher education institutions operating in fields that were neglected by universities (engineering sciences, agronomics, business and commerce, public administration), that escape their control and that still provide most of the French professional and political elites. Again under the Second Empire, in 1868, faced with the underdevelopment of empirical and experimental research in France compared to what was happening in the USA, UK and Germany, the regime decided to create the Ecole Pratique des Hautes Etudes which was designed to fund research and train a new type of professor fit for the modern scientific approach. The EPHE became one of the cradles for the development of modern social sciences in France.

The Third Republic (1875–1940) tried to give power back to universities by authorising the recreation of faculties outside of Paris and releasing the central control on their functioning. However, the harm was already done. Many resources were drained towards the *Grandes Ecoles* and other State sponsored institutions. Most scientific research was conducted there and oriented in order to correspond with the needs of the State. The activities of the new faculties were still limited to the fields on which the Universities had a monopoly, i.e. law and medicine, where activities were oriented towards the transmission of techniques rather than towards research.

It is the very incapacity of universities, due to a lack of financial and human resources, to develop research activities that eventually led the French State to create the CNRS in 1939. The objective was to reunify in a single body all the State-controlled fundamental and applied research centres in order to coordinate the national research effort. The CNRS has three main missions: firstly, to fund the current functioning of the laboratories; secondly to fund research projects through calls and bids; and thirdly, to manage its own research staff (26,000 researchers, engineers and technicians in 2004). Unexpectedly in the French context, the major part in the governance of the new institution is entrusted to the researchers themselves. Indeed, they have the responsibility to orientate the research effort according to what is considered as strategic by the scientific community itself. Somehow, the CNRS created a realm of academic liberties that never really existed in the French universities. CNRS researchers benefit from a civil servant status and a life-time job contract, are entrusted with a mission to develop fundamental research within an institution that preserves their autonomy, and play a key role in its governance.

Nevertheless, the creation of the CNRS did not mean that the State had abandoned any will to control and orientate research activities and had given priority to fundamental research. After WWII, as well as the CNRS, the State created a series of applied research agencies in strategic sectors. The *Centre National d'Etudes des Télécommunications* (CNET) was founded in 1944, the *Commissariat à l'Energie Atomique* (CEA) in 1945, the *Institut National de Recherche Agronomique* (INRA) in 1946, the *Centre National d'Etudes Spatiales* (CNES) in 1961, the *Institut National de la Santé et la Recherche Médicale* (INSERM) in 1964, etc. The most prestigious of those *établissements publics scientifiques et techniques* (EPST) are usually well connected to the French State apparatus. The staffs of ministries and research institutions were usually recruited in the same pond of the *Grandes Ecoles,* which created a strong proximity. This proximity is attested by the budget they can count on. For instance, while in 2004 the global budget of the CNRS was made €0.5 billion, the CEA could rely on more than €3 billion.

The landscape of the French system of research evolved again in the late 1960s due to a first stage of democratisation in the higher education system. The economic development and the rise of the French Welfare State created a call for a more educated workforce. That challenge was taken up by the universities in which new departments of social sciences, sciences and economy were created or reinforced. That democratisation also provoked a significant growth of the academic staff. Universities were emerging as the main staff pool of researchers. That new situation led to the narrowing of universities and CNRS. In 1966, the CNRS decided to create some *unités associées* [*associated units*] to sponsor the research departments created in various universities. Those departments hosted researchers that were both CNRS and university staff. They were linked to the CNRS by a contract that guaranteed them, besides more scientific credibility, funds for administration, equipment and research operations. This narrowing of CNRS and universities was particularly important for the social sciences that were able to strengthen their fragile position.

Nevertheless, the coming together of those two institutions did not favour them in the long term. In the eyes of the preachers of academic reforms, they were seen to embody the weak pole of the French system of innovation. The CNRS represents the autonomy of the scientific community and the orientation towards fundamental research. The Universities have been accused of making no effort to adapt their teaching to the needs of the job markets and to solve the problem of youth unemployment. Thus, so as to orientate research towards 'social needs', a bureaucratic crusade began in the 1960s.

The Early Development of Contract Research and its Unexpected Effects

Very early on, the way the CNRS had been conceived – as an institution dedicated to fundamental research, with its own permanent research staff, and governed by the research community itself – appeared as an anomaly to the bureaucratic and political elite. As far as this elite was concerned, the research effort had to be orientated according to the social and economic needs of the nation. In the 1970s, political pressures compelled the CNRS to reorganise. Industrial demand for innovation support led the agency to create an 'engineering sciences' department. The CNRS was asked to define a scientific strategy and it launched a new policy of calls and bids on targeted themes. The central idea was to orientate researchers to topics considered as socially useful.

Social scientists were also encouraged to pay more attention to the needs of policy-makers through the development of contractual research on the initiative of institutions, such as planning agencies and ministries, whose central activities were not to undertake research. As Amiot (1986) states, contractual research in social science developed with the rise of the *Etat planificateur*, the planning State, through the 1950s and 1960s. What we call the *Etat planificateur* is both a whole set of institutions of agencies and a new way to govern the country. The conviction of its proponents was that modern governance should be based on a solid scientific knowledge, that the State should be endowed with an efficient apparatus able to produce statistics, to conduct economic studies, and to elaborate long term plans (Bourdieu and Boltanski 1976; Fourquet 1980). The Fourth Republic (1946–1958) saw the creation of a national planning agency (the *Commissariat Général au Plan*), a national agency for statistics (INSEE), and bureaus of statistics and economic studies inside key ministries like the Ministry of Finance. Faced with universities that were unable to provide the kind of economic expertise they needed, a set of schools and research centres was also created outside of the universities and CNRS. The French research system in economics was thus progressively organised by the planning networks of the central state and orientated according to its specific needs.

The installation of the 5th Republic in 1958 was an opportunity for the planners and bureaucrats to enlarge their grip on the State apparatus. The restoration of a strong executive power dedicated to the development of the country and the weakening of Parliament was a boon for the planners who had acquired key positions in the government and ministries. Under the new regime, a new device was created in order to orientate the research effort of the country. An inter-ministerial committee for scientific research was created whose mission was to coordinate the way each department was managing its research funds. Besides its coordination mission, it is entrusted with its own funds, the National Fund for Research, which was to give a real boost to contract research (Amiot 1986). This committee was backed by the *Direction Générale de la Recherche Scientifique et Technique* (DGRST), a bureau located inside the Ministry of Finances.

The new role of governmental agencies in the coordination of research continued, with a renewed interest in the social sciences (Bezes 2005; 2009). In the mid-1960s, after having reorganised research in economics, the main concern of the members of the planning apparatus was about the social acceptability of economic change and the identification of non-material needs in society. They then turned themselves towards the social sciences, in the hope that they would help to build the conditions for the social acceptability of the planned change. The planners and bureaucrats 'were asking sociologists to trace for them the limit of the bearable' (Amiot 1986: 79). Their aim was also to reorganise research in the social sciences on the model that they had applied to economics: large research centres oriented to answer to bureaucratic requests (Pollak 1976). They failed. Most sociologists were reluctant to become planners' auxiliaries. However, despite this initial failure, the DGRST and the different ministries launched new calls for research specifically targeted towards social scientists. The idea was explicitly to avoid the transfer of research monies through CNRS and to establish direct relations with research centres in order to drive them towards more applied research. As was now common in France, 'academic institutions have not been dispossessed of their powers; but other powers and other funding sources had been set up, that were not entrusted to them and which objective was to transform the functioning of academic institutions' from outside (Amiot 1986: 87).

The development of contract research opened a period of material opulence for social sciences. Public monies were pouring into departments as never before. Although the CNRS and universities recurrent funds only covered the operating costs of research, funds from government and the ministries were large enough to support ambitious large-scale empirical research programs. Classics in French sociology like Bourdieu and Darbel's *L'amour de l'art* (1969), Crozier's *La société bloquée* (1971), or Touraine's works on post-industrial social movements were drafted from empirical research undertaken under contract to DGRST and research support units in the ministries. French urban sociology was one of the sub-disciplines in the social sciences that secured the greatest benefits from the channelling of governmental funds towards research. Indeed, it took great advantage of the creation, in 1966, of the *Ministère de l'Equipement*; a huge department with functions in the spheres of public works, infrastructures, housing and planning. A bureau for urban research was created inside the ministry that started to allocate large amounts of money to research teams working on the effects of urban planning on populations. With the May 1968 outburst, the funds channelled towards urban research grew even further, reaching 15 million francs per year at the beginning of the 1970s. A large number of sociologists that started their careers in the 1960s and 1970s were thus oriented to work on urban issues.

Unexpectedly, this abundance of contract funds supported research studies that gave birth to the most radical theories French urban sociology has ever produced. Castells and Godard's *Monopolville* (1974), a book based on research conducted between 1971 and 1973 in Dunkirk (a city drastically re-organised by State planners in order to host a large steel industry compound by-the-sea), is probably the best example of the kind of radical theories that contract research funds helped to generate. In this book, inspired by the Althusser's theory of the *Capitalisme Monopolistique d'Etat*, the authors tried to demonstrate how a new kind of city controlled by large industrial companies was emerging with the help of State planning. Dunkirk had been chosen by one of the largest French companies, and by the *Commissariat Général au Plan* within the framework of the 6th Plan (1971–1975) to host a new steel production site. However, at the same time, State offcials were eager to demonstrate their desire to solve the socio-spatial contradictions generated by economic growth. Thus the newly created *Ministère de l'Equipement* was entrusted with the formulation and implementation of spatial policies (planning, housing, transport) that would accompany the construction of the industrial site. Yet the authors argued this new state concern with housing conditions was little more than an exercise in ideological mystification. Production remained the priority, so the official concern for collective consumption (e.g. housing) originated from a desire to provide a support infrastructure for the production process.

In a nutshell, *Monopolville* set out to analyse the extension of exploitation from the sphere of production to the sphere of the collective consumption of commodities and housing – with the state playing an orchestrating role in both processes for the purposes of maximising opportunities for capitalist profit making. Most other research studies conducted in this period displayed a similar critical stance towards the meaning, ideology and methods of State planning (Chamborédon and Lemaire 1970; Lojkine 1974; Topalov 1974; Mehl 1975; Huet et al. 1977). This being the case, it is difficult to understand why the State and, in particular, the *Ministère de l'Equipement*, continued to finance research of this nature but one thing is clear: the trauma among political and administrative elites generated by May 1968, and the fact that many of the staff that were hired by the bureau for urban research had a social sciences background, made them sympathetic to this kind of research. After 1981, the victory of the Left at the Presidential election enabled them to stay inside the ministries and to continue funding critical research.

Nevertheless, this kind of urban research never fully satisfied the bureaucratic elites who commissioned them. Although bureaucratic elites expected social scientists to share their intellectual interests and concerns, they encountered a social scientific community that was constantly trying to challenge their world views and to reformulate the research issues in different ways. For bureaucrats and planners who had been mainly trained in *Grandes Ecoles* to apply solutions rather than to undertake research, and whose vision of science was structured by what they knew about 'exact' research, it was a source of frustration. This frustration might partly explain the subsequent evolution of the State/social sciences relationships.

In this first part I tried to demonstrate that the state's interest in research is not new in France. Indeed, attempts to reorganise the research and academic system according to its own 'knowledge needs' are one of the historic peculiarities of the French State. But what should be noticed is that those attempts almost always resulted in the creation of new institutions, or new funding devices, rather than the internal reorganisation of the existing system. As Amiot put it clearly (1986, 72):

> The conservatism of the medieval universities led to the creation of the *Collège de France* designed to host the new disciplines rejected by universities. Later, the *Académies* […] were juxtaposed next to existing institutions to host the disciplines that did not find any place either inside universities or in *Collège de France*. That sequence ended with the French Revolution that put down the Ancient Regime edifice and designed a brand new one. The history of the academic institutions during the 19th and 20th century offer analogue sequences: on the margins of universities, unable to innovate, the *Ecole pratique des hautes études* was designed under the Second Empire to develop scientific research. The creation of the CNRS testified of the insufficiency of the previous arrangements and the necessity to add another layer.

And so on, until the very last period.

Managerial Assaults on the French Research System

The period spanning the mid 1970s to the mid 1990s did not bring about much change in the relations between social sciences and the State. The economic crisis generated cuts in Ministries' research budgets but the state planners that were in charge of these funds remained active and cultivated their networks. In compensation, the Left-wing government elected in 1981 integrated many of the researchers that were employed on contracts within the CNRS with a civil servant status. This was a period of consolidation for the French system of research and higher education. In 1984, a decree improved the status of the '*enseignants-chercheurs*' (i.e. professors and lecturers working within the universities) by setting up standardised salary grids and teaching duties. However, from the mid-1990s onwards, things began to change. The French polity became more sympathetic to the neoliberal narrative on higher education and research promoted by supranational institutions such as OECD and EU. This narrative was being relayed by domestic actors like Claude Allègre, a renowned geochemist and Minister of Education of the Socialist Prime Minister Lionel Jospin between 1997 and 2000. During this period, a series of silent reforms were implemented that led the French system of innovation to comply with the neoliberal *Knowledge Society* and *New Public Management* agendas. However, the election of Nicolas Sarkozy as President in 2007 has seen an intensification of these efforts to compel French academia to conform to neoliberal and NPM prescriptions.

Knowledge Society and the Redefinition of the Framework of Higher Education and Research Policies

Changes to the research environment in France cannot be understood without taking account of the global neoliberal offensive that has now targeted higher education and research institutions for more than 20 years. This offensive was launched by international institutions such as the OECD and the World Bank who have found allies within the European Commission, national governments and the business world more generally. This ideological offensive found scientific backing from new 'theories' about knowledge production which claimed that researchers' relationship with the state and business should change to comply with the reality of the knowledge economy, i.e. the links between wealth production and knowledge production. The offensive first struck in North America but has recently expanded to higher education institutions in Europe; France included (Laval 2009).

The neoliberal offensive against higher education institutions and research began in the United States in the 1970s. Scientific disciplines with the greatest potential for industrial application, such as biological engineering or computing, were compelled by the state to service business interests. Moreover, as businesses, university managers and academics themselves came to realise the economic potential and benefits of collaboration, a new movement in the privatisation of academic knowledge started. The procurement of patents for scientific achievements became a new priority for researchers, universities and businesses (Krimsky 2004; Duval and Heilbronn 2009) and thus opened the way for a widespread commodification of knowledge and universities (Harvey 1998; Warde 2001; Malissard, Gingras and Hemme 2003). In the 1980s, the fiscal stress imposed on universities by states and the federal governments created a new incentive for the commercialisation of research results and partnerships with private interests. In 1980, the *Bayh-Dole Act* (or *Patent and Trademarks Law Amendments Act*) gave universities and small businesses (that could be created by academics themselves) the right to claim property rights on inventions and scientific achievements that were generated using public research funds. For Slaughter and Leslie (1997), the *Bayh-Dole Act* was the symbol of the official legitimisation of an 'academic capitalism'.

What followed was the intellectual legitimation of this system of collaboration, which was provided by the increasing circulation of collaborating actors between academia, business, and policy networks. The best – and probably most influential-example of this kind of intellectual legitimation is provided by the academic, Michael Gibbons; co-author of the *New Production of Knowledge* (1994)[1] which proposes the 'two modes of production of knowledge' theory.

According to Gibbons, Mode 1 forms of knowledge production prevailed until the 1950s and were characterised by the distance that existed between the scientific world and society. Universities and academics were strictly autonomous, organised in impervious and independent disciplines, and the orientation of research was decided by academics themselves. Interactions between academia and industry were almost non existent. On the contrary, Gibbons argues that Mode 2 embodies the way science works *or should work* in contemporary society. The idea of Mode 2 is based on the claim that the epistemological and institutional independence of scientists is an obstacle to technological innovation and economic growth. The implication of this is that the orientation of research should be decided through a process of dialogue between academics and their political and economic partners. Priority should be given to the accumulation of knowledge that is directly applicable to the needs of government and industry because they are the engines of economic growth. Moreover the governance of universities and research institutions should be revised in order to integrate these new 'stakeholders'.

For the last 20 years, international institutions have sought to articulate and mobilise these ideas through a new set of concepts – the 'Knowledge society' or 'Knowledge economy' – in order to legitimise the restructuring of higher education and research. Although initially elaborated by international institutions such as the OECD, World Bank and UNESCO (Milot 2003), the idea of the knowledge economy is now being relayed by the EU through the 'Lisbon strategy'. This 'knowledge economy' narrative posits the core sectors of the contemporary economy as characterised by constant innovation and a continuous consumption of knowledge

---

1   Burton R. Clark (1998) can be cited as another very influential 'expert' on those matters.

and technologies in the pursuit of the economic growth that will apparently benefit all. Higher education, research and innovation systems are thus a crucial asset because they are axiomatic to national economic competitiveness, which is why it is said that they should be reorganised in order to comply with the new challenges of the 'knowledge economy' (Delanty 2003; Lorenz 2007; Garcia 2008; Winkin 2008). What is interesting here is the way in which the American higher education and research system that has evolved over the last twenty years is presented as the example to follow. The use of this hegemonic example is accompanied by a negative campaign that denigrates universities and researchers that are still stuck to the 'Mode 1' as malfunctioning. The Mode 2 zealots constantly disseminate stigmatising representations of the inner world of the academy (De Montlibert 2008) which they represent as closed to any collaboration with the outside world and composed of researchers that lock themselves away in their 'ivory towers' whilst being protected by life-time contracts.

Compared to its American or British counterparts, the French system of higher education has taken more time to comply with the new requisites of the hegemonic 'knowledge economy' project. But since it has started to do so, its adaptation has been quick. Claude Allègre, Minister of Education under the cohabitation government of the Socialist Lionel Jospin between 1997 and 2000, was a key figure in the mobilisation and imposition of 'Knowledge Society' doctrine on the French academy. He was responsible for the Innovation and Research Act (*Loi sur l'innovation et la recherche*) in 1999 which sought to import the 'enterprise culture' into the French research system. This act authorised researchers to create their own enterprises in order to capitalise on the value of their discoveries. It allowed them to take up to 15 per cent of the shares in their enterprises. It also made it easier for the CNRS and the universities to establish commercial partnerships with businesses (Malissard et al. 2003; Gingras 2003; Laval 2009). Allègre also enhanced the capacity of universities to improve upon their ability to commercialise the knowledge and inventions by endowing them with commercial offices that dealt with property rights and patenting. Finally Allègre also tried to transform the CNRS into a resources agency limiting its activities to the elaboration of calls and bids, distribution of funds and evaluation, and to transfer CNRS researchers to universities, but his attempt was rebuffed by the scientific community (Charle 1999).

On the higher education front, Allègre was one of the initiators of the 'Bologna Process', a commitment signed in 1999 by the Ministries of Education of the EU, to build an integrated and competitive European space of higher education until 2010. The launching of the process occurred one year earlier, on the 25 May 1998, when Allègre invited the Ministries of Education of Germany, Italy and United Kingdom in the Sorbonne University in Paris to celebrate the 800th anniversary of Paris University. The 'Sorbonne declaration' sealed the common will of the ministries to build a 'Europe of knowledge' that would counterbalance the 'Europe of bankers'. In actual fact, the Sorbonne declaration and the 'Bologna Process' allowed the expansion of market principles from economy to research and higher education. Indeed, the 'Bologna process' was soon integrated in the Lisbonna Strategy formulated by the European Council in 2000 and aiming at making of Europe the most competitive and dynamic 'knowledge economy' in the world. Concretely, the process aims at harmonising the European landscape of university diplomas by generalising a 3-5-8 system (bachelor-master-PhD) and by creating a system of credits supposed to facilitate the mobility of students. But beyond these practical arrangements, many of the Bologna process critics consider that the overarching objective is to impose an instrumental vision of research and education in which universities would be academic service providers competing in a deregulated market to attract students, the best professors and researchers and to raise private funds (Neyrat 2007; Lorenz 2007; Schultheis et al. 2008; Garcia 2009). In this free integrated market, consumers would have the 'choice' to select their providers. In order to let them exert their freedom of choice in full transparency, the 'Bologna Process' also proposes to set up 'quality assurance' devices allowing assessing and rating the providers of academic services according to standardised values. Beyond this obsession for quality assurance, many critics foresee the end of values such as academic freedom, the disinterested quest for knowledge, and free access to that knowledge.

The 'Bologna Process' was actually initiated by French actors identified with the Leftwing Party. Indeed, the origin of the process can be traced back to a report written in 1998 by the top civil servant and ex-councillor of Mitterrand, Jacques Attali, on the demand of Allègre.[2] Most of the orientations of Bologna were already in the report: harmonisation of the European university grade systems; the facilitation of mobility, etc. More decisive was the statement that the emergence of a globalised higher education market was urging the rationalisation of the European university systems and especially the French one characterised by a high degree of fragmentation. The report thus recommended the regrouping of forces and the identification of a limited number of 'excellence poles'. As Neyrat (2007: 148) put it, 'from now on, it is the position of France in the world market of higher education that seems to be the ultimate justification of reforms'. That new orientation constitutes a break with the previous philosophy of higher education policy that was aiming mainly at facilitating access to higher education and was – officially – based on a principle of equal treatment of the different institutions. 'Performance, not the maintenance of [territorial or social] balances, has become the principle of equity: what is equitable is to reward the best and not necessarily to share out resources on identical bases' (Musselin 2009: 79).

The second half of the 1990s was a crucial period in which many of the principles that would inspire the reforms of the subsequent period were laid down. The hegemonic project of 'knowledge society/economy' and the narrative about the necessary commodification of higher education and research started to structure discourses and practices of French policy-makers. The influence of international

---

2 *Pour un modèle européen d'enseignement supérieur*, Report of the Commission chaired by Jacques Attali, published on 5 May 1998.

organisations (OECD, World Bank, UNESCO, and the European Round Table lobby) and the mythical example of the American academic and research system played a key role in the process but one should not underestimate the role of French bureaucrats and politicians to import and spread those new principles.

The New Governance of Universities and Research

After 2000 a new period opened for a more systematic implementation of most of the *Knowledge Economy* and *New Public Management* recipes. Those recipes are, roughly speaking: the reduction of the autonomy of the academic community; the limitation of internal corporatist regulations; the reinforcement of bureaucratic control and political steering of universities; research institutions founded on the belief that scientific 'discoveries' can be programmed; the introduction of stakeholders (businesses, consumers) in the governance of academic institutions; constant evaluation and the elaboration of performance measurement instruments; and the development of an entrepreneurial culture among the academic communities through bids, contracts and project management. What Lorenz calls a 'managerial colonization' (2007: 49) of the public service of higher education and research was enforced in France by a series of laws, some of which had academia as a specific target, whereas others were part of broader reforms of the French State that had an impact on the management of universities and research institutions.

Within the latter type of reforms, it is worth mentioning the much commented on 2001 'LOLF' (*Loi organique relative aux lois de finances*) passed under the Jospin government (Bezes 2009). At first sight, this Act aims at reorganising the ways that State funds are allocated, managed and controlled and does not seem to be related to the governance of research and universities. But in actual fact, its implementation has revolutionised the traditional conception of public services and the way they are produced. The LOLF embodies the conversion of French State top civil servants and politicians to the New Public Management. It implies a shift from a logic of resource distribution in which funds are allocated to a department without being clearly associated to specific tasks, to a logic in which funds are allocated to specific programmes for which performance indicators are elaborated in order to ensure the efficient and effective use of funds. The bureaucratic control of funds is no longer concerned with simply the legal authority to spend but also on the economy and efficiency of spending. The LOLF is crucial because the principles it laid down have been implemented within the research and higher education policies. This focus on performance and results has allowed subsequent right-wing governments to point to poor performance in terms of student graduation and publications of French universities. In doing so, they were overlooking the fact that French universities cannot select their students and have thus been in the front line to absorb successive waves of higher education massification while the resources they have been allocated have constantly remained low compared to the level of support given to the *Grandes écoles* system. Recently, this denigration campaign had a concrete outcome with the reform of the funding system of the universities. Until recently, funds were allocated by taking account of the number of students registered at the university and contracts were negotiated between the State and each university in order to take into account the socio-economic characteristics of the university public. With the new system, only the number of students succeeding at the exams and the number of publishing teachers is taken into account. Behind this new system, many critics see a political will to realise the vision of the Attali report: the rationalisation of the French university system to around eight or ten big campuses able to deliver masters and PhDs and the downgrading of the other to the status of 'colleges' delivering only bachelors and deprived of any research structures.

The 2006 Research and Innovation Act (*Loi d'orientation et de programmation sur la recherche et l'innovation*, LOPRI), passed under the right-wing government of Dominique de Villepin, made explicit the application of NPM and neoliberal principles to research and education. The ideological framework of the legislators was clearly presented in the presentation report of the law: 'In a merciless world competition', it is urgent to build up in France uncontested research champions'; 'It is about time to reinforce partnerships between public and private research', and for researchers to get involved in 'economic growth founded on knowledge'. Assuming that private research is more efficient, the law facilitates the possibility for private organisations to get public research funds and to get involved in the funding and governance of public research institutions. As decisively, the law created the *Agence Nationale de la Recherche* (ANR) in 2005; the new centre of the research funding device. The ANR is clearly an instrument meant to erode the model of research organisation stabilised after the WWII and embodied by the CNRS. The purpose is to replace recurrent funds granted to the CNRS and its laboratories by a device of funds distribution based on calls and projects privileging public-private partnerships and allowing a tighter political and bureaucratic control. The 'quest for excellence' is also present in the LOPRI through the creation of *Pôles de Recherche et d'Enseignement Supérieur* (PRES). These poles are supposed to be an energetic response to the first publication of the famous Shanghai ranking that initially revealed the fragmentation of the French research system. Quite simply, they are groupings of universities and schools on a territorial basis that will enable the creation of publications pools to allow them to be 'better' ranked. They can thus be interpreted as a precursor of the reorganisation of the French university systems around a dozen poles. Finally, the law also planned the creation of an evaluation agency for higher education and research (*Agence d'évaluation de la recherche et de l'enseignement supérieur*, AERES), that will be in charge of the application of the principles of 'quality assurance'.

The elaboration of the LOPRI and the very tense climate between the government and the scientific world led to an unprecedented social movement amongst researchers, and to the creation of *Sauvons la recherche*. This association brings together a wide scope of researchers working within the universities, the CNRS and other public research institutions in different disciplines. Since the row about the LOPRI, it has been at the forefront of the contestation of neoliberal reforms led by the successive right-wing governments.

Nevertheless, the election of Nicolas Sarkozy as President of the Republic in 2007 gave a new impetus to these reforms. The novelty with Sarkozy is that he is the first French politician endowed with an executive mandate who explicitly assumes a neo-liberal orientation together with a comprehensive programme of massive cuts in the civil service workforce and a neo-managerial reform of administration (Bezes 2009). Assuming a 'market populist' stance, he has chosen to overtly provoke the socio-professional groups that are supposed to oppose resistance to his program, including the academic community. His speech on research of the 22 January 2009 is a clear illustration of this strategy. This mendacious speech was clearly meant to discredit and isolate an incompetent and conservative academic community in order to get public support for his reforms. French researchers were described as lazy and publishing much less than their foreign counterparts. Yet in reality the rank of France in various publication tables remained more than honourable despite constant underfunding and a structural advantage for English speaking countries. Sarkozy asserted that academics are one of the rare professions escaping regular evaluation. He also claimed that his Government had made unprecedented financial efforts to support research, even though France is the only country of the OECD that had reduced its financial support to research and higher education in the years since 1995.

This speech was preceded by two governmental initiatives that had already aroused the hostility of the academic community. The first was the Act on universities' liberties and responsibilities (*Loi relative aux libertés et responsabilités des universités*, LRU) passed in August 2007. The aim of this new law is twofold: first, to transform universities into 'executive agencies' and second, to weaken corporatist and disciplinary regulations. In the new legal framework, universities are supposed to elaborate their own project and to identify their priorities in terms of research and curricula in close relation with their local and economic environment. For this, more power was given to the Presidents of the universities who became the real bosses of their staff; more emphasis was placed on having socio-economic partners on university councils; and universities got more power over their staff. In actual fact, the autonomy awarded is conditional. It has been granted in exchange for compliance with project management and their involvement in academic competition. Awarding autonomy to the universities is a way for the central administration to disengage from the daily management of programmes and staff, and to gain a 'hands-off' style steering capacity (Neave Van Nught 1991). 'Rather than specifying precisely what is to be done, government establish broad objectives, define several principles framing the action of universities, allocate a part of the resources allowing the achievement of objectives and intervene only *ex post*, if evaluations reveals difficulties' (Musselin 2009: 76). In other words, distant control, the 'governance of conduct' and the control of outputs are supposed to be more efficient than direct intervention and focus on inputs. Such disciplinary power is a good means to reduce the real autonomy of the academic community.

The last brick of the new research and academic governance device imagined by right-wing government has been put down in 2008 and created a mass opposition movement among academics and students. This brick was a decree project elaborated by the Sarkozy's minister of higher education and research, Valérie Pécresse, allowing the presidents of universities to modulate the teaching duty of the academics according to criteria such as research performances, involvement in administrative and political functions, etc. Seen as a new step in the promotion of NPM principles and in the rise of a presidential arbitrary power, the decree project was confronted with huge dissent that compelled the minister to redraft it. Based on a desire to save public funds, the decree project was rooted in the assumption that academic workforce is not efficient and should be 'remobilised' – a typical assumption of the neo-managerial thought. For academics, the flaw of the decree is its tendency to consider the teaching task as a punishment. But more than anything the decree and Sarkozy's speech were seen as public disavowal from their employer that added to the 'market populism' that tends to describe professions whose activity cannot be assessed on simple market criteria as useless and privileged. During the first semester of 2009, the biggest academic social movement since 1968 paralysed most French universities.

Excavating the Future of French Academia in the Anglo World

This last section is dedicated to the exploration of the potential effects of the neo-managerial reforms on research and academic practices. It has been developed from two sources: first, texts that provide an analysis of the evolution of academic practices in the Anglo-American world where the effects of those reforms are already visible; second, a work experience in a British research centre on urban issues located in the Manchester region. I will call it the SKI centre. The SKI centre is a particularly good example of the mutation of British urban research since its activities were in response to 'calls for research proposals' by government and industry. This was necessary because SKI relied on contractual funds to survive, and because most of its members had abandoned teaching activities to dedicate themselves to contract research.

Commodification of Research and Mercantile Manners

A defining characteristic of the Anglo-American research system is contract research. The first problem with this is that increases in contract research funding justify the reduction of public funding to universities; the second problem is that the augmentation of the share of contractual research is at the expense of recurrent funding of research organisations. This reduction of recurrent funding compels researchers to orientate their research towards responses to an external demand rather than what is considered important by the scientific community. This might sound good to economic interests, politicians and bureaucrats but it is well-known from the history of science that research, 'discoveries' and applications, cannot be planned with a linear perspective. As Foellmi (2007) put it: 'No theory of relativity, no GPS'. Einstein's discoveries were essential to the eventual birth of the GPS, but it could not have been invented if Einstein had oriented his research towards this aim. The way science works is totally incompatible with planning or any obligation to respond in priority to corporate or societal needs. Market or bureaucratic steering of research activities usually diverts researchers from essential scientific discussion. The SKI centre was created with a faith in the capacity of researchers both to respond to external demands and to remain active in scientific debate. It proved impossible to do both.

Even more worrying is the phenomenon of 'academic affairism' that developed mostly in the physical and natural sciences, with the development of university-business research partnerships. Krimsky (2004) describes how the development of such business partnerships has led to the transformation of the academic ethos and, in particular, the development of worrying habits. The most worrying one is the trend to adjust research results to the interests of the funding entity. For instance, Stelfox et al. (cited in Duval and Heilbron 2006) have showed that the nature of the judgement of pharmaceutical researchers can be associated with the existence or absence of financial links with the firms producing drugs. In the social sciences, academics with similar links that have reached a large public audience do not hesitate to cash in on their interventions in seminars or conventions, or as consultants for government and thinks tanks. In France, the fact that academic salaries have not been increased for some time has created incentives for them to create consulting agencies thus enabling them to cash in on extra activities, sometimes at the expense of their scientific activities.

Criticism of 'academic affairism' and the greedy behaviour that it encourages should not be seen merely as a moral issue but one that drives to the heart of what academia is about: the interest in 'disinterestedness'. The specificity of scientific activities is that they are driven by 'specific libido and beliefs, irreducible to the sole greed for material gain' (Duval and Heilbron 2006: 9). The accumulation of scientific knowledge is guaranteed by the specificity of the scientific field. In this field, values like truth and commitment to objectivity have more power than anywhere else. Social hierarchy is determined by the judgment of peers and this judgement is based on the evaluation of the researcher's achievements in the quest for truth rather than public success or financial success. As Bourdieu (1994) has put it, researchers have an 'interest in disinterestedness' and that is what makes them contribute to scientific accumulation. Thus, as Krimsky reminds us (2004), scientific accumulation is closely dependent on the maintenance of a strong morale of public interest which is itself guaranteed by institutional arrangements such as substantial and recurrent public funding of research and civil servant status for researchers. On the contrary, the development of private funding, public-private partnerships and the priority put on contractual research and project management has brought about the alteration of academic values. As Stengers (2004) explained, those phenomena tend to transform the way researchers define their own interest.

Such researchers shift from a situation in which their interest is to seek recognition from their peers to a situation in which they seek recognition and rewards from industry, in which the priority is to say something that the industry will consider as 'bankable'.

Academic Individualism

The other effects that neoliberal and neo-managerial rationalisation of higher education and research have brought about are: first, the degradation of the feeling of professional collective belonging among researchers; second, the development of a strong academic individualism.

   One of the first signs of academic individualism appeared in the Anglo-American world as an aftermath of the rush to patents and licenses opened by the laws facilitating the claiming of property rights on scientific innovations. That trend created numerous conflicts in the academic world, conflicts that are increasingly solved in courts. At the end of the day, far from being a fuel for innovation, the generalisation of patenting practices creates obstacles to the circulation of scientific information. More generally, what was one of the foundations of the academic community, i.e. the free circulation of knowledge and its status of collective property, is now at risk (Lawrence 2008; Chamayou 2009). Even if patenting is a very marginal practice in social sciences, the climate of competition that has been imposed in departments and research centres due to publication tables, constant evaluation and individualised job contracts, will probably have the same effects on collaboration between academics. While working in the SKI centre, I was struck by the fact that competition rather than collaboration and fraternal relationships was the rule between academics, especially the youngest ones that had been socialised under the rubric of the Blairite university.

   Paradoxically, while the enforcement of neo-managerial principles aims at making the agents more faithful to their employer and their behaviour more predictable and conforming to what is expected from them, it often has the opposite effect. The best examples might be the effect that publication tables, constant evaluation, individualised job contracts and new forms of work organisation have had on the ethos of British academics and their relations to academic institutions. As Faucher-King and Le Galès (2007: 82) writing on the Blairite 'bureaucratic revolution' put it,

> ... the multiplication of audits erodes the trust in professional ethics and the sense of public service. Such a social control contradicts the idea that everybody is acting in a moral way and laminates the trust in social competence. Within organisations, one of the consequences of the audit procedures is the degradation of the employees' morale and the decline of morality.

Where neo-managerialism has been implemented, it has engendered a propensity amongst academics to use its devices to pursue their individual interests rather than the interests of their institution or science. NPM has a kind of 'performative power'; it creates what it describes. The cynical and calculating rational choice actor, who lies at the heart of NPM conceptions is actually produced by NPM rather than pre-existing it. But s/he often acts at the expense of the institution s/he should be accountable to. Thus British academics that have been subjected to audits and compelled to fill time sheets and to act as entrepreneurs tend now to focus on their career and on the increase in their market value rather than on scientific achievements and the welfare of their organisation. This drives them to avoid non-productive activities such as teaching, to recycle data, to write several articles on the basis of minimal empirical work, and to offer their services to the better endowed universities at the expense of making a durable investment in a department or some other collective research endeavour. While in SKI centre, I was struck to meet professors with absolutely no teaching experience. I was astonished by the incredible turn-over of staff and by the fact that the research centre was a collection of individuals whose pursuit of their own enhanced marketability overrode any desire to join a collective of people that shared a passion for the same object or the same theoretical inclinations.

The fact that the increase of controls engenders attempts to overcome controls is also visible in research centres in Britain. This can be seen in the spatial organisation of office space in some British universities with the emergence of panopticons (open plan offices etc.) that enable a permanent surveillance of the academic workforce. But far from being efficient, such open-offices engender a plethora of escaping strategies such as multiplying tea-breaks whilst endeavouring to inform colleagues about how busy one is. This is at the expense of contributing to a collective work of knowledge accumulation.

Another effect of the rise of academic individualism is the erosion of academia as a community. As some historians have reminded us (Charle and Verger 2007) universities were historically created as self-organised corporations of masters and students strongly bonded together to defend a common ideal: the production of knowledge as an end in itself (Caillé and Chanial 2009). The unity of those strange corporations was also linked to the strong peculiarity of their activities, that is, what Bourdieu called *skholè* (1997), which can be translated by 'leisure'. If academic activities can be compared to leisure it is because in the European university tradition they are ontologically disconnected from any form of social, religious, political or economic utility or necessity. This disconnection allows academics to maintain a distance from the world and to have access to pure knowledge. That is why accountability to 'external agents' is a notion that is barely compatible with university and research and why academia is such a strange world for the rest of society, especially to politicians and bureaucrats for whom accountability is a key concern. The other peculiarity of academic work is that it is composed of a set of activities (reading, observing, contemplating, discussing, writing, etc.) whose common points are that they are difficult to quantify and organise and that are difficult to separate from the private lives of those that undertake them.

Indeed, the scholastic lifestyle implies a certain embeddedness of professional activities into the private and social life of the academic. Academics live with their tools and products and therefore socialise with the people of the academic corporation. More than for any other profession, their jobs are a matter of personal identity construction as much as a means to making a living. The peculiarity of this academic life (autarchic, contemplative and liberated from utilitarian imperatives) is one of things that cements academics into communities whilst also being the guarantee of their ability to produce valuable knowledge. Yet, nowadays, neo-managerial reforms are tearing this life apart. Whilst in the SKI centre, I was appalled by the inexistence of academic sociability, by the strict separation that researchers were building between their professional and personal lives, and by the fact that the researchers' work had no real prolongation in their personal life. This disembeddedness of scholarship from researchers' personal lives, which has been generated by the NPM ethos, has weakened the academic community's capacity to defend itself and has thereby reinforced the trend towards academic individualism, free riding behaviours, and the lack of loyalty to the academic community and its institutions.

In spite of its numerous flaws, the research and higher education systems existing under Mode 1 that were based on civil servant job contracts, standardised salary grids, academic autonomy, and internal regulation were not that inefficient at all. Indeed they were miraculously efficient compared to their actual cost! Their efficiency was linked to the fact that they could rely on a workforce that was faithfully committed to its public service. This workforce was more motivated by its collective sense of purpose, shared inside strong academic communities, rather than by individual rewards. The reforms described in this chapter are destroying this collective sense of common purpose and the dedication of academics to systems of service provision that are not based on profitability but on an ideal of disinterestedness and universal access to knowledge. In an article in which he tries to give sense to the 2009 academics movement resorting to the Lafontaine fable *The wolf and the dog*, D'Iribarne (2009) compares academics to wolves that made the choice of a miserable but free life. For him, the fact that French academics are actually doing their job while they are poorly paid constitutes a miraculous propensity to dedication that the Sarkozy reforms are contributing to dissolve.

> The material situation of university professors is pitiful. Even compared to the standards of high public service (I don't even mention the private sector), their pay slip, bonus included, is ridiculous. No way for them to have a decent office, a business car or even a secretary. They fly in economy class. But they are free. They conceive their courses as they wish; do the research they find interesting. And if some of them (mostly researchers) do not do much, the very fact that they are not sanctioned is the living proof that those who, in large majority, are working hard are doing so on their own free will, without anything constraining them.

That miraculous unconstrained dedication might be the next victim of neo-managerial reforms. And free wolves might turn into cheating dogs.

Conclusion

What is at stake nowadays is the survival of university and scientific research. Indeed the paradox of the so-called 'Knowledge society' is that its advent could also signal the death of university and scientific research. That is exactly what Michael Gibbons had in mind while citing this Douglas Hague's sentence in a report on 'Higher Education in the 21st century' for the World Bank: 'If universities do not adapt, we will do without them'. This is exactly what Sarkozy's government had in mind when refusing to seriously negotiate with the academic and student movements in the first half of 2009.

The most worrying thing is the absolute ignorance of the same élites who proclaim their belief in the 'knowledge society'. Most of them have been trained in *Grandes Ecoles* and have absolutely no experience of research. Their dominant vision of science is a vision where scientific progress is linear, where applications can be clearly foreseen, and thus where research can be planned according to application objectives. The idea of an academic world funded by the State but enjoying a large autonomy is thus unbearable.

The challenge for academics now is to defend principles and organisational arrangements that have become almost unbearable in public opinion and among policy-makers' networks which have been converted to 'market populism'. Those principles embodied in organisations are the same that Veblen (1919) tried to defend at the beginning of the twentieth century while observing the intrusion of businessmen and bureaucrats in the management of universities. He argued that the missions of university and scientific research were incompatible with any commercial imperatives and with any form of hierarchical management. Scientific progress cannot bear any form of commercial or bureaucratic control and hierarchies. That is what makes academics so insufferably ungovernable but that is the price that must be paid. The function of criticism through the delivery of 'non consensual expertise' (Krimsky 2004: 121) is the ultimate vocation of universities which should not bear any form of constraint. It is even more important to defend this principle because, with the increasing dominance of the global media within everyday life, universities are now one of the last places where non consensual expertise can be expressed.

PART III
Conclusions

Chapter 13

Contract Research, Universities and the 'Knowledge Society': Back to the Future

Noel Castree

Introduction

Many chapters in this book focus on contract research (hereafter CR), but mine differs from these in three respects. First, rather than focus on CR in its own right I want to situate it in a much wider landscape of knowledge production, circulation and consumption. My reason for doing so is simple: we cannot possibly form a view on the why and wherefore of CR unless we understand the broader epistemic context in which it currently exists. As we'll see, in this context CR appears as just one instance of a widespread shift to seeing knowledge as a means to fairly well-defined ends. Secondly, I want to pay very close attention to the university as an institution where, it seems, ever more CR is occurring. The increasing prominence of the latter in the former is part of a profound post-1970s shift in the political and moral economy of Western higher education. This sea-change has comprised one very particular answer to the venerable and intimately related questions: 'what is a university?' and 'what is a university for?'. Note that I pose these questions in very general terms. My aim here is not to comment on one or other actually-existing university but, instead, to consider the *modus operandi* of any institution that would take this name as its own (rather than any other). Thirdly, I wish to be highly normative. I am going to present some proposals about what *ought* to happen in the future based on what I take to currently be the case. It seems to me wrong-headed to presume that whatever happens to occur in universities at any given time necessarily constitutes a sufficient answer to the questions just posed.

My argument will be that most or even all CR in universities could and should be located in other institutional environments. This dovetails with my wider belief that universities are increasingly being obliged to do things that detract from important functions that other contemporary institutions are unable (or unwilling) to perform. These functions speak to the role of knowledge in societies that aspire – more than rhetorically – to be democratic in character. Throughout, I will draw upon my experience of the British higher education system. My, perhaps controversial, belief is that most people who currently work in universities are unable to provide an intelligent and considered answer to the two questions posed above. The same might be said of the many constituencies who perceive some need or benefit from paying for the 'services' universities now provide. I therefore hope that readers of this chapter unaccustomed to thinking systematically about the university sector they either inhabit, or turn to for assistance, will benefit from the experience – even if they ultimately disagree with my substantive argument.

Contract Research in the Contemporary University

The Rise of Campus-Based CR

Research undertaken to meet the needs of a client in return for money (or, on occasion, something else) need not occur in universities, but these days seems to more and more. The ESRC seminar series from which this book emerged is testament to the fact: the growth in university-based CR has been such as to raise wider questions about its impacts on academics and academia. One indication of its current institutional significance is the proliferation of research centres of the sort that Gary Bridge (this volume) writes about. Indeed, my own personal experience of CR occurred precisely within the confines of such a centre. At the turn of the millennium I was for three months involved in an interim assessment – funded by the then Office of the Deputy Prime Minister – of the British New Deal for Communities programme as it was unfolding in east Manchester. It was not an edifying experience. The quality of the 'research' undertaken was, in my view, very poor indeed. The reasons for this were rather complex, but did not include a lack of effort or integrity on the part of the research team. As a junior player in the local assessment I took the money and moved on – or rather 'back' to my usual activities as a 'regular' academic employed to undertake both peer review research and educate degree students. My experience as a contract researcher did not noticeably alter my practices as a university lecturer. But nor did it inspire me to want to 'switch roles' again in the future, either by being re-employed by the Centre for Urban Policy Research (CUPS) or by seeking to emulate its director (my Manchester colleague and friend Professor Brian Robson).

I do not offer this anecdote in order to condemn contract research; mine could well be an atypical experience. It would be facile to infer that just because some CR is of questionable quality that the whole enterprise is bankrupt. In any case, CR on a large scale is here to stay, at least for the foreseeable future. Central government departments, charities, foundations, non-governmental organisations, transnational companies, trade associations, local authorities, think tanks, pressure groups, trades unions, and many other organisations today routinely pay for knowledge – be it factual or conceptual, quantitative or qualitative, applied or theoretical, cognitive or moral. They put this knowledge to a diversity of uses – for instance, to alter public debates, to shape government policy, to advance a specific economic agenda, or to train their employees. In short, even those cynical about the quality typical of research undertaken for external clients cannot plausibly argue that we ought to turn back the hands of time and have far less of it – at least not any time soon.

The question then becomes this: if CR is now a major part of our epistemic landscape, then where – institutionally speaking – is it best undertaken? Clearly, many university chancellors, deans, departmental heads and practising contract researchers believe the answer is in 'red brick' institutions like my own or in the kind of 'enterprising university' discussed in Chris Allen and Pauline Marne's chapter. Support for this belief, to the extent that it's been publicly articulated, seems to rest on four arguments. First, universities possess the research capacity that most of those who contract research simply do not possess. Second, because universities' 'core funding' has either remained static or declined relative to rising costs, they are increasingly obliged to generate additional income by becoming service providers. Third, because virtually all universities experience this obligation – at least in highly centralised higher education systems like Britain's – then competition for a share of the lucrative CR 'market' becomes unavoidable (leading to a 'you've got to be in it to win it' mentality). Finally, and more positively, because universities in a country like Britain are overwhelmingly 'public' in character then contract research is deemed consistent with their mission to serve a wide array of actors and institutions in civil society, including the national state apparatus which provides their core funding.

Should CR Occur on Campus?

Those not persuaded by these arguments fall into two camps. Some regard themselves as pragmatists or realists. They aim to make the best of a less than ideal situation. The logic of their argument is pretty plausible, and goes something like this: university-based CR generates much needed revenue, is often intellectually stimulating, offers a chance for researchers to influence non-university constituencies, and is 'relevant' in ways that 'academic research' usually never is. While there is always the risk that the contract researcher becomes servile or, in Allen's (2005) more subtle terms, 'docile', the argument is that this risk is worth taking. After all, in the social relations of contract research, the academic can – depending on the situation – be positioned as a 'partner', a 'consultant' or even an 'expert' to be deferred to (see Manzi and Smith-Blowers, this volume). To suggest otherwise, as Rob Imrie (this volume) rightly reminds us, is to reduce CR to some putative 'essence' that is little more than a caricature, and whose empirical inaccuracy is demonstrated readily. In any case, even if CR does sometimes threaten academics' independence and academic standards, it does not – some say – 'spill over' in its effects *systematically*, and thus 'taint' the conduct of all that research funded without strings attached.

Unlike the pragmatist-realist position, idealists see the recent growth of university-based CR as either compromising or departing from the core mission of a university. I call them idealists, not because they are idle dreamers – far from it – but because their critique bites by virtue of the gap between posited ideals and the actualities of campus life today. One of these is the sociologist and philosopher of science Steve Fuller, who is among the most interesting theorists writing about universities in so-called 'knowledge societies' like our own. In his book *Knowledge Management Foundations* (2002), Fuller suggests that the growing cadre of campus-based contract workers – specifically, those lacking permanent academic contracts – pose a serious threat to the 'proper' identity and role of universities. The thrust of his argument is two-fold. First, he argues that there is no necessary link between universities as institutions and CR: in other words, contract researchers and their managers are usually undertaking epistemic work that could, in principle, occur in independent research institutes, foundations and centres. Their presence on campus is thus entirely contingent, yet this inevitably alters the universities' sense of self as CR becomes a normal part of their business. Secondly, Fuller argues that universities – because of their history and its tangible legacy – often offer contract researchers precious little reason to value them as distinctive or special institutions. For instance, these researchers endure insecure employment on rolling contracts and are materially dependent on the money of external clients; and, to offer a second example, it may be hard for them to use material from a piece of jointly-undertaken CR in the service of, say, a single-authored peer review publication that may help them get a permanent academic post. Whatever an individual contract researcher's personal experience, seen in aggregate they comprise a major section of the large, 'flexible', casualised workforce that now inhabits Western universities. This workforce, Fuller argues, has little reason to see universities as more than convenient locations for the conduct of their professional activities. Indeed, its members may come to resent the 'academic freedom' enjoyed by academics on permanent contracts, and be inclined to support measures that undermine the relative autonomy that many universities have traditionally enjoyed from paymasters, special interests and the visible hand of government interference in their affairs.

I will discuss Fuller's normative vision for the university later. For now, I simply note that his views on contract researchers do not concern the fine details of their relations with clients, and how this may affect the conduct and outputs of inquiry. Interesting though these details might be, they do not speak to Fuller's more fundamental concern. This is with whether institutions that call themselves 'universities' should be in the business of selling knowledge and thus embroiling more and more of their members in contractual relations with myriad other parties. But the marketisation of both research and researchers is, of course, simply one part of a much larger story about universities in the 'knowledge society'. It's a story to which I turn in the next two sections.

Universities in the Twenty-First Century 'Knowledge Society'

Western universities were once elite institutions in which a few scholar-teachers educated a small cadre of would-be leaders. They were relatively insulated from the wider society. This began to change quite rapidly in the 1960s. Four decades on and universities enjoy a greater importance than ever before, both nationally and globally. Such is the scale and diversity of their activities that they've become key institutions for a wide range of what we've learnt to call 'stakeholders'. Universities' centrality to the business of CR is simply one aspect of this. They have made themselves – or, we might say, have been made into – key institutions in a range of other areas too. This has been done by consolidating what, historically speaking, was their far from complete monopoly in two domains: namely, creating and disseminating new high-level knowledge (i.e. research and teaching), and certifying advanced knowledge, advanced skills and those who master them (i.e. awarding credentials and being seen to embody standards of 'truth', 'rigour' 'objectivity' etc.). In the last 30 years, these expanded historic functions have formed the basis of what Alan and Marten Shipman (2006), in their book *Knowledge monopolies*, call 'the academisation of society'. By this they mean that ever-more social actors must now attend, or solicit the services of, universities if they are to realise their own aims and agendas.

If we take Britain, this 'academisation' is obvious at the educational level. During the 1960s only 7 per cent of 18–21 year olds attended university, whereas today it is over 30 per cent (which is itself some way short of New Labour's ambitious 1997 pledge to make it 50 per cent). A minimum of three years degree level study is now a virtual requirement if students are to secure even half-interesting, half-remunerative employment. Many choose to stay on for a master's degree in order to give them a competitive edge in the labour market or simply buy some time before entering it. Not a few pursue a PhD or an MPhil – four times more than 30 years ago, in fact – and for many this is a necessity in order to get an often insecure and not always well paid research or teaching post in a university. This massive expansion in the number of British university graduates has coincided with a sharp increase in the number of overseas students, especially at postgraduate level. For instance, in my own school at Manchester University we educate hundreds of African, Asian and Latin American students who hope to return home and enter the business of 'development'. Likewise, in my next-door building, colleagues at Manchester Business School train and certify candidates from virtually every country on the planet. Examples like these are dime-a-dozen. Where students cannot be educated on-site, universities have set about providing all manner of distance learning courses at certificate, diploma and degree levels.

In addition to their ramped-up teaching and credentialising functions, British universities' research is also enjoying heightened prominence – quite aside from the CR already discussed. The British research councils, for example, pump considerable money into investigative programmes focused on public policy challenges, new technologies, or current issues of consequence (such as climate change mitigation and adaptation). Then there are all those science and business parks that have popped-up adjacent to university campuses, where spin-off companies can be incubated and intellectual property rights (e.g. patents) claimed with the help of new university IP officers. Though an awful lot of 'blue skies' research still occurs (its relative importance being measured in new international league tables, like the Shanghai Jiao Tong ranking that preoccupies my own institution), the academic *zeitgeist* dictates that universities produce knowledge that is 'useful' and 'relevant' in ways that are tangible for various sections of government, the business community or civil society. New Labour has made appreciable sums of 'third stream' funding available to this end. Even the PhD – once a marker of someone's capacity to undertake research independently – is today responsive to socio-economic agendas (as the rise of 'professional doctorates', 'executive PhDs' and 'CASE studentships' attest). Across the board, there is now a lot of talk about 'users' and 'knowledge transfer' – with the latter these days a significant criteria for promotion among permanent academic staff in my own university. It's thus clear that the purported shift to a 'mode 2' style of knowledge production cross-cuts the otherwise clear distinction between contract-only researchers and permanent academic staff ostensibly funded from the public purse. University research in Britain is increasingly important to those who are not themselves in the business of doing research.

In sum, universities in countries like Britain today enjoy a power and prominence unprecedented in their (often long) histories. But has their new-found importance altered their very character? And, if so, is it for the better? In answer to the first question most people with long enough memories would almost certainly say 'yes'. Many believe that Western universities' enhanced domestic significance has come at a price: namely, a creeping subordination of their own ideals and practices to those of external users of the universities' stock-in-trade, knowledge. In both their pedagogic and research functions, the knowledge that universities produce is, it seems, increasingly responsive to others' agendas – as I intimated in the previous paragraph. In the next section I will briefly describe and explain this diminution in relative autonomy, taking the British case once more. Given how many under-30s now work in the British system, and given how many baby-boomers have recently retired, the number of university people who have actually experienced the changes recounted below is fast-diminishing. The result could easily be an incremental loss of critical perspective and critical distance on these changes.

Universities: Measured, Monitored, Managed and Massified

'The ... transformation of universities over the past 25 years', writes Alex Callinicos (2006: 34), 'has been relentless, but it has also been piecemeal. Change has come not abruptly, but through a process of drip, drip, drip'. In the British case, perhaps the most striking feature of this transformation is that it's been externally *imposed* rather than being initiated or led by those who inhabit universities professionally. Specifically, successive Conservative and Labour governments have intentionally redefined the relationship between universities and the wider society. Their success has been achieved, in large part, because of British universities' dependence on tax-payer money for survival: the proverbial piper has been able to call the tune, once it made up its mind to do so. Academics have, by and large, danced to the new music – indeed, many are enjoying successful careers on this basis. So, what is the new moral economy – or, as critic Gillian Howie (2005) would have it, 'company policy' – that academics have been obliged to buy into?

The Instrumentalisation of Academic Knowledge

As many commentators have observed, it is one in which *knowledge is presumed to be useful and/or measurable*. Utility implies that knowledge can meet clearly defined ends external to itself – be they economic, social, cultural, political or environmental. Measurability implies that knowledge can be summarised in one or other metric that comes to represent its utility comparatively or, if not this, then some other thing that can be similarly graded (such as 'quality' or 'excellence'). Though utility is not synonymous with whether or not knowledge aids national economic growth and competitiveness, it's fair to say that this has been a running theme in central government policy on universities. It has been evident in successive pronouncements made by past and present ministers, including David Blunkett, Lord David Sainsbury, Charles Clarke and Peter Mandelson; it's been evident in the language animating the several national reviews of universities this last quarter century (including those by Ron Dearing and Richard Lambert); and, at the time of writing, it's evident in the fact the universities are overseen by a Cabinet minister whose portfolio includes business and industry. Indeed, this minister – in a recent letter to *The Guardian* newspaper – described British universities as 'a *critical* part of our *knowledge economy*' (Mandelson 2010: 37, emphasis added). Of course, these universities have, at some level, *always* responded to central government agendas – since even before the Robbins review of 1963 and Prime Minister James Callaghan's famous 1976 speech at Ruskin College. So what explains central government's determination to make them *even more* responsive since roughly 1988, when the Education Reform Act was passed?

One answer lies in the already-mentioned concept of the 'knowledge society', and the related terms 'knowledge economy' (used by Mandelson) and 'knowledge capitalism'. At a global level, the OECD report *The Knowledge-Based Economy* (1996) and the World Bank report *Knowledge for Development* (1998) helped to popularise an emerging idea among policy-makers that education was an undervalued form of knowledge capital. The argument was that equipping more people with knowledge and skills would bring its own rewards in a hyper-competitive global economy. In Britain, this argument was embodied in the 1999 Department of Trade and Industry White Paper *Our Competitive Future: Building the Knowledge Driven Economy* (a successor document to a 1993 White Paper advancing the idea of an 'enterprise culture'). The suggestion was that Britain's 'post-industrial' future lay in it exporting knowledge-based services and products to the rest of the world. The emphasis would be on higher value-added commodities and on continuous innovation.

On the educational side, it's precisely this argument which has been used to justify the massive increase in the number of students entering university to take one or other academic, applied or vocational course. These students are thereby seen to enhance their 'human capital' and long-term earnings potential, while providing society with new generations of well-educated people accustomed to the idea of 'lifelong learning' (and thus 'flexible' about their skills and occupations). Students are here invited to view themselves as investors in their future and as consumers of an educational service – especially now that so many must undertake paid-employment during their university years and pay tuition fees too. Universities, conversely, are invited to see students as clients whose needs and wants must be satisfied – the new National Student Survey being just one tool through which this is achieved. Indeed, students are seen as a 'market' that universities must compete for, and an especially lucrative one in the case of overseas applicants paying premium fees (Britain is a major destination for such students). It is a moot point whether all this is simply reproducing existing patterns of social inequality, with a few universities accrediting a minority of upper middle class students to be tomorrow's economic and political elite, while students from less fortunate back-grounds end-up as a mass of 'generic workers' with limited prospects. So much for 'widening access'.

On the research side, the idea that knowledge ought to have an exchange value is evident in the several-fold increase in intellectual property claims filed by British academics since 1990 – especially in the physical and biomedical sciences. But the perceived value of research goes well beyond commerce, as much university-based CR attests. Knowledge produced through systematic inquiry is today seen as vital in order to address a range of public policy problems and to serve the needs of diverse civil society organisations. This is now very evident in the way the British research councils address prospective winners of grants. That a commitment to 'utility' in research has seeped into the mind-set of academics is evident in my own discipline, human geography. Just after I embarked upon an academic career, a set of often angst-ridden debates occurred in the pages of peer review journals and at annual conferences. Stretching over several years, they concerned 'policy relevance', 'academic activism', 'participatory research' and engaging with 'publics'. Notwithstanding the differences of detail between these debates, the common presumption was that research can and should *have immediate and tangible effects*. Interestingly, when commentators felt that such effects could not be detected, they worried deeply about the well-being of human geography – with non-effects unthinkingly equated with 'irrelevance'.

Measuring Knowledge, Controlling Academic 'Knowledge Workers'

If utility is now almost a synonym for 'worthwhile knowledge' in universities, the idea that knowledge is measurable has also become routinised. This goes beyond the central state's determination to ensure capital accumulation. It also reflects a belief, articulated during the Thatcher era, that publicly funded institutions must ensure 'value for money' and be run 'efficiently' so that resources are not unduly wasted. This belief survived Thatcherism and the fiscal stringency of the 1980s, living-on during the economic 'boom' that New Labour presided over up until the recent financial crisis. In research, the several RAEs (Research Assessment Exercises) demonstrate as much, with their competitive, banded allocation of non-teaching monies. In teaching, the now defunct Quality Assurance Agency regime introduced the idea of close monitoring of academics' pedagogy. This idea finds contemporary expression in student evaluations of almost every module they take and in routine assessments of entire degree programmes by some mixture of internal and external evaluators. It also finds expression in recently instituted complaints and grievance procedures (for instance, as Head of Discipline I will spend a lot of this summer dealing with student appeals against their final degree classification). The measurement of research and teaching, along with campus facilities, reach its apotheosis in various university national and global league tables. Today, these quantitative exercises assume a degree of authority and importance unimaginable 25 years ago.

Measurement is, of course, of a piece with the 'audit culture' that is today pervasive, not only in universities but in all British public sector organisations. The constant monitoring, checking and assessment of public sector employees' activities performance has become normalised within the space of a generation. The national Time Allocation Surveys (TACs) are one of many examples, with British academics periodically obliged to record the time they devote to different professional activities over two randomly chosen weeks. Another example is the annual PDR (personal development review) undergone by academics at all levels of the university system. At Manchester, to offer a third example, we are currently undergoing an individualised, institution-wide Research Profiling Exercise, a sort of internal RAE (or REF, as it will be called in the future). The essence of audit is that those subject to it must be held accountable, and that accountability can only be guaranteed by frequent exercises in recording performance and feeding the results back to auditees. In universities, audit presently takes two forms: bureaucratic (i.e. professional, peer audit) and consumerist (i.e. client-led). In itself, audit is no bad thing. However, there is a difference between audit that's self-imposed, organic and voluntary – such as the long-standing external examiner system for British university degrees – and audit imposed on those who become subject to its rationalities. Overwhelmingly, British universities' current audit culture is a product of central government diktat.

Remarkably, British academics socialised under pre-Thatcher regimes acceded to all this through the 1980s and 90s, and offered little or no resistance. As I said earlier, their younger successors are equally compliant, often lacking the historic experience with which to measure the degree of systemic change. Unlike their French counterparts, recently in uproar about Nicolas Sarkozy's proposals for university reform (see Pinson, this volume), British academics remain quiescent and thus complicit. We can speculate about the reasons why the imposition of elaborate surveillance systems has been tolerated. It may be the considerable financial power possessed by central government departments and agencies. In real terms, the unit of resource per staff member and student has declined since the early

1980s, and in the competition for public resources it could well be that universities have seen submission to government targets and agendas as being in their short-term interest. Academics' compliance could also have a lot to do with the new, top-down managerialism that has undoubtedly triumphed in British universities, and which concentrates power in the hands of vice-chancellors, deans, departmental heads, and their administrative teams. It has led many (most?) academics to regard themselves as employees rather than members of a professional community. However, this begs the question of why such managerialism was tolerated in the first place. One possibility is that some academics were attracted by the prospect of greater managerial authority over colleagues and supported attacks on the latters' notional equality and historic right to self-governance. Another is that British academics' have a weak track record of collective action and lack the necessary political astuteness to win strategic battles; they have always tended to operate as individuals, albeit within a wider department, faculty or centre. This is especially true in the social sciences and humanities. In that context, the costs of speaking out against new initiatives or refusing to comply with them can be very high indeed.

Regardless of the reasons, the fact remains that British universities today are highly managed and regulated institutions – so much so that they're 'McUniversities' according to some, the academic equivalent of large-scale private firms. Ironically, in a supposedly 'neoliberal era', they have been 'victims of one of the last great experiments in central state planning' (Gamble 2004: 50). With internal control relatively strong, academics have been made to adapt their teaching and research – sometimes willingly, often unconsciously – to the perceived demands of government, business and civil society actors. Many believe that this amounts not simply to their 'deprofessionalisation' but to something more profound: namely, a deep remaking of academic subjectivities.

Reimagining the University I: Looking Backwards

I have suggested that British universities are today institutions of considerable national importance, but that they have bought enhanced influence at a certain price: namely, a diminution in their relative autonomy from non-academic actors and organisations. I have further argued that this erosion of independence has been forced upon universities by successive national governments, eliciting little opposition. Clearly, I have moved well beyond a discussion of CR per se. But this seems to me legitimate, because the significance of CR for the universities where so much of it today occurs can only be understood with reference to the wider context described in the previous two sections. In the rest of this chapter I want to move from a diagnostic towards a normative mode of argumentation. I am going to provide a positive answer to the two questions about universities posed at the outset. I suspect that most readers of this book are like most people who work in universities, or who utilise their services: that is to say, I'd wager they possess few alternative ideas regarding what universities should and could be like. Though there's a very rich literature critical of the changes recounted above, it is not – alas – widely read by those affected by, or leading, these changes. My own case proceeds in four stages. In thinking about the future of British universities, I begin (in this section) by talking about universities in the past. As we'll see, the history is instructive. It provides food for thought for the many university personnel who have little precious little sense of the functional specificity their institutions should arguably possess.

Though some are wont to talk about 'the university' in the singular – as if it has a timeless essence that's more-or-less realised by universities in any given time or place – the reality is that there has never been just one conception of its character and role. Medieval European universities were typically 'autonomous, self-funding, limited liability corporations, with many of the same characteristics as ancient republics' (Fuller 2002: 216). In its original sense, a corporation was an institutionalised community of practitioners willing to abide by certain norms internal to the community itself. As well as universities, guilds, religious orders, and cities were granted 'corporate' status. To join a corporation 'typically required negotiating one's identity through examination or election, as well being willing to become something other than one already is' (Fuller 2003: 121). Corporations bound otherwise different individuals into a collective that emphasised shared goals, standards and duties. By the nineteenth century, this corporate identity – based on an institutional capacity to resist external pressures – had morphed into something rather different. There were three national models, each with a totemic champion.

The British model, based on Oxbridge, regarded the university as a place for educating 'well rounded people'. Academics were largely teachers (not researchers), and related to students in parental mode as members of one university fraternity. By insisting on students' residency in a college, this Newmanesque model made the university a finishing school for the lucky few. In turn, they'd assume leadership roles in the church, politics and the secular professions, while together upholding a strong sense of 'national culture'. In France, by contrast, Napoleon Bonaparte ensured that higher education became hard-wired to the felt needs of government and nation. The system of specialised *grandes ecoles* was created in order to produce new cadres of certified professionals in engineering, mining, the law and so on. These professionals would be specialists, inculcated with an ethic of public service and confident in their own expertise. France's existing universities never really got out from under the shadow of the *grand ecoles* once the latter were set-up. Finally, there was the German model of the university as a place where research and teaching were sides of the same coin. Inspired by Wilhelm von Humboldt, the medieval corporate model was updated so that academics would be free to undertake research which, in and through the act of teaching, would be codified in growing bodies of disciplinary knowledge. Towards the end of their studies students would be addressing the very questions that perplexed and energised their teachers, thus 'thinking for themselves'. This departed from the medieval university model of teaching as, in effect, indoctrination.

The German model, it seems to me, is by no means antiquated. To appreciate its significance, we need to recall the context in which Humboldt's ideas were formed. A child of the Enlightenment, which itself replayed the dissident ethic of the Protestant Reformation; he saw universities as potential embodiments of the Kantian injunction 'Dare to know!' – an injunction whose power arose from the challenge it posed to ecclesiastic, political, monarchical and other forms of authority. For Humboldt, the university would be an agent of change by creating new knowledge and then, through teaching, distributing it to those citizens who had been admitted to the institution before assuming positions in (and perhaps even altering) the wider society. In practice, of course, the Humboldtian ideal was compromised almost from the get go. Because German universities relied so heavily on state funding from the early nineteenth century, they could only buy their independence at a cost – thus rendering it putative. Freedom of research was guaranteed by the government, but only if academics agreed to educate a new national elite drawn from the aristocracy and emerging bourgeoisie. In this way, the dynamism of research became divorced from teaching, whose function was to ensure social reproduction by way of relatively fixed curricula. Indeed, academic research itself soon congealed into various Kuhnian 'paradigms', thus stifling the critical spirit. Meanwhile, growing state demands for 'relevant research' were satisfied after Humboldt's death by the creation of various Kaiser Wilhelm Institutes (now Max Planck Institutes).

This deformation of the German model has occurred beyond Germany. For instance, it has been evident in the British redbrick universities for decades, so too America's most prestigious public and private universities. This reminds us that the supposed post-1990 'break' in the character of Western universities is a myth. In reality, we have to go back much further in time in order to locate the erosion of their institutional freedom. Here, for example, is Anthony Wilden writing from within the US university sector back in 1972: 'not "to publish or perish" in an industry whose product is "knowledge" is unthinkable … The so-called "knowledge explosion" of the last 30 years has little to do with knowledge. It has to do with knowledge as a commodity …' (xxiii–xxiv). In this light, Fuller offers us an interesting insight on the differences between Western universities during the period of 'welfare capitalism' (circa 1945–1979) and that of 'neoliberal globalisation' (roughly 1980–today). In his view, it's not that universities have been made qualitatively more responsive to exogenous demands during the latter era. Instead, it's that the recent sharp decline in the unit of resource provided by the state presents universities with a stark choice: either they more intensively chase alternative sources of income in order to remain as large as they presently are, or else contract and hive-off a number of current functions. I'll return to this choice below since the current retrenchment in public funding makes it an ever more important one.

Reimagining Universities II:
The Umbilical Connection with Republican Democracy

Having briefly considered different models of the university, I want now to discuss political theory. To my mind, it's impossible to discuss the 'proper' identity and role of universities in abstraction from a worked-up conception of how any society should be governed. This is where some traditional defences of things like 'academic freedom', 'pure inquiry' and 'blue skies research' usually come unstuck. For it is unclear why one would have an institution that promotes any of these without some wider theory of their value or purpose. At worst, defences of universities' autonomy can come across as self-serving pleas for career academics to be left alone – as if universities had no wider social role to play. Following Fuller (2000), I would suggest that civic republicanism provides the necessary rationale for their existence today.

Civic republicanism is conception of democratic rule that is, in the twenty-first century, more an ideal than an actuality. To understand why it is an ideal worth fighting for, imagine three opposed scenarios in the production and consumption of knowledge (cf. Fuller, ibid. 11–15). In the first, only those who can pay for knowledge – as either contractors or students/learners – determine its quantity and quality. The market rules and is justified in liberal terms: individuals are entitled to whatever knowledge they want, as long as they can pay. Epistemic workers are thus enjoined to give the market what it wants. In the second scenario, only knowledge that does not pose a threat to existing orthodoxy or established group identities can be produced and disseminated. Anything else is deemed too risky, controversial or destabilising. Epistemic workers thus operate within existing frameworks and steer clear of radically new knowledge. In the third scenario a few especially well-endowed public and private funders pay for research and teaching on their own terms. Epistemic workers are thus disempowered and become ciphers of dominant interests. The problems with all three scenarios are obvious enough. Given the economic inequality characteristic of all contemporary societies, the first scenario equates to financial censorship and the silencing of those who lack the resources to enter the market. In the second scenario the problem is one of ideological censorship: people become afraid to provide alternative insights on the world for fear of offending current opinion or the beliefs of particular social groups. In the third scenario censorship arises because of stark asymmetries of institutional power: a few dominant actors call the epistemic shots for everyone else. Thus, in all three cases knowledge becomes subject to very sharp constraints, be they economic, social or political.

In contrast to all this, a civic republican abhors undue censorship and places a premium on epistemic diversity, dialogue, dissent and the formation of a never-final consensus. Civic republicans regard all adult members of a polity as, in principle, equals in two senses: (i) they have a right to be heard as individuals; and (ii) they have an obligation to comment on matters of common concern insofar as they belong to a society in which their own lives are necessarily affected by the thoughts and actions of other citizens. In respect of the latter, 'the common interest' goes far beyond matters that are formally 'political', such as immigration policy, healthcare provision or environmental policy. It also includes all those questions that speak to the intellectual, emotional and physical lives of contemporary citizens: questions such 'who am I?', 'why is the world as it is?', 'what are my values?', 'are we alone in the universe?', 'how should I live', and 'why do other people not share my own beliefs?'. The civic republican ideal is a genuinely 'open society' where all existing norms, values, beliefs, identities and prejudices can be questioned, not by resort to physical conflict but through discursive conflict – conducted according to agreed standards of rationality and civility. This is very much an ideal – in the sense of an aspiration – because civic republicans are acutely sensitive to the subtle and not-so-subtle ways in which knowledge of all kinds comes to reflect the perverse logics operative in the three above-mentioned scenarios. The ideal's rationale is simple: unless epistemic diversity, dialogue and critique is properly institutionalised, individuals can easily become the victims of others' agendas or else passive believers of others' ideas – often without knowing it.

Clearly, for civic republicanism to be more than an ideal one needs citizens who are not only well educated – that is, both knowledgeable and able to ask pertinent and probing questions. They also need to be secure in their own right to speak, and to be confident enough to learn from others' knowledge and to admit their own errors when necessary. In this context, we get a clearer sense of Humboldt's original vision of the university as a quasi-autonomous institution committed to the unity of advanced research and teaching. Through research new ideas, facts and insights are *created* that may *challenge* existing cognitive, moral or aesthetic mindsets. So long as this research meets standards of rigour certified by the wider research community then it's deemed acceptable, regardless of its precise content. Through teaching, this research is *disseminated* beyond its originators, but *not* as a potential new dogma that will replace current orthodoxy. Instead, through well constructed curricula students are exposed to a range of not necessarily consistent or commensurable knowledge-claims. They learn to accept, reject or synthesise them through a process of careful consideration whose end-point is not 'Truth' but a set of provisional understandings that might, in time, be found wanting and thus in need of revision. In this way they come to embody the ethic of 'the open society'. For them, knowledge is not simply a 'positional good' that confers a personal advantage to those who possess it; instead, it's seen as constitutively social.

Given all this, if the young Humboldt – who was a civic republican – were alive today he would shake his head at the state of British universities. First, he would object to the volume of vocational teaching and training in the sector, most of its divorced from any 'research frontier'. Second, he would object to the number of 'professional schools' found on campus, again because their aim is to inculcate knowledge on an instrumental means-ends basis. Third, he would object to campus-based CR, because it's too often client-driven and divorced from the university's pedagogic functions. Fourth, he would lament the growing divide between research (as measured by the RAE/REF system) and increasingly mechanical forms of undergraduate teaching (which are measured by different metrics, and where text-books, worsening staff-student ratios and fewer tutorials/ seminars are the norm). In the fifth place, he would regard the fracturing of many academic subjects (like human geography) into relatively discrete, mutually indifferent research communities as an abrogation of the critical, dialogical spirit of civic republicanism. He would say the same of disciplines like economics, in which major paradigms crowd-out alternative perspectives and are too powerful. Finally, he would object to the British state's attempt to subordinate universities to the executive's agenda on the following grounds: there ought to be distinction between the state as a public institution which guarantees those public goods necessary for a healthy democracy to function, and the particular ideological aims of any ruling party. Once ruling parties reconfigure public institutions to suit their own partisan ends then the very basis of democracy starts to be eroded.

Let me be clear. Humboldt, like any civic republican, would not object to many of the things that today occur on British university campuses on principle. It's not the practices *per se* that are in question. Instead, the objection would be this: many of those things should occur *elsewhere*, in different institutions with distinct missions – such as the former polytechnics, independent foundations, corporate laboratories, specialist training institutes, government research centres, and so on. For Humboldt, a university is not only a very *specific* institution in terms of its identity and goals; it is also *necessary*, though by no means sufficient, for the achievement of a genuinely self-governing society

Reimagining Universities III: Sustaining the Public Sphere

To round-out this normative vision of the university today, in light of long-term erosion of its institutional autonomy in Britain and elsewhere, let me briefly connect it to the idea and reality of 'the public'. One of the great ironies of contemporary Britain is this: we have more graduates and a supposedly more educated citizenry than ever before in our history, and yet there's a widespread feeling that ignorance, philistinism, and a preference for 'infotainment' define our cultural milieu. This concern has been expressed by liberals and social democrats as much as it has by cultural conservatives. Membership of political parties is in sharp decline; voter turn-outs are appallingly low; trust in politicians, the political process and the integrity of public institutions has reached its nadir; the 'serious' parts of the print, televisual and online media are greatly outweighed by those dedicated to light entertainment, sensationalism and the cult of celebrity; public broadcasting has given way to private provision; shopping and consumption have become central to many people's weekly routines and sense of self; and it seems that 'leisure', in all its forms, has become the dominant activity when people are not at work.

All this would be fine if Britain – like all major capitalist democracies – did not face a set of extraordinary domestic and international challenges. These include:

coping with a major financial crisis and reconfiguring the country's economic base; responding to the twin threats of energy insecurity and the effects of carbon-dependency on the earth-atmosphere system; dealing with a multi-cultural society in which recent immigrants loom large, in the context of the 'war on terror' and radical Muslim insurgency; creating a transport infrastructure that is fast, affordable, reliable and 'clean'; coping with a growing number of retired and elderly people; dealing with persistent social inequality along the axes of class, gender, ethnicity, sexual preference and geographic location; and determining what our role should be in a world where US power in on the wane and the power of major far eastern countries is on the rise. These are, of course, all questions of public policy and politics, but there are others to ponder too. Consider these examples: religious leaders like Archbishop Rowan Williams have persistently asked about the quality and substance of Briton's spiritual lives; environmentalists like George Monbiot have consistently challenged prevailing practices of commodity consumption in the name of social and ecological justice; and social democrats like the journalist Madeleine Bunting have suggested that our 'quality of life' has declined even as many families' material wealth increased through the New Labour boom years. These arguments speak to ever-present questions about the 'good life', about a 'life worth living' and about what is to be human in a world of over 6 billion people whose lives and well-being are profoundly co-dependent.

Williams, Monbiot and Bunting are all, in their different ways, 'public intellectuals' – a species in decline, according to Frank Furedi (2004). That is to say, they speak and write in the hope that people quite unlike themselves will not only consider but possibly be persuaded by what it is they communicate. Like most public intellectuals in Britain, neither Williams, Monbiot nor Bunting are located in a university environment. Does this suggest that British academics have weak ties to the national public and sub-sections thereof? I would argue yes – though this answer, I realise, begs the question of what precisely 'the public' is and why universities should have a relationship with it in the first place. The term public has a close etymological connection to the idea of a republic, a self-governing society of equals in which the interests of individuals and groups must be mediated through the interests of all. It describes a collective willing and able to deliberate on issues of common concern. This collective need not be ethnically or culturally homogenous since a public is not defined by its members' personal or group identity. In Western Europe, where the idea of a public was first made flesh, this collective required a literal and metaphorical 'space' in which it could exist – thus permitting individuals to take-on an identity outside the spheres of the market, the home and the state. Democrats have always insisted on the need for a proper 'public sphere'. But if the public inhabiting it is disinterested, ignorant, dogmatic or fearful of discursive conflict then democracy can become nominal rather than substantive. A robust public is thus a *purposeful creation* not a spontaneous invention: it must be slowly built and actively sustained, and this requires effort and resources.

In recent years, many critics have bemoaned what David Marquand (2004) calls 'the decline of the public' in Britain and many other Western democracies. This is linked to wider worries that democracy is today in crisis, a contemporary travesty of the ideas proposed by its original champions (such as Tom Paine and John Stuart Mill). If these worries are justified, then we see why a rethinking of the university along the lines I've suggested is so important. Universities should be key institutions for equipping individuals to be willing and able members of a genuine public. Their principal role is not to increase national wealth (in the economic sense of 'wealth') nor to train the next generation of workers nor to serve the particularistic needs of various named 'stakeholders'. Ideally, they should equip both their own members, and those who pass through them as students, with the capacity to resist two deformations of 'the public' identified by Andrew Gamble (2004). The first relates to complexity and involves a public becoming *cynical* in the face of a world that seems confusing, contradictory and difficult to fathom. The second also relates to complexity and involves a public choosing *populism* because it offers simple and instant solutions to current problems. To my mind, without institutions that can equip people to resist these deformations of their public role, 'democracy' becomes increasingly weak. The same can be said when any of the three knowledge pathologies described earlier become a reality. Along with organisations comprising the mass media, universities should – in my view – be pillars sustaining the public domain.

This, it seems to me, is the proper context in which defences of university autonomy and academic freedom should be presented and understood. Otherwise, they can be misunderstood as conservative pleas that professors are allowed to do what they like, regardless. The point of autonomy and freedom, I would argue, is not that the wider world be *shut-out*. Rather, it gives universities a special ability to *resist being colonised by one or other agenda, actor or mindset issuing from beyond it*. Despite the changes recounted earlier in this chapter, British universities – especially Oxbridge and the redbricks – still enjoy a degree of autonomy. Likewise, academic freedom is not (yet) either a myth or an anachronism; it still exists and it needs to be enhanced. What a pity that so many people who still enjoy the protections it affords have no real understanding of why it exists or to what ends it ought to be used.

What is to be Done?

In the previous three sections I've made a normative case that amounts to a strong critique of British universities as presently constituted. Clearly, I'm one of the idealists I described earlier in this chapter. It is one thing to present a vision and arguments supporting it; but it's quite another to make this vision come true. In this penultimate section I will present some ideas about how universities might be restructured looking ahead. I'm not saying *every* institution that today possesses the title 'university' should be altered, but that we ensure that we do have institutions whose identity and purpose is consistent with the normative case I've made. My preference is to call these institutions (and *only* these institutions) universities. This preference respects the semantic specificity and history of the term: a university is not a place where all knowledges are synthesised and somehow made complete, but where a wide range of novel or even conflicting evidence, argument, concepts, values and principles are brought into a critical conversation. Note, then, that I see no compelling reason for CR to occur in a university so defined.

British universities, as we've seen, are today 'multiversities'. Their research and teaching together perform a wide range of functions and serve the needs of numerous and varied constituencies. But why do we have so many institutions – over 150 – seeking to do more-or-less the same things more-or-less (un)successfully? Why not encourage these institutions to differentiate and niche themselves? And why continue to have all these institutions beholden to the central state for funding – unless the state can offer guarantees that it will not use all of them as an extension of the specific agendas of elected parties? In light of these questions here are some proposals for change:

1. Create a set of universities whose mission is consistent with that outlined above. These would probably include Oxbridge and a set of redbrick universities, but there may be others too. These institutions should be given a 'fresh start' by having their charters renewed or redescribed.

2. These universities would be genuinely free of undue state interference or the demands of other powerful actors or constituencies. They would be self-governing, implying the end of current managerialist practices, externally-driven audits and a return to democratic decision making.

3. These universities would place a premium on reuniting research and teaching, with both operating in an environment where 'academic freedom' is meaningful. This would achieve a number of things. Academic research published purely for consumption by other academics would decline because 'teachability' would become a key criterion for even the most esoteric research. Students would be exposed to new findings at the 'research frontier', and obliged to evaluate them critically in light of existing bodies of knowledge. This means that textbooks – classically a genre of 'instructional' writing – would find no place in degrees beyond the first year (unless they subverted the monological textbook conventions).

4. These universities would revisit the idea of a well-designed curriculum for all degrees awarded, thus reversing the drift towards pick-and-mix modular programmes that are often less than sum of their parts. The curricula would, for any subject, be constructed with a civic republican sensibility in mind and cultivate knowledgeable, confident, critically minded graduates. Standards would be high, with a lot of emphasis on formative (not just summative) assessment. The volume and frequency of formal student assessment would decline, and the onus ultimately placed on students for their own learning.

5. These universities would publicly reject the idea that their degrees exist principally in order to train students for paid employment. Likewise, they would publicly reject the idea that their research activities serve the particularistic needs of external parties. They would declare themselves to be 'public' institutions – not necessarily part of the 'public sector' but free-standing entities committed to the ideals of the public domain.

6. These universities would down-size, hive-off a number of current activities and simplify their strategic objectives. Funding would be redeployed towards supporting excellent peer review research and excellent teaching. Staff-student ratios would greatly improve, either by hiring more tenured academics or greatly reducing student numbers.

7. If, in support of 1–6 above, state funding is insufficient or deemed undesirable, then these universities should consider going private in the financial sense. This could be achieved by one-off endowments from central government, student fees and contributions from alumni on the Ivy League model of the USA.

8. These universities would be agents of social justice by ensuring fair access for talented students from underprivileged background and talented researchers who do not hail from the usual social groups. Their role would not be the creation of a self-regarding 'elite' drawn from well-off families, but a continuous stream of capable individuals from a mixture of social backgrounds.

9. To the extent that these universities offer 'service' at the local, national or international levels, it should be to and for various publics, not special interests or discrete groups with narrow or specific interests.

10. Internally, these universities would disallow any one Faculty from becoming too large or powerful. Thus, the humanities, social sciences and biophysical sciences would be roughly balanced.

This 'new deal' for a greatly slimmed down British university sector of (say) 15–20 organisations will, I realise, be enormously difficult to implement. It implies that all other British higher education institutions find their own place and purpose within a highly differentiated system of training, education and research. The barriers to change are formidable. But this is, perhaps, a propitious time to think about structural transformation of higher education, in Britain and elsewhere. I say this because of the already-mentioned funding squeeze ahead.

This is a critical juncture in the life of British universities. Swingeing reductions in central government budgets – resulting from the recent financial crisis and subsequent recession – will force them to make some tough decisions. In this light, the response of leading universities to Peter Mandelson's recent funding cut announcement is disappointingly unimaginative. Here is Leeds University vice-chancellor Mike Arthur and director general of the Russell Group Wendy Piatt, writing to Mandelson in *The Guardian*: '... our gold standard system could be replaced with one of silver, bronze or worse ... We live in a world where ideas, innovation and entrepreneurialism are key to prosperity and wellbeing. Our universities are critical to supporting this agenda ... If politicians don't act now, they'll be faced with a meltdown in a sector that is vital to our national posterity' (2010: 30). Behind this seemingly reasonable defence of current state funding levels are some all too familiar ideas, namely: that central government should fund all HE institutions; that all these institutions should pursue their current agendas; and that universities exist to serve the needs of a 'knowledge economy'. As one respondent argued, 'We need a system that recognises the need for different types of equally valued higher and further education (academic and technical, theoretical and practical) ... This is not elitist but does differentiate on the basis of function and objective' (Williams 2010: 43; see also Jenkins 2010).

Conclusions

This has been a chapter of two closely related halves. By setting university-based CR in a wider epistemic context, I sought to characterise our supposed 'knowledge society' and then, on this basis, I took issue with the way British universities are today governed. Having diagnosed current maladies I went on to suggest a new identity and role for universities, inspired by one historic vision (out of several) and the political philosophy known as civic republicanism. I am well aware that my aspirations will appear utopian to many readers, even supposing they concede the force of my arguments. But I'd prefer to be utopian than have nothing to aim for by shrugging my shoulders and accepting the *status quo* uncritically. If nothing else, I hope this chapter has given some readers pause for thought and a reason to reflect more deeply on their own practices within or towards the university.

Chapter 14

Reconstructing the Knowledge Business

Rob Imrie and Chris Allen

The UK research councils are arguably the custodians of traditions that seek to propagate the highest intellectual and academic standards of research conducted by university academics. As much is evident from the mission statement of the Economic and Social Research Council (ESRC 2009: 1) who say that their objective is 'to promote and support, by any means, high-quality basic, strategic and applied research ...'. Other research councils say likewise and concur with the ESRC that a crucial part of their work is 'to advance knowledge and provide trained social scientists who meet the needs of users and beneficiaries, thereby contributing to the economic competitiveness of the United Kingdom ...' (ESRC 2009: 1). Here, the research councils are responding to broader government directives that, in the words of the former Minister for Business, Skills, and Innovation, Peter Mandelson (2009: 2), is to place British 'universities at the heart of policy on our future growth and prosperity and ... that is exactly where they should be'.

This is an unequivocal statement yet, as chapters in this book show, one that flies in the face of Mandelson's (2009: 13) assertion that 'there is no tension between a more strategic view of Britain's universities as critical to our knowledge economy and our future economic growth and their essential autonomy or their cultural and civilisational role'. The chapters in this book take a different view in seeking to show the contradictions in such statements, and highlighting some of the ways in which the academy is entwined in a struggle to (re)define the essence of what scholarship is or ought to be. The insertion of the market into the processes of knowledge production and consumption in the academy is transforming the operations of education, characterised by Mayo (2003) as the supplanting of issues such as social justice with those of marketability. The universities' *raison d'être* is no longer to serve the public interest, broadly defined, but to interact with government and corporate programmes relating to the enhancement of economic competitiveness.

This utilitarian turn can be defined as the emergence of the knowledge business, or strategic changes to the organisational structures and practices of the academy, and in the value dispositions of its members. The objective is to make higher education work better to serve the business community, while, simultaneously, turning the academy into a business to fulfil, in part, Mandelson's (2009: 3) dictate, for the 'universities to focus more on commercialising the fruits of their endeavour'. A manifestation of the knowledge business, as discussed by the chapters in the book, is the orientation of research towards 'useful' and 'applied' programmes of work, increasingly through the context of contracts with government and business partners (also, see Deem 2002; Slaughter and Rhoades 2004). Knowledge, and its production, then, becomes something which is not necessarily defined by intellectual agendas controlled by the academy, but, rather, by the entanglement of academies in a complexity of external organisational settings.

This complexity, for observers such as Mayo (2003: 38), has emerged out of the last twenty years or so of change in higher education, and it is the outcome of the imposition of a hegemonic discourse that is, as he says, 'technical rational and focuses primarily on what works' (also, see May 2005, Slaughter and Rhoades, 2004). Its manifestations, as described in this book, are many, and include the commodification of cultural products, such as learning and knowledge, as part of a broader degeneration of the intellectual content of the academy. This degeneration includes, so contributors to the book argue, dilution of academics' control over setting research agendas, and the increasing prioritisation of mundane, even banal, research questions narrowly focused on the production of a tangible outcome or product. This is not surprising given the business-facing orientation of the research councils, and as George Monbiot (2009) has aptly asked, why is it that the research councils are run by business people from the private sector and operate like 'corporate research departments'?

The answer to this is, in part, government seeking to change the organisational fabric of the academy, as part of a process to transform the values and practices of academics towards making their research relevant. Such sentiments underpin major research initiatives sponsored by government, including the Foresight projects that had their first phase from 1994 to 1999. The objective of the programme was to engage academics in conducting research 'with the avowed purpose of increasing the wealth creation of the UK and ... to improve the quality of life of UK citizens' (Wood, undated). During its initial phase, there were 16 Technology Panels set up to explore different areas of social and economic life, ranging from agriculture to financial services. Academics chaired two panels; the rest were chaired by people from business, including individuals such as Jim Streeton of Standard Life (Ageing Population Panel), Colin Sharman of KPMG International (Crime Prevention Panel), and Keith Clarke of Kvaerner Construction Ltd and Transport (Built Environment Panel).

The notion of relevance, in Foresight and other projects, is precise; it is 'to encourage industry, academia and government to identify research needs and market opportunities and threats for the future' (Wood, undated). This is a forthright approach to interlink the operations of markets with the skills and resources of the academy, and it reflects the government's intent on making the universities work well in relation to the pursuit of agendas relating to economic growth and efficiency objectives. For Peter Mandelson (2009: 1), the appropriate remit of the academy is to 'turn more of the knowledge that is generated in UK universities into jobs and growth, especially by bringing business and universities together to collaborate'. Similar intimations are evident in other countries, such as Sweden, the USA, and Australia, with the former Minister for Higher Education in Australia noting, as far back as 1998, that the country's success 'as a knowledge based economy will depend upon our ability to innovate – to generate new knowledge, ideas and technologies through research' (PMSCIC 1998: 1).

These observations point towards the importance of universities achieving commercial outputs and impacts related to their research, and ensuring there is a closer fit between research agendas and the needs of the business community. A new world view or paradigm appears to have emerged that, as described and evaluated by contributors to the book, includes the understanding that research should align itself with meeting the needs of a modern economy. Part of the paradigmatic shift is institutional and organisational and relates to the new networks that, increasingly, define how research is to be organised and conducted. As academics become entangled in the 'entrepreneurial turn', it appears that, to echo Krimsky (1995: 125), 'a new concept of scientific autonomy and public responsibility is emerging'. This is (re)defining the roles and responsibilities of academics in ways whereby their (moral) obligations are less to do with serving some broader public interest, and more to do with delivering a product or output that is useful to specific and powerful groups of interests.

This is particularly evident in recent changes to the ways in which academics' work is to be measured and judged by government. In 2013, the UK university system will be subject to another round of quality review by government, as part of its process of allocating public funds to the higher educational sector. This review system is, somewhat misleadingly, called the 'Research Excellence Framework' (REF) and its objective is to steer academics so that they can contribute to 'a dynamic and internationally competitive research sector that makes a major contribution to economic prosperity' (HEfCE 2009: 5). Part of the process revolves around pushing academics towards research that can demonstrate 'economic and social impact'. It is proposed that 25 per cent of future research funding will be allocated on the basis of the 'economic and social impact' of research, and, not surprisingly, many academics see this as an attack on the integrity of the academy (see, for example, Bridges 2009; Educators for Reform 2009).

The contributions to this book highlight that what is at stake here is no less than the status of knowledge in society, with one organisation, the University and College Union (UCU, 2009) defending the Mertonian view of the university, or, as they have asserted, 'universities must continue to be spaces in which the spirit of adventure thrives and where researchers enjoy academic freedom to push back the boundaries of knowledge in their disciplines'. For the UCU, the REF's impact agenda is anathema to the Mertonian spirit and, as they have argued, 'as academics, researchers and higher education professionals we believe that it is counterproductive to make funding for the best research conditional on its perceived economic and social benefits'. Similar points have been made by others, with Corbyn (2008) describing how 2,300 academics signed a petition delivered to the Prime Minister's Office in 2008 requesting the reversal of policies to 'direct funds to projects whose outcomes are determined to have a significant "impact"'.

The major concern of academics is that the REF is no more than a disciplinary apparatus to ensure universities' fiscal propriety as part of welfare state restructuring, a process that will lead to, so the fear is, the closure of departments deemed not to be contributing to the outputs as defined by quality audit exercises (see Harley and Lee 1997). These fears are not without substance given what has happened since the last quality audit of UK university research in 2008. This process, entitled the research assessment exercise (RAE), has, in its wake, led to a retrenchment in the UK university environment, with units of assessment not coming up to the mark closed down, and academics judged to be 'off the pace' fired or forced to take voluntary redundancy packages (see Allred and Miller 2007). Over the last 18 months there has been a purge in the UK higher educational system, compounded by government funding cutbacks to universities in the wake of a global recession.

These changes are an inescapable part of the business logic pervading the academy, in which returns to investment, premised on 'picking winners' and investing only where a profit is likely to transpire, is paramount. As much is admitted by Peter Mandelson (2009: 5) who argues that 'the modern global economy puts a premium on specialization'. For Mandelson (2009), this points towards the prioritisation of research activities in universities, particularly in relation to science and technology. As he says, 'low carbon, digital communications, life science, the creative industries: these are all absolutely reliant on high levels of knowledge, skill and innovation. They will also draw heavily on our capacity for research and our ability to commercialise it' (Mandelson 2009: 5). The fear for those academics outside of the chosen winners, or select specialisms, is abandonment and that their subjects, and research, will be deemed to be superfluous, even irrelevant, in the changing university environment.

A further implication is that the new paradigm, in which the REF is its leading exemplar, is part of a continued diminution of scholarship founded on the principles of what the UCU (2009) describe as 'curiosity-driven research'. This observation is particularly salient in relation to the social sciences and arts and humanities, or in subject areas where the intuitive, even instinctual, behaviour of its members is to engage in critique of the objects and subjects of society. Such activities are, potentially, anathema to the knowledge business and, as Nussbaum (2010: 2) has argued, the shrinkage of the arts and humanities globally is not unconnected to the fears that 'educators for economic growth' have of such subject areas. These fears relate to the critical faculties that arts and humanities seeks to instil in those that it educates, and to inculcate its students with what Matthew Arnold referred to as 'the best that has been thought and said (quoted in Reisz 2010: 32).

Such dispositions, or discourses, of what knowledge is or ought to be, are a problem for the new cadre of knowledge managers confronted with the conundrum of how to deal with the inner-worldliness of the intellectual, or what Lewis Coser (1965: 135–136) has described as 'the general tension between the intellectuals' preoccupation with general and abstract values and the routine institutions of society' (also, see Bourdieu 1998; Deem 2002; Lyotard 1995; May 2005). The antithetical relationships between the knowledge business and the intellectual are ones whereby the former requires a closure of questions and the finality of dialogue. In contrast, the latter revolves around the opening up of the world, or what Wilson (1981: 38) describes as a process 'by which assumptions are questioned, early findings re-examined, and new avenues of inquiry identified'.

These orientations pose a threat to embedding the knowledge business into the academy and, as chapters in the book have described, the response by government officials and university managers is the development of widespread programmes of behaviour change through a re-institutionalisation of both pedagogic and research practices. The process is taking its lead from the REF that is premised upon its ability to steer and manage academic performance in ways commensurate with cultivating the knowledge business in the academy. As the REF consultative document says: 'we will be able to use the REF to encourage desirable behaviours at three levels: the behaviour of individual researchers ... research units ... [and] whole Higher Educational Institutes' (HEfCE: 9). For Alldred and Miller (2007: 147), such steerage heralds a system in which 'as academics become increasingly self-conscious of performance indicators and, individually more visible through them, we are more tightly disciplined by them'.

The government's alignment of universities with business and economic values is particularly entwined with the development of instruments or techniques to ensure the delivery of the enterprising academy. Such instrumentation, as documented in some of the book's chapters, include: a realignment of post graduate research training towards serving a definable business-based skills agenda; the mimicking of business organisation, especially in relation to differential pay rates, the development of a bonus culture, and the decentring of fiscal control into cost centres; the development of a cadre of university business managers responsible for (re)organising the academic labour process along entrepreneurial lines; the emergence of a managerial culture based on performance management and disciplinary techniques; and, the re-branding of universities as part of a progressive cosmopolitan agenda that seeks to extend the reach of knowledge to a global customer base.

Each and every one of these 'instrumentations' is symptomatic of, so contributors to the book argue, a shift in values and practices of the academy towards serving external clientele, and setting in place the means to do so. One example is the globalisation of the academy and the fastest growing part of the knowledge business relates to the export-orientation of the universities, a trend highlighted by Peter Mandelson (2009) in noting that 'we will throw our weight behind UK universities looking to export their brands globally'. Few universities fail to claim their 'world class' status and their outward looking persona based on the excellence of their research and teaching. The objective is market expansion and capturing added value by mimicking business organisational behaviour. A study of this phenomenon concluded that the claims to 'world class' by universities were 'vague or even tautological' and emphasised 'reputational aspects rather than concrete examples' (see Levin and Wook Jeong 2006: 3).

Another example of the instrumentation of the academy is outlined in a recently issued management paper at a leading Russell University in the UK, in which the vision for the future in relation to the impact agenda is outlined as closer ties with external organisation: 'Through enhanced partnership, collaboration and networking with public, third and commercial sectors, all departments within [the School] have the potential to sit at the heart of government thinking in developing public policy across a range of specialist areas; to lead the way in the development of organisational management and delivery within the commercial and public sectors'. This can be achieved, so the document suggests, by a mixed menu of initiatives, including the development of consultancy, partnerships, and executive education aimed at external professionals from government, the public sector, and business. The document concludes by telling academics 'to celebrate impact where it occurs'.

An outcome of such (re)institutionalisation is the absorption of academics into a new discourse of knowledge, its production and dissemination, and the development of the organisational basis to enable the transformation in the nature of what the academy is. For Chomsky (2003), the unrelenting managerialism of the universities appears to be creating institutions that are the embodiment of passivity and conformity by virtue of the acquiescence of academics to the knowledge business. This process involves, as contributors to the book have shown, complicity by academics or what Zipin and Brennan (2003) refer to as 'silent self-suppression', including conformity with the emergent values and norms of the knowledge business. Allred and Miller's (2007: 159) critique of performance instruments suggests likewise, and, as they observe, academics' 'commitments have been powerfully reworked so that we have become instrumental in our own exploitation, over-complying or over-zealous'.

The implication of this process is described by Chomsky (2003) as the university betraying its public trust by virtue of its social scientists not acting as counter weights to, and critics of, state and military power. For Chomsky (2003), university social science is failing the public because of its practitioners, both academics and managers, becoming agents of reactionary institutions, set on serving sectional, partisan, interests, in which closure of, and restricted access to, research findings is one of the key features. However, this understanding, while insightful, is qualified by some of the contributors to the book who suggest that academics' attitudes and practices are part of unconscious bodily actions, related to a 'mechanics of power' (Foucault 1975: 138). This is part of a process whereby individuals are rendered docile or, as Foucault (1975: 138) suggests, their bodies are subject to 'a machinery of power that explores it, breaks it down and rearranges it'.

The paradigmatic shift towards assessing impact and encouraging relevance is also seen by some as encouraging sensationalist and second-rate forms of knowledge akin to the development of a 'circus culture'. This is the view of a number of contributors to the book, and these contributions add to the weight of a viewpoint emanating from commentators such as Pierre Bourdieu, Steve Fuller, Frank Furedi and others critical of the alleged devaluation of the status of the intellectual in society. It is suggested that the knowledge business is the 'subordination of knowledge to pragmatic objectives', and is inimical to, as Furedi (2005: 72) puts it, 'experimentation and the development of powerful ideas'. For others, such as Lyotard (1995), the knowledge business is also a 'network of exchanges in which cultural objects are commodities', a process that is part of a broader, societal, shift towards a prescribed or pre-set institutionalisation of what knowledge is or ought to be.

The chapters in the book bear testimony to these observations and show that the knowledge business is antithetical to an inquiring and open persona that understands the world not as closed or fixed, or that is easily amenable to answers or solutions to problems posed by research questions. Rather, as Lyotard (1995) suggests, given the messy and indeterminate nature of human social relations, an objective of the academy is, or ought to be, the 'perpetual displacement of questions' so that 'answering is never achieved'. Instead, Lyotard (1995) calls for a resistance to the market, the commodification of ideas, and the reduction of knowledge to 'the simple and naive exchangeability of things in our world'. This reflects the views of many others, with Robins (2006) noting that the objective of the universities ought to be about promoting the 'democratic intellect', by counteracting cooption of knowledge for partial ends or its use to promote social distinction.

This message is an undercurrent of contributors' chapters, and especially to the fore in the latter part of Noel Castree's intriguing 'reimaginations' of what the university ought to be or become. We would agree with, and subscribe to, Castree's sentiment that the university is significant as it is '*necessary*, though by no means sufficient, for the achievement of a genuinely self-governing society'. For Castree, and other contributors to the book, the appropriate role of the university is not to increase national wealth or train people to fit into the labour market, but, rather, to contribute to the building and sustenance of public life, or a public sphere that is the basis for a functioning democratic society. This requires the university to provide the resources and skills to enable people to acquire the knowledge to resist popular and populist understandings of the world. As Castree rightly suggests, the objective of university education is to resist the production of knowledge that fails to discourage public cynicism and presents 'simple and instant solutions to current problems'.

These observations go to the heart of the question of 'what is a university for', a question that governments, more or less without opposition, are answering for the universities by imposing the market on the teaching, research, and the administration and management of the academy. One of us used to pose the question to candidates invited for interview for academic posts, but never felt that a considered answer was given. Usually, candidates see the academy as the next step on the road to the labour market, and rarely as a place for reflexive learning and engagement. Indeed, the question of what is a university for is seldom asked or discussed by members of the academy, and neither of us can remember it being debated by colleagues in our respective institutions.

We would suggest that the starting point for such a debate is to critique and reconstruct the knowledge business because it is based on values that are, potentially, doctrinaire, dogmatic, and authoritarian and a threat to freedom of speech, thought, and action. Its value-base seeks to define knowledge as something that has to fit into, and serve, the interests of a select, and particular, part of society. But like all doctrines, proponents of the knowledge business present its partiality as a generality and something that is 'good for all'. This is not so, and there is need, we feel, for the universities to rediscover their roots in what Kronman (2007) terms secular humanism, that is, the commitment to free inquiry and the opposition to anything that attempts to censor inquiry or to impose orthodoxy on beliefs and values (also, see Kurtz 1983). The objective is perhaps obvious but is no less than developing the capacity for critical intelligence in both the individual and the community.

Here we are in agreement with Kronman (2007), who suggests that the universities *raison d'être* is to deal with existential issues of fundamental importance to the understanding of the human condition. For Kronman (2007), the significance of secular humanism, as the basis for pedagogic practices and knowledge production is its emphasis on the collective and the public, or what he terms 'our dependence on structures of value larger and more lasting than those that any individual can create'. Such ideas are suggestive about the directions of a debate that, we feel, ought not to be about how we do business with business, but about how we can (re)capture, and re-orientate, our civil institutions and society towards a plurality of educational ideals that can restore the moral integrity of academic research. This integrity ought to be characterised by freedom from interference by powerful and select interest groups seeking to mould knowledge to fit their pre-conceived purposes.

This takes us back, in part, to the Mertonian ideal of science. It seems to us that such ideals can still provide a basis by which to judge, and regulate, the actions of the academy, and its inter actions with the broadcloth of society. If the point and purpose of a university is, in Kronman's terms, to study the value and purpose of life, there has to be trust that the knowledge produced accords with much more than the partialities of a business agenda, or a series of values seeking to promote the reproduction of the capitalist system (also, see Sztompka 2007). Rather, the point of the university, in these so-called 'post academic' times, ought to be the basis for the cultivation of heterogeneous views and values, and the development of individuals' critical capacities to critique the socio-institutional and organisational relations of society.

Bibliography

Academy of Social Sciences/ESRC (2008) *Developing Dialogue: Learned Societies in the Social Sciences – Developing Knowledge Transfer and Public Engagement.* http://www.esrc.ac.uk/ESRCInfoCentre/Images/Develop ing%20Dialogue_tcm6-27125.pdf (accessed 23 December 2009).

Adamson, D. (1996) Estate management, in Warner, D. and Palfreyman, D. (eds) *Higher Education Management: The Key Elements*, Buckingham: Society for Research into Higher Education and Open University, pp. 136–154.

Addams, J. (1968) *Twenty Years at Hull House*, New York: Macmillan (original 1919).

Adorno, T. (1997) Engagement, *Gesammelte Schriften*, 11, pp. 409–430.

Agrawal, A. (2001) University-to-industry knowledge transfer: Literature review and unanswered questions, *International Journal of Management Reviews*, 3(4), pp. 285–302.

Albon, R. and Stafford, D. (1987) *Rent Control*, London: Croom Helm.

Alden, J.D., Batty, M., Batty, S. and Longley, P. (1988) A Socio-economic profile of Cardiff Bay, *Cambria*, 15, pp. 61–87.

Alldred, P. and Miller, T. (2007) Measuring what's valued or valuing what's measured? Knowledge production and the research assessment exercise, in Gillies, V. and Lucey, H. (eds) *Power, Knowledge and the Academy: The Institutional is Political*, Basingstoke: Palgrave, pp. 147–167.

Allen Collinson, J. (2004) Occupational identity on the edge: Social science contract researchers in higher education, *Sociology*, 38, pp. 313–329.

Allen, C. (2001a) On the social consequences (and social conscience) of the "foyer industry": A critical ethnography, *Journal of Youth Studies*, 4(4), pp. 471–494.

Allen, C. (2001b) Criticism of foyers is being stifled, *The Guardian (Society)*, 18 June.

Allen, C. (2005) On the social relations of contract research production: Power, positionality and epistemology in housing and urban research, *Housing Studies*, 20(6), pp. 989–1007.

Allen, C. (2006) 'Minding its own business? The social organisation of entrepreneurial scholarship @ enterprising-university.co.uk'. Paper presented at the ESRC Seminar on social relations of contract research production, King's College London, April 2006.

Allen, C. (2007) *Crime, Drugs and Social Theory*, Aldershot: Ashgate.

Allen, C. (2008) Gentrification 'research' and the academic nobility: A different class? *International Journal of Urban and Regional Research*, 32(1), pp. 180–5.

Allen, C. (2008) *Housing Market Renewal and Social Class*, London: Routledge.

Allen, C. (2009) Silencing dissent: Languages of denunciation for the neutralisation and criminalisation of trouble makers in Liverpool 08, unpublished paper (available from author).

Allen, C. (2009) The fallacy of 'Housing Studies': Philosophical problems of knowledge and understanding in housing research, *Housing, Theory and Society*, 26(1), pp. 53–79.

Amin, A. and Graham, S. (1999) Cities of connection and disconnection, in Allen, J., Massey, D. and Pryke, M. (eds) *Unsettling Cities*, London: Routledge, pp. 7–38.

Amiot, M. (1986) *Contre l'Etat, les sociologues. Éléments pour une histoire de la sociologie urbaine en France (1900–1980)*, Paris: Editions de l'Ecole des hautes études en sciences sociales.

Anderson, I., Kemp, P. and Quilgars, D. (1993) *Single Homeless People: A Report to the Department of the Environment*, London: HMSO.

Arthur, M. and Piatt, W. (2010) Universities face meltdown – and all of Britain will suffer, *The Guardian*, 12 January, p. 30.

Atkinson, P. and Silverman, D. (1997) Kundera's *Immortality*: The interview society and the invention of the self, *Qualitative Inquiry*, 3(3), pp. 304–325.

Atkinson, R. (2002) Does gentrification help or harm urban neighbourhoods? An assessment of the evidence-base in the context of the new urban agenda, *Centre for Neighbourhood Research Paper 5*.

Atkinson, R. and Jacobs, K. (2008) The social forces and politics of housing research: Reflections from within the academy, *Housing, Theory and Society*, pp. 1–15.

Attili, G. (2009) Ethical awareness in advocacy planning research, in Lo Piccolo, F. and Thomas, H. (eds) *Ethics and Planning Research*, Aldershot: Ashgate, pp. 207–218.

Babb, S. (2001) *Managing Mexico: Economists from Nationalism to Neoliberalism*, Princeton: Princeton University Press.

Badley, G. (2009) Academic writing as shaping and re-shaping, *Teaching in Higher Education*, 14(2), pp. 209–219.

Bailey, N., Haworth, A., Manzi, T., Paramanagage, P. and Roberts, M. (2006) *Creating and Sustaining Mixed income Communities: A Good Practice Guide*, York: Joseph Rowntree Foundation.

Ball, M. (1986) Housing analysis: Time for a theoretical refocus, *Housing Studies*, 1(3), pp. 147–165.

Banks, M. and Mackian, S. (2000) Jump In! The water's warm: A comment on Peck's 'grey geography', *Transactions of the Institute of British Geographers*, 25, pp. 249–54.

Bargh, C., Scott, P. and Smith, D. (1996) *Governing Universities: Changing the Culture?* Buckingham: Society for Research in Higher Education and Open University Press.

Barlow, J. and Duncan, S. (1994) *Success and Failure in Housing Provision: European Systems Compared*, London: Pergamon.

Barnes, C. (1996) Disability and the myth of the independent researcher, *Disability and Society*, 11, pp. 107–110.

Bauman, Z. (1987) *Legislators and Interpreters: On Modernity, Post-Modernity and Intellectuals*, Cambridge: Polity Press.

Beals, R. (1969) *Politics of Social Research: An Inquiry into the Ethics and Responsibilities of Social Scientists*, Chicago: Aldine Publishing Company.

Becher, T. and Kogan, M. (1992) *Process and Structure in Higher Education*, London: Routledge.

Becher, T. and Trowler, P.R. (2001) *Academic Tribes and Territories*, Buckingham: Open University Press and Society for Research into Higher Education (second edition).

Beck, U. (1994) Replies and critiques – self dissolution and self endangerment of industrial society: What does this mean? in Beck, U., Giddens, A. and Lash, S. (eds) *Reflexive Modernization: Politics, Tradition and Aesthetics in the Modern Social Order*, Cambridge: Polity Press, pp. 174–183.

Begg, I. (ed.) (2002) *Urban Competitiveness*, Bristol: Policy Press.

Bekhradnia, B. (2001) *20 Years of Higher Education Policy: Looking Back 10 Years and Forward to the Next Decade*, London, Higher Education Policy Institute.

Bell, D. and Baverstock, B. (2006) A bad year for science, *Nuclear Engineering*, February, 1–10.

Bell, E. (1999) The negotiation of a working role in organisational ethnography, *International Journal of Social Science Methodology*, 2, pp. 17–37.

Bell, E. and Read, C. (1998) *On the Case: Advice for Collaborative Studentships – Report for the Research Training Division of the ESRC*. Accessed on 9 July 2004 at http://www.esrc.ac.uk/ESRCContent/downloaddocs/onthecase.doc

Bender, T. (ed.) (1988) *The University and the City*, Oxford: Oxford University Press.

Bender, T. (2002) *The Unfinished City: New York and the Metropolitan Idea*, New York: The New Press.

Beveridge, M. (2004) Inspectors slam Peabody for focus on cutting-edge schemes. *Housing Today.* Accessed on 18 August 2004 at http://www.housing-today.co.uk/story.asp?storyType=10&sectioncode=306&storyCode=3035493

Bezes, P. (ed.) (2005) *L'État à l'épreuve des sciences sociales: La fonction recherche dans les administrations sous la Ve République*, Paris: La Découverte.

Bezes, P. (2009) *Réinventer l'Etat. Les réformes de l'administration française (1962–2008)*, Paris: Presses universitaires de France.

Birch, M. and Miller, T. (2000) Inviting intimacy: The interview as a therapeutic opportunity, *International Journal of Social Research Methodology*, 3, pp. 189–202.

Blackaby, B. (2004) *Community Cohesion and Housing: A Good Practice Guide*, Coventry: Chartered Institute of Housing.

Blair T. (2002) Science matters, *Prime Minister's speech to the Royal Society*, 10 April. Accessed on 24 April 2007 at http://www.number-10.gov.uk/output/Page1715.asp

Blunkett, D. (2000) Influence or irrelevance: Can social science improve government? *Research Intelligence*, 71, pp. 12–21.

Blunkett, D. (2000) *Speech on Higher Education*, 15 February 2000 at University of Greenwich, http://cms1.gre.ac.uk/dfee/ (accessed 20 October 2009).

Bogner, A., Littig, B. and Menz, W. (eds) (2009) *Interviewing experts*, New York: Palgrave Macmillan.

Bok, D. (2003) *Universities in the Marketplace: The Commercialization of Higher Education*, Princeton: Princeton University Press.

Boltanski, L. and Bourdieu, P. (1976) La production de l'idéologie dominante, *Actes de la recherche en sciences socials*, 2(2–3), pp. 4–73.

Booth, R. (2008) Home Office urges architects to design terror-proof buildings, *The Guardian*, Saturday 22 March, http://www.guardian.co.uk/politics/2008/mar/22/terrorism.uksecurity

Bourdieu, P. (1990) *The Logic of Practice*, Stanford: University Press.

Bourdieu, P. (1993) *The Field of Cultural Production*, Cambridge: Polity Press.

Bourdieu P. (1994) *Raisons pratiques: Sur la théorie de l'action*, Paris: Seuil.

Bourdieu P. (1997) *Méditations pascaliennes*, Paris: Seuil.

Bourdieu, P. (1998) *Acts of Resistance: Against the Myths of Our Time*, Cambridge: Polity Press.

Bourdieu, P. (2000) *Pascallian Meditations*, Stanford, CA: Stanford University Press.

Bourdieu P. and Darbel, A. (1969) *L'amour de l'art. Les musées d'art européens et leur public*, Paris: Minuit.

Bourdieu, P. and Wacquant, L. (2001) New Liberal speak: Notes on the new planetary vulgate, *Radical Philosophy*, 105, January–February, pp. 2–5.

Box, R. (2007) Redescribing the public interest, *The Social Science Journal*, 44(4), pp. 585–598.

Boyne, G., Farrell, C., Law, J., Powell, M. and Walker, R. (eds) (2003) *Evaluating Public Management Reforms: Principles and Practice*, Buckingham: Oxford University Press.

Braverman, H. (1974) *Labor and Monopoly Capital: The Degradation of Work in the Twentieth Century*, New York: Monthly Review Press.

Brewer, J.D. (1993) Sensitivity as a problem in field research: A study of routine policing in Northern Ireland, in Renzetti, C.M. and Lee, R.M (eds) *Researching Sensitive Topics*, London: Sage, pp. 125–146.

Bridges, D. (2009) Research quality assessment in education: Impossible science, possible art? *British Educational Research Journal*, 35(4), pp. 497–517.

Briggs, A. (1963) *Victorian Cities*, London: Odhams.

British Academy (1961) *Research in the Humanities and the Social Sciences: Report of a Survey by the British Academy 1958–60*, Oxford: Oxford University Press.

British Academy (2004) Response to the Government's Consultation Paper on *Science and innovation: Working towards a ten-year investment framework*. Accessed on 18 August 2004 at http://www.britac.ac.uk/news/reports/sifresp/sifresp-html.htm

Brown, G. (2007) 'Statement on Security', available at http://www.number10.gov.uk/output/Page12675.asp (accessed 25 July 2007).

Brown G. (2009) *Science and Our Economic Future*, Romanes Lecture given by the Prime Minister at the Sheldonian Theatre, Oxford University, 27 February 2009. Accessed on 9 May 2009 at http://www.number10.gov.uk/Page18472

Brown, T. (ed.) (1999) *Stakeholder Housing: A Third Way Approach*, London: Pluto Press.

Buchbinder, H. and Newson, J. (1985) Corporate-university linkages and the scientific-technical revolution, *Interchange*, 16(3) pp. 37–53.

Bundy, C. (2004) Under new management? A critical history of managerialism in British universities, in Walker, M. and Nixon, J. (eds) *Reclaiming Universities from a Runaway World*, Maidenhead: Open University Press and Society for Research into Higher Education.

Burgess, R. (2000) 'Foreword' in D. Burton (ed.) *Research Training for Social Scientists*, London: Sage.

Burns, D. and Taylor, M. (2000) *Auditing Community Participation*, Bristol: The Policy Press.

Burton Jones, A. (1999) *Knowledge Capitalism: Business, Work and Learning in the New Economy*, Oxford: Oxford University Press.

Byrne, D. (2001) *Understanding the City*, Basingstoke: Palgrave.

Caillé, A. and Chanial, P. (2009) L'université en crise: Présentation, *Revue du MAUSS*, 2009/01(33), pp. 5–30.

Cairncross, A. (1995) Economists in wartime, *Contemporary European History*, 4(1), pp. 19–36.

Callaghan, D. and Jennings, B. (eds) (1983) *Ethics, the Social Sciences, and Policy Analysis*, London and New York: Plenum Press.

Campbell, H. and Marshall, R. (2000) Moral obligations, planning, and the public interest: A commentary on current British practice, *Environment and Planning B: Planning and Design*, (27), pp. 297–312.

Castells, M. and Godard, F. (1974) *Monopolville*, Paris/La Haye: Mouton.

Castles, S. and Miller, M. (2003) *The Age of Migration: International Population Movements in the Modern World*, Basingstoke: Palgrave Macmillan.

Castree, N. (2006) Geographical knowledges, universities and academic freedom, *Environment and Planning A*, 38, pp. 1189–1192.

Cealey-Harrison, W. and Hood-Williams, J. (1998) 'More varieties than Heinz': Social categories and sociality in Humphries, Hammersley and beyond, *Sociological Research Online*, 3(1). Available at http://www.socresonline.org.uk/3/1/8.html

Chamayou, G. (2009) Petits conseils aux enseignants-chercheurs qui voudront réussir leur evaluation, *Revue du MAUSS*, 2009/01(33), pp. 208–226.

Chamborédon, J.-C. and Lemaire, M. (1970) Proximité spatiale et distance sociale. Les grands ensembles et leur peuplement, *Revue Française de Sociologie*, pp. 3–33.

Charle, C. (1999) Université et recherche dans le carcan technocratique, *Le Monde Diplomatique*, November, pp. 24–25.

Charle, C. and Soulié, C. (eds) (2007) *Les Ravages de la 'Modernisation' Uuniversitaire en Europe*, Paris: Syllepse.

Charle, C. and Verger, J. (2007) *Histoire des Universités* (2nd edn), Paris: Presses universitaires de France.

Charmaz, K. and Mitchell, R.G. (1997) The myth of silent authorship: Self, substance and style in ethnographic writing, in R. Hertz (ed.) *Reflexivity and Voice*, Thousand Oaks, CA: Sage, pp. 193–215.

Chartered Institute of Housing (2008) *Qualifications for MCIH: Approved Centres for Postgraduate Programmes, 2008/9*, http://www.cih.org/education/PostgraduateCourseList2008-9.pdf (accessed 10 November 2009).

Chomsky, N. (2003) *Objectivity and Liberal Scholarship*, London and New York: The New Press.

Chrimes, S.B. (1983) *University College, Cardiff: A Centenary History*, Cardiff: University College Cardiff.

Chwieroth, J. (2007) Neoliberal economists and capital account liberalisation in emerging markets, *International Organisation*, 61, pp. 443–463.

Clapham, D. (1996) Housing and the economy: Broadening comparative housing research, *Urban Studies*, 33(4–5), pp. 631–647.

Clapham, D. (1997) The social construction of housing management research, *Urban Studies*, 34(5–6), pp. 761–774.

Clapham, J. (1946) *Economic and Social Research: Report of the Clapham Committee*, London: HMSO.

Clark, B. (2001) The entrepreneurial university: A new foundation for collegiality, autonomy and achievement, *Higher Education Management*, 13(2), pp. 9–24.

Clark, B.R. (1998) *Creating Entrepreneurial Universities: Organizational Pathways of Transformation. Issues in Higher Education*, New York: Pergamon Press.

Clarke, C. (1998) Resurrecting educational research to raise standards: Statement from the new Minister responsible for research, *Research Intelligence: British Educational Research Association Newsletter*, 66, pp. 8–9.

Cloke, P., Cooke, P., Cursons, J., Milbourne, P. and Widdowfield, R. (2000) Ethics, reflexivity and research: Encounters with homeless people, *Ethics, Place and Environment*, 3(2), pp. 133–154.

Cloke, P., Milbourne. P. and Widdowfield, R. (2001) The local spaces of welfare provision: Responding to homelessness in rural England, *Political Geography*, 20, pp. 419–512.

Coaffee, J. (2003) *Terrorism, Risk and the City*, Aldershot: Ashgate.

Coaffee, J. and Diamond, J. (2008) Reflections on the role of the evaluator: Recognising value for money and creative learning within regeneration evaluation, *Journal of Urban Regeneration and Renewal*, 2(1), pp. 86–99.

Coaffee, J. and O'Hare, P. (2008) Urban resilience and national security: The role for planning, *Urban Design and Planning*, 161(DP4), pp. 173–182.

Coaffee, J., O'Hare, P. and Hawkesworth, M. (2009) The visibility of (in)security: The aesthetics of planning urban defences against terrorism, *Security Dialogue*, 40(4–5), pp. 489–511.

Cochrane, A. (2007) *Understanding Urban Policy: A Critical Approach*, Oxford: Blackwell.

Coffey, A. (1999) *The Ethnographic Self*, London: Sage.

Coffield, F. and Williamson, B. (1997) The challenges facing higher education, in Coffield, F. and Williamson, B. (eds) *Repositioning Higher Education*, Buckingham: Society for Research into Higher Education and Open University Press, pp. 1–26.

Cohen, S. and Taylor, L. (1977) Talking about prison blues, in Bell, C. and Newby, H., *Doing Sociological Research*, London: George Allen & Unwin, pp. 67–86.

Cole, I. (n.d.) *The Perils of a Practice Driven Future for Housing Education*, Sheffield: School of Urban and Regional Studies, Sheffield Hallam University.

Cole, I. and Furbey, R. (1994) *The Eclipse of Council Housing*, London: Routledge.

Cole, I. and Nevin, N. (2004) *The Road to Renewal*, York: York Publishing Services.

Coleman, A. (1985) *Utopia on Trial: Vision and Reality in Planned Housing*, London: Hilary Shipman.

Commission on the Social Sciences (2003) *Great Expectations: The Social Sciences in Britain*, http://www.acss.org.uk/docs/GtExpectations.pdf (accessed 23 December 2009).

Coop, S. and Thomas, H. (2007) Planning doctrine as an element in planning history: The case of Cardiff, *Planning Perspectives*, 22(2), pp. 167–193.

Corbyn, Z. (2008) Managers and scholars divided as resistance grows to impact agenda, *Times Higher Educational Supplement*, 5 November.

Coser, L. (1965) *Men of Ideas: A Sociologist's View*, New York: The Free Press.

Cowell, R. and Thomas, H. (2002) Managing nature and narratives of dispossession: Reclaiming territory in Cardiff Bay, *Urban Studies*, 39(7), pp. 1241–1260.

Cox, A. and Mair, A. (1989) Urban growth machines and the politics of local economic development, *International Journal of Urban and Regional Research*, 13, pp. 137–146.

Crookes, L. (2006) Non-statutory objection to the compulsory purchase orders 2006: Written submission. Unpublished paper.

Crozier, M. (1971) *La société bloquée*, Paris: Éditions du Seuil.

Cunningham, V. and Goodwin, J. (2001) *Cardiff University: A Celebration*, Cardiff: Cardiff University.

Davies, H., Nutley, S. and Smith, P. (2000) Learning from the past, prospects for the future, in Davies, H., Nutley, S. and Smith, P. (eds) *What Works? Evidence-Based Practice and Policy in Public Services*, Bristol: The Polity Press, pp. 351–366.

Davis, J.M. (2000) Disability studies as ethnographic research and text: Research strategies and roles for promoting social change? *Disability and Society*, 15, pp. 191–206.

Davis, M. (2001), The Flames of New York, *New Left Review*, 12, November–December, http://www.newleftreview.org/?view=2355 (accessed 12 January 2003).

Deem, R. (1998) New managerialism in higher education: The management of performance and cultures, *International Studies in the Sociology of Education*, 8(1), pp. 47–70.

Deem, R. (2001) Globalisation, new managerialism, academic capitalism and entrepreneurialism in universities: Is the local dimension still important? *Comparative Education*, 37(1), pp. 7–20.

Deem, R. (2001) *'New Managerialism' and the Management of UK Universities' End of Project Report*, University of Bristol: Graduate School of Education.

Deem, R., Hillyard, S. and Reed, M. (2008) *Knowledge, Higher Education and the New Managerialism: The Changing Management of UK Universities*, Oxford: Oxford University Press.

Delanty, G. (2001) *Challenging Knowledge: The University in the Knowledge Society*, Buckingham: Open University Press.

Delanty, G. (2003) Ideologies of the knowledge society and the cultural contradictions of higher education, *Policy Futures in Education*, 1(1), pp. 71–82.

Demeritt, D. (2000) The new social contract for science: Accountability, relevance and value in US and UK science and research policy, *Antipode*, 32(3), pp. 308–329.

Demeritt, D. (2004) Research training and the end(s) of the PhD, *Geoforum*, 35(6), pp. 655–60.

Demeritt, D. (2010) Harnessing science and securing societal impacts from publicly funded research: Reflections on UK science policy. *Environment and Planning A*, 42, 515–23.

Demeritt, D. and Lees, L. (2005) Research relevance and the geographies of CASE studentship collaboration, *Area*, 37(2), pp. 127–37.

De Montlibert, C. (2008) La réforme universitaire: Une affaire de mots, in *Le cauchemar de Humboldt: Les réformes de l'enseignement supérieur européen*, Paris: Raisons d'agir, pp. 27–46.

Dennis, N. (1970) *People and Planning*, London: Faber and Faber.

Dennis, N. (1972) *Public Participation and Planners' Blight*, London: Faber and Faber.

Department for Education and Skills (2003) *The Future of Higher Education*, London: HMSO.

Department for Education and Skills (2004) *Research Forum: The Relationship between Research and Teaching in Institutions of Higher Education*, London: The Stationery Office.

Department of Communities and Local Government (2008) *Establishing Acceptable Standards for Local Environmental Quality*, Reference: RAE 3/6/130, http://www.rmd.communities.gov.uk/project.asp?intProjectID=12211

Department of Communities and Local Government (2009) *Analytical Services Analytical Programme 2009–2010*, London: DCLG.

Dewey, J. (1927) *The Public and its Problems*, New York: Henry Holt & Co.

Dewey J. (1930) *The Quest for Certainty: A Study of the Relation of Knowledge to Action*, London: Allen and Unwin.

Dewey, J. (1958 [1929]) *Experience and Nature*, New York: Dover.

Diamond, I. (2006a) Our job is to ensure research has the maximum impact, *Education Guardian*, 7 March, p. 10.

Diamond, I. (2006b) *Times Higher Educational Supplement*, 10 March, p. 56.

D'Iribarne, P. (2009) Le loup et le chien, *Le Monde*, 10 March.

Donnison, D. (1967) *The Government of Housing*, Middlesex: Penguin.

Donnison, D. and Stephens, M. (2003) The political economy of housing research, in O'Sullivan, T. and Gibb, K. (eds) *Housing Economics and Public Policy*, Oxford: Blackwell, pp. 248–267.

Donovan, C. (2004) The governance of social science, unpublished paper, presented to the Australasian Political Studies Association Conference.

Doohm, S. (2005) Theodor W. Adorno and Jurgen Habermas – two ways of being a public intellectual, *European Journal of Social Theory*, 8(3), pp. 269–280.

Du Gay, P. and Salaman, G. (1992) The cult(ure) of the customer, *Journal of Management Studies*, 29(5), pp. 615–33.

Dunleavy, P. (1981) *The Politics of Mass Housing in Britain 1945–1975: A Study of Corporate Power and Professional Influence in the Welfare State*, Oxford: Clarendon Press.

Durning, B. (2004) Planning academics and planning practitioners: Two tribes or a community of practice? *Planning Practice and Research*, 19(40), pp. 435–446.

Duval, J. and Johan H. (2006) Les enjeux des transformations de la recherché, *Actes de la recherche en sciences sociales*, 164(2006/4), pp. 5–10.

Dwelly, T. and Cowans, J. (2006) *Rethinking Social Housing*, London: The Smith Institute.

Educators for Reform (2009) *The Threat to Britain's Research Base: Response to HEFCE Research Excellence Framework Consultation*, London: Reform.

Elias, N. (1972) *The Civilizing Process*, Oxford: Blackwell.

Engelen, E. (2004) The Rise and Fall of the Swedish Wage Earner Funds: A Cautionary Tale, Haven Center for the Study of Social Structure and Social Change, University of Madison-Wisconsin Real Utopias Archive (edited by

Erik Olin Wright) http://www.havenscenter.org/real_utopias/2004documents/ The%20Demise%20of%20the%20Swedish%20Wage%20Earner%20Funds% 202.pdf

Engels, F. (1892) *The Condition of the Working Class in England*, London: Granada.

ESRC (2000) The Thematic Priorities, also available at http://www.esrcsocietytoday. ac.uk/ESRCInfoCentre/about/what_to_do/OurOrganisationandstructure/ BoardsandCommitees/index.aspx

ESRC (2003) *Annual Report*, Swindon, ESRC.

ESRC (2004) *ESRC CASE Studentship Exercise*. Accessed on 6 July 2004 at http://www.esrc.ac.uk/ESRCContent/postgradfunding/CASE-academic_and_ commercial_partners.asp

ESRC (2005) *Postgraduate Training Guidelines*, also available at http://www. esrcsocietytoday.ac.uk/postgraduate

ESRC (2007a) *The Benefits of Collaborative Research between Academic and Public/Voluntary Sector Partners*. Accessed on 30 April 2007 at http:// www.esrcsocietytoday.ac.uk/ESRCInfoCentre/opportunities/postgraduate/ pgtrainingpolicy/index3.aspx?ComponentId=4681&SourcePageId=5405

ESRC (2007b) *ESRC CASE Studentship Exercise*. Accessed on 30 April 2007 at http://www.esrcsocietytoday.ac.uk/ESRCInfoCentre/opportunities/postgraduate/ pgtrainingpolicy/index2.aspx?ComponentId=4679&SourcePageId=5405

ESRC (2009) *ESRC Researcher Development Initiative*, also available at http:// www.esrcsocietytoday.ac.uk/ESRCInfoCentre/opportunities/postgraduate/ fellowships/training/Eligibility_RDIcall.aspx

ESRC (2009) *Mission Statement*, Swindon: ESRC. Accessed on 4 January 2010 at http://www.Esrc.Ac.Uk/Esrcinfocentre/About/What_To_Do/Mission/

Etzkowitz, H. (1994) Knowledge as property: The Massachusetts Institute of technology and the debate over academic patent policy, *Minerva*, 32(4), pp. 383–421.

Etzkowitz, H. (1998) The norms of entrepreneurial science: Cognitive effects of the new university–industry linkages, *Research Policy*, 27(8), pp. 823–833.

Etzkowitz, H. (2001) The second academic revolution and the rise of entrepreneurial science, *IEEE Technology and Society Magazine*, 20(2), pp. 18–29.

Etzkowitz, H. (2002) *MIT and the Rise of Entrepreneurial Science*, London: Routledge.

Etzkowitz, H. and Leydesdorff L. (1997) Introduction to special issue on science policy dimensions of the triple helix of university-industry-government relations, *Science and Public Policy*, 24, pp. 2–5.

Etzkowitz, H., Schuler, E. and Gulbrandsen, M. (2000) The evolution of the entrepreneurial university, in Jacob, M. and Hellstrom, T. (eds) *The Future of Knowledge Production in the Academy*, Buckingham: Open University Press, pp. 40–60.

Etzkowitz, H., Webster, A. and Healey, P. (1998) Introduction, in Etzkowitz, H., Webster, A. and Healey, P. (eds) *Capitalizing Knowledge: New Intersections of Industry and Academia*, Albany, NY: State University of New York Press, pp. 1–17.

Faberman, H. (1975) A criminogenic market structure: The automobile industry, *Sociological Quarterly*, 16, pp. 438–57.

Fainstein, S., Gordon, I. and Harloe, M. (eds) *Divided Cities: New York and London in the Contemporary World*, London: Blackwell.

Faucher-King, F. and Le Galès, P. 2007. *Tony Blair, 1997–2007. Le bilan des réformes*, Paris: Presses de la Fondation nationale des sciences politiques.

Fink, D. (2006) The professional doctorate: Its relativity to the Ph.D. and relevance for the knowledge economy, *International Journal of Doctoral Studies*, 1, pp. 35–44.

Flyvbjerg, B. (1998) *Rationality and Power*, Chicago: Chicago University Press.

Flyvbjerg, B. (2001) *Making Social Science Matter: Why Social Inquiry Fails and How it Can Succeed Again*, Cambridge: Cambridge University Press.

Foellmi, C. (2007) Sans théorie de la relativité, pas de GPS, *Le Monde*, 4 November.

Foucault, M. (1975) *Discipline and Punish: The Birth of the Prison*, New York: Random House.

Foucault, M. (1977) *Discipline and Punish: The Birth of the Prison*, London, Penguin.

Foucault, M. (2003) *Society Must be Defended: Lectures at the Collège de France, 1975–76*, translated by David Macey, Picador USA.

Fourquet, F. (1980) *Les comptes de la puissance. Histoire de la comptabilité nationale et du Plan*, Paris: Editions Recherches.

Friedman, M. (1990) *Free to Choose: A Personal Statement*, London: Penguin.

Fuller, S. (2000) *The Governance of Science*, Buckingham: Open University Press.

Fuller, S. (2002) *Knowledge Management Foundations*, Boston and Oxford: Butterworth-Heinemann.

Fuller, S. (2004) Intellectuals: An endangered species in the twenty-first century? *Economy and Society*, 33(4), pp. 463–483.

Fung A. (2004) *Empowered Participation: Reinventing Urban Democracy*, Princeton University Press.

Furedi, F. (2004) *Where Have All the Intellectuals Gone?* London: Continuum.

Gamble, A. (2004) Public intellectuals and the public domain, *New Formations*, 53 (Summer), pp. 41–53.

Garcia, S. (2007) L'Europe du savoir contre l'Europe des banques? La construction de l'espace européen de l'enseignement supérieur, *Actes de la recherche en sciences sociales*, 2007/1–2(166–167), pp. 80–93.

Garcia, S. (2008) La construction de l'espace européen de l'enseignement supérieur, in Franz Schultheis et al. (eds) *Le cauchemar de Humboldt: Les réformes de l'enseignement supérieur européen*, pp. 63–85.

Garcia, S. (2009) Réformes de Bologne et économicisation de l'enseignement supérieur, *Revue du MAUSS*, 2009/01(33), pp. 154–172.

Garside, P. (2000) *The Conduct of Philanthropy*, London: Athlone Press.

Gibbons, M. et al. (1994) *The New Production of Knowledge*, London: Sage.

Gibbons, M., Limoges, C., Nowotny, H., Schwartzman, S., Scott, P. and Trow, M. (1994) *The New Production of Knowledge: The Dynamics of Science and Research in Contemporary Societies*, London: Sage.

Giddens, A. (1982) *Profiles and Critiques in Social Theory*, Basingstoke: Macmillan.

Giddens, A. (2002) There is a Third Way, *The Guardian*, 5 December, p. 23.

Gingras, Y. (2003) Idées d'universités. Enseignement, recherche et innovation, *Actes de la recherche en sciences sociales*, 2003/3(148), pp. 3–7.

Glennerster, H. (2007) *British Social Policy: 1945 to the Present*, Oxford: Blackwell.

Goodley, D. and Moore, M. (2000) Doing disability research: Activist lives and the academy, *Disability and Society*, 15(6), pp. 865–882.

Gouldner (1971) *The Coming Crisis of Western Sociology*, London: Heinemann.

Green, C. 2006. *Proof of Evidence of Cath Green (Liverpool City Council)*. Accessed on 5 July 2007 at http://www.persona.uk.com/newheartlands/index.htm

Green, H. and Powell, S. (2005) *Doctoral Study in Contemporary Higher Education*, Buckingham: Open University Press.

Greenaway, D. and Haynes, M. (2003) Funding higher education in the UK: The role of fees and loans, *The Economic Journal of The Royal Economic Society*, 113.

Groves, J. (2002) *Key Findings of the NPC National Survey of Postgraduate Funding and Priorities*, National Postgraduate Committee, also available at http://www.npc.org.uk/features/featuresarchive/keyfindingsofthenpcnational surveyofpostgraduatefundingandpriorities

Gurney, C. (1999a) Pride and prejudice: Discourses of normalisation in the public and private accounts of home ownership, *Housing Studies*, 14(2), pp. 163–183.

Gurney, C. (1999b) Lowering the drawbridge: A case study of analogy and metaphor in the construction of home, *Urban Studies*, 36(10), pp. 1705–1722.

Guy, C. and David, G. (2004) Measuring physical access to 'healthy foods' in areas of social deprivation: A case study in Cardiff, *International Journal of Consumer Studies*, 28, pp. 222–234.

Haas, P. (1992) Introduction: Epistemic communities and international policy coordination, *International Organization*, 46(1), pp. 1–35.

Habermas J. (1984) *The Theory of Communicative Action, Volume 1: Reason and the Rationalisation of Society*, translated by T. McCarthy, London: Heinemann.

Habermas J. (1987) *The Theory of Communicative Action, Volume 2: A Critique of Functionalist Reason*, translated by T. McCarthy, Cambridge: Polity.

Hammersley, M. (1995) *The Politics of Social Research*, London: Sage.

Hammersley, M. (2005) The myth of research-based practice: The critical case of educational inquiry, *International Journal of Social Research Methodology*, 8(4), pp. 317–330.

Hammersley, M. and Atkinson, P. (1983) *Ethnography: Principles in Practice*, London: Tavistock.

Harding, A., Scott, A., Laske, S. and Butscher, C. (eds) (2007) *Bright Satanic Mills: Universities, Regional Development and the Knowledge Economy*, Aldershot: Ashgate.

Harding, S. (1991) *Whose Science? Whose Knowledge? Thinking from Women's Lives*, Milton Keynes: Open University Press.

Harley, S. and Lee, F. (1997) Research selectivity, managerialism, and the academic labor process: The future of nonmainstream economics in UK universities, *Human Relations*, 50(11), pp. 1427–1460.

Harloe, M. (1977) Introduction, in Harloe, M. (ed.) *Captive Cities: Studies in the Political Economy of Cities and Regions*, Chichester: Wiley.

Harloe, M. and Lebas, E. (eds) (1981) *City, Class and Capital*, London: Arnold.

Harloe, M. and Perry, B. (2004) Universities, localities and regional development: The emergence of the 'Mode 2' university? *International Journal of Urban and Regional Research*, 28(1), pp. 212–223.

Harloe, M., Pickvance, C. and Urry, J. (eds) (1990) *Place, Policy and Politics*, London: Unwin Hyman.

Harvey, D. (1989) From managerialism to entrepreneurialism: The transformation in governance in late capitalism, *Geografiska Annaler*, 71(B), pp. 3–17.

Harvey, D. (1998) University, Inc., *The Atlantic Monthly* (October).

Harvey, D. (2008) The right to the city, *New Left Review*, 53, September–October, http://www.newleftreview.org/?view=2740 (accessed 23 December 2009).

Harwood, J. and Moon, G. (2003) Accessing the research setting: The politics of research and the limits to enquiry, *Area*, 35, pp. 106–109.

Hastings, A. (2002) Making discourse analysis explicit, *Housing, Theory and Society*, 19(1), pp. 19.

Hayter, T. and Harvey, D. (1993) *The Factory and the City*, London: Mansell.

Healey, P. (1991) Researching planning practice, *Town Planning Review*, 62(4), pp. 447–59.

Healey, P. (2006) *Collaborative Planning* (2nd edn), Basingstoke: Palgrave Macmillan.

Hedling, E. (2005) *Sydsvenska Dagbladet* (11 March).

Heidegger, M. (1962) *Being and Time*, Oxford: Blackwell.

Heidegger, M. (1988) *The Basic Problems of Phenomenology*, Bloomington, IN: Indiana University Press.

Heilbron, J. (2006) *Naissance de la sociologie*, Marseille: Agone.

Henkel, M. (2007) Can academic autonomy survive in the knowledge society? A perspective from Britain, *Higher Education Research & Development*, 26(1) pp. 87–99.

Her Majesty's Stationery Office (1993) *Realising Our Potential*, London: HMSO.

Herman, E. (1995) *The Romance of American Psychology: Political Culture in the Age of Experts*, Los Angelos and Berkeley: University of California Press.

Hertz, R. and Imber, J.B. (eds) (1995) *Studying Elites Using Qualitative Methods*, Thousand Oaks, CA: Sage.

Higher Education Funding Council for England (2008) *Higher Education – Business and Community Interaction Survey*, London: HEfCE.

Higher Education Funding Council for England (2009) *Research Excellence Framework: Second Consultation on the Assessment and Funding of Research*, London: HEfCE.

Hill-Collins, P. (1990) *Black Feminist Thought*, London: Routledge.

Hillyard, P. and Sim, J. (1997) The political economy of socio-legal research, in Thomas, P.A. (ed.) *Socio-Legal Studies*, Aldershot: Dartmouth, pp. 45–75.

Hillyard, P., Sim, J., Tombs, S. and Whyte, D. (2004) Leaving a stain on the silence: Contemporary criminology and the politics of dissent, *British Journal of Criminology*, 44, pp. 369–390.

HM Government (2006) *Countering International Terrorism: The United Kingdom's Strategy*, London: HMSO.

HM Government (2007) Afternoon Press Briefing, 14 November, available at http://www.number10.gov.uk/output/Page13763.asp (accessed 14 November 2007).

HM Treasury (2002) *Investing in Innovation: A Strategy for Science, Engineering and Technology* (HM Treasury, London). Accessed on 27 January 2005 at http://www.HM Treasury.gov.uk/media/FDD/8D/science_strat02_ch1to4.pdf

HM Treasury (2006) *Prosperity for all in the Global Economy – World Class Skills (Leitch Review of Skills – Final Report)*, London: HMSO.

Holmans, A. (1995) *Housing Demand and Need, 1991–2011*, York: Joseph Rowntree Foundation.

Holmes, C. (2003) *Housing, Equality and Choice*, London: Institute of Public Policy Research.

Home Office (2006) *Countering International Terrorism: The United Kingdom's Strategy*, London: HMSO.

Hooper, A. and Punter, J. (eds) (2006) *Capital Cardiff*, Cardiff: University of Wales Press.

Horowitz, I. (ed.) (1967) *The Rise and Fall of Project Camelot: Studies in the Relationship between Social Science and Practical Politics*, Cambridge, MA: MIT Press.

Howie, G. (2005) Universities in the UK: Drowning by numbers, *Critical Quarterly*, 47(1–2), pp. 1–10.

Hubbard, G., Backett-Milburn, K. and Kemmer, D. (2001) Working with emotion: Issues for the researcher in fieldwork and teamwork, *International Journal of Social Research Methodology*, 4, pp. 119–137.

Hubbard, P. (2006) *City*, London: Routledge.

Huet, A, Péron, R. and Sauvage, A. (1977) *Urbanisation capitaliste et pouvoir local*, Paris: Delarge.

Imrie, R. (1996) Transforming the social relations of research production in urban policy evaluation, *Environment and Planning A*, 28, pp. 1445–1464.

Imrie R. (2004) Urban geography, relevance and resistance to the 'policy turn', *Urban Geography*, 25, pp. 697–708.

Imrie, R. (2009) The knowledge business in academic planning research, in Lo Piccolo, F. and Thomas, H. (eds) *Ethics in Planning Research*, Aldershot: Ashgate, pp. 71–90.

Imrie, R. and Raco, M. (1999) How new is the new local governance? Lessons from the United Kingdom, *Transactions of the Institute of British Geographers*, 24(1), pp. 45–63.

Imrie, R. and Raco, M. (2001) A critique without a focus: A response to Ward's reinterpretation of urban politics, *Transactions of the Institute of British Geographers*, 26(1), pp. 121–126.

Irwin, A. and Michaels, M. (2003) *Science, Social Theory & Public Knowledge*, Milton Keynes: Open University Press.

Jacob, M. (2000) 'Mode 2' in context: The contract researcher, the university and the knowledge society, in Jacob, M. and Hellstrom, T. (eds) *The Future of Knowledge Production in the Academy*, Buckingham: Open University Press, pp. 11–27.

Jacob, M. and Hellstrom, T. (eds) (2000) *The Future of Knowledge Production in the Academy*, Buckingham: Open University Press.

Jacob, M. and Helstrom, T. (2000) From networking researchers to the networked university, in Jacob, M. and Hellstrom, T. (eds) *The Future of Knowledge Production in the Academy*, Buckingham: Open University Press, pp. 81–94.

Jacobs, K., Kemeny, J. and Manzi, T. (2005) *Social Constructionism in Housing Research*, Aldershot: Ashgate.

Jenkins, S. (2010) It's another 1988 moment. Universities can break free, *The Guardian*, 27 January, p. 31.

Johnes, M. (2006) Inventing a county: Cardiff, South Glamorgan and the 1974 reorganization of local government, *Welsh History Review*, 23(2), pp. 153–174.

Johnes, M. (2007) Applied and commissioned histories: A cautionary tale of a researcher, a subject and a university, unpublished paper, available from author, Swansea University, UK.

Johnson, L., Lee, A. and Green, B. (2000) The PhD and the autonomous self: Gender, rationality and postgraduate pedagogy, *Studies in Higher Education*, 25(2), pp. 135–147.

Jones A. and Seelig, T. (2004) *Understanding and Enhancing Research-Policy Linkages in Australian Housing: A Discussion Paper*, Melbourne: AHURI.

Jones, D.R. (1988) *The Origins of Civic Universities*, London: Routledge.

Jones, G. (2006) Review of Mike Ungersma (ed.) *Cardiff: Rebirth of a Capital*, in *Planet: The Welsh Internationalist*, 175.

Jordanova, L. (2000) *History in Practice*, London: Arnold.

Karn, V., Kemeny, J. and Williams, P. (1985) *Home Ownership in the Inner City: Salvation or Despair?* Aldershot: Gower.

Karran, T. (2009) Academic freedom: In justification of a universal ideal, *Studies in Higher Education*, 34(3), pp. 263–283.

Katznelson, I. (1986) Rethinking the silences of social and economic policy, *Political Science Quarterly*, 101(2), pp. 307–325.

Kearns, A. and Turok, I. (2004) *Sustainable Communities: Dimensions and Challenges – ESRC/ODPM Postgraduate Research Programme Working Paper 1*, London: ODPM.

Keith, M. (2004) Knowing the city? 21st century urban policy and the introduction of local strategic partnerships, in Johnstone, C. and Whitehead, M. (eds) *New Horizons in British Urban Policy*, Aldershot: Ashgate.

Kemeny, J. (1992) *Housing and Social Theory*, London: Routledge.

Kemeny, J. (1995) *From Public Housing to the Social Market*, London: Routledge.

Kemeny, J. (1996) *Abolition of the Swedish Institute for Building Research: Social Change and the Politics of Compromise*, Gavle: Institute for Housing Research Research Report 2, Uppsala University (75 pp.).

Kemeny, J. (1997) The abolition of the National Swedish Institute for Building Research: Social change and political compromise, *Scandinavian Housing and Planning Research*, 14(3), pp. 133–147.

Kemeny, J. (2005) 'The Really Big Trade-Off' between home ownership and welfare: Castles' evaluation of the 1980 thesis, and a reformulation 25 years on, *Housing, Theory and Society*, 22(2), pp. 59–75 (Focus Article plus comments and author's response), pp. 76–93.

Kemeny, J. and Lowe, S. (1998) Schools of comparative research: From convergence to divergence, *Housing Studies*, 13(2), pp. 161–176.

Kerr, C. (2001) *The Uses of the University*, Cambridge: Harvard University Press.

King, P. (2003) *A Social Philosophy of Housing*, Aldershot: Ashgate.

King's College London (2009) *Guidelines on Good Practice in Academic Research*, London: King's College London.

Klein, N. (2007). *The Shock Doctrine*, London: Penguin.

Krimsky, S. (1995) Science, society, and the expanding boundaries of moral discourse, in Gavroglu, K. et al. (eds) *Science, Politics, and Social Practice*, Kluwer Academic Publishers, pp. 113–128.

Krimsky, S. (1995) Science, society, and the expanding boundaries of moral discourse, in Gavroglu, K., Stachel, J., Wartofsky, M. (eds) *Science, Politics, and Social Practice*, Kluwer Academic Publishers, pp. 113–128.

Krimsky, S. (2004) *La recherche face aux intérêts privés*, Paris: Les Empêcheurs de Penser en Rond/Seuil (original edition: *Science in the Private Interest*, Lanham, Rowman & Littlefield, 2003).

Kronman, A. (2007) *Education's End: Why Our Colleges and Universities Have Given Up on the Meaning of Life*, New Haven: Yale University Press.

Kuhn, T. (1962) *The Structure of Scientific Revolutions*, Chicago: University of Chicago Press.

Kuhn, T. (1970) *The Structure of Scientific Revolutions* (2nd edn), Chicago: University of Chicago Press.

Kurtz, P. (1983) *In Defense of Secular Humanism*, New York: Prometheus Books.

Laffin, M. (ed.) (1998) *Beyond Bureaucracy: The Professions in the Contemporary Public Sector*, Aldershot: Ashgate.

Lambert, R. (2003) *Lambert Review of Business-University Collaboration*, London: HM Treasury. Accessed on 30 June 2004 at http://www.HM Treasury. gov.uk/media//EA556/lambert_review_final_450.pdf

Landmark Chambers (2006) Closing submission on behalf of Liverpool City Council to public inquiry into the compulsory purchase of houses in Newheartlands, Liverpool, July 2006.

Latour, B. and Woolgar, S. (1979) *Laboratory Life: The Social Construction of Scientific Facts*, Princeton NJ: Princeton University Press.

Laval, C. (2009) Les nouvelles usines du capitalisme universitaire, *Revue du MAUSS*, 2009/01(33), pp. 173–184.

Lawless, P. (1994) Partnership in urban regeneration in the UK, *Urban Studies*, 31, pp. 1303–1324.

Lawrence, P. (2008) Lost in publication: How measurement harms science, *Ethics in Science and Environmental Politics*, 8(1), pp. 9–11.

Leathwood, C. and O'Connell, P. (2003) 'It's a Struggle': The construction of the 'new student' in higher education, *Journal of Education Policy*, 18(6), pp. 597–615.

Lee, A., Brennan, M. and Green, B. (2009) Re-imagining doctoral education: Professional doctorates and beyond, *Higher Education Research & Development*, 28(3), pp. 275–287.

Lee, P. and Nevin, B. (2002) *Renewing the Housing Market of Liverpool's Inner Core*, Birmingham: CURS.

Lee, R. (1997) Socio-legal research – what's the use? in Thomas, P. A. (ed.) *Socio-Legal Studies*. Aldershiot: Dartmouth, pp. 76–98.

Lee, R.M. (1993) *Doing Research on Sensitive Topics*, Sage: London.

Lee, R.M. and Renzetti, C.M. (1990) The problems of researching sensitive topics: An overview and introduction, *American Behavioural Scientist*, 33(5) pp. 510–533.

Levin, H. and Wook Jeong, D. (2006) What is a world class university? Paper presented to the *Conference of the Comparative & International Education Society*, Honolulu, Hawaii, 16 March.

Levin, M. (2007) Knowledge and technology transfer: Can universities promote regional development? in A. Harding, A. Scott, S. Laske and C. Butscher (eds) (2007) *Bright Satanic Mills: Universities, Regional Development and the Knowledge Economy*, Aldershot: Ashgate, pp. 39–52.

Levi-Strauss, C. (1966) *The Savage Mind*, Chicago: University of Chicago Press.

Lo Piccolo, F. (2009) Multiple roles in multiple dramas: Ethical challenges in undertaking participatory planning research, in Lo Piccolo, F. and Thomas, H. (eds) *Ethics and Planning Research*, Aldershot: Ashgate, pp. 233–254.

Lo Piccolo, F. and Thomas, H. (2008) Research ethics in planning: A framework for discussion, *Planning Theory*, 7(1), pp. 7–23.

Loftman, P. and Nevin, B. (1998) *Evaluation for Whom? The Politics of Evaluation Research*, Birmingham: University of Birmingham School of Public Policy Occasional Paper 15.

Logan, J. and Molotch, H. (1987) *Urban Fortunes*, Berkeley: University of California Press.

Lojkine, J. (1974) *La politique urbaine dans la région lyonnaise (1945–1972)*, Paris/La Haye: Mouton.

Lorenz, C. (2007) 'L'économie de la connaissance', le nouveau management public et les politiques de l'enseignement supérieur dans l'Union européenne, in *Les ravages de la 'modernisation' universitaire en Europe*, Paris: Syllepse, pp. 33–52.

Louis, K.S. and Anderson, M.S. (1998) The changing context of science and university-industry relations, in Etzkowitz, H., Webster, A., Healey, P. (eds) *Capitalizing Knowledge: New Intersections of Industry and Academia*, Albany, NY: State University of New York Press, pp. 73–91.

Lovering, J. (1999) Theory led by policy: The inadequacies of the 'New Regionalism' (illustrated from the case of Wales), *International Journal of Urban and Regional Research*, 23, pp. 379–395.

Lovitts, B.E. (2001) *Leaving the Ivory Tower*, London: Rowman and Littlefield.

Lyotard, J.-F. (1984) *The Postmodern Condition: A Report on Knowledge*, University of Minnesota Press.

Lyotard, J. (1995) Resisting a discourse of mastery: A conversation with Jean-François Lyotard, *JAC*, 15(3).

McConkey, J. (2004) Knowledge and acknowledgement: 'Epistemic Injustice' as a problem of recognition, *Politics*, 24(3), pp. 198–205.

Maclennan, D. and Williams, R. (eds) (1990) *Housing Subsidies and the Market: An International Perspective*, York: Joseph Rowntree Foundation.

Macmillan, R. and Scott, A. (2003) On the case? Dilemmas of collaborative research, *Area*, 35, pp. 101–109.

Magnusson, C. (2006) Why Only Men?, *Svenska Dagbladet* (30 July), p. 5.

Maguire, P. (1987) *Doing Participatory Research: A Feminist Approach*, Center for International Education: University of Massachusetts, Amherst.

Major, P. (2008) *CPO Report to the Secretary of State for Communities and Local Government: Urban Regeneration Agency (Edge Lane West, Liverpool) Compulsory Purchase Order (no. 2) 2007*, Bristol: The Planning Inspectorate.

Malissard, P., Gingras, Y. and Gemme, B. (2003) La commercialisation de la recherché, *Actes de la recherche en sciences sociales*, 148(2003/3), pp. 57–67.

Mandelson, P. (2009) Higher ambitions, *Speech to the CBI-HE Conference*, London, 9 October, http://www.bis.gov.uk/higher-ambitions

Mandelson, P. (2009) Higher education and modern life, *Speech at Birkbeck University*, 27 July, available at http://www.dius.gov.uk/news_and_speeches/speeches/peter-mandelson/universities

Mandelson, P. (2010) Our universities are not under threat, *The Guardian*, 14 January, p. 36.

Mannheim, K. (1993) The sociology of intellectuals, *Theory, Culture, and Society*, 10, pp. 69–80.

Marginson, S. (1995) The economics of education as power-knowledge: Subjects and subjugation, *Australian Association for Research in Education, 25th Annual Conference*, Hobart, 26–30 November 1995.

Marginson, S. (2000) Rethinking academic work in the global era, *Journal of Higher Education Policy and Management*, 22(1), pp. 23–35.

Marginson, S. and Considine, M. (2000) *The Enterprise University: Power, Governance, and Reinvention in Australia*, Cambridge: Cambridge University Press.

Marquand, D. (2004) *Decline of the Public*, Cambridge: Polity Press.

Marsland, D. (1996) *Welfare or Welfare State? Contradictions and Dilemmas in Social Policy.* Basingstoke: Palgrave Macmillan.

Marston, G. (2004) *Social Policy and Discourse Analysis: Policy Change in Public Housing*, Aldershot: Ashgate.

Marston, G. (2008) Technocrats or intellectuals? Reflections on the role of housing researchers as social scientists, *Housing, Theory and Society*, 25(3), pp. 177–190.

Martin, R. (2001) Geography and public policy: The case of the missing manifesto, *Progress in Human Geography*, 25, pp. 121–137.

Martin, R. (2001) Geography and public policy: The case of the missing agenda, *Progress in Human Geography*, 25(2), pp. 189–210.

Mason, C. and McKenna, H.P. (1995) How to survive a PhD, *Nurse Researcher*, 2(3), pp. 73–79.

Mautner, G. (2005) The entrepreneurial university: A discursive profile of a higher education buzzword, *Critical Discourse Studies*, 2(2), pp. 90–120.

May, T. (2002) *Qualitative Research in Action*, London: Routledge.

May, T. (2005) Transformations in academic production: Content, context, and consequence, *European Journal of Social Theory*, 8(2), pp. 193–209.

May, T. (2007) Regulation, engagement and academic production, in Harding, A., Scott, A., Laske, S. and Burtscher, C. (eds) *Bright Satanic Mills: Universities, Regional Development and the Knowledge Economy*, Aldershot: Ashgate, pp. 119–132.

Mayo, P. (2003) A rationale for a transformative approach to education, *Journal of Transformative Education*, 1(1), pp. 38–57.

Meadmore, D. (1998) Changing the culture: The governance of the Australian pre-millennial university, *International Studies in Sociology of Education*, 8(1), pp. 27–45.

Meen, G., Gibb, K., Goody, J., McGrath, T. and Mackinnon, J. (2005) *Economic Segregation in Britain: Causes, Consequences and Policy*, York: Joseph Rowntree Foundation.

Mehl, D. (1975) Les luttes de résidents dans les grands ensembles, *Sociologie du Travail*, 4, pp. 351–371.

Mello, M., Brian R. Clarridge, B. and Studdert, D. (2005) Academic medical centers' standards for clinical-trial agreements with industry, *The New England Journal of Medicine*, 352, p. 21.

Merton, R. (1957) *Social Theory and Social Structure*, New York: The Free Press.

Millichope, R. (2001) Doctorates awarded from United Kingdom higher education institutions, *Statistics Focus: Higher Education Statistics Agency*, 3(2), pp. 23–30. Accessed on 2 July 2004 at http://www.hesa.ac.uk/acuk/publications/statistics_focus_volume3_issue2.pdf

Mills, C. (1959) *The Sociological Imagination*, Oxford: Oxford University Press.

Milot, P. (2003) La reconfiguration des universités selon l'OCDE. Economie du savoir et politique de l'innovation, *Actes de la recherche en sciences sociales*, 148(2003/3), pp. 68–73.

Mirowski, P. and VanHorn, R. (2005) The contract research organization and the commercialization of scientific research, *Social Studies of Science*, 35, pp. 503–548.

Monbiot, G. (2009) Captive Knowledge, *The Guardian*, 12 May.

Mowery, D.C. and Shane, S. (2002) Introduction to the special issue on university entrepreneurship and technology transfer, *Management Science*, 48(1), pp. v–vx.

Mullins, D. and Murie, A. (2006) *Housing Policy in the UK*, Basingstoke: Palgrave Macmillan.

Mullins, D., Reid, B. and Walker, R. (2001) Modernisation and change in social housing: The case for an organisational perspective, *Public Administration*, 79(3), pp. 599–623.

Musselin, C. (2009) Les réformes des universités en Europe: Des orientations comparables, mais des déclinaisons nationals, *Revue du MAUSS*, 2009/01(33), pp. 69–91.

Musselin, C. (2001) *La longue marche des universités françaises*, Paris: PUF.

Mustar, P. and Larédo, P. (2002) Innovation and research policy in France (1980–2000) or the disappearance of the Colbertist state, *Research Policy*, 31(1), pp. 55–72.

Nadin, V. (1997) Widening the gap between the haves and the have-nots, *Planning Practice and Research*, 12(2), pp. 93–97.

Neave, G. and Van Vught, F. (1991) *Prometheus Bound: The Changing Relationship between Government and Higher Education in Western Europe*, Oxford: Pergamon.

Nelson, R. (1993) *National Innovation Systems: A Comparative Analysis*, New York: Oxford University Press.

Nevin, B. (2006) *Proof of Evidence of Brendan Nevin (Ecotec Research and Consulting Ltd)*. Accessed on 5 July 2007 at http://www.persona.uk.com/newheartlands/index.htm

Nevin, B. (2006b) Rebuttal to the Proof of Evidence of Professor Chris Allen (unpublished).

Nevin, B., Lee, P., Goodson, L., Murie, A. and Phillimore, J. (1999) *Changing Housing Markets and Urban Regeneration in the M62 Corridor*, Birmingham: CURS.

Neyrat, F. (2007) Le 'LMD' en France: Loin de l'utopie de l'universitas médiévale, les effets d'une réforme économique libérale, in *Les ravages de la 'modernisation' universitaire en Europe*, Paris: Syllepse, pp. 145–172.

Niskanen, W. (1973) *Bureaucracy: Servant or Master?* London: Institute of Economic Affairs.

Novick, P. (1988) *The Noble Dream*, Cambridge: Cambridge University Press.

Nussbaum, M. (2010) *Not For Profit: Why Democracy Needs the Humanities*, New York: Princeton University Press.

O'Brien, M., Clayton, S., Varga-Atkins and Qualter, A. (2008) Power and the theory-and-practice conundrum: The experience of doing research with a local authority, *Evidence and Policy*, 4(4), pp. 371–90.

ODPM and Home Office (2004) *Safer Places: The Planning System and Crime Prevention*, London: HMSO.

ODPM and Home Office (2004) *Skills for Sustainable Communities: The Egan Review*, London: ODPM.

Okely, J. (1992) Anthropology and autobiography: Participatory experience and embodied knowledge, in J. Okely and H. Callaway (eds) *Anthropology and Autobiography*, London: Routledge.

Oliver, M. (1996) *Understanding Disability: From Theory to Practice*, London: Macmillan.

Olssen, M. and Peters, M.A. (2005) Neoliberalism, higher education and the knowledge economy: From the free market to knowledge capitalism, *Journal of Education Policy*, 20(3), pp. 313–345.

Osborne, T. (2002) On mediators: Intellectuals and the ideas trade in the knowledge society, Bristol: University of Bristol (unpublished paper).

O'Shea, R.P., Allen, T.J., Chevalier, A. and Roche, F. (2005), Entrepreneurial orientation, technology transfer and spinoff performance of U.S. universities, *Research Policy*, 34, 7, pp. 994–1009.

Östros, T. (2004) Chronicle, *Tvärsnitt*, 3/04 (rear cover).

Ozga, J. (1998) The entrepreneurial researcher: Re-formations of identity in the research market place, *International Journal in Sociology of Education*, 8(2).

Pal, L. (1990) Knowledge, power, and policy: Reflections on Foucault, in Brooks, S. and Gagnon, A. (eds) *Social Scientists, Policy, and the State*, New York: Praeger Publishers.

Pawson, R. (2001a) *Evidence Based Policy: 1. In Search of a Method*, London: ESRC UK Centre for Evidence-Based Policy and Practice Working Paper 3, King's College London.

Pawson, R. (2001b) *Evidence Based Policy: II. The Promise of 'Realist Synthesis'*, London: ESRC Centre for Evidence-Based Policy and Practice Working Paper 4, King's College London.

Peck, J. (1999) Grey geography, *Transactions of the Institute of British Geographers*, 24, pp. 131–5.

Percy-Smith, J. with Burden, T., Darlow, A., Dowson, L., Hawtin, M. and Ladi, S. (2004) *Promoting Change through Research: The Impact of Research in Local Government*, York: Joseph Rowntree Foundation.

Performance and Innovation Unit (2002) *Social Capital: A Discussion Paper*, London: Cabinet Office.

Phillipson, N. (1988) Commerce and culture: Edinburgh, Edinburgh University, and the Scottish Enlightenment, in Bender, T. (ed.) *The University and the City: From Medieval Origins to the Present*, Oxford: Oxford University Press, pp. 100–118.

Pollak, M. (1976) La planification des sciences socials, *Actes de la recherche en sciences sociales*, 2(2), pp. 105–121.

Power, A. (1993) *Hovels to High Rise: State Housing in Europe since 1850*, London: Routledge.

Power, A. and Houghton, J. (2007) *Jigsaw Cities: Big Places, Small Spaces*, Bristol: Policy Press.

Prime Minister's Science, Engineering and Innovation Council (1998) *University-Industry Linked Research in Australia*, Canberra: PMSCIC.

Raco, M. (1999) Researching the new urban governance: An examination of closure, access and complexities of institutional research, *Area*, 31(3), pp. 271–279.

Rait, R.S. (1912) *Life in the Medieval University*, Cambridge: Cambridge University Press.

Rallis, S. and Rossman, G. (2000) Dialogue for learning: Evaluator as critical friend, *New Directions in Evaluation*, 86, pp. 81–92.

Rappert, B. (1999) The uses of relevance: Thought on a reflexive sociology, *Sociology*, 33(4), pp. 705–723.

Ravetz, A. (2001) *Council Housing and Culture: The History of a Social Experiment*, London: Routledge.

Readings, B. (1996) *The University in Ruins*, Cambridge: Harvard University Press.

Reagan, M. (2006) Blast proof city, in *Planning in London Yearbook*, Manchester: Excel Publishing, pp. 22–24.

Rees, G. and Lambert, J. (1981) Nationalism as legitimation? in Harloe, M. (ed.) *New Perspectives in Urban Change and Conflict*, London: Heinemann Education.

Reid, B. (1999) Reframing the delivery of local housing services: Networks and the new competition, in Stoker, G. (ed.) *The New Management of British Local Governance*, London: Macmillan, pp. 128–144.

Reisz, M. (2010) The core connection, *Times Higher Educational Supplement*, 7 January.

Research Council Economic Impact Group (2006) *Increasing the Economic Impact of Research Councils*, London: DTI.

Research Councils UK (2006) *Report of the Research Councils UK Efficiency and Effectiveness of Peer Review Project: Executive summary*.

Rex, J. and Moore, R. (1967) *Race, Community and Conflict: A Study of Sparkbrook*, London: Oxford University Press for Institute of Race Relations.

Richardson, J. (2006) Talking about gypsies and travellers: The notion of discourse as control, *Housing Studies*, 21(1), pp. 77–96.

Robbins, D. (2006) *On Bourdieu, Education and Society*, Oxford: Bardwell Press.

Roberts, G. (2002) *Review of Research Assessment*, London: HM Treasury.

Roberts, G. (2002) *SET for Success: The Supply of People with Science, Technology, Engineering and Mathematics Skills – The Report of Sir Gareth Roberts' Review*. Accessed on 30 June 2004 at http://www.HM Treasury.gov. uk/documents/enterprise_and_productivity/research_and_enterprise/ent_res_ roberts.cfm

Roberts G. (2003) *Review of Research Assessment: Report by Sir Gareth Roberts to the UK Funding Bodies*. Accessed on 24 April 2007 at http://www.ra-review. ac.uk/reports/roberts.asp

Robertson, D. (2008) *Looking into Housing: A Practical Guide to Housing Research*, Coventry: Chartered Institute of Housing.

Robertson, D. and McLaughlin, P. (1996) *Looking into Housing: A Practical Guide to Housing Research*, Coventry: Chartered Institute of Housing.

Ross, A. (2003) Higher education and social access: To the Robbins Report, in Archer, L., Hutchings, M. and Ross, A. (eds) *Higher Education and Social Class: Issues of Education and Inclusion*, London: Routledge, pp. 21–44.

Rothblatt, S. (1988) London: A metropolitan university, in Bender T. (ed.) *The University and the City: From Medieval Origins to the Present*, Oxford: Oxford University Press, pp. 119–149.

Rothschild, Lord (1971) *A Framework for Government Research and Development*, London: HMSO Cm 4814.

Rothstein, B. (2005) Bengt Westerberg shows willing as the government's poodle (authors translation), *Dagens Nyheter*, 8 May (in Swedish).

Rothstein, B. (2006) Social Democratic Commissars direct Swedish research (authors translation), *Dagens Nyheter*, 5 June (in Swedish).

Rothstein, B. (2008) Research with the wrong goals (authors translation), *Sydsvenska Dagblad*, 3 November.

Routledge, P. (2004) Relational ethics of struggle, in Fuller, D. and Kitchin, R. (eds) *Radical Theory/Critical Praxis: Making a Difference Beyond the Academy?* Vernon and Victoria, BC: Praxis Press.

Rupp. (1998) A dialogue on university stewardship: New responsibilities and opportunities, Government–University–Industry research roundtable, *Proceedings of a Roundtable Discussion*, Washington, DC.

Said, E. (1994) *Representations of the Intellectual: The 1993 Reith Lectures*, London: Vintage.

Sainsbury, Lord (2007) *The Race to the Top: Review of Government's Science and Innovation Policies.* London: HM Treasury. Accessed on 9 May 2009 at http://www.HM Treasury.gov.uk/d/sainsbury_review051007.pdf

Saunders, P. (1990) *A Nation of Home Owners?* London: Unwin Hyman.

Sayad, A. (1996) L'immigration et la pensee d'Etat: Reflections sur la double peine, Delit d'immigration, *COST A2*, pp. 11–30.

Sayer, A. (2000) *Realism and Social Science*, London: Sage.

Schultheis, F., Escoda, M.R. and Cousin, P.-F. (eds) (2008) *Le cauchemar de Humboldt: Les réformes de l'enseignement supérieur européen*, Paris: Raisons d'agir.

Scott, J. (2005) Sociology and its others: Reflections on disciplinary specialisation and fragmentation, *Sociological Research Online*, 10(1). Also available at http://www.socresonline.org.uk/10/1/scott.html

Scott, P. (1995) *The Meaning of Mass Higher Education*, Buckingham: Open University Press.

Seddon, T. (1996) The principle of choice in policy research, *Journal of Education Policy*, 11(2), pp. 197–214.

Sharp, S. and Coleman, S. (2005) Ratings in the research assessment exercise 2001: The patterns of university status and panel membership, *Higher Education Quarterly*, 59(2), pp. 153–171.

Shepherd, J. (2006) Staff cash in on consultancy, *Times Higher Educational Supplement*, 6 January.

Shepherd, J. (2008) So, what's the attraction? *The Guardian* (Education Section), 20 May, p. 1.

Shils, E. (1988) The University, the City and the World: Chicago and the University of Chicago, in Bender, T. (ed.) *The University and the City*, Oxford: Oxford University Press, pp. 210–230.

Shinn, T. (2002) Nouvelle production du savoir et triple hélice. Tendances du prêt-à-penser les sciences, *Actes de la recherche en sciences sociales* (2002/1), pp. 21–30.

Shove, E. (2000) Reciprocities and reputations: New currencies in research, in Jacob, M. and Hellstrom, T. (eds) *The Future of Knowledge Production in the Academy*, Buckingham: Open University Press, pp. 63–80.

Siegel, D.S., Veugelers, R. and Wright, M. (2007), Technology transfer offices and commercialization of university intellectual property: Performance and policy implications, *Oxford Review of Economic Policy*, 23, 4, pp. 640–660.

Sjoberg, G. (ed.) (1967) *Ethics, Politics and Social Research*, Cambridge: Schenkman.

Skeggs, B. (2001) Feminist ethnography, in Atkinson, P. et al. (eds) *Handbook of Ethnography*, London: Sage, pp. 426–442.

Slater, T. (2006) The eviction of critical perspectives from gentrification research, *International Journal of Urban and Regional Research*, 30(4), pp. 737–57.

Slaughter, S. and Leslie, L. (1997) *Academic Capitalism: Politics, Policies and the Entrepreneurial University*, Baltimore: Johns Hopkins University Press.

Slaughter, S. and Rhoades, G. (2004) *Academic Capitalism and the New Economy*, Baltimore: Johns Hopkins University Press.

Smith, J. (2007) House of Commons Debate, 14 November, Col. 45WS.

Social Research Association (2003) *Ethical Guidelines*, http://www.the-sra.org.uk/documents/pdfs/ethics03.pdf (accessed 30 March 2006).

Solesbury, W. (2001) Evidence-based policy: Whence it came and where it's going, London: ESRC UK Centre for Evidence Based Policy and Practice Working Paper 1, King's College London.

Solesbury, W. (2002) The ascendancy of evidence, *Planning Theory*, 3(1), pp. 90–96.

Solovey, M. (2001) Project Camelot and the 1960s epistemological revolution: Rethinking the politics-patronage science nexus, *Social Studies of Science*, 31(2), pp. 171–206.

Somerville, P. (1994) On explanations of housing policy, *Scandinavian Housing and Planning Research*, 11, pp. 211–230.

Sprigings, N. (2010) The fictions of the fallacy paper: A verifiable response, *Housing, Theory and Society*, forthcoming.

Spring School of Oxford (2009) *Quantitative Methods for Social Research*. Available at http://springschool.politics.ox.ac.uk/spring_school/aims.asp

Stack, C.B. (1972) *All Our Kin: Strategies for Survival in a Black Community*, New York: Harper and Row.

Standish, P. (2005) Towards an economy of higher education, *Critical Quarterly*, 47(1–2), pp. 53–71.

Stark, A. (2004) The mathematics of research applications, *Tvärsnitt* 3/04, pp. 32–33.

Stelfox, H., Chua, G., O'Rourke, K. and Detsky, A. (1998) Conflict of interest in the debate over calcium-channel antagonists, *New England Journal of Medicine* (338/2), pp. 101–106.

Stengers, I. (2004) Préface. La mouche et le tigre, in Krimsky, S., *La recherche face aux intérêts privés*, Paris: Les Empêcheurs de Penser en Rond/Seuil, p. 5–18.

Stephens, M., Whitehead, C. and Munro, M. (2005) *Lessons from the Past, Challenges for the Future for Housing Policy: An Evaluation of English Housing Policy, 1975–2000*, London: HMSO, http://www.communities.gov.uk/documents/housing/pdf/138130.pdf (accessed 9 November 2009).

Stewart, W.A.C. (1989) *Higher Education in Postwar Britain*, London: Macmillan.

Stoker, G. and Mossberger, K. (1994) Urban regime theory in comparative perspective, *Environment and Planning C: Government and Policy*, 12, pp. 195–212.

Stoker, G. and Young, S. (1993) *Cities in the 1990s*, Harlow: Longman.

Stone, C. (1989) *Regime Politics: Governing Atlanta 1946–1988*, Lawrence: University Press of Kansas.

Stone, C. (2005) Looking back to look forward: Reflections on urban regime analysis, *Urban Affairs Review*, 40(3), pp. 309–341.

Svensson, L.E. (2008) A Discourse Analysis of Innovation Policies for Economic Growth, Doctoral Dissertation, Gothenburg University.

Swedish Research Council (2004) *Strong Basic Research in Sweden: The Swedish Research Council's Research Strategy for 2005–2008* (in Swedish).

Sztompka, P. (2007) Trust in science, Robert K. Merton's inspirations, *Journal of Classical Sociology*, 7, p. 211.

Taylor, J. (2001) Private property, public interest, and the role of the state in nineteenth century Britain: The case of lighthouses, *The Historical Journal*, 44(3), pp. 749–771.

Taylor, J. (2008) Home Office architecture contest 'fosters culture of fear', *The Independent*, 24 November, p. 17.

Taylor, M. (2003) *Public Policy in the Community*, London: Palgrave Macmillan.

Taylor, M. and Hoggett, P. (1994) Quasi-markets and the transformation of the independent sector, in W. Bartlett, C. Propper, D. Wilson and J. Le Grand (eds) (1994) *Quasi Markets in the Welfare State*, Bristol: SAUS, pp. 184–206.

Thomas, H. (1998) Spatial restructuring in the capital: Struggles to shape Cardiff's built environment, in Fevre, R. and Thompson, A. (eds) *Nation, Identity and Social Theory – Perspectives from Wales*, Cardiff: University of Wales Press.

Thomas, H. (2003) *Discovering Cities: Cardiff*, Sheffield: Geographical Association.

Thomas, H. (2005) Pressures, purpose and collegiality in UK Planning education, *Planning Theory and Practice*, 6(2), pp. 238–247.

Thomas, H. (2008) Book Review: Hooper, A.J. and Punter, J. (eds) *Capital Cardiff 1975–2020*, Cardiff: University of Wales Press, *Urban Studies* 45, pp. 239–241.

Thomas, H. and Imrie, R. (1999) Urban policy, modernization and the regeneration of Cardiff Bay, in Imrie, R. and Thomas, H. (eds) *British Urban Policy: An Evaluation of the Urban Development Corporations* (2nd edn), London: Sage, pp. 106–127.

Thompson, E.P. (1970) *Warwick University Limited*, Harmondsworth: Penguin.

Thrift, N. (2008) University reforms: The tension between form and substance, in Mazza, C., Quattrone, P. and Riiccaboni, A. (eds) *European Universities in Transition*, Cheltenham: Edward Elgar, pp. 17–30.

Tooley, J. (2001) *Analysis: Unreliable Evidence*, transcript of BBC Radio 4 broadcast, 29 July, BBC, Tape Number, TLN129/01VT1030.

Topalov, C. (1974) *Les promoteurs immobiliers. Contribution à l'analyse de la production capitaliste du logement en France*, Paris/La Haye: Mouton.

Torgersen, U. (1987) Housing: The wobbly pillar under the welfare state, in Turner, B., Kemeny, J. and Lundqvist, L. (eds) *Between State and Market: Housing in the Post-Industrial Era*, Stockholm: Almqvist and Wiksell.

Townsend, P. (1979) *Poverty in the United Kingdom*, London: Penguin.

United Nations Chernobyl Forum (2006) *Scientific Facts on the Chernobyl Nuclear Accident*, Vienna: International Atomic Energy Authority.

University and College Union (2009) *Response to the Research Excellence Framework*, London: UCU.

Van Manen, J. (1988) *Tales of the Field: On Writing Ethnography*, Thousand Oaks, CA: Sage.

Vatin, F. and Vernet, A. (2009) La crise de l'Université française: Une perspective historique et socio-démographique, *Revue du MAUSS*, 1(33), pp. 47–68.

Veblen, T. (1919) *The Higher Learning in America*, New York: B. W. Huebsh.

Vellani, F. (2006) Disability and higher education, unpublished PhD thesis, Department of Geography, Royal Holloway University of London.

Veysey, L. (1965) *The Emergence of the American University*, Chicago: University of Chicago Press.

Wacquant, L. (2004) Critical thought as solvent of *doxa*, *Constellations*, 11(1), pp. 97–101.

Walker, R. (1987) Perhaps minister: The messy world of in-house social research, in Bulmer, M. (ed.) *Social Science Research and Government: Comparative Essays on Britain and the USA*, Cambridge: Cambridge University Press, pp. 141–165.

Walker, R. (2000) Can social science evaluate New Labour's policies, paper presented to the Royal Statistical Society, 4 July.

Wallace, M. and Wray, A. (2006) *Critical Reading and Writing for Postgraduates*, London: Sage.

Wallis, R. (1977) The moral career of a research project, in Bell, C. and Newby, H. (eds) *Doing Sociological Research*, London: George Allen & Unwin, pp. 149–169.

Walshok, M. (2004) The transformative role of universities in a knowledge society, Bynum Tudor Lecture, Kellogg College, Oxford University, Oxford, November.

Walters, R. (2003) New modes of governance and the commodification of criminological knowledge, *Social and Legal Studies*, 12(1), pp. 5–26.

Walters, R. (2006) Critical criminology and the intensification of the authoritarian state, in Barton, A., Corteen, K., Scott, D. and Whyte, D. (eds) *Expanding the Criminological Imagination: Critical Readings in Criminology*, Oxford: Willan, pp. 15–37.

Waluszewski, A, Hasselberg, Y. and Rider, S. (2008) Science's gold for sale (authors translation) *Svenska Dagblad*, 10 November.

Ward, K. (2005) Geography and public policy: A recent history of 'policy relevance', *Progress in Human Geography*, 29, pp. 310–319.

Warde, A. (1988) Industrial restructuring, local politics and the reproduction of labour power: Some theoretical considerations, *Environment and Planning D: Society and Space*, 6, pp. 75–95.

Warde, I. (2001) L'université américaine vampirisée par les marchands, *Le Monde Diplomatique*, October–November, pp. 20–21.

Washburn, J. (2005) Rent a researcher: Did a British university sell out to Procter & Gamble? *Slate Magazine*, December 22, http://www.slate.com/id/2133061/

Watson, S. and Austerberry, H. (1986) *Housing and Homelessness: A Feminist Perspective*, London: Routledge.

Webb, B. (1979) *My Apprenticeship*, Cambridge: Cambridge University Press.

Weiss, C. (1990) The uneasy partnership endures: Social science and government, in Brooks, S. and Gagnon, A. (eds) *Social Scientists, Policy, and the State*, New York: Praeger Publishers, pp. 97–111.

Wenger, E. (1998) *Communities of Practice*, Cambridge: Cambridge University Press.

Whiteley, R., Aguiar, L. and Martin, T. (2008) The neo-liberal transnational university: The case of UBC Okanagan, *Capital and Class*, 96, pp. 115–142.

Wilden, A. (1972) *System and Structure*, London: Tavistock.

Wilkinson, D. (2005) *The Essential Guide to Postgraduate Study*, London: Sage.

Willensky, J. (2000) *If Only We Knew: Increasing the Public Value of Social Science Research*, London: Routledge.

Williams, N. (2010) Letter to the editor, *The Guardian*, 15 January, p. 43.

Wilson, J. (1981) Policy intellectuals and public policy, *Public Interest*, 64, pp. 31–46.

Winkin, Y. (2008) L'esprit de Bologne: Si les universités ne s'adaptent pas, on se passera d'elles, in Franz Schultheis et al. (eds) *Le cauchemar de Humboldt: Les réformes de l'enseignement supérieur européen*, pp. 199–203.

Wood, P. (n.d.) *UK Foresight Programme: A Panel Chairman's View*, available at http://www.nistep.go.jp/achiev/ftx/eng/mat077e/html/mat0774e.html

Worthington, F. and Hodgson, J. (2005) Academic labour and the politics of quality in higher education: A critical evaluation of the conditions of possibility of resistance, *Critical Quarterly*, 47(1–2), pp. 96–110.

Young, M. and Wilmott, P. (1957) *Family and Kinship in East London*, London: Routledge and Kegan Paul.

Zipin, L. and Brennan, M. (2003) The suppression of ethical dispositions through managerial governmentality: A habitus crisis in Australian higher education, *International Journal of Leadership in Education*, 6(4), pp. 351–370.

Index